W. W. H. DAVIS.

HISTORY OF DOYLESTOWN, OLD AND NEW.

FROM ITS SETTLEMENT TO THE CLOSE

OF THE

NINETEENTH CENTURY.

1745---1900.

ILLUSTRATED.

BY

W. W. H. DAVIS, A. M., M. M. S.

AUTHOR OF EL GRINGO, OR NEW MEXICO AND HER PEOPLE; SPANISH CONQUEST OF NEW MEXICO, 104TH PENNSYLVANIA VOLUNTEERS, HISTORY OF THE HART FAMILY, LIFE OF GENERAL JOHN LACEY, HISTORY OF THE DOYLESTOWN GUARDS, LIFE OF JOHN DAVIS, HISTORY OF BUCKS COUNTY, FRIES REBELLION, &C.

INTELLIGENCER PRINT,
DOYLESTOWN, PA.

– Notice –

The foxing, or discoloration with age, characteristic of old books, sometimes shows through to some extent in reprints such as this, especially when the foxing is very severe in the original book. We feel that the contents of this book warrant its reissue despite these blemishes, and hope you will agree and read it with pleasure.

THIS VOLUME
Is respectfully dedicated to the memory of those whose history is recorded herein, and to the present and future generations who may find pleasure in reading its pages.

TO THE READER.

In submitting this volume to the public, the author takes occasion to say, that its preparation was more than "a labor of love," for difficulties met him at every step.

No one had ever before written, or attempted to write, the history of Doylestown. The ground lay fallow; there was no material at hand to write it from, but it had to be picked up, a bit here and a bit there, like the gathering of threads to weave into a piece of cloth, and was the work of several years.

Among other authorities consulted, were the bound files of the *Bucks County Intelligencer* and *Doylestown Democrat*, reaching through a century. We have related events consecutively, and spoken of persons and things correctly; but, to make them clear, have occasionally resorted to repetition. They who declined to open their storehouse of the past, must not blame the author for inaccuracy. Under the circumstances, we have made the best possible use of our material, and, if we have accomplished nothing more, we have saved valuable material for the future historian.

W. W. H. DAVIS.

Doylestown, Pa., October 31, 1904.

CONTENTS.

CHAPTER		PAGE
I.	The First Step in Civilization	1
II.	The Formative Period	9
III.	Early Business Life	15
IV.	Becomes the County Seat	24
V.	Historic Walk	34
VI.	Typhus Fever Panic	42
VII.	The School and the Church	49
VIII.	Pioneer Newspapers	57
IX.	In the Twenties	71
X.	In the Thirties	80
XI.	A Noted Murder Trial	88
XII.	A Prosperous Period	96
XIII.	Doylestown a Summer Resort	104
XIV.	The Stage and the Mails	114
XV.	Our Public Inns	127
XVI.	The Bench and the Bar	143
XVII.	Social Life in the Past	155
XVIII.	Mercantile Life	166
XIX.	Our Industries	173
XX.	More of Our Industries	184
XXI.	Opening of Streets	194
XXII.	A Group of Churches	201
XXIII.	Middle of the Century	211
XXIV.	Doylestown in the Civil War	223
XXV.	Our Schools	240
XXVI.	Art in Doylestown	254
XXVII.	Our Military History	271
XXVIII.	Beneficial Societies	284
XXIX.	Our Medical Life	296
XXX.	Historic Families	304
XXXI.	A Building Period	324
XXXII.	Bi-Centennial Decade	337
XXXIII.	Fires and Fire Department	348
XXXIV.	Odds and Ends of History	354
XXXV.	Farewell to the Nineteenth Century	365

ILLUSTRATIONS.

		PAGE
1.	Frontispiece, W. W. H. Davis.	
2.	Kirkbride-Chapman Farm House	4
3.	Doyle's Tavern, 1745	10
4.	Nathaniel Shewell, 1860	16
5.	Scheetz's Store House, 1830	20
6.	Old Court House, 1812	28
7.	The Russell House, 1810	34
8.	DuBois Homestead, 1807	36
9.	Old Presbyterian Church, 1815-1845	42
10.	Old Jail, 1812	50
11.	Asher Miner, 1804	56
12.	John S. Bryan	64
13.	The Ross Law Office, 1829	74
14.	Francis B. Shaw	80
15.	Mina, 1832	88
16.	Doylestown National Bank, 1897	96
17.	Charles H. Mann, 1860	106
18.	William T. Rogers	112
19.	The Stage and the Mails	120
20.	The Ship Tavern, 1840	128
21.	The Fountain House, 1853	136
22.	Eleazer T. McDowell, 1840	144
23.	Henry Chapman, 1850	152
24.	Samuel F. DuBois, 1852	160
25.	Hellyer's Store, 1897	168
26.	Fisher's Smith Shop	176
27.	Spoke Factory, 1884	184
28.	New Jail, 1884	194
29.	The Opening of Streets	200
30.	Salem Reformed Church	208
31.	Public School Building	216
32.	Lieutenant McDowell, Killed at Fair Oaks	228
33.	School Board, 1897	240
34.	Art in Doylestown	254
35.	The Harvey House, 1812	274
36.	Office of Judge Fox	288
37.	Dr. Charles H. Mathews	296
38.	Dr. George T. Harvey	300
39.	John Fox, 1840	304
40.	George Lear at 60	314
41.	Beeks Exhibition Building	320
42.	New Presbyterian Church	330
43.	Union Academy	340
44.	Samuel Hall	360
45.	Monument 104th Regiment	370
46.	Linden Female Seminary	372

Doylestown, Old and New.

I

The First Step in Civilization.

If the reader could have taken his stand, at what is now the crossing of Broad and East Court streets, Doylestown, one hundred and fifty years ago, and swept the horison with his glass he would have beheld an almost houseless panorama.

Looking down the long slope into the valley of Pine Run, he might have seen the Kirkbride farm house, subsequently the Chapman homestead, and a few others wideley scattered, but not a single village dwelling. To the east he could have looked across the intervening mile of field and forest to the ridge whereon was later built the Burges farm house; had our "looker on in Vienna" turned his glass to the southeast and southwest into the valley drained by the Neshaminy, he would have seen the modest homes of the Flacks, Isabella Crawford, the Magills, the Scotts and a few other pioneers recently settled there, and would have likewise seen a small licensed inn not far from where the two highways crossed each other, now State and Main streets, had the timber not prevented; had he turned his glass to the west there would have been but little to be seen for the obstructing forest, but, near at hand, on the east side of Dyer's Mill road, now North Main street, was the Fell smith shop later enlarged into the Ross Mansion, and more recently the site of the new building of the Doylestown National Bank, and farther in the same direction he would have seen the pioneer homes of the Johnsons[1] and the Riales and nearer by that of the Doyles.

The pioneers, who settled the wilderness west of the Delaware, were not unmindful of the Roman maxim: "The first step in civilization is to make roads," for the opening of roads was one of their first concerns, and they were often projected and laid out when there were but few to travel them. Roads, in their uses, hold the same relation to a community as the arteries and veins hold to the human body, a proper system of the former being as necessary to a prosperous condition of society as the latter to the life and health of man. The opening of roads was the initial step in founding Penn's Quaker Empire west of the Delaware.

The first public road running through the future site of Doylestown, nearly north and south, and known to many at the present day as the "Easton Road," was opened from "Round Meadow," now the Willow Grove, to the Montgomery County Line, 1720. This was to enable Sir William Keith, the Provincial Governor of Pennsylvania, to reach his plantation of "Graeme Park." In 1722 it was extended to Dyer's Mill, two miles above Doylestown, this section being called the "Dyer's Mill Road;" and was subsequently laid out and opened to Easton, making a continuous highway from Philadelphia to the "Forks of Delaware." While the Easton Road joined the Upper and Lower Delaware in common interest, it was still necessary to unite the Delaware with the Schuylkill that bounds the peninsula on the west. This was done in 1730 by opening a road from Coryell's Ferry, the present New Hope, to the fords on the Schuylkill, intersecting the Easton road at the site of Doylestown, then only the crossing of two roads in the wilderness. It remained this and nothing more for three-quarters of a century, and until a road was laid out and opened, 1807, from the Swamp road to the Dyer's Mill road, the present Court street, and the County seat was located here three years later. In the meanwhile an occasional settler was dropping in and taking up land and building a cabin or a farm house, these roads

---

1 In Doylestown, late Warwick, March 21, 1819, in his 87th year, David Johnson. He was a native of Ireland, but had resided from early life in this county and, by the blessings of Heaven, his industry and economy had acquired a competency. A suitable discourse was delivered by the Rev. Mr. DuBois.

leading to what, in after years became the capital of Penn's beloved Bucks.

In laying out their highways the projectors "builded better than they knew." Their point of intersection became an ideal site for a country village and the future county seat. It is within a mile of the geographical centre of the county; the four roads radiate from it toward the cardinal points of the compass, tapping the Delaware on the northeast and south, and the Schuylkill on the west. The Court House stands a few feet less than six hundred above tidewater; the Neshaminy and its branches, adorned with flowery meeds, hug the plateau the town is built on; sweet valleys and gentle hills are seen in the distance, and from the cupalo of the Court House the eye sweeps over an agricultural region of unsurpassed beauty, with the distant Blue mountains for a back-ground.

Doylestown is built on the tract William Penn conveyed to the "Free Society of Traders," 1682, originally containing 20,000 acres, 8,612 acres laying in the contiguous townships of Warwick, New Britain and Hilltown. The area was twice reduced prior to 1726, when the remainder, containing about 2,000 acres, in Warwick and New Britain, on both sides of the present Court street, then the line between these townships, was purchased by Jeremiah Langhorne, Middletown. Of Langhorne's purchase, Joseph Kirkbride, Falls township, bought several hundred acres in New Britain, the south-eastern boundary being the present Court street. At this time these two proprietors owned every acre of land within the present borough limits.

Jeremiah Langhorne, one of the earliest owners of the ground Doylestown stands on, was the son of Thomas Langhorne, Westmoreland county, England, who settled in Middletown township, 1684. The homestead, called Langhorne Park, containing eight hundred acres, lay on the Durham road below the present borough of Langhorne. Joseph Kirkbride, Langhorne's fellow owner of the site of Doylestown, ran away from his master in England when a youth of twenty, and came over in the Welcome, starting for the new world with a wallet, containing some clothing, and a flail. He was first employed at Pennsbury but soon removed to New Jersey; was twice married and lived to become an influential and wealthy man, and a leading minister among Friends. At his death, 1738, at the age of seventy-five, he left 13,439 acres to be divided among his children,

Colonel Joseph Kirkbride, who lived in Falls township and prominent in the Revolution, being a grandson.

By 1725-30 a number of settlers had found homes in the neighboring townships, including the Jameses and other Welshmen in New Britain, James Meredith at Castle Valley, Walter Shewell, who built Painswick Hall; Benjamin Snodgrass, the Riale family descended from John Riale, born in England 1687, who bought 300 acres from Joseph Kirkbride in New Britain, his tract touching the northwest corner of the borough, and dying 1748 in his 60th year, leaving a widow and five children; Joseph Kirkbride a purchaser in the Valley of Cook's Run, with a sprinkling of Friends and Scotch Irish Presbyterians on the southeast.

Doylestown began life at the intersection of these two highways, and was born of a road-side inn and a log house or two. Great interest attaches to the Doyle family, not only because they were among the first settlers on the village site, but were present at its birth and christening, and gave name to the infant settlement.

The Doyles were in the county as early as 1696, and the Fourth-month ninth of that year Clement Dungan conveyed to Edward Doyle a tract of 50 acres: "Beginning at a corner tree by the side of the river Delaware, thence by land of the widow Dungan's N. N. W. 320 pole, thence by Clement Dungan's land S. by W. 25 pole, thence by land of Joseph Large 320 pole to a tree standing by the river Delaware, thence up the Delaware to the place of beginning." The consideration was £5. Edward Doyle, by will dated Seventh-month sixteenth, 1702, devising said tract to his wife and executrix, Rebecca Doyle. The will was proved before the Register General of the Province; and Rebecca Doyle, widow and executrix of Edward Doyle, conveyed said tract to Tobias Dymock and Sarah his wife, Third-month twenty-fifth, 1703, consideration £20. This Edward Doyls was the father of the Edward and Clement Doyle, who settled at Doylestown.

Three of the Doyles, Edward, William and Clement were here in 1730, and are thought to have been brothers, but this is a mistake, Clement and Edward were the sons of Edward, who settled on the Delaware about 1696 and marriad Rebecca Dungan; and William, the pioneer tavern keeper, was the son of Edward the younger. On March 30th, 1730, Edward Doyle bought of Joseph Kirkbride a narrow strip of land a mile long and less than a quarter of a mile wide, containing 150 acres, extending from West Court street northwest

KIRKBRIDE-CHAPMAN FARM HOUSE.

down into the valley of Cook's Run, and up the farther rise to the second cross roads. In the borough the width was from Hamilton street to the southwest boundary, and comprised the farms of Isaac and Richard Riale, Rachel White and Samuel Heckman. Edward Doyle is thought to have lived in the old stone house of Isaac Riale, at present the property of James Biglan, or in a house on its site. Doyle was not prosperous. His will, dated September 9th, 1763, was filed in Philadelphia, where he died 1770. His will mentions four children, William, Jeremiah, Edward and Rebecca Freeman, and a granddaughter Elizabeth, daughter of Elizabeth Reese. Edward Doyle, son of Edward Doyle, Jr., kept tavern in Philadelphia and his son William was assessed, 1779, "a Shoemaker without lands."

In 1737 Edward Doyle bought of Joseph Kirkbride another long, narrow strip of 42 acres, covering a portion of the late Armstrong farm on the southwest side next to the old Methodist church. It was only 342 feet wide, but a mile long. Edward Doyle owned this strip all his life and, after his death, 1770, his son Edward came into possession of it. In October, 1776, the latter made an assignment to his uncle, William Doyle, brother of Edward Doyle, Jr., who sold it to Daniel Hough, "Innkeeper." At that time Daniel Hough had removed to Plumstead. With the 42 acres William Doyle sold Hough, he also conveyed to him the two acres adjoining on the south side of Court street, then the Warwick–New Britain township line, and covering the triangle before mentioned and lying between Court, Hamilton, State and Main streets, extending along the latter street 320 feet, and including the site of the Fountain House. The following month Hough sold this triangle to Richard Swanwick, the Tory, for $600.

The Swanwick property was put up at public sale by the State, August 24, 1779, and sold to Samuel and Joseph Flack, of Warwick, the deed from the State to the Flack brothers being dated June 8, 1780. The deed, which we have seen, is a beautifully inscribed document.

In 1779 the Supreme Executive Council confiscated Swanwick's land, which was sold at public sale to Joseph Flack, probably the same who had kept the ship tavern on the site of Lenape Building, 1778 and later. The Flacks owned both the forty-two acres and the triangle until 1792, when they sold the former to John Shaw; 1794, Shaw to Enoch Harvey; 1798, Harvey to Charles Stewart; 1802, Stewart to Dr. Hugh Meredith; 1803, Meredith to Enoch Harvey; 1832, Harvey sold thirty-nine acres to Samuel Yardley; 1848, assignees of Yardley to Thomas Ross, and in 1849 Ross sold fifty-three acres to Jesse Armstrong.

The Armstrong corner, of which so much has been said in the past, and is not likely to be lost sight of in the future, has a separate history. It was part of 100 acres bought in 1737 by William Doyle, the tavern keeper, of Joseph Kirkbride. It ran back a mile, and was 825 feet wide, covering the late Ross Mansion, site of the Court House, the Monument House and the Miner* property. The Armstrong corner, 17 acres, was sold by Willlam Doyle 1750 to Israel Pemberton, and by the latter, 1752, to Edward Doyle, Jr., and John Robinson got it in 1771 after the sheriff had sold the estate of Edward Doyle. In 1779 John Robinson was taxed for only two acres and sixty perches, and was "an invalid." He was in Doylestown as early as 1756, when he bought half an acre of Archibald Crawford in Warwick. In 1760 he bought 28 acres of Israel Pemberton in New Britain, and 10 acres of Nathan Preston, 1771. In 1779 Robinson sold 40 acres to Jesse Fell, storekeeper, and Joseph Fell, blacksmith. Joseph Fell came into his brother's share, and removed to Wilkesbarre. In 1789 he sold 36 acres to Dr. Hugh Meredith, who built the stone farm house of the Armstrongs, which stood on the corner for ninety years, or about 1879, when new buildings were erected. In 1806 Hugh Meredith sold the house and 17 acres to William Watts, and in 1813 Watts sold it to Samuel Yardley. In what manner Yardley was dispossessed of it has already been stated. Subsequently, April 13th, 1819, Thomas N. Meredith and wife conveyed to William Watts the triangular tract shown by the annexed draft, and, appended to the deed, was a conveyance by Charles Meredith and Isabella, his wife, conveying all their right, title and interest to the said William Watts "as shall lie northeastwardly of a line beginning at the said Horse Block, (corner North Main and Court) and running hence a southerly course so as to strike its opposite side line in the centre between the two extreme points as will appear by a dotted line."

We have now accounted for two of the Doyle brothers, who were among the pioneer settlers on the site of Doylestown, Edward and William; but shall have more to say of the latter later on, and will now deal with the third brother, Clement. He probably settled here about the same time, 1733, and bought 148 acres of Joseph Kirkbride in Pine Run Valley, just south of Swartzlander's mill. On the

---

* Now the Mrs. N. C. James property.

DOYLESTOWN, OLD AND NEW. 7

southwest it was bounded by the Chapman farm, including the Carwithian farm, and we believe his homestead was on that part of the tract. Clement Doyle was the owner of this farm about forty years and to his death, 1772, leaving a widow and three sons. He was a Baptist, and himself and wife were two of the twenty-three constituent members of the New Britain Baptist church, 1734. Clement Doyle lived two miles northwest of Edward and William and was probably the most prosperous member of the family that had the honor of giving name to the future county seat. William Doyle built the Hiestand grist and carding mills, and carried on business there for several years. One of his sons is said to have read law with Abraham Chapman, and died at the age of forty, but, as his name is not among the law students admitted to the bar, he probably did not conclude his studies. The wife of the late Robert Smith, Doylestown, was a daughter of Jonathan Doyle. The Doyles intermarried with the Fells. Elizabeth Doyle's marriage certificate shows she was married to Joseph Fell, at Buckingham Meeting House, Third-month tenth, 1711. She is referred to as of Middletown township, where she was born, 1688. Her father was an Irishman and her mother born in Rhode Island. It is possible the Doyle brothers, who settled at Doylestown, were influenced to come here by the Kirkbrides and Langhorns, who had land to sell.

Joseph Fell took up a tract east of the borough, extending out to Pool's corner, including the Frank Mann farm. In 1775 the land owners immediately around the town, and a portion of whose holdings are now in the built up portion of the borough, were Edward and William Doyle, Joseph Kirkbride, Joseph and Samuel Flack, William and Robert Scott, Isabella Crawford and Robert and Henry Magill. The Magills made their appearance here 1768, when Archibald Crawford conveyed two lots to Robert and Henry Magill. Henry released to Robert, 1776, and died intestate leaving one child, William. William Magill likewise died intestate, 1824, leaving five children, Alfred,[2] Louisa C., William D., Robert M., and Benjamin Morris, all their holdings vesting in them in fee.[3]

What was remaining of Joseph Kirkbride's tract, northwest of

---

[2] At Philadelphia, February 28, 1828, Alfred M. Magill to Mrs. Jane S. Mann, daughter of John S. Mann, both of Doylestown.

[3] The Magills land was in the triangle formed by South Main and West State streets, one piece of the property being still in possession of the family. Charles Howard Magill, of Doylestown, is the only living male representative of this colonial family. See a further reference to the Magills in the chapter entitled "Our Highways."

the present Court street, and a large quantity of other lands in the lower end of the county was left to his children at his death. Some of them held the ancestral acres for two or three generations, but it is said not an acre at present is known to be in the possession of their descendants. The last of the New Britain tract, in the valley of Cook's Run, was sold to Abraham Chapman, 1814, and is still in this family. Kirkbride is not known to have ever lived in this part of the county, and doubtless kept his home in Falls township, where he settled.

At Jeremiah Langhorne's death, 1742, in disposing of his extensive real estate by will, he made provision for his negro slaves. Of the 2,000 acres, in Warwick township, purchased of the Free Society of traders, and covering the site of Doylestown south of Court street, 310 acres were devised to Cudjo and Joe for life, Cudjo's title being extinguished by the executors, 1757, and sold to Isabella Crawford. It lay in the triangle formed by South Main and East State street, and she held it in 1775.

A member of the Society of Friends, named Joseph Beal, bought land in New Britain, touching the Buckingham line, before 1750. His will was proved March 11th, 1752, dying young, leaving a widow, Grace, and three minor sons, Thomas, Joseph and William, and daughters Sarah and Elizabeth. His wife was a daughter of Mathew Gill. This tract was owned by Timothy Smith at one time, and subsequently by John Lloyd. The present owner is James Bertles. It lay on the north side of the "Academy Lane," an extension of Court street. Beal's widow survived until 1794, when she willed the farm to her sons Joseph and William and they sold it to John, for 235£. Fronting the Lloyd place, separating it from the Academy Lane, was a narrow strip in New Britain, which, in Colonial times, belonged to a plantation in Warwick, the late Pickering farm. In 1805 the will of the late John Pennington, then owner of the Pickering farm, ordered sale of so much of his farm as laid in New Britain.

Doylestown, Old and New.

II
The Formative Period.

The history of Doylestown is a blank from 1730 to 1745, in so far as our having knowledge of what was going on within its narrow limits. We may presume, however, there was a gradual increase in the number of settlers in this semi-wilderness country; there were marrying and giving in marriage, farms were opened, dwellings erected and old comers and new, the first run of the traditional "Nation Makers" were hard at work earning a living for themselves and families. At the Cross roads an occasional log or rough frame house went up and the owner moved in; now and then a Conestoga wagon from the Durham furnace or the Forks of Delaware passed down the Easton road to Philadelphia, returning with a load of necessaries for the settlers on that then distant frontier; at other times, more frequently on a Sunday, we have, in our minds eye, the picture of a venerable man[1] on horseback riding through this cross-road hamlet on his way to preach the word to his "Upper Congregation" at Deep Run meeting house.

The year is now 1745, and a new step is taken in the life of the hamlet to increase its attractions and develope its growth. For some time the want was felt of a place whereat "creature comforts" could be obtained for man and beast, and steps were now taken to supply this want.

At the March term of Court William Doyle, the settler of 1730,

---
[1] The Reverend William Tennent, pastor at Neshaminy in Warwick, from 1726 to 1738, who supplied the Congregation at Deep Run, Bedminster township, once a month.

went down to Newtown, the then county seat, with a petition to the Court of Quarter Sessions in his pocket, praying for license to keep a public house on the sight of the present Doylestown. It was stated in this petition that Doyle lived "between two great roads, one leading from Durham to Philadelphia," the other "from Well's Ferry toward the Potomack," and "there was no public house within five miles." The petition was signed by fourteen of Doyle's neighbors and friends: David Thomas, William Wells, Thomas Adams, Thomas Morris, John Marks, Hugh Edmond, Clement Doyle, Joseph Burges, Nathaniel West, William Dungan, Solomon McLean, David Eaton, and Edward Doyle. The license was granted, and renewed, from time to time, until 1775, when Doyle gave up the occupation. He had kept a public inn for thirty years and retired on his laurels.

Just where this pioneer hostelry was opened would be interesting to know after the lapse of one hundred and sixty-seven years. At that time William Doyle lived on the New Britain side of Court street, which would bring his dwelling in one of the great angles formed by the crossing of the present Main and State streets, and it is reasonable to suppose the new tavern was near enough to the cross roads to command patronage from both. He may have set up a bar in his own dwelling, for ought we know to the contrary, until he rented or purchased a more suitable place, and, in such case, the new location would most likely be south and east of Court street, and near one of the corners where Main and State streets cross.

At this time the hamlet could hardly have had more than a half dozen houses, log at that, and without a name until a licensed house was opened. Then, very naturally, it took the name of "Doyle's Tavern," which stuck to it for thirty years. In 1752, seven years after William Doyle received his first license, he purchased 19 acres and 7 perches of Isabella Crawford, including what is now "Randall's Corner," the southeast corner of Main and State streets. Two or three locations lay claim to the site of Doyle's first tavern; one, the former Scheetz dwelling, is on West Court street, the residence of Wynne James. This claim is fortified by an old covered well in the middle of the street, and the recollection of an old horse-block, near the corner of West Court and North Main, used for mounting and dismounting by the frequenters of the tavern, if it stood at that location. Among the persons recommended for license, 1774, was William Doyle, of Warwick, a fact that proves he was then south of Court street. The site of the present Fountain House is claimed by

DOYLE'S TAVERN, 1745.

some as the location of "Doyle's Tavern." There was a tavern there early and Daniel Hough at one time kept it. Warren S. Ely, good authority, thinks Doyle vacated the Fountain House property when he removed to Plumstead, 1775.

Since the above was written as to the location of " Doyle's Tavern" a bit of paper fell into our hands that throws light on the subject. This was the return of New Britain retailers for 1755, which reads as follows:

" I return William Doyle, Arthur Thomas and John Housekeeper for retailers of strong liquors by small measure." (Signed) Per James James, constable of New Britain." But, despite this, there is still a doubt as to the location of the Doyle Tavern. In a list of persons, recommended by the Court for license at the June term, 1774, for the year ensuing, William Doyle is set down as being "in Warwick," which would preclude him keeping in New Britain, unless the Court allowed him to keep two taverns at the same time, one in Warwick, the other in New Britain. We repeat, in conclusion of the subject, that it would be highly interesting to know the exact location of " Doyle's Tavern" of 1745 and after, for it would let us into the secret where the young Doyles, Dungans, McLeans, Wests, Johnsons, Flacks, Greirs, Snodgrasses, Riales and other scions of the leading families hereabout at that day, spent their evening, and indulged in

" Sport, that wrinkled care derides,
And laughter holding both his sides.
Come and trip it as ye go,
On the light fantastic toe,"

with their rustic sweethearts, but we have no Oedipus to unravel the secret.

That Doylestown took its name from the Doyle family, and that the name of their tavern was the immediate ancestral name of the village is unquestioned. It has had various spellings, beginning with "Doyle's Tavern," then "Doyle's Town," next "Doyletown," and last Doylestown, the name and spelling of to-day. Soon after the British army took possession of Philadelphia, 1777, their engineers made a map of the country twenty-five miles around the city, and which seems to be correct as to roads and streams. This then log hamlet had its proper location at the "crossing of two great highways, one running from Durham to Philadelphia, the other from Wells' Ferry to the ford on the Schuylkill." On this map we note a new spelling of the village name. It is no longer " Doyle's Tavern" but "Doyltown," the same spelling as the present with the exception of the syllable "es" between the "l" and the "t." When it was first called by this name we know not, the engineers doubtless, not inventing this spelling, but borrowing it from some previous map or other authority.

We now come to another interregum in the history of Doylestown, if we may be allowed so to speak, a period when we absolutely know nothing of what was going on, in or around it. This was of longer duration than the first, embracing thirty-two years, 1745-1777, two years after the colonies took up arms against the mother country. The sources of information casting light on this period are very few and hard to get at. In the absence of the church and the school, there was no centre in the neighborhood where its history could be embalmed for future use. While the tavern of William Doyle became a resort for the settlers, they were not of a class likely to preserve local history while making it. In truth, they had neither the leisure nor the inclination to engage in such work. Almost without an exception they had enlisted in the battle of life, and young and old were "fighting it out on this line" summer and winter. A cross-roads hamlet, in a semi-wilderness country, with tavern and smith shop, but without church, school or newspaper, is not a locality where passing history is apt to be preserved, or have purveyors to hand it down to those who shall come after them. This accounts for our want of knowledge of the formative period of the county capital at that early day.

This brings us down to the Revolutionary period, when the battle was on between the colonies and mother country. While our hamlet was in touch with these stirring times it played but a very modest part in the war for independence.

In the fall and winter of 1777-78, while the British army occupied Philadelphia and the Continentals lay at Valley Forge, General John Lacey, recently commissioned a Brigadier General of Militia, was placed in command of the Delaware-Schuylkill peninsula, to prevent the country Tories carrying supplies to the enemy in the city, and prevent small parties of the British from raiding the country districts. Doylestown was Lacey's depot of supplies, with a small guard to protect them, and sometimes it was his headquarters. He was here March 19, 1778, and, in brigade orders, the detail for guard duty mentions, three captains, three sergeants, four corporals and forty-eight privates. His duties were arduous. In this order, the name of the village is spelled the same as at present. While here Lacey's troops did not suffer for rations, and of a good quality, the receipts of the purchasing commissary covering payments for veal, beef, mutton, flour, whiskey, turkey and fowls, articles to be found in a Bucks county larder in peace or war. In addition to the above, there was an occasional passage of small bodies of American troops through the village and possibly the meeting of a neighboring company of Associators for drill, but there is no record of the enemy ever having visited the immediate vicinity, or come nearer than the Crooked Billet. Why the British did not attack Lacey's force at Doylestown, or make an attempt, is strange. It is evidence he was on the alert that does him credit as a commander.

The largest force passing through Doylestown at any one time was the Continental army in June, 1778, on its march from Valley Forge to intercept the British in their retreat from Philadelphia to New York. The advance of six brigades, under Lee, crossed the Delaware at Coryell's Ferry the evening of the 20th, Washington, with the main army, encamping at Doylestown the same evening. The weather being stormy, he remained until the next afternoon, a newspaper[3] account saying: "The army occupied three encampments, the first in rear of a row of cherry trees, extending southwestward from the site of the Mansion House, corner of State and Main street, a log cabin being occupied during the night as headquarters and bearing the imposing words "Cakes and Beer." The second brigade was placed near where the Presbyterian Church stands, and the third on the farm of Mr. Callender about half a mile from the village, on the New Hope road. The army was accompanied by a few warriors of the Seneca nation seeking the release of a captured chief and attended by friendly Oneidas and Tuscaroras.

The same newspaper account continues: "As far back as 1778, a period of near fifty-five years, there were but two or three log buildings in the place; the oldest occupied and kept as a public house, standing nearly, or perhaps quite, on the site where the handsome new building of Pugh Dungan now stands. No trace of this venerable building was to be observed for a number of years saving a small cavity which designated the spot occupied by the cellar and a well which has been re-opened by Mr. Dungan. The next was a low log building which subsequently gave place to the "Mansion Houes" of

---

3 Bucks County Intelligencer January 7, 1838.

Mrs. Magill. These were perhaps the only buildings in the place at that time."

One source of information, about the period of which we write, comes from the county records[4] the name of the land owners within two miles of Doyle's Tavern in 1776, in the respective townships around it, portions of which were cut off to make Doylestown township in 1818;

New Britain: Moses Aaron, Alexander Brown, Joseph Barton, William Beale, Thomas Barton, Christopher Day, Jr., John Dungan, William Dungan, David Dungan, Nathan Dungan, Daniel Evans, Benjamin Evans, Isaac Evans, James Evans, Abraham Freed, Thomas Good, Jr., Joseph Hair, Daniel Hough, James James, Conrad Keil, Robert Kirkbride, Benjamin Love, John Morris, Mennonite Meeting, Hugh Meredith, John Meredith, Jonathan Mason, Benjamin Mathews, John Mathews, New Britain Baptist Church, Nathan Preston, Richard Riale, Joshua Rowland, Henry Rosenberger, David Rees, Jacob Stout, William Stephens, David Stephens, Benjamin Stephens, Evan Stephens, Walter Shewell, Rich Swanwick, James Thomas, Jonathan Worthington, Samuel Worthington, John Williams, Casper Yoder.

Warwick: William Beale, Thomas Barton, Joseph Dungan, John Dungan, Jonathan Dungan, George Ewer, Jonathan Fell, John Fell, Joseph and Samuel Flack, James Hair, John Hough, Joseph Hough, Daniel Hough, Jacob Lapp, Robert and Henry Magill, William Miller, John McIntyre, Thomas Meredith, Simon Meredith, Samuel McKinstry, Edward and John Pool, Joseph Rodman, William Rodman, John Robinson, Ludwig Switzer, James Snodgrass.

Buckingham: Abner Bradfield, John Bradfield, John Burgess, Alexander Brown, Christopher Day, Jonathan Fell, Zenas Fell, George Fell, David Henderson, Thomas Jones, John Leinberger, Nathan McKinstry, John Samuels, George Walters, Henry Wierman, Thomas West.

Plumstead: Abraham Freed and Christopher Day, Jr.

One thing worthy of note, in this connection, is the fact that none of the Doyles are mentioned among the list of land owners in 1776, within two miles of the cross roads that subsequently became Doylestown. It will be remembered, however, that William Doyle removed to Plumstead township in 1776, and parted with his land at the time, and other members of the family doubtless had previously sold theirs.

---

4 Furnished by Charles Hall, Esq.

Doylestown, Old and New.

III

Early Business Life.

The first record, of the business life of Doylestown, carries us back to 1779, possibly a year or two earlier, when Jesse Fell was keeping store at the cross-roads. In that year he purchased forty acres of land of John Robinson, who was designated in the deed as "storekeeper." He was a brother of Joseph Fell, the blacksmith, on the site of the Ross mansion, and a son of Thomas and Jane Fell, Buckingham, where he was born April 16, 1751. He removed to Wilkesbarre about 1790, where he became quite prominent. He made the first successful experiment of burning antharcite coal in a grate; held several public positions, including Associate Judge, and died August 11, 1830. The next venture in store keeping, at Doylestown, was in 1785, one hundred and seventeen years prior to this writing, when Christian Wirts, Jr. kept a branch store here in connection with his father at Philadelphia. The Durham furnace records show that it did considerable business with the Philadelphia Wirts, the earliest purchase being made at Doylestown, September 26, 1788, of seven Indian blankets, £3.16.6. The bill was made out to "Richard Backhouse, Esq.," then owner of the furnace, but is not receipted. It would be interesting to know where this early store stood, and when it opened. We have trace of a store, or shop, at Doylestown prior to this, to supply the wants of the neighborhood, but the date is meagre and uncertain. We learn from John S. Wirts, of Philadelphia, that Christfan Wirts, Jr., was the son of Christian Wirts (Wurts) who was born in Germany, 1737, and a Major at

Lancaster during the Revolution. Christian Wirts, Jr. married Maria Helina Wynkoop, one of the daughters of Judge Wynkoop, of Newtown.

Nathaniel Shewell was also a pioneer store keeper at Doylestown, and one of the earliest we have met with. We cannot tell when he opened, but he was in business here in 1790, on the site of Randall's Hardware store, southeast corner of State and Main streets, and closed out his stock of goods at public sale on November 2, 1810, and retired. He was now forty years old, and if he had kept store continuously, since 1790, he would have spent half his life in the business. Possibly the building he occupied was the frame in which William Doyle had kept tavern. Nathaniel Shewell was a son of Robert and grandson of Walter Shewell, born in New Britain township, November 22, 1770, married Cynthia, daughter of Thomas Fell, February 3, 1795, and died 1860.

He was prominent in business and politics, elected to the Assembly in 1809-10, and was subsequently Sheriff of the county. He kept a tavern several years at Doylestown, and owned the ground the public buildings were built on, 1812. The Shewells came to America from Gloucester, England, 1729.

There was no visible improvement, as the last decade of the century came in. The Embryo county seat was credited with half a dozen dwellings, two taverns, a store or two and a smith shop, these making up the hamlet. George Stewart kept a store here in 1805, and lived in a log house on the site of *The Intelligencer* office, afterwards known as "Barton Stewart's shop."[1] Hugh Meredith was at or near Armstrong's corner in a stone house with frame office attached; a small stone tavern, "The Ship," was on the sight of Lenape building, which Christian Wirts[2] bought in 1791 and kept it some time; on Main street, adjoining, was a frame store; on the opposite corner of State and Main streets, on the site of the old Mansion House, was a frame: a log house stood on the west side of West State street on the site afterwards occupied by the old brewery; it had no occupant at that time, but, soon afterward, one Joseph Pool kept a groggery

---

[1] At Doylestown, January 10, 1813, at the house of her son-in-law, Barton Stewart, Mrs. Rebecca Sandham, widow of the late Mathias Sandham, of Blockley township, Philadelphia county.

[2] He was no doubt the Christian Wirts who kept store here in 1785, in connection with his father in Philadelphia, although his name was spelled differently. It must be borne in mind that the Doyle Tavern was licensed in 1745, and was probably kept at or near where the two roads crossed.

N. SHEWELL.

there, and Joseph Fell whose shop was in the southwest corner of a little stone structure that subsequently grew to be the "Ross Mansion." This was the make up of Doylestown one hundred and eleven years ago, obtained from the most reliable sources, but, humble as it was, it possessed the seed, everywhere sown in this country, from which spring towns, cities, and great metropolisses.

A visible sign of improvement and progress, as the last decade of the eighteenth century expired, was the running of a stage, through Doylestown, between Easton and Philadelphia. This was put on ten years prior to the opening of a post office here, and eight before the century expired. John Nicholaus[3] was the earliest proprietor, and the line commenced running April 29, 1792, making weekly trips, down on Monday and up on Thursday, fare $2.00. There is hardly a doubt it carried the mail. In the spring of 1794, Lawrence Erb, of Easton, put on an opposition line to Philadelphia, both running down the Easton road, and through Doylestown on the same days. The fare was the same, Erb's line allowing passengers ten pounds of baggage. As early as 1800, a semi-weekly stage ran from Philadelpha through Doylestown, to Bethlehem, but whether it carried the mail is not known. These stage lines were the pioneers between the lower Delaware and the Lehigh, and the region beyond to the Susquehanna, and there is hardly a doubt they were the first to supply that far away frontier with its mail matter. A more extended account of the mails and stages centering at, or running through, Doylestown will be found in a subsequent chapter, entitled "The Stage and the Mails."

By the close of the century there had been some additional progress made, and the little town of the Doyles seemed disposed to exchange its swadling clothing for the garments of sturdy boyhood.

As the new century turned its back on the old we find Charles Stewart keeping a tavern on the site of the Fountain House, and probably the present building was part of it, where the Bethlehem mail stage stopped for dinner; Jacob Thomas was saddler, cap, holster and harness maker; and Joseph Stewart carried on the same business, "on the Swede's ford road the first house below Doylestown." The site of the village was well-wooded. Timber extended up both sides of Main street, from Broad to the Dublin road, reaching back some distance; on the north side of Court street out to the

---

3 Nicholaus died at Easton, 1807.

borough line, and the Riale and Armstrong farm were covered w
timber.

In the course of researches we come upon a document of so
interest, of which the following is a copy: "In three months after d
I promise to pay to William Magill, or order, the just and full sum
seven pounds current lawful money of Pennsylvania with law
interest from the date for value received, as witness my hand and se
September 16th, 1799.

    Witness present,   (Signed) JNO. ROSS.
      ROBT. MURRAY.   (Sea

We have already mentioned the Kirkbride estate on the nor
western confine of the borough, and that his vast realty was inheri
by his heirs. One of these was Robert Kirkbride, probably a gra
son, who owned the Chapman farm. His executors, shortly after
death, made a sale of building lots, including both sides of the slope
the Germany hill. This was in 1799, the first public sale of lots
Doylestown, and among the purchasers, were Elijah Russell, Willi
Magill, George Stewart, John Byerly and Eleazer Fenton. This
the south end of the plantation.

Down to this time we have refrained from discussing the quest
of population, a subject difficult to handle in a hamlet without recor
as we are about to pass into a new century it is well to give
reader the best estimate of the population we are able to make,
with the figures we give the authority. In 1856, the late Thor
Lewis, Buckingham, who died that year at the age of eighty-tw
told William J. Buck that he had known Doylestown all his life,
the houses, at 1790, did not exceed twenty. If we accept this as
number of dwellings, and allow five to a family, it gives a populat
of one hundred persons. As Mr. Lewis lived near the village,
doubtless was frequently at it, and was sixteen years old at 1790,
is a competent witness, and we doubt if one more reliable can be p
duced. It is safe, then, to set down the population of Doylestow
1790, at one hundred souls, men women and children. The increa
for the next ten years, is altogether a matter of conjecture, but
make a liberal allowance in estimating it at 25, giving a population
125, when we turn out of the old century into the new.

Everything considered, its lowly birth, humble beginning a
surroundings, the absence of outside help, and the fact that t
country was recovering from a long and exhaustive war, it will be co
ceded that our hamlet had been fairly successful in the race of li

but the coming decade will emphasize its future hope. A period of ten years, that brings to a cross-road village a newspaper, a post-office with mail facilities, a classical school and a public library, lays the foundation of a church and is declared the future county seat of one of the original counties of the commonwealth, deserves to be called prosperous. At this day villages grow with much greater rapidity, but, it must be borne in mind, that was a very conservative period, and now towns, cities and villages grow up like mushrooms.

As the eighteenth century turned into the nineteenth, a newspaper made its appearance at the cross-roads village, the *Farmers' Weekly Gazette*, published by Isaac Ralston, of which more will be said in the eighth chapter, on the "Newspaper Press." It throws but little, if any, light on the period, of the hamlet or where published ; it contained not a line of the village life or its business life except the following reference: "The Bethlehem mail stage, running to Philadelphia, will dine at the house of Charles Stewart[4] in Doylestown; a saddle and bridle were found near Doylestown, and the Republican citizens of Bucks county met at Charles Stewart's tavern on Saturday, the 22nd of November, 1800."

By this time the hamlet had grown to a village of 125 inhabitants, according to our estimate, and the first recognition, that it had come to stay, was the opening of a post-office in January, 1802, and the appointment of Charles Stewart as post-master.

We now reach the year 1804, an important period in the life of the hamlet of the Doyles, by the arrival of two new factors that added strength to its young life, the building of the Union Academy, and the establishment of a second newspaper, The *Pennsylvania Correspondent* and *Farmers' Gazette,* by Asher Miner,[5] the one set up in 1800 having given up the ghost. The chapter on newspapers will likewise have more to say of the *Correspondent*.

The coming down of the Rev. Uriah DuBois from Dublin, and the opening of the Union Academy, in 1805, were matters of great import. The erection of the Academy may be set down on the credit side of Mr. DuBois' account; he was the moving spirit, and some of the officers and members of his church were active in the work. A man of his culture would naturally be the motive power of such an

---

4 Present Fountain House.

5 At West Chester, Pa., February 9, 1831, Mary Minor, wife of Asher Minor, aged about 50 years.

enterprise. In this building one room was reserved for religious worship, and the meetings held there were the germ of the Presbyterian church that was founded ten years later. It is an interesting coincidence and creditable to the period, that two such powerful agents, as the church and the press, should drive in their stakes the same year at this country hamlet. Was there a Providence in this coincidence? The Academy and the newspaper were the parent of the culture of the period and their influence extended beyond their local boundaries. The first issue of Miner's paper was July 7, 1804.

The village was now well equipped with mechanics, dealers, traders et al. to carry on the affairs of the new-born community, and the paper informs us who and what they were. The list is headed with Daniel Farley "from the cities of New York and Philadelphia," who advertised as "sign and portrait painter, glazier and paperhanger," and, through printers ink, "solicits a share of public favor," and expresses his gratitude " for the commands he has received since his residence in Doylestown." He had his "shop," not studio, directly over the " new printing office." What a gap there is in art from "sign" to "portrait" painter! George Stewart in 1805, who carried on making saddles "at the old stand a few rods southwest of the two taverns,"[6] probably the same who kept store here that year; Andrew Dennison, Simon Jameson, Meshash Minerer, Jr., and William Huntsmen were village cobblers, who called a meeting of the Master Shoemakers, "who feel interested in the proper regulation of the prices." By 1805, Doylestown had a hatter, in the person of John Knight; a taylor, in Goden Hall, a cousin of the late Samuel Hall, who "makes Ladies Great Coats in the newest fashion;" Benjamin Drake was blacksmith but had to leave October 12th; and Daniel M'Intosh had lately commenced the business of "spinning wheel and windsor chair making."

Asher Miner announces in his newspaper, now a year and a half old, in the issue of December 2nd, 1805, that he had removed his printing apparatus " to the new and convenient building just erected, adjoining his dwelling house at the upper end of the village, and

---

6 The "two taverns" were what is now the Fountain House, and the "Ship" on the site of "Lenape Building". And a few rods southwest would be a short way out West State street.

SCHEETZ'S STORE HOUSE, FOUNDED 1830

directly opposite the Academy;"[7] and that over the printing office, Zerick Titus "made and repaired saddles, bridles and harness." In the fall of 1804, David Kirkbride advertises for sale a tract of 30 or 40 acres adjoining the village, "on the stage road from Easton and Bethlehem to Philadelphia principally covered with timber," and is " probably one of the best stands in the county for a tan yard, there being a large spring upon it." This embraced the slope of "Germany" hill, the " Clear Spring" hotel property, and, beyond, part of the Chapman farm.

The second sale of building lots, in Doylestown, was held on Saturday, February 8th, 1806, by John Black, "on the main road from Norristown to Coryell's Ferry." This was somewhere on State street, but there is no indication as to location, price, or purchasers' names if any lots were sold.

The factors of progress were constantly added to. In January, 1805, the representative in Congress, from this district, had an act passed for the opening of two post routes through the county; one from Bristol, via Newtown, and Doylestown to Quakertown; and the other from Coryell's Ferry, via Doylestown to Lancaster, both of great convenience to Miner's newspaper, the post-office and the public generally. Prior to this there was but a single mail route through the county, from Philadelphia, via Doylestown to Bethlehem and Easton. The progress made in the village, in the past few years, was more than respectable, quite astonishing for the period, and gave evidence of enterprise; a newspaper, an Academy, a public library, a post office with three mail routes, several mechanics, two taverns, that many or more stores, grouped about the cross roads fairly well equipped the coming village.

By 1807, the prospect looked so encouraging for the future, it was thought best to open a new street, or road, and this led to the laying out and opening of the "Academy Lane," the present Court street, on the township line of New Britain and Warwick, from the Easton road to Buckingham line, 33 feet wide. The landholders,

---

[7] The location of the new building is easily fixed. Asher Miner lived in the stone house that stood on the site of the dwellings of N. C. and J. D. James, on the west side of North Main street, back of the Court House, and the new printing office, frame, almost joined the house. In this building the *Bucks County Express* was last published. It was "directly opposite the Academy" for, at that early day, there was nothing to obstruct the view across the intervening field, and neither Court nor Broad street was yet opened. This was before "Germany" was founded, and the Court House built.

along the new highway were as follows, beginning at the Easton road, now Main street: On the south side, Barton Stewart, Nathaniel Shewell, the Union Academy, Jonathan and Daniel McIntosh, Asher Miner, Dr. Hugh Meredith and John Pennington; and, on the north side, also beginning at the Easton road, Nathaniel Shewell, John Black, Samuel Wigton, John Shaw,[8] John Worman, Uriah DuBois, Septimus Evans, Josiah Y. Shaw, Israel Vanluvanee and John Pennington. This was followed, 1811, by the laying out and opening of the present Broad street, from the New Hope road to the Easton road on the line of lands of Septimus Evans and Uriah DuBois; on the east side of the site for the public buildings, Nathaniel Shewell and Isaac Hall on the west.

The question of a County Alms House was agitated as early as 1790, the main argument, in its favor, being the less expense and greater convenience in keeping the poor. Under the old system the county was divided into districts, each keeping its own poor, which proved expensive and troublesome. The proposed change met with great opposition from the Germans, as they furnished few paupers. The bill was signed by the Governor, April 10th, 1807, was approved by the Court, Grand Jury and Commissioners at the next term, and Thomas Long, William Watts, William Ruckman and David Spinner were elected Commissioners to erect the buildings at the following October election. Several townships were exempt from the provisions of the Act of Assembly, but were authorized to share its benefits by paying their pro rata of the cost of the erection of buildings, etc. Eighteen townships were named in the act, all below and including, Plumstead, New Britain and Hilltown.

On the passage of the bill, the Alms House war was waged with increased bitterness, and every possible influence brought to bear against the purchase of a site. Although the act was passed three years prior to that for the removal of the county seat, it was a warning to its friends what they might expect when that question should be pressed. The effect was to unite them against the Alms House scheme, but without avail. On December 20th, 1808, the Commissioners purchased of Gilbert Rodman,[9] the "Spruce Hill" farm, then in Warwick township, of 360 acres at £20 per acre, a large portion being covered with timber.

The purchase of the farm renewed the opposition that had some-

---

8 The Burges map.
9 In Doylestown, August 26th, 1835, Hannah Rodman, daughter of the late Gilbert Rodman.

what subsided, and John Watson wrote several violent articles against it over his own signature.   Meetings were held and lampooning handbills issued and circulated. A meeting, to sustain the purchase, was held at the public house of Septimus Hough, Warwick, at which several depositions were taken to prove the farm was well-watered, well-timbered and the soil fertile. All opposition failed to set aside the purchase, which the Court confirmed, and arrangements were made for beginning the work. The corner-stone was laid May 4th, 1809, and it was pushed to completion as actively as possible.

The corner-stone laying was made an event of some significance which the correspondent recorded as taking place "In the presence of the assembled workmen, and a number of neighboring gentlemen; a 'libation,' consisting of liquors of several kinds, was provided for the occasion by the directors and two other gentlemen at their private expense: the corner-stone was laid by Mr. Hall,[10] Master Mason." The buildings were finished in less than a year, the entire cost of material, erection, furnishing and stocking the farm, being $19,029, which, added to the price paid for the land, $19,280,00, made the entire cost $38,309.13. During its erection the directors paid $94.77½ for whiskey for the workmen. The first death in the new Alms House occured April 23, 1810.[11]

Among the deaths at the Alms House[12] was that of Dr. William Bachelor, of Moreland township, Montgomery county, April 4th, 1826. He was a surgeon in General Gates' army at the battle of Saratoga, and, after the war, settled in Bucks county and married Eleanor Hart, daughter of Silas Hart, Warminster. He was buried in the Vansant graveyard. Dr. Bachelor had a good practice, but ruined himself and wasted his estate by dissipation. He was a man of many excentricities and some of his actions are still rehearsed. He was a native of Massachusetts.

---

10 Isaac Hall, father of the late Samuel Hall, Doylestown.

11 This was a black woman, named "Dinah," a native of this county, formerly a slave of Jeremiah Langhorne, and supposed to be 116 years old.

12 At the Alms House, November 21st, 1812, Catharine Leonard, aged 102 years. Since she arrived at 100 she had spun 200 dozens of flax yarn.

Doylestown, Old and New.

IV
Becomes the County Seat.

The first effort to remove the county seat from Newtown to Doylestown, was made as early as 1784, petitions being presented to the Legislature that session. The petition, from this vicinity, was read March 28th, and, with a single exception, they were all couched in the same language and the same reason assigned:

"The great disadvantage of having the Courts of Justice held in a place very 'uncentral' in said county, whereby the expense of attending on juries and other occasions fall very unequally on the freemen of said county; the present Court House and prison are old and decaying, and must soon be rebuilt from the foundation which makes the present a proper time to apply to your Honorable House for leave to build a Court House and prison on a better plan at Doylestown," etc.

A draft of the village accompanies the petitions, but that has disappeared. To this petition were the names of 114 signers, among them those of Dungan, Greir, Hines, Meredith, Wigton, James, Harris, Mathews, Stephens, Flack, Shewell, Darrah and others well known at the present day. There were eight petitions in all, containing 284 names, and, as a whole, the signers, were men who controlled public sentiment in their respective neighborhoods. On one of the petitions was the name of Zebulon Pike, Solebury, father of General Zebulon M. Pike, killed at the capture of York, Canada, 1813. The draft of the village was with the Doylestown petition, and also a subscription list of some £300 toward erecting the new Court House and prison. Jesse and Joseph Fell, of Doylestown, were the heaviest subscribers, who also pledged themselves to give a suitable piece of ground to erect the public buildings on.

Other subsequent and unsuccessful efforts were made to change the location of the county seat before it became an accomplished fact. There was one in 1795, when the same reasons were given, but almost a generation elapsed before the county seat was changed to its present eligible site. Soon after the nineteenth century came in, the agitation, for the removal of the county seat to Doylestown, was renewed and continued until success crowned the effort, by the Governor approving the bill. The movement, this time, was general except in the lower end of the county, the project for erecting a new jail and Court House at Newtown, giving it emphasis. The fight was a bitter one, minister and layman taking part in it, one of the most active, for removal, being the Rev. Nathaniel Irwin, pastor of Neshaminy Presbyterian church, Warwick. After the removal was accomplished, some wag of an artist depicted the part the parson had taken, by a charcoal sketch on the walls of the old Court House, representing him with a rope across his shoulders and around the building and he tugging away as for dear life toward Doylestown. The Governor signed the bill, February 28th, 1810. The success of the friends of the measure aptly fitted a familiar quotation from Shakespeare, "There is a tide in the affairs of men which, taken at the flood, leads on to fortune."

The act of Assembly, authorizing the removal of the county seat, empowered the Governor

"To appoint three discreet and disinterested persons, one from the county of Northampton, one from the county of Chester and one from the county of Berks, not holding any real estate in the county of Bucks, whose duty it shall be to fix on a proper and convenient site for a Court House, prison and county offices to be erected not more than three miles from Bradshaw's corner, where the roads leading from Wilkinson's tavern[1] to the Cross Keyes, intersects with the public road leading from Doyls Town to Vanhorn's tavern, admitted to be the centre of said county."

The Governor named as Commissioners, Edward Darlington,

---

[1] Wilkinson's tavern was then at Bushington, and Vanhorn's at Centreville and "Bradshaws Corner," the present Pool's Corner, on the New Hope turnpike a mile from Doylestown.

Chester; Nicholas Kern, Northampton, and Gabriel Hiester, Berks county, who were required to view the respective site and transmit their report to the County Commissioners, on or before the first Monday in June. The Deputy Secretary of the Commonwealth forwarded the commissions in care of the Prothonotary of the respective counties with an authenticated copy of the Act of Assembly.

The Commissioners met at Doylestown, May 12th, 1810, and viewed the sites recommended, three in all; at Doylestown, the Turk, a mile south of Doylestown, and at Bradshaw's Corner, a mile to the east. Strong influence was brought in favor of each location, the friends of the Turk, then called "Houghville," laying out a prospective village, the original plot of which belongs to the author, and a copy hangs in the museum of the Bucks County Historical Society; but Doylestown, already quite a considerable village, with an academy and a newspaper, was selected unanimously, its fine healthy location being within a few hundred yards of the geographical centre of the county, and at the intersection of two great highways, were doubtless the factors that decided the question. The report was made out and signed the same day, in which the Commissioners say they had "fixed upon a lot of land, herein after described, situated in the township of New Britain, in the said county of Bucks, in or near the village commonly called Doyls Town." This report was accompanied by a draft of the land recommended for a site for the public buildings, as surveyed and drawn by George Burges.[2]

The land selected for the public buildings was the triangular lot on which the Court House now stands, and where the old jail stood, belonging to Nathaniel Shewell, in New Britain, containing 2 acres and 121 perches. The transfer of the property to Jacob Weaver, Thomas Jenks and John Corson, the Commissioners of the county, was made the same day the site was agreed upon; the deed was acknowledged before John Shaw, Esq., and the witnesses, Edward Darlington, Gabriel Hiester, and Nicholas Kern, the three Commissioners to select the site. The land was practically a gift to the county, the consideration in the deed being one dollar. The boundary of the tract was as follows:

"Beginning at a corner in the post road leading from Easton to Philadelphia; thence along a street by land of Septimus Evans, south-

---

[2] It will be noticed the draft is signed May 11th, the day before the Commissioners met, indicating that the friends of this location were sure of getting the decision before the site was viewed.

east 32 perches to a corner in a public road, being a corner of land appropriated for the use of an Academy, thence southwest by other land of Nathaniel Shewell 19 perches; thence along other land of said Shewell northwest 15 perches to middle of said post road; thence north along the same 28 perches to the place of beginning. [3]

From this draught, it would appear that Nathaniel Shewell, Charles Meredith, Asher Miner, Serick Titus and Septimus Evans were the only land owners bordering the property conveyed to the county, but there were probably others. Shewell owned the land from Broad street to Pine on Court, and also what was afterward the Ross property. Although Broad street was not opened until the following year, it is dotted as if already opened, and the same is the case with Pine. Pine was probably intended to go through to Main, but never opened farther than Court, and we believe about the time the village was made the county seat.

In the meantime an effort was made to extend the time for the erection of the public buildings, a movement of its enemies for delay, but it failed in its purpose; whereupon James Chapman, clerk to the board of County Commissioners, advertised, March 23rd, 1811, for "Proposals, in writing, for furnishing material, and for mechanics and workmen for the erection of the necessary public buildings, at Doylestown." The carpenter work was given to Levi Bond, Newtown, and the mason work to Timothy Smith, Doylestown, the wages being fixed at $1 a day, the hands to work without regard to hours. [4] Samuel Q. Holt, a journeyman mason, who worked on the public buildings, was living, and quite active, in 1876, and, so far as is known, the only one then living.

As soon as the contracts were signed, and the material delivered, ground was broken and the work of erecting the buildings begun. In the issue of Miner's *Correspondent,* April 13th, 1812, we find the following notice of the progress on the work:

"The sound of the hammer and the hum of the building may be witnessed on the public grounds in this village. The carpenters and masons commenced their operations during the past week, under the

---

3 This lot was part of the 30 acres Joseph Fell bought at Sheriff's sale, 1788, and was conveyed to Nathaniel Shewell by Fell's administrator, 1802. The property belonged to William Doyle, 1750, when he sold it to Israel Pemberton.

4 The proposals were received by the Commissioners and opened at the public house of Enoch Harvey, Doylestown, at 10 A. M., April 8th, and the County Commissioners met at the same place, in November, to close the contract for furnishing the stone for the jail wall, lime, sand, iron, work, etc.

superintendency of Jonathan Smith, Esq.[5] Sheds for the workmen are erected, and the cellar of the Court House is progressing. May success attend their exertions! The work was pushed and the buildings finished in the spring of 1813, almost three years from the time the site was selected. On April 20th, when the new buildings were about completed, and the offices on the point of being removed to Doylestown, the following notice was made public : " Whereas, the records and papers in the Register's, Recorder's, and Prothonotary's offices in Newtown will soon be packed up for removal to their new apartments, in Doylestown, no business will be done in their offices, from the 10th to the 24th of May, and the next Court will be held at Doylestown on the 31st of May."[6]

The Bucks County *Intelligencer* of January, 1833, in an article speaking generally of Doylestown, says of the erection of the public buildings of 1812-13:

"Preparations for building were commenced in the latter part of the year 1811, and they were completed in 1813. They were built of the best material and in a superior manner; and are, perhaps, unequalled by any County Court House and jail in the state. The amount for erecting the entire building is $38,007.31, since which time alternations have been made, the more recent of which were in 1831, when the Court House underwent a thorough repair, the expense amounting to $2,111.74."

The last Court held at Newtown was a Criminal Court in March, 1813, and arrangements were shortly under way for a transfer to the new county seat. Judge Bird Wilson issued a proclamation April 28th, from Newtown, for a Criminal Court at Doylestown May 31st, the first held in the new Court House. The last business done in the public offices at Newtown was on May 10th, and, meanwhile, to May 31st, the records were removed, and the Court held as announced. The first prisoners to escape from the new jail were John H.

---

[5] One of the Commissioners.

[6] The old public buildings, at Newtown, were sold at public sale by the Commissioners, January 25th, 1813. The property was divided into four parcels, the Commissioners reserving the Court House bell, the iron doors in the offices; all the stoves belonging to the county, the books, papers, cases, boxes, chairs, etc. Lots 1, 2 and 3, on which stood the Court House, jail, the old office and stable, were struck off to John Hulme at $1,600, and No. 4, the new office, now occupied by the Newtown National Bank, to William Watts at $900.

OLD COURT HOUSE, 1812.

Hayes and Samuel Trumbower, March 16th, 1816, but were pursued and captured after a fight.[7]

The removal of the county seat to Doylestown caused considerable bitterness; with some it lasted for years, with others through life. The change of the seat of justice touched some in the pocket, the most sensitive part of one's personality, but the removal was for the public convenience. The following paragraph from the *Patriot* of July 18th, 1825, shows the feeling at that time: "We have seen petitions in circulation for the removal of the seat of justice of Bucks county from Doylestown to Easton."

The removal caused some activity in real estate at Doylestown, and several pieces of property were offered for sale. On January 1st, 1813, the dwelling of Rev. Uriah DuBois, now the property of Judge Yerkes, corner of Broad and State streets, was offered for sale, and Lot Carr also offered a house, with 40 perches of land attached, "near the centre of business on the main stage road," and a lot adjoining on which are a new two-story frame house and a comfortable shop for a mechanic;" and Daniel McIntosh offered a handsome lot of 2 acres and 18 perches, " fronting almost 20 rods on the stage road, on which are erected a two-story frame house, a convenient work-shop for a mechanic and a good stable, the buildings all nearly new."

The transfer of the Courts, public officers and their families, to the new county seat was quite an event; and many friends and neighbors assisted. The author frequently heard his father speak of this moving, at which he was present. He was then a young man of twenty-five. In the afternoon, after the men of the party had their dinner, a number of them went into the jail yard and engaged in the old ball game known as "Fives," popular at that period, but not practiced now.

No sooner was the county seat changed, than an active effort was begun to divide the county, with a view of first making Newtown and then Bristol the seat of justice of the new county. This was kept up for forty years, and the question was raised in more than one political campaign. The late C. N. Taylor was the leader, and, sometimes

---

7 They were cutting wood in the yard, and while the jailor had his back turned, skipped out through the kitchen, fastening the door behind them, and then through the dwelling into the street. In their recapture Hayes had his arm broken and Trumbower wounded in the head. Four prisoners escaped the night of March 15th, 1827, and two the night of December 3rd, 1830.

came very near success, but the constitution of 1874 has made t division practically impossible.

The last effort to divide the county, and which came near be successful, was in 1855. It passed the House and reached the Co mittee of the Senate, which was said to be in its favor. In the ea spring of 1855, Enos Prizer and Henry T. Darlington, two you printers from Chester county, bought the Bucks County *Intelligenc* and, of course, were against a division of the county. On a Sunday March they drove down to Davisville and requested the late Gene John Davis to go to Harrisburg and try to prevent the passage of bill. He went with reluctance, although opposed to division, rea ing the Capital early in the evening. The first man General Da called on was his old friend Simon Cameron, to whom he stated case. Cameron consented to do what he could, but stipulated t they, Cameron and Davis, must not be seen together. When Senate Committee met, those for and against division were hea including General Davis and Caleb N. Taylor, the latter the gr champion of division, but General Cameron was nowhere to be se He had done his work outside. The committee was unanim against division and so reported. The people of Bucks are indebted General Cameron for preventing the mutilation of Penn's old coun At that time, Howard K. Sagers, of Northampton township, was Senator from Bucks and opposed division.

In after years the county jails of the state got into such a repute as to cleanliness and good management, that visitations w made to them. In the 40's, Miss Dix, a noted philanthropist of N York, visited the Doylestown jail and Alms House, of which spoke in the following terms:

"Bucks county jail at Doylestown is a well-built prison in go order and repair, the departments being comfortable and decent. found here four prisoners, two men and two women, committed immoralities, all occupying one room by day. It would appear t " if evil communications are corrupting, they were not likely to le the prison with amended purposes or repentent minds."

" The County Poor House is in Warwick township, three m from Doylestown. The situation is elevated, pleasant and health The farm is large, productive and well cultivated. All things p taining to it are creditable to the Superintendent." Since that per there has been great improvement in the management of such institutions.

When the seat of justice was transferred to Doylestown, the local members of the bar, with two exceptions, came with it, there being but eight practicing attorneys at that time. It was the custom for Philadelphia attorneys to attend the Courts of neighboring counties, and some of them were present at Newtown at every term. This custom was continued for a number of years, after the county seat was removed, but gradually relinquished. They who followed the county seat to Doylestown and are designated the pioneer bar, were the following with the date of their admission: Abraham Chapman, 1790; Francis B. Shaw, 1800, Enos Morris and William McIlheny, 1801; John Fox, 1807; Mathias Morris, 1809; John D. Roney, 1812, and William W. Hart, 1813. Mr. Hart was Clerk of the Orphan's Court, having been appointed to succeed the Rev. James Boyd, deceased.

Enos Morris remained at Newtown making it his permanent home, and died there. He was a member of the Southampton Baptist Church, and a regular attendant. Of John D. Roney we know nothing. Francis B. Shaw, born in New Britain, and son of John Shaw, divided his time, for a few years, between Philadelphia and Doylestown, but finally made the latter place his home. He was deprived of his sight, for two years, by a cataract, but an operation by Dr. Phisick, Philadelphia, restored it in 1815, and he returned to practice. He passed the remainder of his life at Doylestown occupied with his profession and journalism, for which he had a taste, dying in 1832, at the age of fifty-six. "Frank" Shaw, as all his acquaintance called him, and by which name he is still known by the few survivors of that period, was a man of ability and, in some respects, a picturesque character.

Abraham Chapman was born in Wrightstown, and his wife, a daughter of Dr. Hugh Meredith, in Doylestown. She, being an invalid, they came up from Newtown in advance of the bar and court, and she died at her father's home. Mathias Morris was born in Hilltown, where the family settled at an early day. He entered politics and served one term in Congress and one in the State Senate, but continued the practice of the law to his death.[8] On the expiration of John Fox's term as Deputy Attorney General for the county, 1821, Mathias

---

8 At Doylestown, November 8th, 1839, Mathias Morris, aged fifty-four years.

Morris was appointed in his stead, January 2nd. William W. Ha[r]
the youngest member of the pioneer bar, and born in Southampt[on]
township, was a nephew of William Watts, after whom he was name[d]
Mr. Fox, the only one of the number who reached the bench, surviv[ed]
them all.

Bird Wilson was President Judge when the change of the seat
Justice came, but never resided in the county, making his home
Norristown. He was born at Philadelphia, January 8th, 1777, sat [on]
our bench from February 28th, 1806, to January 1st, 1818, when he r[e]
signed to enter the church, and died April 14th, 1859. He was t[he]
son of James Wilson, a signer of the Declaration of Independence, a[nd]
also of the Convention that formed the United States Constitutio[n]
and Washington called him the "father of the Constitution." Wils[on]
was third President Judge of this district under the then judicial sy[s]
tem, his predecessors having been John D. Cox and James Bidd[le]
The associates at the removal were Samuel Hart and Robert Smit[h]
and John Fox, the prosecuting officer, called "Deputy Attorney Ge[n]
eral." The coming of the members of the bar, and court officials,
Doylestown with their families, increased the sparce population of t[he]
village and was an addition to its social life.

Mr. Fox was probably the ablest of the lawyers that came
from Newtown and we do not believe he had his superior in any th[at]
followed him. He read law with Alexander J. Dallas, Philadelphi[a]
and commenced practice at Newtown as soon as admitted. He w[as]
a well-read lawyer, booked in the political history of the country, a[nd]
familiar with English literature. When he addressed the Court [or]
jury he dealt in facts, leaving fancy to others, and what he said we[nt]
home straight as the arrow flies. He made his mark on the bench.
the Mina-Chapman trial, 1832, with which the science of chemistry h[ad]
much to do in reaching the truth, the experts found him their equ[al]
His opinion, delivered in the case denying the right of negroes to vo[te]
in Pennsylvania, 1838, attracted wide attention, and was quoted [by]
DeTocqueville in his "Democracy in America."

The removal of the seat of justice was shortly followed by t[he]
organization of a new township encircling the county seat, 181[8,]
taken from the three contiguous townships of Buckingham, N[ew]
Britain, and Warwick. The line of these townships run through t[he]
middle of the village, which frequently led to great inconvenienc[e.]
In 1818, the inhabitants awoke to the necessity of a change in t[he]
matter and a petition was presented to the August Quarter Sessio[ns]

Court. In response to the prayer of the petitioners, Thomas G. Kennedy,[8] Thomas Yardley and Thomas Story were appointed Commissioners to "lay out a new township, of which the Court House should be the centre as nearly as might be convenient." They reported in favor of a new township to be called Doylestown, to the November Sessions; the report was confirmed at the following term, 1819, and the township laid out accordingly.

The area of the township, according to the survey, was 10,050 acres, of which 5,350 were taken from New Britain, 1,185 from Buckingham, and 3,515 from Warwick, but the area was subsequently enlarged and the lines changed. The first election for township officers was held at the Court House, Friday, March 19th, 1819, with the following result: Constable, John D. James, received 89 votes, Isaac Benner, 58 and Stephen Brock, 58. The remaining officers elected were Joshua Riale and John Mann, supervisors; Abraham Geil, Timothy Smith and Moses Dunlap, settlers; and Benjamin Morris, Jr., town clerk.

In 1821 Doylestown township, including the village, had 339 taxables. The report of the Commissioners, which laid it out, was accompanied by an elaborate map, including several of the surrounding townships, drawn by Thomas G. Kennedy, but it has never fallen under our notice and do not know what has become of it. Mr. Kennedy was a distinguished engineer of the period. It is just possible the map, here alluded to, is confounded with the map Kennedy drew of Bucks county in 1817, for the State, two years before Doylestown township was laid out, and for which he received $500. A copy of this map, obtained from the office of Internal Affairs, Harrisburg, hangs in the room of the Bucks County Historical Society.

---

8 At Erwinna, May 24, 1819, by the Rev. Uriah DuBois, Thomas G. Kennedy, Esq., of Newtown, to Mrs. Julianna Dick, daughter of William Erwin, of Erwinna.

At Erwinna, May 14, 1836, Thomas G. Kennedy, aged fifty-three years.

Doylestown, Old and New.

V
Historic Walk.

Before moving on with the progress of events at Doylestown, and preparing for the advent of the county seat in the near future, we purpose to take a glance at the village about the opening of the nineteenth century. The most satisfactory way of doing it will be for the reader to accompany the author on a tramp around town and keep his eyes open. This will give him a better knowledge of the cross roads hamlet an hundred years ago; enable him to make a more intelligent comparison of old Doylestown with the new, and appreciate the latter's growth in the past century. We begin our walk at the north end of Main street in, "Germany," and come south.

Standing by the Clear Spring hotel and looking across the street to the east, we notice a small log-clapboard building on the knoll almost opposite. This is known as the "Russell house," and is, undoubtedly, the oldest dwelling in the borough. The lot was bought by Elijah Russell,[1] in 1800, of David Kirkbride at public sale and was formerly a part of the Chapman farm. The house was probably erected the same year of logs, and, in more recent years clapboarded. It has had a number of owners, the present one being Ernest Werner, a carpet weaver. We begin our historic walk by turning south up Lyman's hill. Passing Kramer's store, at the junction of Church street, we reach what was the Musgrave house in

[1] At Doylestown, Pa., April 9th, 1826, Sarah, wife of Elijah Russell, aged seventy-two years; interment at New Britain.

THE RUSSELL HOUSE, 1810.

the long ago. It stands on the east side of Main street, and was also built of logs, but has been so modernized its identity is gone. The Musgraves, father and son, were Canadians, coming here about the time of the Russells, and carried on watch-making and wheelwrighting on their premises. Continuing down North Main street up Chapman's hill, we next reach the Titus-Chapman-Lyman house, recently purchased by the late Frank Kolbe, who lived in it at his death. It is on the northeast corner of Broad and Main streets, and was built by Zerick Titus,[2] between 1800 and 1810, and, in a shop, that stood in Mrs. O. P. James' front yard, carried on his trade, that of saddler and harness maker. The house was bought by Abraham Chapman after coming here with the county seat. When Asher Miner built his new printing office, on the west side of North Main street, just south, Titus occupied a room in it. The north end of the Chapman-Lyman house was built by Mr. Chapman, who occupied it until his death, 1865. The dwelling, to some extent, was rebuilt, and very much repaired by Mr. Lyman, 1873. He was a member of the prominent Connecticut family of that name, and settled here on marrying the daughter of Mathias Morris, and spent the remainder of his life in Doylestown, Mrs. Lyman dying suddenly in 1902.

The dwelling across Main street, on the east corner of Broad, the home of Webster Grim, was built by Septimus Evans, 1810, for a public house and kept as the "Green Tree" for almost half a century, of which a fuller account will be given in the chapter on taverns. It had undergone little change until 1897, although occupied several years as a dwelling. The new owner, Mr. Grim, made many alterations and improvements, and thoroughly modernized it, but the outside walls are the same. It is a subject of regret no one thought of taking its likeness while it was in the flesh, as its original appearance has been wholly changed. We now turn into Broad street, going southeast, every house along it, on the east side, being modern dwellings, and void of history. On the west side were the open lots on which the Court House and jail were built 1810-13. At the northeast corner of Broad and Court we note the Union Academy, built in 1804, of which more will be said in another chapter.

We halt here a few minutes, to take a view of the old Fox house, now the pleasant home of George P. Brock. It has undergone some change since it came into the possession of the present owner, a few

---

[2] At Doylestown, Saturday evening, May 20th, 1808, by the Rev. Uriah DuBois, Mr. Zerick Titus to Miss Jane Fell, daughter of the late Joseph Fell.

colonial touches being added to it. This house has an interesti[ng] history, but we have only the space and time to rehearse a small pa[rt] of it. The ground, it stands on, belonged, at one time, to Cudjo a[nd] Joe, two of the negro slaves of Chief Justice Langhorne, but, abo[ut] the close of the eighteenth century, came into the possession [of] Jonathan and Daniel M'Intosh, emigrants from the Valley of Virgin[ia]. They sold it to the Rev. Uriah DuBois, who had just moved do[wn] from Dublin to the village to take charge of the new Academy, an[d] in 1807, he built a dwelling upon it, at a cost of $2,000, on the Co[urt] street front and next to the Academy. He lived there until 181[?] when he sold the house to William Watts[3] who had come up [to] Doylestown with the new county seat. Mr. DuBois now moved [to] a new house he had built at the southeast corner of East State a[nd] Broad streets. Judge Watts sold the house to John Fox, 181[?] another new comer from Newtown, who was married[4] the same ye[ar] and spent the remainder of his life there, dying 1849, Judge F[ox] became a prominent figure and was the bosom friend of Samuel Ingham, Jackson's Secretary of the Treasury, and his confident[ial] adviser in the Cabinet trouble. While the author was reading l[aw] with Judge Fox, he used to see Mr. Ingham's horse hitched to [the] fence opposite the Judge's house he having driven over from [his] beautiful home at "Ingham's Spring," Solebury township, to ta[lk] county, state and national politics. When taking our historic wa[lk] there was not a dwelling from the Brock house all the way [to] Court street.

Continuing our walk down Broad street to State, we halt op[po] site the DuBois homestead, built in 1808, and where the Revere[nd] Uriah DuBois died, September 10th, 1821. In its day, this dwelli[ng] was much the best house in the village, large and built of stone. [It] was owned and occupied many years by the late James Gilkyson, f[ol] lowed by his son-in-law, Henry T. Murfit, deceased. At a rec[ent] public sale the property came into the possession of Judge Yerkes. [In] the front yard a large pine tree is still standing, planted by Mr. D[uBois]

---

3 At Doylestown, May 3rd, 1838, in his seventy-ninth year, Willi[am] Watts, son of Arthur Watts of Southampton. He was several years Proth[on] otary and Clerk of the Quarter Sessions and Associate Judge. He was faith[ful] and impartial. He was a member of the Southampton Baptist Church ab[out] fifty years. He died without children. He was a descendant of the Rev. Jo[hn] Watts, the first pastor of the Pennepack Baptist Church.

4 On June 6th, 1816, by the Rev. Uriah DuBois, John Fox, Esq., Attor[ney] at Law, Doylestown, to Miss Margery Rodman, daughter of Gilbert Rodm[an] Esq., Bensalem.

DUBOIS HOMESTEAD, 1807.

Bois, the year he built the house to mark the birth of his son Samuel, the artist. We now turn into State street, going west, and the first old dwelling we strike, is the west end of the Hall homestead, built 1800 by Isaac Hall,[5] father of the late Samuel[6] and grandfather of Charles Hall, shortly after moving over from New Jersey. Until recently it had never been occupied by any other family. We next stop in front of the Nightingale stone house, with pointed front, one door east of Pine, south side. It was built 1821, and in it the Doylestown National Bank was organized, 1832-33, whence it removed to the new bank building on west side of North Main street, now occupied by the Doylestown Trust Company, which purchased it of the National Bank in recent years. The Nightingale house, too young to join in the procession that welcomes the county seat to Doylestown, will have to look on at a distance, was owned many years by the late Mrs. Kuhn, a daughter of the Reverend Samuel Nightingale. It has been so much changed, by the addition of modern mechanical furbeloes, neither the architect, nor builder, would be able to recognize it could they see it.

At the intersection of State and Main streets we strike a group of interesting buildings, and venerable with age. These were known, in the long ago, as "The Three Taverns." The oldest was the "Ship," on the site of Lenape Building, first licensed about 1775. The second of the group is the present Fountain House, that has rounded out a century, and was called the "Fox Chase" seventy years ago, while the third, and youngest, was the "Mansion House," built about 1810 by William Magill for a tavern, and licensed and kept as such over half a century. A log house is said to have occupied the site when the Continental army encamped one night at Doylestown, 1778. The walls are the same as when kept for a public inn, but has been occupied for a bakery and ice cream saloon several years. The prospect of the county seat being removed to Doylestown hastened the erection of the Mansion House. A couple of hundred feet across West State street stood an old stone smith shop, Fisher's of recent years, probably the oldest building in town when taken down in 1898. As it was near the cross-roads we believe it to have been the pioneer blacksmith shop of the neighborhood, and erected soon after the two public roads were opened. We now turn down

---

5 At Doylestown, May 5, 1833, Isaac Hall, the father of Samuel Hall, aged upward of 60 years.

6 At Doylestown, October 6, 1896, Samuel Hall, at the age of 85.

South Main street and halt a square below, where we find an old stone house on the northeast corner of York street, in which John Pugh formerly lived, and where his grandson, John P. Rogers, was born. It was probably built about 1808, but whether by Josiah Y. Shaw or Mr. Pugh is not so clear. It is now part of the Keller property. On the opposite corner, across York street, and now the property of Dr. Benner, is the house in which Josiah Y. Shaw died and where he spent many years of his life. It is a very old house and there is no doubt Mr. Shaw built it, but the time is not known. Opposite the Pugh house, on the northwest corner of Main street and Oakland avenue, is the old Nathan Cornell stone-pointed house were he carried on his trade of making hats for many years, and in which himself and wife died.[7] He advertised his business as early as November 28th, 1820. The property belonged to General John S. Bryan a number of years, and in it himself, and subsequently Samuel Johnson Paxson published the Doylestown *Democrat*. This house was built by Isaac B. Medary, 1814, and he lived in it a number of years. It is still in good condition.

In addition to the houses we have mentioned as being in the flesh to welcome the advent of the county seat, there were others built prior to 1813. On, or near the Armstrong corner, stood the stone dwelling of Dr. Hugh Meredith which he built, about 1789, and died in it 1815, also the McCoy dwelling, North Main street, built by Dr. Hugh, for his son Dr. Charles Meredith, but the exact year we do not know. In it the late Dr. G. R. McCoy spent the greater part of his professional life, and there died. Dr. Hugh Meredith also built the small stone house that stood on the site of the Mrs. N. C. James' dwelling, North Main, and although it did not stand parallel with the street, the McCoy house was laid out on the same lines. It is said that Dr. Charles Meredith,[8] the son, for whom the house was being erected, got up in the night and straightened the lines without his father's knowledge, saying "I will not have my house spoiled." The appearance of the house bespeaks its age. In this category are the old Asher Miner stone house on North Main street, opposite the Court House, that many of us remember, the Ross stable, and the

---

7 At Doylestown, March 27th, 1824, Mrs. Hannah Cornell, wife of Nathan Cornell, at the age of thirty-five. At Doylestown, November 7th, 1841, Nathan Cornell, at the age of fifty-four.

8 At Doylestown, July 29th, 1831, Dr. Charles Meredith in his fifty-seventh year: At Philadelphia, February 7th, 1832. Mrs. Isabella, relict of the late Dr Charles Meredith, of Doylestown.

old brewery on West Court street. The "Ross Mansion" was enlarged from a smith-shop, 1811, and that and two other public houses were licensed in view of the seat of justice coming here, the "Mansion House" and the "Green Tree." The Harvey house, a nice old semi-colonial dwelling at the northwest corner of North Main and West Court streets, recently taken down, was erected 1813, just in time to welcome the removal hither of the Courts and Court officers. The dressed stone, for the front and corners of the Harvey house, was probably the finest bit of masonry in old Doylestown. If we add to these Barton Stewart's [9] two log houses on the south side of East Court street opposite the monument, occupying the site of the *Democrat* and *Intelligencer* offices and Elias Carver's dwelling, we have named about all the buildings that witnessed the advent of the county seat, 1813, if not in being, 1810, when the Act of Assembly was passed for the change. Of course we except out-buildings.

Shortly before the late Samuel Hall died we had a conversation with him about the oldest buildings in Doylestown, and he not only confirmed what we have said of the pioneer houses as to date of erection, etc., but named others here at his earliest recollection, say 1818-1820, some of which may have been built prior. Of these were the M'Intosh house, now Mrs. Darlington's, at Maple Avenue and East State street, built shortly after 1810, and soon after the family came here; the stone house on the south side of East State street in which James Wigton then lived, subsequently where George Murray kept his famous boys' school, and more recently the property of the Barber family; the frame on the site of the Ruckman new stone dwelling, south side of East State; the Keichline frame nearly opposite, the Joshua Beans house north side of same street four doors from Main, in which he lived and died, and where Cameron and Mifflin published the *Democrat* 1819-20; the little frame, a few doors west of corner of State and Printer's Alley, north side where Thomas J. Stewart kept a confectionery seventy-five years ago, a genial man but very much under size; the Donnelly house, South Main street the home of Judge William Watts three quarters of a century ago; the E. T. McDowell house, built of pointed stone masonry now rough

---

9 At the house of her son-in-law, Barton Stewart, January 10th, 1813, Mrs. Rebecca Sandum of Blockley township, Philadelphia county, also: At Horsham, May 2nd, 1816, by the Rev. Robert Belville, Barton Steward, Doylestown, to Miss Margaret Dun, of Horsham, Montgomery county, also: At Doylestown, April 20th, 1828, of consumption, at the age of nineteen, Sylvester M., son of Barton Stewart, a student of Medicine with Dr. Miner, of Wilkesbarre.

cast, east side of North Main, erected by Dr. Hugh Meredith, who died in 1815. When this house was built it faced south, as there were no buildings to obstruct the view down to the corner of Main and State streets; the small Magill stone house with an A gable to the street, a story an a half high, on the west side of South Main, just above Green, was built by William Magill, who died in 1824, and in which his son Alfred taught school. It is still owned by one of the name, and has been longer in the same family than any other house in town except the Hall dwelling.

The Ross Mansion was the most interesting, if not the oldest dwelling in Doylestown, when it took its place in history. It occupied the apex of the triangle bounded by Main, Broad and Court streets, the lot joining the Court House property on the northeast, and was taken down, 1896, to make way for the erection of the new banking building. The land was included in Joseph Kirkbride's purchase from Jeremiah Langhorne, 1729, and passed into the hands of Nathaniel Shewell about the end of the century. The dwelling grew from a modest beginning. On what was then the northeast corner of East Court street and Monument Place, was a small blacksmith shop in the Revolutionary period, and for several years after. By whom erected there is doubt, but Joseph Fell carried on the trade there before the end of the century, but when it was assured Doylestown would become the county seat, Nathaniel Shewell, the then owner, enlarged the smithy to a two story attic house extending the southwest front to Main street, two rooms on each story. This improvement could be plainly distinguished. Further additions were added before or after the house got license, including a hall, sitting and dining-rooms. The kitchen and library were built after the property came into the possession of the Ross family.

When the house was being torn down to make way for the bank building, on two of the beam fillings, at the top of the Court street wall near the southwest corner, scratched in the fresh mortar, were the letters "N. S." and "G. S., 1811," the former, the initials for Nathaniel Shewell,[10] the latter the initials of some other member of the family, probably his wife. In the middle of the building, where the two sections united, there was found a heavy stone wall extending up to the comb of the roof and on it was a dressed chimney top. The

---

10 In Doylestown township, December 23rd, 1823, Robert Shewell in his 84th year.

house was probably extended to its northeast limit, 1811, for when Shewell offered it for sale, 1812, he described it as "a new stone house 50x32, having three fronts; a stone barn[11] with convenient double shed 95 feet long, and a stone smith shop." A new smith shop was probably built across Main street on what is now the Hellyer property, where charcoal and other debris of a smithy, were turned up fifty years ago in digging a foundation for a new hay scale.

In 1813, the Ross mansion was licensed as a public inn under the name of the "Indian Queen," and Frederick Nicholas or Nicholaus became the landlord. It was subsequently occupied by several landlords down to 1824, when it was purchased of William Watts; next by John Ross, recently appointed President Judge of the District. The deed was executed May 24th. This historic building now entered upon its third life, that of a dwelling, and as such is relegated to history at the end of its earthly career, a century and a quarter after the seed were sown in the little smith shop. It was occupied by a single family, the Rosses, whose male members were bred to the profession of the law, four generations of lawyers being sheltered under the roof, a record few dwellings make.

Some of our readers have a vivid recollection of the lovely woman who presided over the Ross Mansion for many years; of the pride she took in her intellectual sons, and with what grief she mourned the daughter of the house, cut off in the pride of womanhood. Many pleasant and sad memories are connected with the history of the old mansion.

We are now on the home stretch from our "Historic Walk," and, while descending Germany hill, have time to note a few things we have missed. As we pass the "Green Tree," we recall to mind that Jacob Kiple, who kept it about 1820, hanged himself in the stable. The Clear Spring tavern, not in our count, a Springfield Opp kept in the teens, nor the tannery adjoining that property. We omitted the Thompson stone house, demolished some years ago to make way for improvements; the old Doyle house, also in the borough, these all go to make the general aggregate. If we have duplicated any in our count, that does not matter, for history hath its license as well as poetry.

---

11 The building known as the "old Ross barn." It was grey with age when taken down.

Doylestown, Old and New.

VI
Typhus Fever Panic.

A panic visited Doylestown in the winter of 1815, by the breaking out of that much dreaded disease, typhus fever, which soon became epidemic. Several deaths occured, the whole number we do not know, nor the name of the first victim. The second death was that of John L. Dick,[1] who was the first person buried in the graveyard of the Presbyterian church, then building. Mr. Dick and three sisters, children of a Presbyterian clergyman of Belfast, Ireland, settled here prior to 1812. He purchased the tannery in "Germany," where he was carrying on business at his death. He was a young man of education and refinement, and highly respected. One of his sisters was the wife of Dr. Charles Meredith, at whose house he died, the dwelling now belonging to the widow of the late Dr. John Rhoads, on the east side of North Main street, just below Court. The next victim to the fell disease was William W. Hart, the young member of the bar of whom we have spoken, the intimate friend of Mr. Dick, and was with him when he died. Young Hart, having occasion the next day to write a letter to his brother-in-law, the late General John Davis, of Davisville, spoke of the death of his friend Dick, in the following pathetic terms :

"My friend, John L. Dick, died to-day at two o'clock p. m., of typus fever. How frail is man! Ten days ago he was in the vigor of

---

[1] At Doylestown, on Saturday, February 18th, 1815, at the house of his brother-in-law, Dr. Charles Meredith, John L. Dick, aged twenty-seven years.

OLD PRESBYTERIAN CHURCH, 1815.

health. Alas, how visionary our hopes of earthly happiness! But two months since he married Miss Erwin,[2] the daughter of the richest man in the county. How soon their fondest anticipations of future bliss and domestic felicity were destroyed." As I have already stated, Mr. Hart, the writer of the letter I have quoted from, and the next victim, was the nephew of William Watts, subsequently Associate Judge of our Courts, and boarded with him. He lived in the house now owned and occupied by George P. Brock. Young Hart was seized almost immediately and died six days after his friend Dick.

William Watts Hart, son of Josiah and Ann Hart, born January 2nd, 1790, and, being intended for the bar, was educated accordingly. He was a student at the Union Academy, Doylestown, 1806-07, completed his academic studies at Philadelphia, read law in the office of Enos Morris, Esq., at Newtown, and was admitted to the bar, June 3rd, 1813. He opened an office at Doylestown, to which place he came with the removal of the county seat, and began practice. He was Deputy Recorder, 1810, under his cousin, Dr. William Hart, Deputy Register and Recorder under John Pugh, 1813, and commissioned Clerk of the Orphans' Court by Governor Snyder February 28th, 1814, dying while holding that office.

There were five victims, to this fatal fever, in the same house within a few days. The next to die after Mr. Hart was his mother, Mrs. Ann Hart, of Southampton township, who had come to Doylestown to nurse her son. She was taken sick about the time he died, when her daughter, Mrs. Sarah Miles, of Bustleton, Philadelphia county, came to nurse the mother. Mother and daughter followed the son and brother to the grave in a few days, and they by Eliza Jones, a young cousin of thirteen, and a negro boy, belonging to the family, five in all stricken down in the same house in less than three weeks. They were all taken to the Southampton grave-yard for burial, the funeral services being held by the pastor, the Rev. Thomas B. Montanye, grandfather of Judge Yerkes, of Doylestown.

The author has, in his possesion, the letters written by Mr. Watts to Mr. Montanye, after the death of each victim, asking him to make arrangements for the burial of the dead and provide refreshments for the mourners. We never remember to have read more distressing

---

[2] At Erwinna, Thursday evening December 19th, 1814, by the Rev. Uriah DuBois, Mr. John L. Dick of Doylestown, to Miss Julianna Erwin, daughter of William Erwin, Esq.

letters. The first, written February 24th, announcing the death of Mr. Hart, says:

"You can more easily conceive my situation than I express it, when I tell you that William Hart is expired, his mother very ill with the same complaint, and the black boy, who was so brisk last evening, perhaps much worse—three of us down and the rest worn out." In the second letter Mrs. Watts writes: "The black boy died about half an hour after Mrs. Hart;" in the next, "Eliza Jones[3] is gone," Mrs. Miles having died meanwhile. On the death of Mr. Hart the Rev. Uriah DuBois was appointed his successor as Clerk of Orphans' Court, evidence that ministers of the Gospel were not overlooked, at that day, when political favors were to be distributed. Of three incumbents of the office, in the same number of years, two were clergymen. Laymen were more generous then than now in the giving out of office.

We copy from Asher Miner's *Correspondent*, of that date, the death notices as they appeared in that paper at the time and are part of the local history of Doylestown, of the period.

At Doylestown, on Friday evening, February 24, 1815, William W. Hart, Esq., Attorney-at-Law and Clerk of the Orphans' Court, after an illness of five days, aged twenty-five years.

"O how pretentious is prosperity!
How Comet-like it threatens while it shines,
Few years but yield us proof of Death's ambition,
To cut his victim from the fairest fold,
And sheathe his shafts in all the pride of life."

"At Doylestown, March 2, 1815, Mrs. Ann Hart, of Southampton, aged 55 years, relict of Josiah Hart, late of Montgomery county, and mother of William W. Hart, whose death was announced last week. She was taken ill the night previous to his death, and survived him but six days."

"Vain Man thy fond pursuits forbear,
Repent, thy end is nigh :
Death at the farthest can't be far,
Oh think before you die."

---

3 Eliza Jones and her younger sister, Anna L. Jones, were the daughters of Colonel Jones, civil engineer, and the first surveyor appointed for Ohio. Anna L. married Charles Yardley, brother of Samuel Yardley, many years ago the leading merchant of Doylestown. Charles Yardley was clerk to Samuel until he went into business for himself at Newtown, 1826, and died in Doylestown, 1840. Mrs. Anna L. Yardley died at Bethlehem, March 24th, 1897, in her ninety-second year. The Misses Jones were related to the family of Judge Watts by marriage.

> "The voice of this alarming scene,
>   May every heart obey,
> Nor be the Heavenly warning vain,
>   Which calls to watch and pray."
>
> "Great God, Thy Sovereign Grace impart
>   With cleansing, healing power;
> This only can prepare the heart,
>   For death's surprising hour."

"At Doylestown, March 7th, 1815, Mrs. Sarah Miles, of Moreland township, and sister of William W. Hart, Esq."

"At Doylestown, March 8th, 1815, Eliza Jones, aged thirteen years, a relative, and died in the same house."

The following acrostic appeared in the *Correspondent* on the death of Miss Jones of the same date:

> Every age and every station,
> Live exposed to Death's arrest,
> In a pious resignation,
> Some with easy grace are blessed,
> All her hope was in her Saviour
> Being reconciled to die,
> Even in her last behavior,
> This appeared to standers by.
> Hear, she speaks to those around her,
> Just before her dying breath,
> 'O my dear young friends remember,
> Now in youth prepare for death,'
> Eternity of bliss I now have full in view,
> So dear young friends I bid you all adieu."

While Doylestown has been generally free from contageous diseases since 1815, it had two subsequent frights from Asiatic Cholera, 1832 and 1849. The former was during its first visit to America, and the alarm was universal. Every possible precaution was taken against it. In July, an article addressed "To housekeepers, and particularly those in Doylestown," appeared in the Bucks County *Intelligencer*, urging them to be prepared for the cholera. The article advised them to "get at the foundation of cleanliness, the *celler*." The town remained healthy despite the scare, without a case, and, in consequence, more than the usual number of city people spent the summer here to escape the disease.

The cholera's visit to this vicinity, 1849, centered at the Alms House, two miles below town, and was confined there except a few cases in the immediate vicinity, and two or three in Doylestown with a death or two. Dr. Ferguson, who lived on East State street, fell a victim to it; and also a student of medicine, reading with Dr. Hendrie. As both were assisting at the Alms House, they contracted the disease there. Over one hundred of the inmates died in a few days, some being found dead on the road-side, having wandered away when attacked. Among the victims was William Edwards, steward of the Alms House. Davis E. Brower, Bridge Point; Nelson MacReynolds of the neighborhood and others, whose names we do not recollect, distinguished themselves as nurses.

In a period at which this chapter opened, the second decade of the last century, the people were more observant of national days than at present. The 4th of July, Washington's birthday and the 8th of January, the anniversary of the battle of New Orleans, were not allowed to pass unnoticed. All down through the century, to the Civil War, much note was paid to these days, but since then there has been a great falling off in their observance. In evidence of this we cite three celebrations that took place at Doylestown on the 4th of July, 1815, 1817 and 1823 respectively. It seems it would be hardly possible to organize such demonstrations now on a purely patriotic basis.

In 1815 the day was marked with great eclat. At 12, noon, a procession was formed at the centre of the town in the following order;

Advance Guard.

Officer of the Day, Major Watts, assisted by Major Shaw.

Band of Music from Philadelphia.

Bucks County Rangers, under command of Major Magill.

Clergymen, orator of the day and citizens two and two. A favorite National Air was struck up by the band and the procession moved to the public ground; when in front of the Court House, the military opened to the right and left, and the citizens walked into the Court room followed by the Rangers.

The services consisted of a prayer by the Rev. Uriah DuBois; the Declaration of Independence was read by Mr. Miner, and Samuel D. Ingham delivered the oration.

From the Court House the procession moved to a table erected in a neighboring piece of wood, where a cold collation had been prepared by Messrs. Enoch Harvey and Mathew Hare. Robert Smith

Esq., was called to preside, assisted by Jonathan Smith, John Fox and Samuel Sellers, Esqs., as vice presidents.

After dinner toasts were drunk, eighteen in all, one for each State, with music. Two Volunteer toasts were drunk: By the president, "To General Andrew Jackson and his followers;" by John Fox, "To the people of France." About one hundred ladies partook of an elegant entertainment in the Grand Jury room. The exercises of the day were concluded by music in the Court House, and congratulations.

In 1817 the celebration was repeated at the same place, Josiah Y. Shaw presiding; A. H. Griswold read the Declaration, and toasts were drunk at the Mansion House. A report of the occasion said— the general sentiment appears to be:

> "A day—an hour of virtuous
> Liberty,
> Is worth a whole Eternity of
> Bondage."

The celebration of the Fourth, in 1823, broke all previous records for a "flourish of trumpets" which we condense from Miner's *Correspondent:*

Mathias Morris was Marshall; Captain Robbart's troops, dismounted; Captain Magill's artillerists and Captain Roger's Bucks County Rangers were the escorts. The literary exercises were held in the Court House; Rev. Charles Hyde was Chaplain; Robert Bethel, Esq., read the Declaration of Independence and Eleazar T. Mc Dowell delivered the oration of which the report says: "With an action, an emphasis and a pathos becoming the subject, and gave evidence of a talent for public speaking by no means discreditable to his native county of Bucks." Afterward the procession marched to a "shady retreat" where preparations had been made and where toasts were drunk.

The same afternoon a comany dined at the Court Inn, Watts's, another at the Fox Chase, Marple's, now Fountain House, and a third at the Bucks County Inn, Kohll's.

A paragraph of the day's proceedings, says:

"A numerous company of young ladies and gentlemen, under the superintendence of Messrs. Charles E. DuBois, Gilbert Rodman and Henry Chapman, a committee of arrangement, and under the umbrageous foliage of the towering oaks and the wide spreading sycamores, partook of a collation prepared by Joseph Burrows, our neighbor of the Green Tree. Here appeard to be enjoyment without alloy. A portion of the youth, the activity and the sprightliness here concentrated. After partaking of the good things of life provided by mine host of the Green Tree, and interchange of sentiment and the patriotic songs which the occasion called forth, the exercises of the day were harmoniously concluded by several cotillions and country dances on the green, the musical band having politely attended with their instruments."4

---

4 Hamilton Dick of Doylestown, a seaman on board the India ship Asia, of Philadelphia, was washed overboard off the Cape of Good Hope, in the fall of 1809. He was probably a brother of John L. Dick.

Doylestown, Old and New.

VII
The School and the Church.

The first Academy built in Bucks county, under an Act of Assembly passed for that purpose, was erected at Newtown, 1798, at a cost of $4,000, and in it the Rev. Alexander Boyd kept a noted classical school for several years. This was the ninth Academy in the State, and the charter provided that the trustees shall cause ten poor children to be taught gratis at one time. The Union Academy at Doylestown, erected, 1804, the second in the county, was partly built by subscription and partly by lottery, $6,000 being raised by the latter means, the Commissioners being Andrew Dunlap, Christian Clemens, John Hough, Thomas Stewart, Hugh Meredith, Nathaniel Shewell and Josiah Y. Shaw. The lot on which it was built, at the southeast corner of Court and Broad streets, was the gift of John Hough, Warwick township, and the deed was executed, September, 1804, to Charles Meredith, New Britain. In the conveyance the object of the gift was stated to be, "with a view, and to the intent, that a building should be erected thereon as a school or seminary of learning," one clause reserving a room for religious worship.

The building was probably begun in 1803, before the deed was executed, as it was ready for occupancy by July, 1804, when the Rev. Uriah DuBois, pastor of the Presbyterian church at Deep Run, Bedminster township, was invited to take charge of it. He moved down sometime that summer, and occupied a dwelling of Mrs. Thomas Stewart on the site of that owned by the late Joshua Beans, north side of East State street, bounded by Printer's alley on the east. The Academy was of stone 53x35 feet, 30 feet to the square and 36 to the peak of the roof. On the top was a small belfry with a bell in it. The first board of trustees consisted of the same persons as the lottery Commissioner, except Andrew Dunlap. The building was finished sometime in 1806, from the proceeds of the lottery. In the announcement for the opening of the school, the village is spoken of as being "delightful and healthy with many natural advantages," and it was stated, as an additional inducement, that "the Easton and Bethlehem stages run through the town twice a week." The assistant of Mr. DuBois was Robert Patterson, his brother-in-law, a graduate of the University of Pennsylvania, and subsequently Professor of Natural Philosophy at the University of Virginia, and Director of the United States Mint. The school soon became a noted one, and pupils were in attendance from the various states and the West Indies. The first public examination was held in January 1805. On the evening of Tuesday, October 28, 1806, the parents and others, who intended continuing their children at the Academy, were invited to meet and "consult on a proper and certain plan of furnishing the school with wood." It was both a boarding and day school, the boarders living in the family of the principal.[1]

Mr. DuBois held frequent religious meetings in the room set apart for this purpose and, after being relieved of his Tinicum congregation, 1808, he preached alternately in the Academy and at Deep Run. In this room in the Academy, the first Sabbath school in Bucks county was organized, and there Mr. DuBois laid the foundation of the Doylestown Presbyterian church, of which he was the first pastor and officiated until his death.

Doylestown had been settled almost three quarters of a century, before a church of any denomination was organized here, and then the Scotch-Irish Presbyterians were the pioneers. The first step toward having religious service at Doylestown, was taken at a meeting of the Deep Run Congregation, February 2, 1804, when three "referees" were chosen to confer with such as may be sent from "Doyal Town"

---

[1] While the Rev. Uriah DuBois was in charge of the Academy, Samuel Aaron opened a mathematical school in the building the first Monday of March, 1821; and, to encourage him, Mr. DuBois announced in the *Bucks County Messenger*, edited by Simon Cameron, that Mr. Aaron, "a young man, whose mathematical acquirements were formerly respectable, has returned to his native county from a celebrated school in which his whole attention has been given to mathematics."

OLD JAIL, 1812.

and "may tend to have the gospel preached to both." At a subsequent meeting, on the 29th, delegates were present from "Doyal Town," where a resolution was passed giving the "Doyal Town people one-third of Mr. DuBois' time." This movement led to the founding of a Presbyterian church here, which has grown to be one of the strongest in the State.

When the Rev. Uriah DuBois moved down from Dublin to Doylestown, 1804, to take charge of the newly built Academy, it was a cross roads hamlet. It may have had one hundred inhabitants, but we doubt it. There was no church, or other place of religious worship here and never had been, the nearest being the New Britain Baptist Church three miles southwest, Neshaminy Presbyterian in Warwick, six miles, the Newtown Presbyterian, fourteen, and his own charge at Deep Run, six miles. Mr. DuBois was a strong man, a great accession to Doylestown; and, during the seventeen years he spent here, was an able leader and worthy of followers. He looked after his school in the Academy, which grew stronger in number and in usefulness through his efforts, and held religious services in the reserved room in the building Sunday afternoon and evening. Gradually he gathered a congregation about him, and the outcome was the founding of the Presbyterian church and the erection of a suitable building in the graveyard and nearly on the site of the present one.

Work was begun on the building, August 1813, and was dedicated the same month, 1815. It was built of stone, 45x55 feet, plain in appearance and cost $4,282. The lot was bought of John Shaw for $409. The subscriptions were principally in small sums, that of Dr. Samuel Moore[2] $200, being the largest, two other gentlemen giving $100 each. At the dedication were the Reverends Jacob Janeway, Philadelphia, and Robert B. Bellville, Neshaminy. At this time the united membership at Deep Run and Doylestown was but 30 and had only increased to 48 by 1818. The first session consisted of the pastor, Thomas Stewart, James Ferguson[3] and Andrew Dunlap,[4]

2 At Steubenville, Ohio, May 28, 1825, Mrs. Lydia Beatty, wife of Rev. Charles Beatty, and daughter of Dr. Samuel Moore, of Bridge Point, Doylestown township.

3 At Doylestown, February 28, 1817, James Ferguson, aged about sixty years. He had lately removed from his farm in Plumstead to be near a church and school. He was buried in the Presbyterian Church yard and a discourse preached by the Rev. Uriah DuBois.

4 At Doylestown, January 18, 1835, Andrew Dunlap, aged seventy-seven, a ruling elder in the Presbyterian Church.

The Rev. Robert Dunlap, (son of Andrew Dunlap,) born at Doylestown, 1803, and a minister of the Presbyterian Church, died at Pittsburg, March 21, 1847.

ruling elders at Deep Run for many years. The graveyard was opened for interment several months before the building was finished, and the first person buried there was John Ledley Dick, who died at Doylestown, February 18, 1815, of typus fever. The church was not incorporated until 1816. The congregation met on Saturday, August 26, 1815 for the purpose of making a selection of seats. The first notice of Thanksgiving in Doylestown was that of 1818, and held in the "Presbyterian Meeting House."

The old church building was twice repaired, at one time much changed in appearance, and subsequently a new one erected. It was last repaired in 1852, when it was made almost a new building, at a cost of $4,339.03, a trifle more than the original building cost. In 1871 a handsome brown stone edifice was erected almost on the site of the old one, more than one-half the cost being defrayed by a charitable and liberal woman, about $25,000, including furnishing. Of this church we shall have more to say in a subsequent chapter. Mr. DuBois' pastorate was closed by his death in 1821.[5] He was a man of broad influence in the church and out of it, and his death was a great loss to the community. Since that time, a period of eighty-two years, the church has had but five pastors.

In order to discover what the newspapers of that period had to say about the erection of the first church at the county seat, we carefully examined the columns of the *Pennsylvania Correspondent*, the only paper published at Doylestown, or in the county. In the issue of August 21, 1815, we find the following and nothing more:

"At a meeting of the congregation of Doylestown, agreeably to public notice, held in the new church, on the 17th instant to elect a board of trustees; on motion resolved, by the trustees present forming a quorum, in concurrence with the unaminous consent of the meeting that there be public invitation given to all whom it may concern, to meet in the Doylestown church on Saturday the 26th inst at two o'clock p. m. for the purpose of making a selection of seats."

Extract from the minutes.

Mr. DuBois was succeeded by Charles Hyde, of Connecticut, who was called in 1823 and ordained the 19th of November. He

---

5 The Rev. Uriah DuBois, who died Monday, September 10, 1821, in his fifty-fourth year, was born in Salem county, N. J. One of the papers said of him: "As a preacher of the gospel, the Presbyterian Church, of Doylestown founded under his pastoral care, will be an appropriate monument to his memory." The Rev, Mr. Engels, Philadelphia, preached a funeral discourse in the church, September 23rd.

resigned 1829, and returned to his native state, where he died in
1871. There was now another vacancy of two years, when the Rev.
Silas M. Andrews was called, 1831, who enjoyed a long and prosperous ministry. At the fortieth anniversary, commemorated on a Sunday in November, the audience was large and attentive, the pastor preaching a sermon from the words of Moses as recorded in Deuteronomy, chapter XXIX, and 6th verse: "And I have led you forty years in the wilderness." The sermon was mainly taken up with a review of his pastorate, in which he mentioned the forms of church government dominating the world. During the forty years of his pastorate, Dr. Andrews had administered the Lord's Supper 240 times, baptised 179 adults and 350 children, received into communion 651 persons, married 841 couples, attended 940 funerals, and from the pulpit, or in lectures, had preached 6,871 times—a most remarkable record of intellectual work for one man. He was a model pastor in every respect; possessed great executive ability, and administered every department of his great charge with consummate skill. Few churches, of any denomination, have been equally blessed.

The Reverend Silas M. Andrews, D. D., was born in Rowan county, North Carolina, March 11, 1805, and graduated from the University of that state; then taught school until 1828, when, having selected the ministry for his life occupation, he entered Princeton Theological Seminary. He was called to the Doylestown Presbyterian church, his first and only charge, November, 1831, prior to his graduation, and installed the 16th.[6] He entered upon his great work in May, not waiting to complete his course at the Seminary. His parish consisted of the two congregations of Doylestown and Deep Run, for which he labored with unwearied faithfulness. Dr. Andrews was twice married his first wife being Matilda, a daughter of the Rev. Uriah DuBois, his second Miss Harriet Waller, Wilkesbarre. The latter survived him, also two children by his first wife, his son William, a graduate of Lafayette College, who served three years in the Civil War in Durrell's battery.

After a pastorate of almost half a century, Dr. Andrews died suddenly of a brief illness, at Doylestown, March 9, 1881, and was buried on the 11th in the cemetery at this place of which he was long president. The services were held in the Presbyterian church, and

---

[6] The following is the first marriage notice of Mr. Andrews that appeared in the newspapers; February 27, 1834, by the Rev. Silas M. Andrews, of Doytown, Andrew Kelley to Ruth Grasson, of Philadelphia.

every foot of the large audience room was occupied by those who loved and respected the deceased while living. The coffin was borne up the aisle at eleven and deposited in front of the pulpit, carried by six church members and followed by the deacons as honorary pall bearers. The exercises were opened by the choir singing "Nearer My God to Thee;" the Rev. Dr. Cattell, President of Lafayette College, made the opening prayer, and read a portion of scripture Dr Murphy, Frankford, a life long friend of the deceased, preached the funeral sermon; and Dr. Knox, Bristol, delivered the closing prayer. There were seventeen clergymen present, and the occasion was one of great solemnity and interest. Many of the vast congregation were moved to tears.[7]

Dr. Andrews was very formal, and not a little diplomatic in sending marriage notices to the local press. He had a printed form and to fill up the blank and send it to the papers was almost the first thing he did after the newly married couple had left the parsonage. Occasionally there was a mite of history connected with this clerical duty When he had married his 1199th couple, he announced he would marry the 1200th couple gratis. Several weeks elapsed without an applicant to have the matrimonial knot tied, until one day two couple came together and both were married "without money and without price." This was a little rough on the Doctor but there was no room left for him to discriminate.

Upon the death of Dr. Andrews, the church called the Rev William A. Patton the following April, 1881, who took formal charge sometime in the summer. He was pastor almost nine years, resigning March 1, 1890, to accept a call from a church at Wayne, Pa. Mr Patton was succeeded by the Rev. W. Hayes Moore, the following September, who resigned after a pastorate of seven years on account of ill health, November 1, 1899, to accept a call at Santa Fe, New Mexico. The present pastor of the Doylestown Presbyterian church the Rev. Robert M. Labaree was born in Persia, and is the son of an American missionary.

There are two important factors in this church for the work in hand, the Female Bible Society, auxiliary to the County Society and the Female Library, both organized 1816. The Bucks County Bibl

---

[7] The following is a copy of the last marriage notice of Dr. Andrews published in our local papers just prior to his death: At his residence 81 East Court street, Doylestown, February 26, 1881, by Rev. Silas M. Andrews, No 1242, John A. Myers and Mrs. Mary L. Myers, both of Plumstead, Bucks county Pennsylvania.

Society was organized in this church, 1815, its fourth anniversary meeting being held there, 1819; among the members were the Revs. Robert B. Belville, Thomas B. Montanye, Uriah DuBois, Jacob Larzelere, Joseph Mathias and Silas Hough, with the following laymen : Samuel D. Ingham, Samuel Moore, Enos Morris, John Pugh, Nathaniel Shewell, William Watts, John Hart, William Purdy, Robert Beatty and William Long, all prominent men long since deceased. In these years 640 copies of the Bible, 30 of them in German, had been distributed and $545 received into the treasury. At the eleventh annual meeting, held in the church, October 3, 1826, the Rev. Jacob Larzelere, Southampton, preached the sermon, the Rev. Joseph Mathias, Hilltown, elected president, William Watts, treasurer and E. Smith, secretary. In the intervening years the temporal and spiritual affairs of the church prospered, and the congregation grown to be one of the largest of this denomination in the state.

The earliest debating society, at the new county capital, developed by our investigation, was the "Union Debating Club" that was in full blast in 1819. How much earlier these young Patrick Henry's were spouting here there is no way of telling. On the evening of June 26, same year, the question for discussion was: "Has Nature or Education had the greatest share in forming the human character?" The place of meeting was probably in the Academy, and doubtless the students were instrumental in organizing the Society.

In the summer of 1823, the widow of Captain John Rily who had been buried in the Presbyterian grave-yard, presented the church two handsome brass chandeliers for the pulpit, two brass candlesticks for the clerk's desk attached to mahogany stands, several tin sconces for candles, and a handsome pair of snuffers and tray.[8] In a previous issue of the *Pennsylvania Correspondent*, Asher Miner's paper, I find the following reference to the burial of Captain Rily:

"March 31, 1822, the body of Captain John Rily, a practical navigator of Philadelphia, was deposited in the grave-yard of the Presbyterian church Doylestown, on Saturday last, in compliance with his own request expressed shortly before his decease. Captain Rily's age was about sixty years. He left a widow but no children. His funeral was attended from the dwelling of Josiah Y. Shaw, Esq., and our fellow citizens offered suitable testimonials of respect to the mem-

---

8 What has become of these relics of the first church building?

ory of a deceased stranger. The Rev. Mr. Potts, Philadelphia, made some very appropriate observations at the grave, calling the attention of the living to the necessity of preparing for death."

ASHER MINER,

Doylestown, Old and New.

VIII
Pioneer Newspapers.

In previous chapters, covering the present period, we took note of the founding of an Academy, the removal hither of the seat of justice and the organization and erection of the pioneer church. These were important factors of improvement and progress that came in with the nineteenth century, but there is another agency equally vital to the spread of human intelligence, and calculated to make men better, wiser and happier. This is the newspaper press, which will receive proper notice in this chapter. The pioneer newspapers at the cross-roads hamlet, now Doylestown, were the *Farmers' Weekly Gazette*, established 1800, and the *Pennsylvania Correspondent*, 1804, both in evidence that the young village was forging ahead. The first of these journalistic ventures was by Isaac Ralston,[1] who issued the first number of his paper from the "Centre House," July 25, 1800. It was printed on a medium sheet, and, at its head, floated the hackneyed motto. "Open to all parties but influenced by none."[2] The subscription price was two dollars, with twenty-five cents additional when delivered by private post. How long this paper was published no one knows, for it left no record behind. We have seen a few numbers, the latest No. 27 of volume one, bearing the date of January 29, 1801. The first issue, coming under our notice, September 5,

---

[1] A careful examination of the records in the Register's office failed to reveal the name of Ralston, and Isaac Ralston was doubtless a stranger to the county.

[2] In Mr. Ralston's salutatory he assures the public that "nothing of a personal nature, nor in the least, tends to corrupt a single moral obligation, shall ever be allowed in the paper."

1800, had an entire page taken up with the proceedings of the Irish Parliament. Soon after the *Gazette* appeared, Mr. Ralston issued proposals for publishing a monthly of fifty pages, at twenty-five cents, but it never made its appearance. Who this pioneer journalist of Bucks county was, we have never been able to find out, whence he came nor whither he went. He passed completely out of sight, as much so as if the earth had opened and swallowed him. His advent was comet-like, quick to appear and quick to disappear.[3]

The next venture on this line was by Asher Miner,[4] a Wilkesbarre yankee, who came to Doylestown in May, 1804, and established the *Pennsylvania Correspondent* and *Farmers' Advertiser*. The first issue made its appearance on July 7, from a back room in Barton Stewart's log house, on the site of the present *Intelligencer* office at the corner of Court street and Printer's Alley, and Miner lived in a small stone house on North Main street near the site of Mrs. N. C. James' dwelling. The subscription was two dollars. He said in his address to the public: "The editor is by birth an American, in principle a Federal Republican. His private sentiment, with regard to the administration of the Government of the country, he will mantain and avow as becomes a freeman. In his public character, as becomes the conductor of the only newspsper printed in the county, he will act with that impartiality which prudence and justice require.[5] It is related of Miner, that one of the first men he called upon to ask assistance of, in pushing his paper, was the Rev. Nathaniel Irwin, a Democrat and a power in the county. The good parson declined on the ground he did not like Mr. M's politics. The latter said he would publish "an independent newspaper," to which Mr. Irwin replied: "Yes, you say so, but you look toward Buckingham," the strongest Federal township in the county.

The appearance of the *Correspondent* created something of a sensation, and the first issue was largely given away. The first number

---

3 After the lapse of a century it would be interesting to know something abount the father of the newspaper press of the county.

4 Asher Miner was born at Norwich, Connecticut, in March, 1777, learned the trade in the office of the *Gazette* and *Commercial Intelligencer*, at New London and settled at Wilkesbarre, Pa., 1799. Here he published the *Luzerne County Federalist* with his brother Charles until May, 1804. In 1800 he married Polly Wright, of Wilkesbarre, whose mother was a daughter of Josiah Dyer, of Dyerstown two miles above Doylestown.

5 At Doylestown, January 15, 1822, Seth Miner, aged seventy-seven years, father of the editors of the *Correspondent* and the *Village Record*. He was a soldier of the Revolution.

contained but a single advertisement, but patronage gradually grew, and, after the removal of the county seat to Doylestown, the improvement, in both advertising and subscription, was more perceptible. The enterprise proved a success; there was an increase in Mr. Miner's worldly goods, and his young family grew from two to twelve.[6] In 1806 the paper was enlarged to a royal sheet. Miner established the *Star of Freedom*, at Newtown, 1817, but it did not survive a year. The late General William T. Rogers learned the trade in the *Correspondent* office.

After an active editorial career of twenty years, Miner sold the *Correspondent* to Edmund Morris and Samuel R. Kramer of Philadelphia, September 24, 1824, and removed to West Chester where he formed a partnership with his brother in the publication of the *Village Record*. They sold out the *Record*, 1834, and returned to Wilkesbarre, where Asher Miner died, 1841.

Of the new proprietors of the *Correspondent*, Edmund Morris was born at Burlington, N. J., 1804, and learned the trade in the office of the *Freemen's Journal*. He had a fondness for literary pursuits, and after leaving Doylestown, was connected several years with the Philadelphia press. He returned to Burlington and divided his time between rural pursuits and literature, and dying there. Kramer was a native of Philadelphia, where he learned his trade in a book office, and also died there. He was fond of reading and a close observer of men and things.

The office, at the time Asher Miner sold his newspaper, is thus spoken of by one who knew it, a strong contrast with printing offices of the present day:

"It was a small two story building with the second story large enough to hold an old Ramage press, with a stone bed on which the paper was worked by using the old fashioned ball, the stands and cases containing job and newspaper type. The type was old and worn. The outside form consumed so nearly all the letter, the inside could not be set up until the outside was distributed. The lower story was supplied with huge bins, into which the subscribers emptied their subscription in the shape of corn, flour, oats or whatever article the subscriber should bring. All was received as cash."[7]

---

[6] At Doylestown, April 27, 1821, very suddenly, Miss Anna Miner, sister of the editor of the *Correspondent*, in the forty-ninth year of her age.

[7] At Doylestown, Sunday evening, April 19, 1819, by the Rev. Uriah DuBois, Dr. Abraham Stout, of Northampton county, to Miss Anna Maria Miner, daughter of Asher Miner, editor of the *Correspondent*, Doylestown.

The new proprietors of the *Correspondent*, changed the name of the paper to the *Bucks County Patriot* and *Farmers' Advertiser*, the first issue appearing October 4, 1824. They were not long in business together, dissolving by mutual consent in February, 1827. Mr. Morris conducted the paper alone until October 1, same year, when another change took place, by the sale of the paper to Elisha B. Jackson, a native of Columbia county, Pa., and James Kelly,[8] an Englishman by birth, both graduates of the *Village Record* office. They changed the name of the paper to *Bucks County Intelligencer* and *General Advertiser*, which made its first appearance in a new suit of type. Kelly was an active, pushing man and the paper prospered under his management. He was a bitter partizan, and being of English birth had a tendency to aggrivate the friction between him and the *Democrat*. In March 1835, Kelly took William M. Large,[9] a graduate of the office, into partnership with him. The paper was now enlarged to a double medium sheet. This co-partnership was dissolved, January 3, 1837, by its own limitation, when Kelly assumed control. He conducted the paper until March 14, 1838, when he sold the plant to his late partner, Large, who became sole proprietor, with Hugh M. Henry,[10] a young member of the bar as editor. This arrangement continued until March 17, 1841, when the paper was sold to Samuel Fretz,[11] a graduate of the office. At this time the paper was published in a brick building on Main street nearly opposite the Doylestown Trust Company.

The next change of ownership was a fortunate one for both the purchaser and the paper, passing into the hands of John S. Brown, March 8, 1843. Mr. Brown, born in Plumstead township, 1815,

---

8 Kelly was married, at West Chester, November 20, 1827, to Mary Hodgson, of the same place. He had one sister Jane, and there may have been others, who married Samuel Harbison, and died February 26, 1836. Mr. Kelly reached some prominence. In April 1838, he was appointed Clerk of the Court of Quarter Sessions to succeed John Dungan, holding the office a few months; was defeated for the State Senate 1826, and died at Doylestown, May 4, 1839. His only son, James Miner Kelly, died here August 13, 1834.

9 William M. Large was the son of a Buckingham farmer and learned the trade in the *Intelligencer* office. After he sold out he began farming at which he spent the remainder of his life, on his handsome place near Doylestown, where he died.

10 Hugh M. Henry was a young man of ability, and died at Doylestown at the early age of twenty-nine. The Court adjourned, and, with the bar, attended the funeral in a body.

11 Fretz was born in Plumstead township. In 1840 he and Oliver G. Search established the *Literary Chronicle* at Hatboro, but Fretz left it when he bought the *Intelligencer*. He died in Spawlding county, Ohio, December 25, 1884, at the age of sixty-six.

was a descendant of Thomas Brown, an immigrant from Barking, County Essex, England, 1700-1701, and settled near Dyerstown, about 1712. Learning his trade in the *Intelligencer* office, Brown bought the Hunderton County, (N. J.) *Gazette*, which he published some time. On selling the *Intelligencer*, 1855, he entered the Guarantee Trust and Safe Deposit Company, Philadelphia, of which he was an incorporator and was an official several years, living in the city. He subsequently removed to Swarthmore, where he died, October 1, 1898, in his eighty-third year.

While John S. Brown owned the *Intelligencer* it was much improved, and there was soon a friendly rivalry between it and the *Democrat*. About this time local items began to make their appearance in country newspapers, and the *Intelligencer* was one of the first to take this advanced step. It is still an unsettled question which of the two papers, the *Democrat* or *Intelligencer*, first opened its columns to this species of local intelligence. Brown did much for the paper, and, when he stepped down and out from the editorial chair, left it better than he found it. In 1848, he removed the *Intelligencer* to the new frame office he built, at the corner of Court street and Printer's Alley.

Mr. Brown sold the *Intelligencer* to Enos Prizer and Henry T. Darlington, in the early spring of 1855, their first issue bearing date March 6. They were from Chester county; both learned their trade in the *Village Record* office, and while apprentices, had for office mates Bayard Taylor, Judge William Butler and Ex-Chief Justice Edward M. Paxson of the State Supreme Court. The new editors and proprietors were well equipped for their work; they had been trained for the business and were successful journalists. Mr. Prizer was of German descent on both sides, and Darlington of Quaker ancestry, a nephew of the distinguished Dr. William Darlington. The co-partnership lasted until the death of Mr. Prizer, 1864, when Mr. Darlington purchased the plant and real estate. In 1876, Darlington took Alfred Paschall, Chester county, into business with him as junior partner, and, a year later, S. Edward Paschall, his brother, was taken into the firm. The paper was now published under the firm name of H. T. Darlington and Co. until Mr. Darlington's death, November 24, 1878. He was seized with apoplexy the day before in front of the Court House and lived but twenty-four hours. He was buried on the 26th, in the Doylestown cemetery followed to the grave by a large number of relatives and friends.

Mr. Darlington was an excellent man, a good citizen and public spirited. He was the friend of all local improvements; one of the most active in the erection of the Doylestown Seminary, the introduction of water into the borough and the erection of Lenape building. He was also active in urging the building of a new Court House and jail, but did not live to see the latter built. Previous to his death, arrangements had been made to issue a daily paper, but the project was abandoned; the semi-weekly discontinued July 1, 1879, and the weekly resumed. Subsequently, 1884, a daily was issued, the first in the county, and continued to the present time. Since then there have been two changes in the firm names, Alfred Paschall and Co. and the Intelligencer Company, under a charter in recent years, with Mr. Paschall as editor. In 1876 the *Intelligencer* built a new brick office on the site of the old frame. In 1902 another change was made, by which Arthur K. Thomas, a graduate of the *Democrat* office, who had previously become a member of the firm and business manager, purchased a controlling interest of the stock, and Mr. Paschall retired.

A sketch of our newspapers would be incomplete without proper notice of two of their most conspicuous graduates, the late Hiram Lukens who was dean of the Bucks county press for many years, to his death and Rowan Foulke, both dying, 1897. Mr. Lukens had probably worked longer at the case than any other printer in the state, entering the office of the *Bucks County Intelligencer* under James Kelly, June 21, 1832, the day the Spaniard Mina was hanged for the murder of Dr. William Chapman, of Bensalem. There he spent his life, dying November 19, 1897, in his seventy-sixth year, lacking but two days of having worked in the same office for sixty-five years and five months, being foreman about forty years. He was born in Montgomery county, Pa., of Quaker parents, December 16, 1821. Mr. Lukens possessed an agreeable personality, was a pleasant companion, attached to his friends, devoted to Masonry, and respected by all who knew him. He was buried in Doylestown cemetery, November 23, the funeral being largely attended.

Mr. Foulke was a few years the junior of Mr. Lukens. He was born at, or near, Doylestown, of Quaker parents, 1827, and served his apprenticeship in the *Intelligencer* office. He went to Philadelphia about 1850, worked in the larger book printing offices, and was a compositor on the *Ledger* for several years, in which his son, Albert R. was employed. During the Civil War Mr. Foulke entered the military service as a private soldier, and was subsequently commissioned First Lieutenant in Colonel Peter Ellmaker's 119th Pennsylvania regiment. He also worked on the *Press* for a time and was foreman on the *Daily Chronicle*, Washington City, for several years, Colonel Forney's paper, and died in his seventieth year.

Down to 1816, the Democratic party had no organ in the county, Asher Miner having the field to himself. The *Correspondent* claimed to be independent, and Miner flattered himself he could satisfy both parties, but as this double-headed arrangement pleased neither, the Democrats established a paper of their own. The *Doylestown Democrat* appeared September 18, 1816, issued by Lewis Deffebach [12] and Co. The original size is not known, but the 46th number, July 29, 1817, was 19x23½ inches. The *Democrat* had a varied experience in early life. It was issued from a brick building on the east side of North Main street, nearly opposite the Fountain House, but before the year was out the word "Co." was dropped and Mr. Deffebach became sole proprietor. Following the custom of other papers, he announced, in the 42d issue, that he "will receive wheat, rye, oats, hay and all kinds of country produce in payement of debts."

Owing to a division in the Democratic party, an opposition paper was issued, July 28, 1819, called the *Bucks County Messenger*, or the "Yellow Fever" paper from the color of the paper it was printed on. Simeon Siegfried, the proprietor, was born in New Britain, 1797, and learned the printing trade with Asher Miner. From Doylestown he went to Bridgeton, N. J., where he established the *Advertiser*; then to Ohio, where he became a minister of the Gospel. He issued the first number of the *Ohio Luminary*, at Cadiz. He married Mary Johnson, of Newtown, 1817. An effort was made to issue a German paper from the *Messenger* office in August, 1821, but was a failure. As two Democratic newspapers could not be supported at the county seat, they were consolidated in January, 1822, under the name of *Bucks County Democrat*, and Simon Cameron and Benjamin Mifflin placed in charge. Mr. Cameron subsequently became one of the most prominent men in the country, was Secretary of War under Mr. Lincoln and Minister to Russia. Mifflin was born in Philadelphia, whence he came to Doylestown, and whither he returned, and died there. He was subsequently connected with the publication of the *Pennsylvanian*. The consolidation of the two papers harmonized the Democratic

---

12 From Doylestown Deffebach went to Philadelphia, where he published *The Peoples' Guardian* in 1821. Governor Snyder appointed him Armorer for the state, keeper of the Schuylkill Arsenal and Deputy U. S. Marshall, 1817.

party, and, the following December, it was bought by William T. Rogers.[13] At this time the paper was issued from a small frame on the east side of North Main street and Court, later the Shearer building, and site of the present Ziegler building. Rogers changed the name of the paper to the *Democrat* and *Farmers' Gazette.*

In 1829, the *Democrat* changed hands, Rogers selling it to Manassah H. Snyder.[14] Snyder was proprietor but two years, when it again changed hands, this time being sold to William H. Powell in in 1831, who married a daughter of Enoch Harvey of Doylestown, and published the paper until 1834, when he sold it to John S. Bryan, son of William Bryan, Springfield township, who was born 1758, and was an early settler there. Powell returned to Norristown and died there. The *Correspondent* and *Democrat* were the only two papers established in the pioneer period, which came to stay, and none others are in existance that were not started in more recent years. Meanwhile, new papers appeared, and disappeared after a brief life. John S. Bryan,[15] who succeeded William H. Powell, learned his trade in the office. During this period there was no marked change in the paper, except in the increase of business, both in subscription and advertising and job work, and the paper maintained its good repute in the state. During Bryan's ownership the *Democrat*, after having occupied several homes, got back to the old frame it is said to have started in, on the east side of North Main street, opposite the Fountain House, where the plant was burnt out in the winter of 1836. It was shortly after issued frrom the stone house on the northwest corner of South Main street and Oakland avenue, where it was published for thirteen years.

In May 1845, General Bryan sold the *Democrat* to Samuel Johnson Paxson, son of the late Thomas Paxson, Buckingham township,

---

13 William T. Rogers, son of William C. Rogers, was born in Philadelphia and brought up in Warrington township, Bucks county. He learned the trade in Miner's office and was prominent in politics and the Volunteer Militia; served eight years in the State Senate, was collector of tolls on the Delaware Canal at Bristol, Brigade Inspector, Major-General of Militia and died 1869.

14 Snyder was born in Lehigh county, and learned the trade in the office of the *Adler* at Reading. During the Civil War, he served in the Signal Corps of the Union Army, and when peace was declared, returned to his trade. He married a daughter of Elnathan Pettitt, Doylestown, sixty-five years ago proprietor of the Fountain House.

15 General Bryan became a prominent and popular man, and filled numerous public stations; Prothonotary of the county, Associate Judge, Clerk to the U. S. Senate Committee on Printing, Brigadier General of Militia and Democratic candidate for State Senate, but defeated at the polls.

JOHN S. BRYAN.

and was born and died three. After receiving a good English education, he and his brother, Edward M. Paxson, bought the *Literary Chronicle*, of Newtown, changing the name to *Newtown Journal*, which they published for some time. During the Civil War, and politics ran high, Mr. Paxson, who lived on the New Hope turnpike between Doylestown and Centreville, nailed a board on his gate at the road with the inscription: "A friend of the Constitution and the Union lives here." When Mr. Buchanan was elected to the Presidency, 1856, Mr. Paxson announced the fact in the *Democrat* in this wise: "A bachelor in the White House and all the old maids tickled to death." It was republished in the *London Times*.

The first issue of the *Democrat*, under Mr. Paxson's management, which appeared on May 14th, was awaited with no little interest. Having had some previous experience in country journalism, and being a man of great energy of character, he put new vim into the business. He was an innovator on old customs in every department. He allotted space for local news in each issue of the paper, and claimed to have been the originator of what is known as the "Local Item" column, but this claim was disputed by the *Intelligencer*. However this may have been, the local column shortly became a popular feature of every county newspaper. Mr. Paxson was not only aggressive, from a business standpoint, but full of humor, and drew upon this bank at frequent intervals. Under his management of the *Democrat*, the circulation of the paper and advertising both increased. He introduced the first Hoe printing press into the county, and printed the first newspaper by steam. In 1848, he erected the brick building, now Thompson's restaurant, south side of East Court street, and moved the printing machinery and material into it. Subsequently, Paxson erected the adjoining building on the east, into which he moved, 1852, and where the *Democrat* is still published.

In May, 1858, Paxson sold the *Democrat* plant to W. W. H. Davis, who had recently returned from a four years residence in New Mexico. While there, he had control of the *Santa Fe Gazette*, which he published in Spanish and English, and, becoming fond of journalism, made up his mind to obtain possession of the *Democrat* on his return. He was editor and proprietor for thirty-two years, and editor alone, forty-two years. He bought the real estate, 1863. During this period country journalism was more prosperous than at any time before or since; real estate was high, advertisements and job work in plenty and prices good. Mr. Davis assumed control of the

Democrat shortly after the purchase, and his first issue was May 25th. His salutatory was looked for with some interest, because of the split in the Democratic party on the Kansas-Nebraska question. As the views of the new editor did not coincide with those of the National administration, an opposition paper was established, of which more in another place. There was strong rivalry between the *Democrat* and *Intelligencer*, from a business and political standpoint, but this did not interrupt the harmony that prevailed between the editors and proprietors. While the editor of the *Democrat* was absent three years and a half in the army during the Civil War, the paper was in charge of Dr. John D. Mendenhall, a native of Chester county, but had resided several years at Bristol, in Bucks county in the practice of his profession, that of a dentist.

In the spring of 1890, Mr. Davis sold the *Democrat* plant, and everything thereunto belonging, except the real estate, to a syndicate, which subsequently became an incorporated company under the name of "The Doylestown Publishing Company," the late owner remaining as editor. News and job presses, and divers other machinery, were purchased, and the *Democrat* started on its new career as well, if not better, equipped than a majority of country newspapers, in the state. During a period of sixty-seven years, 1834-1901, the *Democrat* had but four proprietors and three editors, and, in this regard, broke the record in the county. In August 1890, a daily was issued and has completed its thirteenth year. The weekly is continued. In June, 1901, the *Democrat* plant was leased to J. C. Dimm, of Juniata county.

The *Bucks County Express*, established 1827, by Manassah H. Snyder, the first German newspaper printed in Bucks county, survives under the name of *Express and Reform*. The *Express* had several owners; belonging to the *Democrat* for fifteen years, and was subsequently owned by O. P. Zink,[16] Edwin Fretz,[17] Charles Price and Adam Daubert. In 1866, the paper was purchased by Dr. Mor-

---

16 O. P. Zink was born in Germany, and coming here when young, learned the printing trade in the *Adler* office, Reading. He served through the Civil War in the 6th Pa. Cavalry (Rush's Laners) and died at the Soldiers' Home, Dayton, Ohio, May 7, 1883.

17 Fretz and Price were both born in Bucks county and learned their trade in the *Democrat* office, of which the former was foreman. He was a Lieutenant in the 104th Pa. Regiment in the Civil War; worked at his trade several years in Philadeldhia, where he died October 2, 1901, and was buried in the Doylestown cemetery.

witz,[18] Philadelphia, and is now owned and published by his son. He also owns the *Bucks County Mirror*, established at Quakertown, 1870, and subsequently removed to Doylestown. In 1835, Joseph Young [19] issued the second German paper published in Doylestown, *Der Morgenstern,* which had but four owners down to 1890, when it was discontinued. Joseph Young, Moritz Loeb,[20] Naiman and Daubert.

Other newspapers appeared in Doylestown, from time to time, of longer or shorter life, some hardly surviving their baptism. Taking them in the order of their birth, we have first the *Political Examiner,* by Francis B. Shaw, 1827, which met its death, 1832, after boxing the political compass and three changes of editors; the *Jackson Courier,* 1835, by the late Thomas Ross, and in charge of Franklin Mills; the *Public Advocate,* by Franklin Sellers, 1837-8; and the *Independent Democrat,* the last on the roll of old newspapers; started by M. H. Snyder, 1847, sold to C. N. Bryan, 1848, purchased by a syndicate, 1852, who placed it in the hands of William P. Seymour, and its death followed. He changed the name to the *Watchtower*, and remained here until 1856-7. He was now lost to view until the outbreak of the Civil war, when he turned up at Washington, as Lieutenant-Colonel of the 99th, Pa. Regiment, from which he shortly resigned and left the service. He went west and died in Indiana, 1886, where, we understand, he cut a respectable figure. His widow, in more recent years, was a matron at the "Old Woman's Home," Erie, Pa., but as we have not heard from her for some time, presume she is dead.

There were two papers, published at Doylestown in the past, bearing the name of *"Olive Branch,"* the first by Asher Miner in connection with the *Correspondent*, the first issue bearing the date of July—, 1821. It occupied the fourth page and was filled with semi-literary matter, with the motto.

<blockquote>"Variety's the spice of life
That gives it all its flavor."</blockquote>

How long it lasted we do not know. Franklin P. Sellers, who established the second *Olive Branch*, twenty years later, learned his

---

18 A German by birth; established the *German Democrat*, and owned it to his death.

19 Joseph Young was born in Lehigh county, and was not twenty when he established the second German paper at Doylestown, *Der Morgenstern* under the name of *Der Bauer*. He married Amanda Lay, of Nockamixon, May 13, 1847, and has been dead many years.

20 Moritz Loeb, a German by birth, came here when young; learned his trade in the *Morgenstern* office and then bought the paper. He was a scholarly man.

trade in Asher Miner's office, and, after that, worked on the *Democrat*. Sellers issued the first number of his *Olive Branch*, June 2, 1842, and, the first of the next March, Sellers removed the paper and the *Bucks County Temperance Herald*, published in connection with it, to a frame on the west side of North Main street, back of the Court House, the same building in which Joseph Young's *Morgenstern* was published. The paper had been previously issued from one of the frame houses on the south side of East State street about opposite the Murfit building.[21] On February 22, 1844, Sellers was married to Mrs. Rachel G. Mathews, daughter of Samuel Godshalk, of Doylestown township; the paper removed to Norristown, 1850, the name changed to the *Independent* and was sold out by the Sheriff, 1874.

The last of July, 1842, Joseph Young and Company, of Doylestown, issued a prospectus for publishing a new German paper to be called the *"Bucks County Farmer,"* the first number appearing August 26th. Its fate we do not know, but doubtless it died in infancy. The first of June, 1842, a prospectus was issued for the publication of the *Bucks County Whig* at Doylestown, by Adam D. Luz and William Keesey, but the paper never made its appearance. In June, 1839, Franklin S. Mills, formerly a compositor on one of the Doylestown newspapers, formed a partnership with Joseph Justice to publish the *Trenton Emporium*, which proved a success. This was the same Mills who bought out the *Jackson Courier* for Thomas Ross.

In 1852, a small paper, called *The Spy*, was started, being set up in the offices of the *Democrat* and *Intelligencer*, and printed on one of the presses *sub rosa*. It was the brightest sheet ever issued in the county and lasted about three years. Ryner T. Donat, a compositor on the *Intelligencer*, was the ostensible editor, but John Harton, foreman in the *Democrat* office furnished both the wit and the brains for this sparkling, little journal. We had understood a bound volume of this paper was in the possession of Frank Harton, son of the late John Harton, but have recently been told, by a member of the family, this is an error, which we learned with regret. It was a little jewel in the newspaper line.

In 1859 the friends of President Buchanan established the *Democratic Standard* in opposition to the *Doylestown Democrat*, because the latter would not support his Kansas-Nebraska policy. Henry P. Ross, then a student of law in his father's office, was the editor, and

---

21 When the *Olive Branch* was published at this place C. C. Cox was roller boy for Frank Sellers.

J. Mathias Beans and Julius Kuster, both graduates of the *Democrat* office, were proprietors and business managers. The paper was ably edited, but ceased to exist when the Civil War broke out. The morning Captain Davis left Doylestown, with the Doylestown Guards, at the outbreak of the war, he bought the *Democratic Standard*, put the material in his own office, and enlisted Julius Kuster, one of its late business managers, in the Guards, with the rank of Corporal. This assisted to close the breach in the Democratic party.

Bernard McGinty, who came to Doylestown with the *Mirror*, left that paper, opened a job office on the property of the Court Inn, and shortly started the *Court Gazette*, which he published until 1890, when he sold out to the syndicate that purchased the *Democrat*. In February, 1883, Howard Morris, a graduate of the *Democrat* office, began the publication of a small sheet called *The Cricket*, which lasted about six months. It was neat and sprightly. It is an open secret that its publication was discontinued because a form was "pied." Julius Kuster was on its staff. The latest newspaper to be born into our local journalistic world of Doylestown, was the *Daily Republican*, 1893, the outcome of a quarrel in that party, and, ostensibly, in the interest of Mr. Quay. Those interested made the plant a stock company under the name of the "Republican Company," and it publishes both a weekly and daily. In addition to the above mentioned papers, the Baptist church published the *Sower and Reaper*, a small religious monthly, and the National Farm School, two miles out of town, issues *The Gleaner*.

One of the editors of a Doylestown paper, became a very prominent journalist in the south. This was John S. Heart, who conducted the *Political Examiner* for Frank Shaw. He was born in Philadelphia, and, from Doylestown, went to Washington, to take charge of the *Spectator and Young Hickory*, organs of the Calhoun Democracy. From Washington, Heart went to Charleston, South Carolina, becoming one of the editors and joint-proprietor of the *Mercury*, September 1, 1849, the firm being Heart and Taber. On July 1, 1851, Heart sold his interest of the *Mercury* to Colonel Rhett and returned to Washington, where he was appointed superintendent of the Printing Bureau. He went back to Charleston at the outbreak of the Civil War and to Memphis, Tennessee, at its close, where he established the *Commercial*.

Our newspaper offices have done more or less book printing in the course of their business life, but not to any great extent. The earliest book published by any of the offices in Doylestown, so far as we can learn, was issued by Asher Miner 1808. This was a volume of the works of Boethus, "Concerning the Consolation of Philosophy." It was written about 1300 years ago, and translated from the Latin by Paul Preston, a self-taught genius of this county. It is a volume of four and one-half by six and one-half inches, of fifty-three pages, and also contains twenty-six verses on "The Captivity of Benjamin Gilbert and Family by the Indians, in 1780." Since that time many books have been issued from the county press, quite a number in German. In 1814 Asher Miner published a volume containing the "Confession of Faith of Mennonists," in German. Following these, our German offices printed, in that language, a number of books between 1834 and 1848, of which the following are the titles:

A Mirror of the Baptism, 1834, J. Zornig; True Righteousness, advocated by A. Gottschall, 1837, J. Young and Krapf; The Prophet, 1838, J. Young and Krapf; Description of the New Creation, by A. Gottschall, 1838, J. Young; The Small Prayer-Book, by J. Habermann, 1839; Catechism, 1844, J. Young; Six Different Discourses (or Dialogues), 1845, J. O. Brecht; Christian Conversations, 1848, J. Young; The Small Religious Harp of the Children of Zion, fifth edition ; by order of the Mennonite Congregations, Doylestown, 1848, printed by Young and Loeb. [22]

While W. W. H. Davis owned the *Democrat* office, he published several volumes there of which he was the author: "The History of the Hart Family;" "Life of General John Lacey;" "History of Bucks County," (type set up in office, press work done in Philadelphia:) "The Spanish Conquest of New Mexico;" "History of the Doylestown Guards;" "Life of General John Davis" and "The Fries Rebellion," the latter being issued from the office after it had passed into the hands of the Publishing Company.

---

[22] The titles of these books, in German, were sent to the author fifteen years ago, by the late Horatio Gates Jones, Esq., Philadelpeia, and Mr. Frederick Constantine, of the *Bucks County Mirror*, translated them into English.

Doylestown, Old and New.

IX

In the Twenties.

While the removal, of the county seat to Doylestown, was an excellent thing for the ultimate prosperity of the village, it was a long time feeling the new impulse. There was little improvement for a number of years, and it had probably less life between '20 and '30, than in any like period of the first fifty years of the century.[1] An occasional building was erected, and a small increase in population, while every thing else moved along on very conservative lines. The village newspapers make no mention of any material improvement until the spring of 1828, when the *Intelligencer* of April 21, says:

"We may here properly notice the general spirit of improvement prevailing in various parts of our town; several new houses are being erected, old ones undergoing repairs, the walling in, fencing, and planting ornamental trees on the grounds attached to the public buildings, and a daily stage to Philadelphia, Easton, Bethlehem and Allentown, give quite an active and business appearance to the village."[2]

While "small favors are thankfully received," as a rule, this was nothing to brag of. A community, that waits fifteen years before

---

[1] In Doylestown, February 20, 1820, John Backhouse, son of Richard Backhouse, former owner of Durham furnace, aged 34 years.

[2] On March 15, 1821, Crispin Blackfan, of Doylestown, Prothonotary of the Court of Common Pleas, to Hannah, daughter of Colonel Elisha Wilkinson, of Buckingham.

planting trees on the grounds of its public buildings and erecting a fence around them, is conservative to the point of lacking public spirit. A boom had long been anticipated, but it did not come until the decade had expired and the century turned into the 30's. In the meantime, however, we come to a period when there is some criticism, the first we have met with, on the general appearance of the county capital. As this is part of the village history we refrain from withholding it. In the summer of 1829, there appeared, in the *Patriot* of June 22nd, over the signature of "Cid Hamet Benengeli," the following:

"Before all other villiages and towns commend me to our charming nob, Doylestown. I admire, exceedingly, its commanding situation; its beautiful appearance when seen from a distance; its winding streets and acute angles; and, above all, the judicious intermingling of fronts, corners, rears and gable-ends, which line the way. Care has evidently been taken, in erecting houses, to avoid the monotony of method. They stand like the 33d regiment P. M. in motly array, front-rank and rear-rank, a little in or a little out, as fancy or convenience may dictate. This, certainly, imparts the flavor of that pleasant spice variety, and, to my eye, constitutes the beauty of a country town, that should not endeavor to look like a great one. There should be something odd; something to take the eyes, and elicit a passing remark from the traveler. Doylestown is quite odd, and must, therefore, I conceive, 'be quite the thing.'"

* * * * * * * * *

"For the origin of Doylestown it is in vain to fix a date. Certainly it is a place of high antiquity—'the memory of man runneth not to the contrary.' To search the Records and wipe away the clouds of doubt and dust, 'I thank my stars is not my task.' The town, however, derives its name from William Doyle, formerly a proprietor of a part of the hill on which it stands, and instead of 'Doylestown' was anciently written 'Doyle-Town.'"

"Not long since, some difficulty arose as to the precise situation of certain important corner-stones. Grubbing hoes and Dutch shovels were set to work to settle the matter, but the principal one, at the junction of the Easton and Newtown roads, was not to be found. So that (quoad hoc) whatever is must necessarily be right. Several years ago somebody undertook to dig for *gold* in a large field near the town. Nothwithstanding the most persevering industry (and at the right age of the moon, too) not a particle of gold was discovered; of course the enterprise fell through, and the proprietor had nothing but his labor for his pains."

"The plan upon which Doyle-Town was laid out was unique. It is doubtful indeed, whether any plan was ever made, for, if such had been the case, I should think the town would have been arranged with more regard for right lines and right angles. The main street makes a very palpable curve, running in a north-westerly course as far as Mr. Morris' hotel, thence curving round to the north, something like a scythe blade, until it gets out of town. The Newtown road and the old Township Line road [3] (there are no names for these streets) cross the main street, running against each other at the west end of the town.[4] There are several other streets or lanes in the town, such as Shaw's lane, the "Dutch Lane,"[5] "Church Lane,"[6] and the "Lane of Desolation." As for the side walks, by your leave, Mr. Editor, I will make but little mention of them, as the least said is the soonest amended. I must say, however, that they die very like Jeremiah's Figs. Strangers, walking in the main street after dark, are cautioned to lift their feet higher than usual, to avoid stumbling over an artificial precipice in the side-walk, near the centre of the town. A more ingenious mantrap was never invented."

* * * * * * *

"Doylestown has no Mineral Springs to make it a great summer resort (as they have at Willow Grove) but they have a fountain of mineral water at Mr. Field's a thousand times more palatable, and I dare say equally beneficial."

The next to critisize the village was a "Sojourner" in the issue of a village newspaper of November 9, 1829, who says:

"I am a stranger in Doylestown and its neighborhood, and for one good reason, I am glad of it. In my passage through your village, the mail, as usual, stopped at Mr. Marples,[7] and, having some little walking to do in the town, it was with the greatest difficulty I could get along in some places, on account of the muddy condition of the streets. One place, in particular, the hill just below Mr. Marples,[8] is a disgrace to so wealthy a place as Doylestown. How the ladies

---

3 Court street.
4 Crossing at Clinton street.
5 Extenuation of Broad street.
6 Church street.
7 Now the Fountain House.
8 The descent of Main street from State.

manage to walk I don't know, though I fancy, if the truth were known, they are obliged to stay within doors."

We allow a couple additional witnesses to take the stand and testify in favor of muddy streets before we close this side of the case. A newspaper of the town, date and name not remembered, says:

"We shall soon be supplied with our winter's supply of mud; and unless the walks are mended, we have nothing to expect but a repetition of the same melancholy and protracted scene of wading splashing and splattering, dirty boots and clumsy overshoes."

Another authority says:

"It is some amusement to witness the manœuvering of the Doylestown people in picking their way through the wretchedly muddy streets in this season of the year. A journey of a square and a half is a most rueful undertaking, and the safe accomplishment of the whole tour of the town would be little better than a miracle."

The severe criticism on the street condition of the town probably had its effect, for we find, that at a public meeting held in the early winter of 1829, to take action toward the incorporation of the village something was done to "amend" them. Measures were inaugurated to effect an improvement of the side walks. The streets were turned over to the supervisors, and Timothy Smith, Enoch Harvey and James S. Rich, were constituted a committee to supervise the work. What, if any, improvement this brought about is not known.

While we fear there was more than a grain of truth in what "Ci Hamet," and the other witnesses, had to say about the condition of the streets of the town of Doyle, at the close of the twenties; nevertheless if they could return in the flesh, and walk the streets of the Doylestown of 1903, almost three quarters of a century intervening we believe they would be willing to recall their previous testimony take off their hats and make the amende honorable.

But the 20's were not allowed to turn the corner into the 30' without a visible sign of improvement, for, in 1827, the first German newspaper in the county, was born into the journalistic world, *The Bucks County Express*, of which more is said in a previous chapter.

To show the attention paid the 4th of July at that period, we give a report of the celebration in the Court House, Doylestown, 1822 held under the auspices of the Artillery, Capt. Magill. Josiah Y Shaw was president of the day, Dr. James S. Rich, vice president and Frank Shaw the orator. Dinner was served in the woods east of the Presbyterian church.

THE ROSS LAW OFFICE, 1829.

The *Correspondent*, Asher Miner's paper, says of it:
"The welcome morning was ushered in by the ringing of the bells and thunder from the cannon. The County Hall (court room) the afternoon previous had been decorated in a style the most enchanting for rural scenery, and displaying, in point of effect, a degree admirably appropriate to the occasion. The interior was darkened with the tall green forests of spruce and laurel most tastefully disposed. The large folding doors, at the entrance of the hall, were thrown wide, and the citizens passed in under wreathed arches of laurel. Every window in the hall was ornamented in the same manner. The large semi-circular recess, occupied by the Judge's Bench, was adorned in the most imposing style. The background presented a thick forest showing, in some degree, the mist of distance, over which was seen towering in bolder approach a grand arch about 21 feet from point to point in its base, and about 10 feet to its centre, formed of the richest foliage of the laurel, and upon which was displayed, at equal distance, the thirteen stars, with radiance of seven inches, representing the thirteen states, that united in the Declaration of Independence, Pennsylvania being the key and centre, and immediately under the centre, in large letters and figures appeared, "July the Fourth 76." This was the 46th Anniversary of Independence. The only citizen, whose toast is reported, was that of Samuel Kachline, who drank: "Our Farmers, Mechanics, Manufactures and Merchants; Independence is their boast; if the country be prompt in furnishing them with arms, they will be prompt to defend it." One gun six cheers.

Seven years later, 1829, a pretentious institution came into being in the village, "The Academy of Natural Sciences," the meeting, for organization being held February 11th, with Abraham Chapman in the chair. What was done is not recorded, but, at a subsequent meeting, held in the Academy the evening of February 25, a committee was appointed to draft an address to the citizens of the county. The next meeting, we find mention of, was held April 29, and the constitution and by-laws were completed at that or a subsequent session. This completing the organization, the first meeting under the constitution, was held for the election of permanent officers, May 25, with the following result: President, John Moore; Vice President, William H. Johnson; Recording Secretary, Albert Smith; Corresponding Secretary, Jonathan C. Jones; Curators, Dr. James S. Rich and Robert P. DuBois; and Treasurer, Rev. Samuel Aaron. The Society held monthly meetings, and at the first, June 6, a lecture

was delivered in the Court House on Botany, at 4 p. m., by M
Jones, Corresponding Secretary. Daniel Longstreth, Warmins
township, delivered a lecture on Entomology at a meeting he
August 28, and, on September 25, Captain John Robbarts, N
Britain, brought to the meeting a chicken with four legs. The i
troductory lecture, on Mineralogy, was delivered before the Socie
by Dr. Hugh Meredith, February 27, 1830, at which time t
membership was thirty, and, in 1836, thirteen women belonged to
The Dr. Meredith, who delivered this lecture, was the nephew of L
Hugh Meredith, senior, who it will be recalled, died in 1815.
the first year of the Society, both the president and correspondi
secretary died, and a resolution of regret was adopted at the ann
meeting, May 22, 1832. The minute book gives a catalogue of t
minerals in the cabinet of the Society, 181 specimens in all with
names of the givers. The last recorded meeting was held January
1837, with Abraham Chapman in the chair, the exercises on t
occasion consisting of a lecture on "Electricity," by S. J. Paxso
and an essay on the subject of "New Year's Day," was read by C.
DuBois. The Society probably came to an end between this ti
and 1840. Subsequent to this we find some trace of the "Bu
County Academy of Natural Sciences," but the two organizatio
were probably one and the same under different names. Two ca
of minerals, belonging to the "Academy of National Sciences," w
deposited in the Ingham Female Seminary, but what became of th
is not known.

In reading what is said about Doylestown, at this period,
reader should not forget "there are two sides to every question,"
least the legal profession inculcates this idea when there is a good
at stake, and, they contend no question should be decided with
hearing both sides. So we think on arriving at the true condition
our "nob Doylestown," when bidding adieu to the 20's and ab
entering the 30's. It was not as black as the other side had pain
it by a good deal, and this we will now prove, at least to our o
satisfaction, if not to our readers, by the witnesses we put on
stand. A writer of the village had the following to say of it; its s
roundings and the people, about 1830, and we rest the verdict on
testimony:

"The charming appearance of the town, particularly at this sea
of the year, will be found an excellent inducement for summer visito
it lies on a most delightful route; leaving Philadelphia we pass thro

Jenkintown, Willow Grove, Hatboro, all pleasant villages, and can stay all night, if they choose, at any of the six hotels of Doylestown; from thence to Bethlehem, Allentown, or the charming borough of Easton. Here the traveler has his choice for Mauch Chunk or Schooley's mountain or, indeed, wherever he may prefer to go. Assuredly, no direction from Philadelphia can be so pleasant to travel as that we have described. Unfortunately, we have, as yet, no mineral spring to constitute a source of attraction; but a solution of Glauber salts(which is much the same thing) can be found at any time. Pleasanter substitutes, such as ale, lemonade, etc. are always in readiness. Last year we had the benefit of a fountain of artificial mineral waters at Mr. Field's, but we are sorry to learn his interesting apparatus does not propose to give another blow-out this season."

"There are some elegant afternoon drives from this place: Would mention, for instance, Prospect Hill, where the view is truly beautiful; New Hope properly No "Hope," where the eye may be regaled with a sight of that national blessing, the Delaware Divison of the Pennsylvania Canal; where also may be seen the Banking house of a very prosperous institution, the New Hope Delaware Bridge Company; an interesting drive may be made to Lumberville and Point Pleasant; to Montgomery Square or to Newtown, which is not so new as the name would indicate. For shorter trip we ride out to the Cross Keys; Colonel Wilkinson's;[7] Major Carver's; to the old Turk[8] (revised) and to Stephen's.[9] One class of people may find this place, on some accounts, particulary agreeable; we mean young ladies. The "Stock Company" of the town are not proportioned in number to the young men; consequently the appearance of a few stars is always waited with eagerness. We dare not do more than throw out a hint upon this subject, for a certain class of the population, will be found no wise anxious for any such addition to society as we have mentioned and will "play the mischief" with us if we are too bountiful in our invitations. We are desirous to keep in their good graces."

A representative of the *Philadelphia Chronicle* says of Doylestown:

"The village contains about 125 dwelling houses, constructed of different materials, some of brick, some of stone, and others wooden

---

[7] Centerville.

[8] One mile below Doylestown.

[9] A mile out of town on the Upper State road; this tavern and the Turk long since out of license.

frame. The houses are generally well built, many of them in modern style with a front yard enclosed." * * * "This is the seat of justice for the county; of course there are a Court House, a prison and county offices. These are of solid and durable construction, erected in the year 1812, upon the summit of the town and are enclosed by a wall and paling in a public lot, which, except on the walks, is well covered with grass and shaded with trees."

*   *   *   *   *   *   *   *

"Among the most favorable signs of the intelligence and spirit of the people of this place and surrounding country, is the encouragement given to the puplic press. There are four newspapers issued here weekly—two in the English, the *Bucks County Intelligencer* and the *Doylestown Democrat*, of the largest class of county journals, and two in the German language, both respectable for matter of size."

It is a fortunate thing for the author, as it will be for the future historian, that the newspapers of the period give such accurate account of the progress of the county capital from time to time. One of the newspapers, speaking of Doylestown at the beginniug of the 30's, says:

"In our village there are upwards of one hundred dwelling houses—three of brick put up the last season; the residue substantial stone and frame buildings, one-half of which are yearly rented to mechanics, laborers and others. At present there are six taverns, five stores, three printing offices, twelve lawyers, four physicians, two cabinet makers, five shoemakers, three tailors, four teachers, two stone masons, one master carpenter, one master hatter, two wheelwrights, two blacksmiths, besides a tanner and currier, tinman, bookbinder, milliner, stonecutter, chairmaker, coachmaker, painter and glazier, iron foundry, saddler, butcher, fanmaker, a brickyard and about twenty journeymen mechanics, forty apprentices, and twenty daily laborers."

"Doylestown and the surrounding country is one of the most healthy and pleasant places we know of; situated nearly equi-distant between Philadelphia and Easton, and the stages pass daily through the village for Philadelphia, Easton and for Pottsville and New York. Persons desirous of purchasing real estate, can now have an excellent opportunity as some of the best farms in the neighborhood of the village are offered for sale, as well as numerous town lots, which may be had at fair prices. Those wishing to purchase, or mechanics desirous of procuring situations, will be cheerfully afforded every information by addressing the editor of this paper." [10]

In 1833, just after the county seat had turned out of the twenties and enrolled itself in the thirties, an unknown correspondent wrote of our town of Doyle:

"Doylestown, the seat of Justice of Bucks county, is twenty-six miles North of Philadelphia in Doylestown township, situated upon a high hill and has a commanding view of a delightful and fertile country which surrounds it, and is not less remarkable for salubrity than for the beauty of its location. The public buildings consist of a commodious stone Court House, in which are the county offices, and a capacious stone prison. There are in the town about one hundred dwellings, five stores, and six taverns. Two daily stages pass through it to Easton. A branch of the Neshaminy creek passes near to and east of the town. There is here a Presbyterian church, an Academy, which is incorporated and has received several donations from the state, an Academy of Natural Sciences, an Agricultural Society and four weekly newspapers; the *Bucks County Intelligencer*, the *Bucks County Republican*, the *Doylestown Democrat* and the *Doylestown Express*, the last a German paper. With this evidence in favor of our charming "nob," despite the testimony on the other side, the verdict must be in favor of our town of Doyle." [11]

---

10 *Democrat*, November 30, 1830.

11 In this decade one of the most distinguished members of the Doylestown bar was admitted to practice, the late Thomas Ross, Esq. This was in 1829, and from that time to his death, 1865, he played a leading part, not only at the bar but also in politics, representing this district two terms in the Congress of the United States. His two grandsons, the fourth generation in descent from Judge John Ross, are in practice at this bar, something unusual; and hold up their end worthily. Thomas Ross is thought to have built the law office, whose likeness assists to illustrate this chapter, about the time he was admitted to the bar.

Doylestown, Old and New.

X
In the Thirties.

In October, 1830, Francis B. Shaw, a member of the Doylestown bar, something of a journalist and son of Josiah Y. Shaw, made a step on the line of improvement, by purchasing the "Underhill Farm,"[1] cutting a portion of it into building lots and offering them at public sale on the 18th. It joined the village on the south and embraced a strip of woodland on the west side of the Easton road, now South Main street. The lots were advertised as "beautiful for building and convenient for business." More or less of them were probably sold but we have not been able to get any account of the sale. Since that time a number of buildings have been erected on the slope, including a hotel, industrial plants, railroad station etc., but the town's growth has not been in that direction. The author remembers when this part of the town was known by the soubriquet of "Ireland," as the north-section is still called "Germany."

The issue of the newspaper announcing the purchase of the "Underhill Farm," the *Bucks County Intelligencer* of October 11, 1830, calls for the following mechanics and others most needed in Doylestown to boom its fortunes: "a tobacconist, a soap and tallow chandler, a brewer and bottler, brickmakers and bricklayers, a brush-maker, clock and watch maker, tinsmith, oak and cedar cooper, and a gun and lock smith." We infer, from these workmen being called

---

[1] This was the old Shaw farm just below the borough, on the west side of the turnpike leading to Philadelphia, and was owned for many years by the late Josiah Hart.

FRANCIS B. SHAW.

for, none of them were here, or the supply was not equal to the demand. At this period,[2] and we believe the same year, 1830, an historic building was erected on the Ross property, on the north side of East Court street where Pine street enters it and adjoining the public grounds. This was an Attorney's office built of brick and still standing, in which three generations of the family, grandfather, sons and grandsons have practiced their profession, consulted their clients and prepared their briefs, which does not often occur under the same roof. Among the cases was the celebrated Mina-Chapman murder, 1831-2, tried by Thomas Ross, then Deputy Attorney General for the county. Of the Attorneys of the Ross family, which occupied this historic office, one served two terms in the House of Representatives of the United States, another sat on the bench of the adjoining counties of Bucks and Montgomery, and a third served two terms in the Senate of Pennsylvania. The office and its distinguished occupants are alike entitled to a place in our volume.

In the *Bucks County Intelligencer*, of December 10, 1832,[3] a resume of the village improvements of that period says:

"There appears to be a renewed vigor and spirit of enterprise here. There have been newly erected several valuable brick dwelling houses, some of them in modern and superior style. It is expected from the late purchase and transfer of lots and the corresponding arrangements, that next summer there will be a number of spacious dwellings as well as other houses of a smaller class erected. There seems an auxiliary and immediate impulse given to trade and business from the establishment of a bank now shortly to go into operation."

The brick dwellings, spoken of as "newly erected," were those of the Misses Buckman and Mr. Freed, next door to each other, south side of East Court street. The former was built by the late General William T. Rogers, the latter by Mrs. Morris, mother of the late John Lloyd, and in the summer and fall of 1832. After the Rogers' house was completed, he got the Rev. Samuel Aaron to calculate the number of bricks in it, which footed up 36,533, of all quality, giving the number in each part of it, viz: partition wall, cellar, 1700; north-

---

2 At Doylestown, February 11, 1830, Mrs Emilie D. Aaron, wife of Rev. Samuel Aaron and daughter of the late Rev. Uriah DuBois, in her 27th year.

3 In Philadelphia, March 8, 1832, after a short illness, Caroline Hyde, formerly of Doylestown, aged thirty years. Miss Hyde lived several years in Doylestown, and was noted for her benevolence, and her disinterested interest for her neighbors. At the time of her death she was teaching an infant school in the Northern Liberties, Philadelphia.

east end, 9,700; the front wall from basement to chamber floor, 2,613; southwest end, 14,702; back wall from basement to chamber floor, 2,613; same from chamber floor to square, 2,263. There were a number of smaller measurements, and the report was made to General Rogers, May 10, 1832, about the time the walls were up. The double brick, on the north side of West Court street, was erected about the same time by Samuel Yardley, in one end of which Robert M. Yardley, Esq., lived.

The first occupant, of the east end, was William Watts, late Associate Judge and there he died. At his death, 1838, his grandfather's clock, given him by his father, Arthur Watts, was sold at public sale to Samuel Yardley, but the much prized clock cannot be traced any further. When these dwellings were erected, the author was a boy at school in Doylestown, and he and other boys had many a good romp in the shavings.

* * * * * *

"We want clock and watch-makers, brewers, plasterers, paperhangers, brick-makers and brick-layers, book-binders, tanners and curriers, and other operators, if we may be allowed to use the term. There remains but little doubt, that in a short time the increasing population and improvement will call for board and coal-yards and an additional store or two, especially an apothecary and druggist. Most of these we already have among us, but competition, like punctuality, is the life of trade, and, instead of diminshing employment and profit, tends to increase both."

The brick dwelling, owned and occupied by Dr. Frank Swartzlander, the elder, on the south side of East State street, was built in 1832 by William Cox, and after his death was bought by William Stokes, who lived in it to his death, January 30, 1850, in his eighty-second year. The brick on the northeast corner of State and Pine, occupied by Dr. Swartzlander, the younger, was built in 1830; sold by the Sheriff and bought by Samuel Yardley, the leading merchant of the village.

In a subsequent issue of the *Intelligencer*,[4] a further view of the improvements going on in Doylestown is given:

"There was probably never a greater degree of prosperity in our town than is exhibited at this time. No less than ten houses are in a state of forwardness, and preparations are making for the erection of

---

4 May 27, 1833.

several others this season. These buildings are all to be erected in a style that will materially add to the beauty of the place, being principally for the occupancy of those who are putting them up. Among those of a larger class we may particularize that of the new bank, the dimensions of which are 36x40 feet, to be two stories high, of stone and plastered in imitation of marble. It is on the Main street between the late Enoch Harvey's dwelling and his tavern house, now Mr. Brock's. The masons have got the cellar walls up. Nearly opposite, Charles Harvey has pulled down his store house on the corner, and is building a beautiful house of suitable dimensions for a store and dwelling.[5] This is of brick and the work tastefully and neatly executed. On the lots fronting the southeast side of the Court House, two brick houses are to be erected which will materially beautify that part of the town. On the southwest side of the lot, facing the public buildings, a house is to be erected by about 26 by 30, as an office for the Clerk of Orphans' Court. A spirit of improvement is visable around several of the older houses, many of which are undergoing material alterations."

Prior to the spring of 1833, there was not a house of any kind on the square "fronting the southeast side of the Court house," bounded by Court, Broad and Pine streets and Garden Alley. The open square was the play ground of the Academy boys where they indulged in shinny and other amusements. When the Court house was erected, 1812-13, the block was owned by Nathaniel Shewell but subsequently sold and built on. On the first of April, 1833, Thomas Shewell, Philadelphia, sold the northeast corner lot to Dr. Hugh Meredith,[6] of Doylestown township, a nephew of old Dr. Hugh Meredith who died 1815. The price was $606.57, and the size 50 feet by 153 feet 5 inches, reaching down to Garden Alley. This house was built the same year the lot was bought, 1833, for when Dr. Meredith advertised his farm in the township for sale, 1834, he included "a large two story brick house on Court street fronting the public square, erected the last season and finished in first rate style. There is a frame office of two stories attached to the main building." This described the house in question as the author remembers it. It was bought by Caleb E. Wright, who had come here to practice law and subsequently by George Lear who tore down the frame office and

---

5 Randall's corner, State and Main.
6 December 21, 1831, Dr. Hugh Meredith, of Doylestown, to Miss Anna D. Rose, formerly of Charleston, S. C.

added a brick to the dwelling as we now find it. The property passed to the possession of Charles H. Magill in recent years.

The DuBois dwelling, the next door west but one, was built the same year, and carried the date, 1833, on the head of the water spout until a thoughtless painter painted over it. No other family has lived in this dwelling. Mrs. Charles E. DuBois[7] died in March, 1901, at the age of 88, and her two daughters and a sister now occupy it.

This house has been longer occupied, continuously, by the same family, than any other dwelling in the borough, and by the family that built it than the Hall dwelling. The next lot purchased on this block, facing the public ground, at the northwest corner, at Pine and Court, was by William Carr, who had recently come here as Clerk of the Orphans' Court. He bought it of Thomas Ross, the then owner, and the size of the lot was 60 feet on Court street by 153 feet 5 inches in depth to Garden Alley. This purchase was made April 25, 1833. Mr. Carr probably built on the lot the same season, for we are told by the family of the late John L. DuBois, Esq., which owns and occupies it that the water spout head formerly had the date, "1833" on it, and that the same date was carved by a diamond on one of the window panes. Mr. Carr cut this lot in two, and, some years after, built a dwelling on the east half in which he had his office, and rented the dwelling part. In the forties it was purchased by George H. Michener, Esq., a member of the bar, who occupied it, until his death, and his family after him. It was purchased of the Michener family by Dr. James Groff, 1895, who erected a new dwelling on the site[8] the following summer at a cost of $8,000.

The next person, to get possession of one of the eligible building lots on Court street, facing the public buildings and ground, was Dr. Charles H. Mathews, who purchased the third lot from the corner of Pine of Thomas Shewell, April 1, 1833, fifty-one feet nine inches by one hundred and fifty-three feet five inches for which he paid $603 and 71 cents. When Dr. Mathews erected a dwelling on the lot we are not informed, but in the near future, and in it he died. At his death the house passed to his son, Charles H. Mathews, Esq.,

---

7 In Philadelphia, June 24, 1831, by the Rev. William Latta, Charles E. DuBois, Esq., of Doylestown, Attorney at Law, to Miss Mary, daughter of the late Rev. John E. Latta, of New Castle, Delaware.

8 The Bucks County *Intelligencer*, of May 27, 1833, says of the buildings to be erected the coming season, "On the lots fronting the southeast side of the Court house, two brick houses, will materially beautify that part of the town." We might infer from this but two were to be erected.

of the Philadelphia bar. The latter sold it, in the eighties to Judge Harman Yerkes, who enlarged and improved it, and it is now one of the handsomest dwellings in the borough.

The last, of the original houses to be erected on this block, was that by Stokes L. Roberts, Esq., 1844, next but one to the corner of Court and Broad streets. He bought the lot of Charles E. DuBois, Esq., 1843. Mr. Roberts sold the house to W. W. H. Davis, 1859, who has lived in it to the present time. Since the house was built, now fifty-nine years, it has had but two occupants, and, until the present occupant made the house his home, neither a birth, death nor marriage had taken place in it. This completes a brief history of the six dwellings on the block facing the Court House and public ground. About 1830, it was intended to erect a building at the corner of Pine and Court for the accommodation of one of the county offices but the idea was abandoned. When these lots were sold, 1833, the present Pine street was called "Shewell street." [9]

Doylestown, in the past, as at present, was abreast with other communities in pushing the column of reform in morals. It was well in the lead in the cause of temperance, but the tone of her people has always been conservative. Probably the first meeting held in Doylestown, to promote the cause of temperance, was at the Academy, the evening of March 3, 1830, at least so far as our investigations have revealed the movement. Andrew Dunlap was called to the chair and Samuel Yardley and George Murray appointed secretaries. A committee, consisting of John Fox, Charles E. DuBois, Albert Smith, E. T. McDowell and Dr. Hugh Meredith, was named to prepare a Constitution, to be reported at an adjourned meeting. This was held the 10th, when the Constitution was adopted, an organization effected, with John Pugh for President; Dr. James S. Rich, Vice President; E. T. McDowell, Corresponding Secretary and Jeremiah S. Rich, Recording Secretary. Mr. McDowell was appointed to deliver an address at the first annual meeting.

In the next issue of the *Democrat* the editor, M. H. Snyder, made the following comments on the temperance movement:

"We certainly do not approve of the present system of anti-

---

[9] Why Shewell street was changed to "Pine" no one knows, for there is nothing connected with it that could suggest the name. When streets were laid out through the Pollock suburb, 1898, the author suggested, in the *Democrat*, that one of them be called "Shewell." H. C. Mercer took it up and advocated it before the Council, which accepted the suggestion, and one of the streets was called "Shewell Avenue," a fitting tribute to the man who did much for Doylestown.

fogmatics, pleghm-cutters, mint julips, and the whole tribe of liver murdering preparations that infest our country, but we hold with Anacreon, Horace and Tom Moore, that the juice of the grape is not to be eschewed. We are poor devils of humanity altogether, and if a glass of Champaign or Madeira or Port will drive away the clouds of care, why should we not indulge it? The world cannot appreciate half the troubles of an editor. To loose a dozen subscribers, to read *turkey tracks*, which some correspondents call writing, to be dunned for ink, etc.—this is the unkindest cut of all—to eat our pudding cold, in short, to do all things we must do, and to submit to all the grievances our state imposes on us—all these things must be taken into consideration."

"Gentlemen, gentlemen, you of the committee, and you so hard of heart as to forego the pleasure of hot whiskey punch at the sign of Fox Chase![10] Think of it before you condemn it. We will dispense with brandy even though it be the "pure Naiad of the Phleghethonic rill, with gin, although it is called the true Hippoerene; but whiskey punch! It will never do, depend upon it."

> "Let us have whiskey punch and mirth and laughter;
> Sermons and soda water the day after!"

In spite of the *Democrat's* philippic against the temperance movement of 1830, the effort resulted in the formation of a society for the suppression of intemperance with the officers already named. This was the commencement of a pretty active period of temperance reform, that was maintained many years and a good work accomplished. At that early day prohibition was hardly thought of, and, if ever talked about, it was with bated breath. That was the period when the decanter was found on almost every sideboard, and the first thing done, when a guest entered a house, was an invitation from the host for him to "take something," and, to decline, was almost equivalent to an insult. When this custom is recalled there is some excuse, if not justification, for the *Democrat's* critcism on the temperance movement.

In this movement *temperance* was the end sought, not *prohibition*. It was too early for the doctrine of "touch not, taste not handle not;" that came later. A history of the work of the societies, following this pioneer movement in the cause of temperance, would be deeply interesting, but we have not the material at hand from which

---

10 The present Fountain House.

to write it. The men and women who, at that early day, and against public sentiment, endeavored to hold in restraint by moral suasion, the appetite of their fathers sons and brothers, deserve to have their names engraved on tablets of gold and it will doubtless be done some day.

Among the temperance organizations, that came into existence from this movement, was the "Sons of Temperance," which, in a few years grew into a powerful body, and were formed in almost every state. In this county there were several such organizations. In Doylestown we had the "Olive Branch Division," 1845, which celebrated its first anniversary in the Presbyterian church, the ladies presenting a bible to the order. The speakers were the Revs. Samuel Nightingale, S. M. Andrews and a Mr. Gillette. The division was probably named after the *Olive Branch* newspaper, a temperance organ published here by Franklin P. Sellers. It was a very spicy paper on temperance and other subjects, and, as the editor had suffered from the effect of intemperance, he knew whereof he spoke. While there is less outward temperance display at this day than half a century ago, the cause is advanced by more agencies, and quieter, and the result more encouraging. [11]

---

[11] October 9, 1838, Miss Mary B. Dunlap, daughter of the late Andrew Dunlap. At Doylestown, March 10, 1839, Hannah Austin, wife of William Austin.

Doylestown, Old and New.

XI

A Noted Murder Trial.

Among the most exciting criminal trials, that ever took place in the Bucks County Courts, was the Mina-Chapman murder case, 1831-32. It attracted great attention throughout the country, and takes rank with the most celebrated murders by arsenic, in our criminal jurisprudence, and the profession yet talks about it. The defendants were charged with poisoning Dr. William Chapman, a reputable person of Bensalem township, one of the guilty parties being his own wife. The following modest notice of Dr. Chapman's death appeared, without date, in one of our county papers and was the first information the public received of the crime:

"At his seat in Andalusia, Bucks county, Pennsylvania, Dr. William Chapman, aged fifty-three years, a native of Buckinghamshire, England, the discoverer of the cure for stammering."

A few days prior to Dr. Chapman's death, who died June 23, 1831, a Spanish vagabond, representing himself as Don Lino Amilio Espos Y. Mina,[1] son of the Governor of Lower California, came to the Chapman residence and asked to stay over night. He was taken in and cared for, and Mrs. Chapman being infatuated with the rascal he was allowed to remain. In a few days, the Doctor sickened and died under suspicious circumstances. After his death Mina left, but the interest of the neighbors being aroused, he was pursued, arrested

---

[1] The real name of this villain was Entrealgo, whose family went from the Spanish Main to Cuba, where his father held the office of Fiscal or Constable.

MINA, MURDERER OF DR. CHAPMAN.

at Boston, and lodged in the Doylestown jail Thursday evening, October 6. Mrs. Chapman, who was charged with being a party to the crime, was arrested at Erie, Pa., and brought to Doylestown in the stage, Sunday morning, December 11, in custody of Thomas Mehaffy. She is represented as "large in person, with a strongly marked and rather forbidding countenance."

In the issue of the *Bucks County Intelligencer*, of September 19, 1831, the editor says:

"We understand that Mr. Ross, prosecuting attorney of the county, has had an interview with Recorder McIlvaine, of Philadelphia, and there is strong reason to believe that a murder has been committed through the means of poison. The individual charged has been arrested at Boston through the prompt measures of Recorder McIlvaine, and the active interference of High Constable Blaney, to both of whom much credit is due. The matter is now in the hands of the Attorney-General of this county, and will, we have no doubt, be thoroughly investigated by him."

While awaiting trial, Mina escaped from the jail by burning a hole through the floor of an adjoining cell, into which he managed to get, and, from that, made his way to the jail yard. There he was assisted in breaking the lock off the outer gate with an axe by William Brown, another prisoner, and both made their escape. They were seen by Sheriff Morris and some of his family, but succeeded in getting away. The alarm was immediately given and pursuit made. Brown was found secreted in a pile of bark in a woods a mile from town, and taken back to his old quarters. A reward of $40, and "all reasonable charges paid," was now offered for Mina, who was arrested at the tavern of A. H. James,[2] Hilltown township, a few miles from Doylestown, brought back and more securely confined.

The case of Mina and Lucretia Chapman was called for trial Tuesday morning, February 14, 1832, the Hon. John Fox, President Judge, on the bench, bills having been found at December term. Thomas Ross, a young lawyer of Doylestown, Deputy Attorney General, and William B. Reed, of Philadelphia, appeared for the Commonwealth; E. T. McDowell, of Doylestown, and S. Rush, of Philadelphia, for Mina, and David Paul Brown and Peter McCall, of Phila-

---

[2] This account of Mina's arrest is taken from a Doylestown paper, but another account says he went into the store of John O. James to buy a pair of shoes, and was arrested there, the late Dr. Wm. S. Hendrie, of Doylestown, assisting.

delphia, for Mrs. Chapman. The morning was consumed in arguing a motion for separate trials, and, when concluded, the court adjourned for consultation. On re-assembling in the afternoon Judge Fox read the opinion of the court granting the application. Mrs. Chapman was now put upon her trial and the panel called for a jury. Twenty challenges were made by the prisoner and two by the Commonwealth, when the following persons were agreed upon as the jury, all of whom affirmed except one, William M. White, of Warminster township; Joseph Paul, Henry Lecey, John B. Balderson, John Shutt, Joseph Watson, Henry Hartzell, John Palmer, John Yardley, Lewis Kinsey, Robert Phillips, Richard Leedom and William M. White.

During the first three days the court room was packed, many being unable to gain admittance. The examination of witnesses commenced on Wednesday morning, and, on Saturday, when the court adjourned, eighteen had been upon the stand. On Wednesday the court laid an injunction on the newspaper reporters, not to publish matter relating to the trial, and could have a bearing upon it, during its progress. The jury returned to the court, with a verdict of "Not Guilty," on Saturday evening, February 25, at 11 o'clock, when the defendant was discharged and returned home. During the rush to get into the court room, to witness the trial, William Reeder, constable, of Wrightstown, was pushed with such force against the railing of the stairs, his ribs were seperated from the back bone, and two or three of them broken. His life was despaired of for some time, but he finally recovered.

Mina's trial came on at the April term; the room was again packed with people and the deepest interest manifested to its close. The jury rendered a verdict of "Guilty of murder in the first degree," and the court passed sentence of death on the defendant on the first day of May in the presence of several hundred persons assembled to witness it. The scene was a solemn one. McDowell, one of Mina's counsel, read a statement made by the prisoner, the latter sobbing aloud. Judge Fox, while passing the sentence, was visibly affected, and the court room was almost still enough to hear a pin drop. Mina stated that he had a little daughter four years old. Great indignation was expressed at the acquital of Mrs. Chapman, many believing her the guiltier of the two. The editor of the *Bucks County Intelligencer*, in speaking of the Mina-Chapman trials remarked :

"We have seldom witnessed a more sacred and patient regard to the end of strict justice, tempered with mercy, than has been witnessed in the progress of these two trials." The death warrant was read to the prisoner on Friday, May 18, and the time for the execution fixed Thursday, June 21. The two trials were printed in pamphlet form at the office of the *Bucks County Intelligencer*, and sold for 12½c a copy, but it has long been out of print.[3]

The execution of Mina took place on the Alms House farm three miles below Doylestown, in the presence of an assemblage variously estimated from 5,000 to 10,000. Everything attending it seems to have been made as dramatic and spectacular as possible for such occasion. The military of the county was called out, without any precedent to sanction it, and what should have been a solemn affair was made a civil and militay frolic and holiday. The poor wretch was taken from the jail to the place of execution in an open wagon, with a large military escort and martial music, to say nothing of the great throng on both sides of the road. The parade was more befitting the triumphal march of a conquering hero than to wait on a miserable convict to the place of death.

The turn out of volunteers were the largest ever seen in the county, embracing Colonel Simpson Torbert's fine Regiment of Infantry and the Centre Union Battalion of Bucks, besides several visiting companies from outside the county, twenty companies in all; First Montgomery troop, Captain Mathews, Second troop, do, Shamline, United States Huzzars, Eckel, Washington troop, Bucks county, Captain Overbeck, Lehigh county troop, Captain Cooper, Montgomery county Grays, Captain Ramsey, Liberty Guards, Bucks county, Captain Hart, Alert Rifles, Captain Praul, Union Rifle Rangers, Captain Joseph Morrison, Yardleyville Blues, Captain Slack, Alert Light Infantry Blues, Captain Clarke, Jefferson Guards, of New Hope, Captain Merrick, Company of Infantry, Captain Logan, Captain Mc Kinstry's Infantry, of Major James' Battalion, Captain Maugle's Infantry, Captain Penrose's rifle Company, Captain Apples' do, Captain Sassman's do and Captain Calvin's Company under Major Bertles.

Sheriff Morris was severely criticised for calling out the military for which there was no necessity—the *Easton Argus* intimating that the landlord of Doylestown and the police had some under-

---

3 We know of but two copies of this trial in existence, but there are undoubtedly others. Of these one belongs to the Bucks County Historical Society, presented to it by Joseph Yates Long, New York, but a native of Bucks county; the other is owned by the author.

standing. After her acquittal, Mrs. Chapman adopted a vagabond life traversing the country with her children, who had been tenderly reared, giving exhibitions. She came to Doylestown once after the trial on some matter of business, and was reported as dying in Florida the spring of 1840, where she was wandering as a strolling player. No woman ever realized more fully than she, that "the wage of sin is death." One of her sons was a student at Lafayette College, Easton, studied dentistry and began practice in Philadelphia, but we have no knowledge of him afterwards.

It subsequently became known that Mrs. Chapman was a daughter of Thomas Winslow, Massachusetts, a noted counterfeiter, and the family notorious in the annals of crime; that she was a member of the gang and signed the bills. It is further said she was under the surveillance of the police at the time of her arrest, for her connection with these counterfeiters and forgers.

Down to this period, there was but one church organization in Doylestown, the Presbyterian, but the next to come was the Friends. From the first settlement there were followers of Penn in the vicinity, and, increasing from year to year, the nearness of Buckingham inviting them across the line, but no organized effort was made to erect a place of worship prior to 1834. That year the Buckingham Monthly gave the Friends of Doylestown and vicinity, permission to hold an Indulged Meeting on First day, and it was doubtless first holden at private houses.

This was followed by steps to erect a suitable place of worship and a lot, purchased on York street, now Ashland. A meeting house was built upon it the following year at a cost of $1,654.50, and the first meeting held December 30, 1836. From that time to the present services have been held and the society kept intact. The Friends in the town and vicinity are not numerous enough for a large congregation, but, when a distinguished minister holds forth, as is occasionally the case, the building is well filled, a few of other denominations being generally present. This little congregation of the followers of Fox and Penn have pursued the even tenor of their way and, wherever their influence reaches, it is found on the side of orthodoxy in religion, and culture and conservatism in secular life. The Doylestown society is under the general care of Buckingham, the parent meeting.

The founding of the Methodist Episcopal Church followed closely the erection of Friends' Meeting House, 1834-1838. Of the latter

we have already spoken, and will now speak of the former. At this
time the population of Doylestown was approaching 800, more
places for public worship were required, and the aggressive Metho-
dists met this want. The nearest church, of this denomination, was
nine miles away, and the few of this communion, settled here, seldom
heard a minister of their own faith preach. Our village was occasionally visited by a missionary, who held service in the room set
apart for religious worship in the Academy, and on July 30, 1830,
the Reverend Mr. Rains, Philadelphia, preached in the Court House.

Somewhat later in the thirties, the Philadelphia Conference
established here the "Doylestown and Allentown Mission of the
Philadelphia District;" on April 24, 1838, the Reverend James
Hand came here to take charge of it, and, on the day of his arrival,
made the following note in his diary:

"There is no Methodist meeting house within nine miles of this
place in any direction, and on the north and west none for twenty-six
or thirty miles. There are Methodist churches at Lumberville, New
Hope and Pennsville, each about nine miles. There is preaching in a
school house at Bushington, three miles, and one still nearer, but no
regular preaching in the town. There is a Presbyterian and one
Quaker meeting house in the place and that's all."

Mr. Hand[4] soon gathered the nucleus of a congregation about
him and set to work. The Reverend Silas M. Andrews, with his
broad views of Christian duty, extended a helping hand to these
pioneers of Methodism, by opening the doors of the Presbyterian
Church to them. One of the earliest converts was Samuel Hall, long
a Presbyterian, who remained with the Methodist the rest of his life,
almost half a century. The others, who were Mr. Hand's most active
lieutenants when help was needed, were Philip Quick and wife,
Samuel Wetherill, Mrs. John Hellings and Samuel and Independence
Moser. At a later date, Henry P. Sands was an active member of
the church, and William Frankenfield led the choir many years, and
to his death, 1895. The congregation was a feeble band for several
years, but faith and work triumphed, as they always will.

When the number was sufficient to justify the erection of a
church building of their own, a lot was purchased on West Court
street, on the site of their late home, and a building erected that and

---

4 Mr. Hand married Sarah Rodman, daughter of Samuel Rodman, Doylestown township. He was a trustee of the church many years after giving up
preaching.

the following year, 1838-1839, and dedicated, with proper ceremonies August 11, of the latter year, the services being held afternoon and evening.

As this was mainly the work of Mr. Hand, he naturally became the first pastor, and administered the affairs of the young church. In his effort he had fair success, and evidence was not wanting, that Methodism had come to Doylestown to stay. Mr. Hand's pastorate extended through 1838-39, with H. H. Sisty his assistant, and again in 1845-46 with D. L. Patterson and Alfred Cookman,[5] assistants. In the interim, Reverend C. J. Crouch, with D. E. Gardner, as assistant was pastor in 1840-41, and Reverend Dallas D. Lore, with J. Ruth assistant, in 1842-43 the Reverend J. J. Elsegood succeeding Mr. Lore

The calling of Mr. Lore was fortunate for the church. He was an able young man, and eloquent speaker, and the congregation increased under his ministrations. He was pastor for three years, and 1846, was appointed missionary to Buenas Ayers, South America. On June 6, previous to sailing for his new field of labor, Mr. Lore was married to Miss Rebecca Toy, Burlington, N. J. He gained distinction in the church and died in recent years, long after his return from South America. The church building was twice repaired, the first time at an expense of $2,000, and again, while Mr. Lorah was pastor, 1891-'92. The activities of the church, outside of religious services, are the Senior and Junior Epworth League, Ladies' Aid Society and Sunday School.

In the first fifty years, of the Methodist Church at Doylestown 1847-1897, the following pastors administered at its altar: George Quigley, J. Turner, H. H. Sisty, R. Owen, William Major, William McMichael, J. F. Gracey, Noble Frame, R. W. Humphrews, William J. Stephenson, H. A. Cleveland, J. L. Taft, Joseph Welsh, S. N Chew, C. H. McDermont, F. E. Church, William J. Mills, N. C McComas, H. H. Bodine, Samuel Howell, L. Brown, A. W. Pichop J. Baudon, H. R. Robinson, George H. Lorah, S. T. Bisca Crocke and A. P. Hodgson. Turner, Wood and Owen were assistants and Mr. Lorah was the longest in charge. In 1892, the congregation too steps to erect a new church building. A lot was purchased on the east side of South Main street below York ; A. Oscar Martin, Arch

---

[5] The Rev. Alfred Cookman was a son of Chaplain Cookman, of the U. S House of Representatives, and preached his last sermon, before that body March 3, 1841. A few days later, he embarked on the Steamer President for England, and the vessel was never heard from. The author was present, and heard Mr. Cookman's farewell sermon to Congress.

itect, of Doylestown, given charge and it was dedicated the 21st day of June, 1903, with appropriate services and ceremonies. The building is a modern structure and an ornament to the town.

In 1898, during the pastorate of Mr. Hodgson, the Church celebrated its sixtieth anniversary. This took place in September and continued a week, opening on Sunday the 18th and closing on Sunday the 25th. The services began with a Love Feast at 9.30 A. M. and closed the following Sunday with two sermons, and an address by the Reverends Messrs. Groff, Fetter and Bergey of Doylestown, the closing sermon being by the Reverend W. L. McDowell, D. D. Each day and evening the services and exercises were of a somewhat different character On Monday evening, they were "Songs in the Night," by the Church choir, Tuesday, anniversary services by the Sunday School, Wednesday, a Reunion of former Pastors and Members, Thursday, exercises by the Senior and Junior Epworth League, etc. On each day and evening there were appropriate religious services. The occasion was one of great interest, the Church was appropriately decorated and attendance large.

In 1835, the "Union Horse Company" was organized at Doylestown, for the detection of horse theives and other villians. The first meeting was held in January, when the officers elected were General Samuel A. Smith, president, John D. James, Secretary, and other preliminary work transacted. The organization is still maintained in working order, and the members eat their annual dinner at the Fountain House.

Doylestown, Old and New.

XII
A Prosperous Period.

One of the most prosperous periods Doylestown had known prior to the middle of the century, was from 1830 to 1840. Among the signs of prosperity, in these ten years, were the chartering and opening of a bank of discount and circulation, the organization of a Beneficial Society and the erection of a suitable building to conduct its affairs in, the charter of an Insurance Company and commencement of business, the incorporation of the village into a borough, the second in the county, two additional churches organized and erected, Friends Meeting and Methodist Episcopal, and the erection of more than the usual number of dwellings and places of business, several of them brick.

The Doylestown Bank, the first financial institution at the county seat, was opened in 1833. The first meeting, in its favor, was held at the court house Friday evening, December 1, 1831, with Abraham Chapman in the chair, and Henry Chapman and William T. Rogers secretaries. Committees were appointed to look after the preliminary work, and the bill, introduced into the Legislature, became a law April 23, 1832, fixing the capital stock at $150,000, in shares of $50 each. The commissioners, named to carry the act into effect, were John Pugh, Abraham Chapman, Samuel D. Ingham, John Fox, Elias Ely, Joseph Hough, Jesse Johnson, Samuel Yardley, Thomas Stewart, Samuel Hart and Abel H. James. A meeting to organize was held May 31, 1832, at William Field's tavern, the books for stock subscription were opened at the court house July 25, the whole amount being taken in six days; the election for directors was held November 9, 1832, when the following persons were chosen: Abraham Chapman, John Robbarts, Benjamin Hough, Sr., E. T. McDowell, Mahlon K. Taylor, Christian Clemens, John Blackfan, John T. Neeley, William T. Stokes, Timothy Smith, Samuel Kachline, Elias Ely, and Samuel Yardley, Jr. The board organized the same day at Worman's tavern, and Abraham Chapman was elected president, unanimously; Daniel Byrnes, of Wilmington, Del., cashier, and Mahlon Long, clerk. The bank notes were printed, meanwhile, by Draper, Underwood, Bald & Spencer, of Philadelphia, the vignets of the five dollar notes representing Justice and Mercy, the end margins being decorated with the likenesses of Franklin and Penn.

The bank commenced business Jan 7, 1833, in the stone house of Samuel Nightingale on the south side of East State street, second door from Pine. It was fitted up temporarily, as the directors contemplated the erection of a new banking house. They shortly bought a lot on the west side of North Main street, next door above the Fountain House; work begun as soon as spring opened, was under roof by July 22, and occupied in the fall. The bank occupied this building for sixty-five years, and, by careful management and strict integrity, grew in financial strength and importance. In 1847 the stockholders accepted the extension of the charter authorized by the Legislature. In 1848 the bank building was considerably improved, inside and out, a part of the expense being born by Josiah Hart, the cashier, who then occupied the house part as a dwelling. At a stockholders' meeting, January, 1848, Charles E. DuBois was elected president; Josiah Hart, cashier, and John J. Brock, clerk. Daniel Byrnes, the first cashier, died at Wilmington July 11, 1845, aged 79.

The bank remained at its location on Main street until the autumn of 1897, when it removed to its new building at the crossing of Main and Court streets on the site of the Ross Mansion. This location was purchased at public sale, 1897, and on it was erected a handsome and unique building, 50 by 82 feet, and height from the ground 55 feet. The site is one of the most eligible in the borough, facing Monument Place and flanked by the two most important streets in the village. The exterior walls are laid in red granite and Pompeian brick; the finish, inside and out, is of the most substantial character, while a massive vault contributes to the safety of the institution, modern improvements add to the comfort and conveniences of its officers. The banking room, 50 feet square, is not surpassed in the state. The following directors composed the board which authorized the new building : Eugene James, Watson F. Paxson, J. B. Rosenberger, Dr. Harvey Kratz, Henry Lear, Rienzi Worthington, J. Simpson Large, John D. Walter, Samuel A. Firman and John L. DuBois and Mr. Lear President. The bank, meanwhile, had been a prosperous institution, and its acceptance of the Act of Congress, changing it to a National Bank, with authority to increase the capital to $300,000, added to its already large volume of business and broadened its usefulness.

In its long life the bank has had but four Presidents and five Cashiers; of the first, were Abraham Chapman, Charles E. DuBois, George Lear and Henry Lear; and Cashiers, Daniel Byrnes, Josiah Hart, John J. Brock, Lewis P. Worthington and George P. Brock elected to succeed Mr. Worthington.

Twenty-four years now elapsed before another financial institution made its appearance in Doylestown. This was in 1857, when Josiah Hart, George Hart, Richard Watson, William M. Large and Jonas Fretz commenced the banking business under the name of "J. Hart & Co., Bankers." They opened in the small frame on the east side of North Main street, formerly the law office of E. T. McDowell, Esq., but the following year erected a new office on the same site. While this was being built, the business was carried on in the office of George Hart, Esq., and the new building was not occupied until about the close of the year.[1] Watson Large and Fretz withdrew from the firm about 1863, and the business was continued by Josiah and George Hart until the latter's death, 1875. John Hart a son of Josiah Hart, was now admitted into the firm, and the business continued by them until 1882, when Frank Hart, another son of Josiah, became a partner. Josiah Hart died, 1885, but the sons carried it on until 1896, when they discontinued the business started by the father, being wound up by the sons, after almost forty years.

The Doylestown Beneficial Society was organized, September, 1832, and incorporated by the Surpreme Court, 1834. Next to the Benevolent Lodge of Masons it was the the earliest organization on this or kindred lines, that appeared in the community. The officers were a president, vice-president, secretary, treasurer and messenger, " with

---

[1] In the *Democrat* of December 8, 1858, J. Hart & Co. announce: "The subscribers have now moved into their new Banking House on Main street, &c."

such other officers and Committees as the Society may see proper to appoint, from time to time by their By-Laws." The admission fee ranged from $1 at 21 years, to $5 from the age of 40 to 50. Fines were imposed for non-attendance, and surplus funds were invested at interest. It was the duty of the Stewards to visit the sick members and report to the Society.

In 1844 the society erected a brick building on East State street, the same now occupied by the Masons. It was an imposing edifice for the times, the audience room having a seating capacity of about 300. The building was dedicated to the uses for which it was erected on Christmas Eve, in the presence of a large audience, and the event was one of no mean importance. The hall was handsomely adorned with evergreen wreaths festooned around the walls, and about the chandaliers and windows. At the top of the stairway, at the entrance, was an arch nine feet high covered with evergreen; on the top of the arch was an eagle with a wreath of roses in his beak, on either side thirteen stars, in the rear resting on wood-work, thirteen beautiful evergreen wreathes interspersed with flowers, representing the original states. The Doylestown brass band furnished the music.

The exercises consisted of reading a portion of the scripture, prayer, singing an ode, written by Samuel D. Patterson, of Norristown, by a company of young ladies and gentlemen, followed by an address by the Reverend Silas M. Andrews. The room was filled, and everything passed off agreeably. After the dedication exercises were over, a fair was held in the basement, consisting of refreshments, etc., the receipts for the benefit of the society, the refreshments being the gift of the ladies. On New Year's night, 1845, the brass band gave a concert in the hall for the benefit of the institute.

The Society was a benefit to Doylestown in several ways, and, in a short time, the town was astonished it had done so long without it. Meetings of various kinds were held in the hall; it was a place for lectures and exhibitions, and there "Tom Thumb" made his first appearance before a Doylestown audience, May 4, 1849, and Signor Blitz, June 30, 1851, afternoon and evening. In this hall the Protestant Episcopal congregation held its meetings until their church was ready for occupation. In 1845, the trustees of the Institute arranged for a course of lectures in the hall during the fall and winter, the first lecture being delivered by Colonel John W. Forney, Saturday evening, November 22, admission, ten cents. July 21, 1851, G.

L. Swift lectured in Beneficial hall, on "Electricity and Electro Magnetism" with various experiments.

The Beneficial Society was quite prosperous until 1856, when old members dying off without a corresponding addition of new ones, it was thought best to wind up its affairs. This was done, and whatever was left, after paying the debts, was divided among the surviving members. Of the 77 members belonging to the Society in 1854, it is not known that more than a half dozen are living, three being in Doylestown. Shortly after the Beneficial Society closed its affairs the building was bought by the Masonic Lodge. The late Generals, Wm. T. Rogers and John S. Bryan were among the most active members in organizing the Society. Prior to the erection of this building there was no place in Doylestown for holding public meetings, except in churches, or court house, that would accommodate fifty persons.

The following article, on Doylestown, appeared in the editorial column of the *Saturday Evening Post*, Philadelphia of October 12, 1833:

"A correspondent begs leave to observe that during a short excursion into the country he spent a few days at Doylestown, in Bucks county, Pennsylvania, delightfully situated on a commanding eminence, where the air is pure and salubrious, and everything is of the most inviting kind. Society is refined, social and literary; and a most commendable spirit of enterprise and improvement was observable all over the village. There was in progress, a handsome Banking House, and nearly twenty very neat dwelling houses and other buildings. In passing up Court street soon after I entered the town, I observed (nearly opposite the Court House,) a conspicuous sign with the following inscription:

CITIZENS TEMPERANCE HOUSE
by Joseph Burrows.

This house having a neat external appearance, I walked in, and found the interior to correspond with the exterior. Wishing to show my approbation, and encourage temperance Inns, for the accommodation of travellers, I put up there. It being Court week, the house was nearly full of company, yet it was as quiet as a private dwelling.

"Doylestown is becoming one of our handsomest inland villages, and a very desirable situation for gentlemen of fortune, who are seeking retirement from the busy scenes of a city life."

The Doylestown Insurance Company organized 1835, was an outcome of the boom period. The Commissioners, named in the Act of Assembly to open books for subscription to stock, met at

Williams Field's tavern, Wednesday, May 6, to make arrangements for discharging their duty. The whole number of Commissioners was 171, but all were not present at this meeting. They agreed to meet to open the books at Field's on Thursday, June 4, the number of shares authorized being 3,000, at ten dollars each. The following names were signed to the notice for this meeting: John H. Anderson, Charles E. DuBois, William Carr, Charles H. Mathews, Caleb Foulke, Hugh B. Ely, James Kelley, E. T. McDowell and John S. Bryan. Two thousand shares were subscribed the first day, and the remainder the second.

The meeting to elect a board of Directors was held at Field's tavern, July 8, when the following persons were chosen: Charles H. Mathews, Hugh B. Ely, Merrick Reeder, John H. Anderson, Morris Buckman, Michael H. Jenks, John Davis, Caleb Foulke and Charles E. DuBois. The board elected Charles H Mathews, president and William Watts, secretary. The Company immediately began business and had a successful career. The office at one time, was in the Dr. Rhodes dwelling east side of North Main street next door above the old Doylestown Trust Company building. Upon the death of William Watts, 1838, George Hart was appointed secretary, and wound up its affairs when the time came. This was the first Insurance Company in Doylestown, long before the day of the Mutual companies.

Several attempts were made to incorporate Doylestown before that end was reached, the first in 1826, when a bill passed the Senate, but failed because boundaries were not given to the proposed borough. The second was in 1829, when several meetings were held but nothing came of it. The movement was renewed, 1830, at a meeting held at Henry Scholl's tavern.[2] November 24, Abraham Chapman, Chairman and Charles E. DuBois, Secretary. On motion it was Resolved :

"That it is proper and expedient to incorporate the village of Doylestown," several committees were appointed among which were the following :

"To fix the boundary and superintend the survey of the same : Josiah Y. Shaw, James S Rich, Enoch Harvey, John Pugh, and Charles E. DuBois.

"To draw an act of incorporation:" Abraham Chapman, Timothy Smith, E. T. McDowell, Samuel Aaron and Samuel Yardley.

"To draw a petition and circulate it:" Lester Rich, Samuel

---

[2] The court inn was a frame on the site of the Monument House.

Kachline, Conrad Shearer, Benjamin Morris, Jr., and George R. Grantham.

The report of the committee, to survey and lay out the proposed borough, was made December 4, and adopted on the 9th, accompained by two drafts; one giving the courses and distances of the borough lines, the other the streets. The former gave the names of the landowners lying contiguous on either side as follows : Samuel Yardley, Enoch Harvey, Richard Riale, John Foulke, Timothy Smith, Francis B. Shaw, Christian Clemens, Josiah Y. Shaw, Abraham and John Gargas, Benjamin Morris, David Rodrock, Charles E. DuBois, William T. Rogers, Barton Stewart, Hugh Ferguson, James Clark, Abraham Chapman, Dr. Charles Meredith and Eleanor Preston. On the second draft the streets are laid out and their names given, one, only, bearing the name "street" the others called "roads" or "lanes." [3] At this meeting E. T. McDowell read the sections of the act of incorporation, and petitions were given the committee to get signatures.[4] A bill passed the House in February, 1834, but got no farther, the opposition being too strong.

There was now a lull of four years in the effort for incorporation, in the meantime the opposition being overcome. Application for a charter was renewed at the session of 1837-'38; passed without opposition and was approved by the Governor, April 16. It conferred upon the inhabitants of the village the usual corporate powers, to which a couple of supplements were added the two following years; one changing the corporate name, the other relative to elections.

An election, to accept, or reject the act, was held at William Field's tavern, May 17, and the vote was nearly unanimous in its favor. On the following Monday, May 21, an election for borough officers was held at Leedom's tavern, with the following result: Chief Burgess, Abraham Chapman; Assistant Burgess, William Field; Council, Caleb E. Wright, Samuel A. Smith, Nathan Cornell, William Stokes, John B. Pugh, Asher D. Bennett, Nathaniel Hubbard, Moses Armstrong and Benjamin Vanluvenee, and Constable, Thomas Dungan.

The first Council meeting was held in the Court house, June 25, 1838, whereof Caleb E. Wright was elected president, and A. M.

---

3 "Easton Road," the present Main street, "New Hope Road," now State street, "Dutch Lane," now Broad street, Court street, "Academy Lane," and the present York street was called "Front street."

4 The original drafts were found a few years ago, by the late H. C. Taylor, among the papers of Josiah Y. Shaw his grandfather.

Griffith, clerk. At this meeting four ordinances were adopted, the first naming the streets, viz : "Maine street, Green street, York street, State street, East street, West street, Broad street, Pine street, Court street, Church street, Mechanics street and Garden alley." The lines and grades of the streets were established by J. Gillingham Fell, a civil engineer, who boarded at the time, with C. E. Wright, his brother-in-law who lived at the southwest corner of Court and Broad streets, which C. H. Magill now owns and lives in.

Of the other ordinances, the second related to horses, cattle, sheep and swine running at large, the third to dogs and the fourth for the "prevention of shows and other nuisances in the borough of Doylestown." The latter ordinance has been amended to death or allowed to lay a dead letter on the statue book. Josiah Y. Shaw was the second president of Council.

Doylestown, Old and New.

XIII
Doylestown a Summer Resort.

Our county capital turned into the forties in much better shape than it entered the thirties. The improvements, the past ten years, were unusual for a country village despite the fact it was the county seat, and made it more desirable as a permanent or temporary residence. Our newspapers, ever faithful chroniclers of the town's attractions, never hesitate to sound its praise and invite strangers to visit it.

The *Democrat* of July 7, 1841, made a pathetic appeal to the people of Philadelphia to come and spend the summer at Doylestown, and names the ways of getting from and back to the city. There were four lines of stages: one daily up the turnpike; a second over the same route; a third connecting at Bristol with the steamboat and thence to Doylestown, via Hulmeville and Newtown; and the fourth connecting with the railroad at Norristown, the only rail travel within reach, and by stage via Centre and Montgomery Squares. The article concludes:

"The town is handsomely improved, affording, in most of the streets, delightful shady walks; a beautiful promenade in the public grounds; and we have first rate ice creams and mineral waters, not exceeded even by the Chestnut street venders. Our landlords, we know, have a few spare well-furnished rooms, and we have no doubt, would do all in their power to render city visitors *very* comfortable and at *very* reasonable prices. Those who prefer private board can be accommodated."

The *Democrat* of July 19, 1843 repeats its invitation for the city folk to come out and spend the heated term among their country cousins :

"We present an annual invitation to our Philadelphia friends to come up and breathe the pure atmosphere of the hill during the summer heat. If retirement from care and bustle be the desired object in a rural retreat, here is quiet; if enfeebled by heated and impure air, ours is healthy; if the country is sought for exercise, we have drives, little fishing and small game. What in fact is not good in the country! Air and rain, food and feeling, heaven and earth, all is fresh and animated."

These appeals were not in vain. At that period the seaside mountain and lake system of resorts had not been invented, and, when people desired to escape the summers' heat of the city, they visited the near by resorts in the country, which they could reach by stage, the only way of getting there. The Doylestown hotels, for several years, were crowded with city boarders, and the village gay with company. A pleasant class of people resorted here. Among the strangers, from a distance, who came in the summer were James Gordon Bennett, of the *New York Herald*, and wife. They were here two or three seasons, boarding at the "Doylestown Hotel," now the Fountain House. About this period Doylestown was quite a resort, and the newspapers did much to induce strangers to come here. The *Bucks County Intelligencer* sang the borough's praises by saying: "Who has not heard of the Vale of Cashmere sings the poet; who has not heard of Doylestown?" The praises of the village are then sung in varied strains, one of its chiefest virtues being that "The stage runs daily and weekly through the borough to Philadelphia and Easton, besides we are incorporated and have a vigilant police." Again :

"We do not mean to boast of the many inducements held out in the way of rural scenery, fine hunting and fishing grounds, elegant drives, fine accommodations at cheap rates, pure water for the temperate, mint and ice for those who live upon vegetable diet, etc. Suffice it to say we hold an elevated position, as a resort for city folks. Come up and see."

As the decade came in, literature had new attractions for a class of her people. In November, 1840, a Society, called the "Doylestown Institute," was organized for the purpose of "public lecturing during the winter;" C. E. DuBois, Esq. was elected president, Reverends S. M. Andrews and Samuel Nightingale, vice presidents and John Robinson, secretary. How this succeeded, we have no means of telling. Literary matters took something of a spurt about this time, and in the *Doylestown Democrat* of December 8, 1841, under the head of "Our Borough; its Literary Aspects," the following appeared:

"The Literary Association," Auxiliary to the National Society of Literature and Science, the Central Society being located in New York. The Auxiliary, in Doylestown, was founded on a "Library of Reviews and Magazines:"

"The Doylestown Lectures," the Reverend Samuel Nightingale, president; "Female Library Society" in connection with the Presbyterian church, the library being kept in the church, about 600 volumes :

"Mechanics Institute," C. H. Mann, Secretary;

"Mechanics Debating Society;"

"Union Academy," in which a classical school is kept by John Robinson, and two common schools, one by Miss Sharpless and the other by Miss Hibbs;

"The Ingham Female Seminary," an incorporated institution, for boarding and day pupils under the care of Dr. C. Soule Cartee and wife, and connected with it, is a cabinet of minerals and other curiosities, and a valuable school library; two select Boarding Schools for boys; one kept by George Murray and the other by the Reverend S. M. Andrews."

In addition to the above are the "Beneficial Society," designed to afford relief to its members, and their families in case of sickness, &c. Also two "Temperance Societies," one the "Mechanics' Temperance" Society, whose members are mechanics and laboring men.

A military encampment was held at Doylestown in August, 1843, on what was subsequently the grounds of the Doylestown Agricultural and Mechanics' Institute. The turnout of troops was good and attendance large. This will be referred to at greater length in a subsequent chapter.

The Democratic celebration in Doylestown, January 8, 1845, the thirtieth anniversary of the American victory at New Orleans over the British army, was a typical one. There was a procession at noon, marshalled by Colonel Isaiah James, followed by a meeting in the Court house, where A. M. Griffith, Esq., read the "Kentucky Resolutions of 1798," and Colonel Reah Frazer, of Lancaster, delivered an oration; in the evening there was a banquet at the Mansion house. Dr. Charles H. Mathews, presiding, number of toasts were drunk, among them the following: By Horatio G. Sickel:

CHARLES H. MANN.

Thomas Dorr, "May the same power which sent down food to the children of Israel, cause the chains of slavery to drop from his limbs."

W. W. H. Davis: "Democracy, may its benign rays be felt in the body politic like the enlivening influence of the summer's rain on parched vegetations, and a stranger gave the toast of the evening:" "Woman, First in the kitchen, first in the parlor, first in the arms of her countrymen."

On the death of Andrew Jackson, 1845, the Doylestown Grays and Beneficial Institute passed resolutions of national condolance and the Reverend Dallas D. Lore, pastor of the Methodist church, delivered an eulogy on the General's life and character.

The setting up and operating a magnetic telegraph instrument at Doylestown, 1845-6, was for this conservative community, "something new under the sun" to every body. Work on a telegraph line, between New York and Norristown, via Doylestown, was begun in September, Alfred Goell, the agent and principal engineer of the company, was here early in the month, examining the proposed route across the peninsula, and inviting proposals for supplying white oak and chestnut poles to string the wires on, requring 27 poles to the mile. This was a section of the first telegraph line between New York and Washington, and was expected to have been finished by the 10th of November, but was not. Mr. Goell was assisted by James L. Shaw, of Doylestown.

At that early day it was called the "Magnetic telegraph." On Wednesday, January 7, 1846, the batteries were set up in Doylestown, and in operation by nine the next morning and messages transmitted. This was the first transmission of messages in the county, and probably in the Delaware-Schuylkill peninsula, as it was the earliest line built across it. It attracted great interest, and there was no little excitement. When the first replies over the wires, in response to a message were received, there were not a few who declared the whole thing a "darned humbug, an effort to impose on country people."

This was a test of the wires, which were copper, as it was thought at that early day, no other metal would carry the electric current. The experiments were entirely successful and the line was pushed forward as rapidly as possible. The batteries set up in Doylestown were placed in a front room facing State street of the Mansion house, south-west corner of Main and State streets, then kept by

---

In Philadelphia, June 18, 1846, John Clemens, of Doylestown, to Emma, daughter of William Heiss, of the Northern Liberties of Philadelphia.

Thomas Sands, and now a bakery into which it was altered the walls being the same.

The batteries were removed to Lambertville, N. J. the following Saturday. Alfred Goell of whom we have spoken, was a Russian by birth and a pet of Postmaster General Amos Kendall. He subsequently built several telegraph lines, among others that from Philadelphia to Wilkesbarre, via Doylestown. This was in 1848.

The first telephone made its appearance in Doylestown, 1878-'79, being an improvised apparatus made in Philadelphia and experimented upon by Silas A. Selser. He had charge of the Western Union line here, and made some experiments between that office, in the Billerbeck building, South Main Street, and Taylor & Hulshizer's drug store, in Lenape building. Seeing it was successful, Selser tried it with Thos. T. Frazer, operator at Quakertown. The only instrument at that time was the receiver, which, for this purpose, was used both as transmitter and receiver, and operated without a battery. On Sunday afternoons, when business was slack, Selser and Frazer "cut out" the Western Union wires, connected their phone and did their talking. Sometimes Selser, who was something of a musician, would delight Frazer with sacred music or solos on the cornet. One afternoon, these telephoners were startled by a third voice, "chipping in." This alarmed the illict phoners, who thought the Western Union was on their track, and the rival company went out of business. It was afterward discovered the unknown voice was the Lansdale operator.[1] On the evening of January 19, 1899, when all danger from discovery had passed, Mr. Selser gave an exhibition of the work of the first telephone in Doylestown, in the lecture room of St. Paul's Episcopal church.

Among the literary socities that came into being in the borough, in 1846, was the "Doylestown Scientific and Literary Institute." It met in the hall of the Beneficial Institute, and the author remembers attending debates there. The following question was advertised to be discussed on the evening of March 27, '46: "Did the wars of the Holy Crusades prove beneficial to Europe?" As the Reverend S. M. Andrews lectured before the Institute, that evening, the debate was postponed.

The breaking out of the Mexician war, May 1846, created some excitement at Doylestown, especially in military circles. Charles H.

---

[1] Doylestown Republican, January 18, 1899.

Mann had recently been elected captain of the Doylestown Grays,[2] a crack company of the village. On May 27, the Governor issued his proclamation for the formation of six regiments of infantry, to await any call that might be made upon the state. The Grays met at the Academy, Monday evening June 1, and took immediate steps to get ready to offer its services. The company was reorganized and regular drills instituted. During the summer and early fall, there was much activity among the members of the Grays, and squad and company drills were frequent. A favorite place of drill was on the broad brick pavement in front of the Court house, and some nights kept up to a late hour. One of the youngest recruits was Charles C. Cox, a Doylestown youth of fourteen, who afterwards saw actual service in the Civil war as Adjutant of an Ohio regiment. Dr. George T. Harvey, a Lieutenant in the Grays, was one of the most active, opening recruiting offices at New Hope, Newtown and Attleborough, now Langhorne. The author was appointed second sergeant, and did his best to keep up his end of the line. When the President called on Pennsylvania for two regiments of Infantry to serve during the war, a strong effort was made to have the Grays accepted, but the offer of the Company was too late, the requisition had been filled. This was a sad disappointment to our embryo heroes, but several of them had an opportunity to test their metal in the Civil war. Two of our young men saw service in the Mexican war.[3 & 4]

Sergeant Davis, of the Guards, who had entered Harvard College about the first of September, 1846, enlisted in the Massachusetts regiment and went out as Colonel Cushing's Adjuant, serving to the close of the war. Before his regiment sailed, he came home to bid good bye to his family and friends and, while here, the Grays presented him a handsome dress sword, the affair taking place in Beneficial Hall, Saturday afternoon, January 31. Dr. Charles H. Mathews made the presentation speech, the recipient making a response. Dr. Mathews said in part: "Lieutenant Davis: Sir, On behalf of the officers and members of the Doylestown Grays, I have the honor to present this token of their regard, on

---

[2] The Doylestown Grays laid aside that name, for the Doylestown Guards, by virtue of on Act of Legislature, of March 16, 1847.

[3] At Perote, Mexico, June 3, 1847, while a soldier in the United States Army, William Day, formely of Doylestown.

[4] At Pueblo, Mexico, August 24, 1847, while a soldier in the United States Army, William H. Harvey, son of Mary Harvey, of Doylestown, in his 25th year.

your depature for the seat of war. Had their services been accepted by the Government, when offered, you would have shared with them the privations and honors of a manly struggle for the nation's right. When you found that both regiments from Pennsylvania were full, and your own company not included, from a sense of duty, and an ardent love of country, you united with the volunteers of another state. Permit me here, sir, to congratulate you on the honorable position which has been conferred upon you, by the distinguished commander of the Massachusetts regiment, and with them you go to the scene of trial."

In reply, Lieutenant Davis said, among other things:

"The honor, which you have this day conferred upon me, in presenting this sword in the name of the "Doylestown Grays," is as unexpected as it is gratifying. I cannot flatter myself that it is deserved from any merit of my own, but only given on account of the deep interest you feel in the cause in which I have the honor to be engaged—the cause of our common country.

* * * * * * *

"It would have been my pride and pleasure to have marched to the scene of strife with my friends and neighbors; to have stood shoulder to shoulder with my companions in arms. But the force of circumstances ordered it otherwise, and it was not until I saw there was no chance of the Grays participating in the glorious struggle, that I enrolled my name in the Massachusetts regiment. I see nothing wrong in fighting in the ranks of another state when all are engaged in the same great cause. In the Revolution, Massachusetts and Pennsylvania stood side by side in defense of their Country's liberties, and the bones of their sons now mingle in the same grave upon many a well-fought field."

* * * * * * *

"Allow me, gentlemen of the "Grays" to bid you an affectionate farewell, and, although my field of action will be distant from you, I will still hold in grateful rememberance the manifestation of esteem and friendship you, this day, have shown toward me."

The sword was made expressly for the recipient and bears the following incription: "Presented, by the officers and members of the Doylestown Grays, to their fellow member, Lieutenant W. W. H. Davis, on his departure for the seat of war, January 30, 1847." The hall was filled with people of both sexes.

The death of Ex-President John Quincy Adams, who died in

April, 1848, was properly noticed by the Doylestown Beneficial Institute, which passed appropriate resolutions of respect, the Revd. Heman Lincoln, pastor of the New Britain Baptist Church, delivering an eulogy on his character and public services in the Hall of the Institute on the evening of April the 8th.

Notwithstanding Doylestown sent no troops into the field, during the Mexican war, her citizens were not unmindful of their duty to the indigent families of the soldiers who went from other parts of the state. When called upon them they contributed $125.50, as follows : John Fox, $10; John White, $2; C. H. Mann, $5; John Clemens, $5; John S. Bryan, $5; C. H. Mathews, $5; W. T. Rogers, $5; James Hibbs, $5; S. L. Roberts, $5; A. J. Paxson, $5; C. E. Wright, $5; John Lloyd, $5; S. A. Smith, $5; Wm. Percey, $5; Joseph Young, $2; Jno. Maugle, $5; George Lear, $5; William Beck, $5; Dr. Hendrie, $5; Jos. Harvey, $5; Chas. E. DuBois, $5; Jas. Cummings, $5; Joel Vasey, $1; B. Gregg, 50c; Jos. Sands, $1; Wm. Kachline, $1; M. Yardley, $2; Theadore Kinsey, $1; Thos. Ross, $5, amounting in the whole $125.50. At the bottom of the subscription list was the following : "Received of J. Fox, by C. E. DuBois." The author had a personal acquaintance with each of these thirty subscribers, all of whom died long since.

As a sample of the martial poetry at the breaking out of the war with Mexico, we insert the following :

SONG
OF THE
CADWALLADER GRAYS.

BY THOMAS P. RAKESTRAW.

TUNE—"*Boatman Dance.*"

Sweet peace has left our land at last,
The clouds of war are gathering fast,
Each musketeer and gallant Ranger,
Must spring to arms and scorn the danger ;
 Then charge ! my brave ones, charge !
 Upon the foe we'll charge ;
 We'll fight all day till the sky turns gray,
 And sleep on our arms till the morning.
  Heigh ho ! we'll march and go, ⎫
  On our route to Mexico.   ⎭ *Repeat.*

Our Northern bands are hard and tough,
We fear not storms or weather rough—
Each heart is high for battle frays ;
We come, the fighty Caddie Grays.
 Then charge ! my brave ones, charge, &c.

> Each leaves his calm and peaceful home,
> At duty's call afar to roam—
> By mountains paths and torrents roar,
> Resistless on the foe we'll pour.
>   Then charge, &c.
>
> When o'er the Southern plains afar,
> We urge the horrid front of war,
> Let mercy still our actions crown,
> That we may win a high renown,
>   Then charge, &c.
>
> Oh ! never strike a fallen foe,
> The fate of battle lays him low—
> Or let a female shrink with fear,
> And name us with the Buccaneer.
>   Then charge, &c.
>
> Let honor shine upon each crest,
> And plant it deeply in each breast;
> We fight our country's rights to urge,
> And prove her justice by our charge.
>   Then charge, &c.

The Doylestown Guards took part in the public reception, Philadelphia gave the Pennsylvania Volunteers, on their return from the Mexican war, July 24, 1848. They went to the city in wagons, and brought home with them Sergeant Peter Opp, who had served in the 1st Pennsylvania Regiment. On reaching Doylestown the Mexican veteran was given a formal reception.

Prior to this period, a cemetery for burying the general public, was a long felt want at Doylestown, the only grave yards here being those belonging to the Presbyterian and Methodist churches, the former opened for interment February 28, 1815, the latter, 1838. The increasing demand for a public cemetery took shape November 1, 1849, by William T. Rogers, Charles E. DuBois, John S. Brown, Samuel Johnson Paxson and the Reverend Silas M. Andrews, purchasing, at public sale, ten acres of land on the ridge just northeast of the village, within the borough limits and facing Court street. The situation is beautiful, commanding an extensive view of the surrounding country with a dry, sandy soil. It was laid out at once and improvements begun. When one hundred lots were subscribed for, a charter was obtained March 22, 1850. The incorporators now met and organized by the election of General Rogers, president; Rev. Silas M. Andrews, secretary and treasurer and Charles E. DuBois, solicitor. The board completed its work by laying out and opening streets and planting trees.[5] In 1870 a plot of ground adjoining, and

---

[5] The first interment, in the Doylestown cemetery, took place on Saturday, January 4, 1851, being the body of a Mr. Trueman who died at Manayunk.

WILLIAM T. ROGERS.

about the same size, was purchased for a similar purpose and incorporated under the name of "Hope Cemetery," the incorporators being Dr. O. P. James, Henry D. Livezey, N. P. Brower, Davis E. Brower and N. C. James. These two cemeteries were conducted separately until August 25, 1893, when their interests were made one by the Hope conveying its real estate and franchises to the Doylestown cemetery for the consideration of $4,000. Since that time the grounds have been much improved and beautified by the erection of monuments and other memorials. Few villages in the state have a more sightly burial place, or with a better location. In 1890, the surplus, in the hands of the treasurer, amounted to $16,000, and the fund is to be kept intact until the interest will meet the expenses.

The spirit of improvement, in the forties, was creditably maintained, and, among the most notable dwellings erected, were those of Henry Chapman, 1844, northwest corner of Main and Broad streets, Stokes L. Roberts, on the south side of East Court, second door from Broad, the same year, and that of John B. Pugh, corner of East Court and Printer's alley, the latter now owned by Hugh B. Eastburn. Into each of these new dwellings young brides were taken, and all are deceased except Mrs. Roberts.

An occasional visitor at Doylestown, in the forties, to call on his college mate, Edward J. Fox, was George Northrop, of Philadelphia. He read law with George M. Dallas, admitted 1845, and was in practice fifty years, dying, 1896. He was a lawyer of great ability and an influential citizen; was a member of Council, candidate for Congress, 1864, against William D. Kelley, and subsequently a candidate for City Solicitor. The charm of Mr. Northrop was his personal qualities.

Doylestown, Old and New.

XIV
The Stage and The Mails.

While a complete history of the stage and mail routes in, through, and from Doylestown in the past, connecting with the outside world, would make a volume of itself, we have only collect material enough for a single chapter. The reader will find the subject briefly alluded to elsewhere.

The first stage through Doylestown, coming down the Easton road from the Forks of Delaware, and continuing down to Philadelphia, was put on April 29, 1792 by John Nicholaus.[1] It made weekly trips, down on Monday and returning on Thursday, fare $2. He probably died at Easton, 1807, and was succeeded by his son Samuel, who moved down to Danboro to take charge of the stages. In the spring of 1794, Lawrence Erb, Easton, put on a stage to Philadelphia with the same running time and fare, allowing each passenger ten pounds of baggage. It ran through Doylestown and changed horses at Craig's tavern four miles below, stopping over night at Jenkintown going down, and at Abraham Driesbach's, Stony Point, returning.

While the Easton road was the direct route from the lower Delaware to the Lehigh, the earliest stages between these two points ran the Bethlehem road. The first "stage wagon," of this line, was that of George Klein, put on 1763, and continued running until relieved by railroads. One of the drivers, almost seventy-five years ago, was

---
[1] Was Nicholaus, the stage proprietor, a relative of Johann Nicholas Wellerhatt, who arrived at Philadelphia, Oct. 22, 1754, in the ship Halifax Thomas Coatman, captain?

John Feuerbend, a soldier of Napoleon, who survived the Russian campaign to die in the Northampton Alms House, 1874.

One of these stage lines left Bethlehem every Thursday and Monday morning at 5 o'clock by the following route: breakfast at the house of William Posten, dine at the house of Charles Stewart, Doylestown, where there was a change of horses; then proceeded to the house of William McCalla, Jenkintown, and arrived the same evening at the house of George Lesher, North Second street, Philadelphia. John Brock and Charles Stewart, Doylestown, were two of the proprietors of this line of stages. It carried the mail, but there was no post office at Doylestown.

There was a semi-weekly stage from Philadelphia, through Doylestown to Bethlehem as early as 1800, fare $2.75, stopping at Stewart's tavern for dinner. We do not know when it was taken off, but it ran for a number of years. In 1822, Samuel Nicholaus was succeeded by James Reeside, the great "Land Admiral," as he was called, Nicholaus probably selling out to him. Reeside formed a partnership with Jacob Peters, and subsequently with Samuel and John Shouse, Easton. He placed new Troy coaches on the road, the first in this section of country. The line was continued down to the completion of the Belvidere-Delaware railroad, 1854.[2] A line of daily stages was running from Philadelphia, through Doylestown to Easton, Bethlehem and Allentown, in 1828. We do not know how long they ran, but were taken off prior to 1853, when passengers, wishing to go from Doylestown to Bethlehem, took a cross-country stage to Montgomery Square and there made the connection.

We cannot learn of any local stage line, between Doylestown and Philadelphia, prior to the removal of the county seat, 1813, and do not believe there was one, but it had not long been the county's capital before a local stage line was put on. May 17, 1813, John Brunner commenced running the "Doylestown Coachee" twice a week, down Monday and Thursday returning Wednesday and Saturday, fare $1.37½ each way. It started from Mathew Hare's "Ship" tavern, site of Lenape Building. In 1817 the line fell into the hands of Joel Doane when the route was extended to the Cross Keys, a mile

---

2 In 1824, the stage on the Easton route left the old road at the Harrow tavern, forty miles from Philadelphia, and struck the River road eleven miles below Easton. The post office, called "Spring Mills," was sometime discontinued but re-established under the name of Monroe, and John Johnson reappointed postmaster. This place is now called Lehnensburg after Mathias Lehnen, an officer in the 104th regiment, Civil war.

above Doylestown with the same running time, stopping on the wa down at the Indian Queen, Doylestown. In September, 1818, th "Coachee" was bought by Jonathan Michener, starting from Kohl tavern, making three round trips a week, leaving Monday, Wednes day and Friday. In 1819, Ephraim Fenton became the proprieto and the name was changed to the "Doylestown Stage." Fento drove and the fare was reduced to $1.25. The stopping place, i Philadelphia, was at John Dungan's Buck tavern, Second stree leaving there at 9 a. m. and reaching Doylestown at 3 p. m. Th "Coachee" was still running in 1826 when it is lost sight of.

In 1827 a new line, between Philadelphia and Easton, was put o by John Moore & Co. starting from the Rotterdam hotel, No. 2 N. 4th street, running daily, Sundays excepted, leaving at 6 a. n reaching Easton at 6 p. m., fare $3.00, and $1.25 to Doyles town, breakfast at Jenkintown and dinner at Ottsville. Returning, th stage left Easton at 5 a. m., reaching Philadelphia 5 p. m., breakfa at Monroe and dinner at Willow Grove. Latteral lines connecte with this stage at several points. The fare was reduced to $2.0 in 1829.

The "Doylestown Coachee" had not been long running before met with opposition, called the "Doylestown Pilot," starting fro Frederick Nicholson's tavern at the same hour, eight o'clock. O August 30, 1830, the Pilot commenced running three times a week starting from the same place, the Indian Queen, then kept by Israe and Alexander McCalla, and occupying the present site of the Doyle town National Bank. In 1823 Shaw and Evans put on the Doyles town post coach three times a week to Philadelphia and back; star ing from Jacob Kohl's Bucks County Inn, stopping in the city John Dungan's Buck tavern. The route was via Hartsville, Hatboro Willow Grove, etc. etc. Fare $1.25. In November, 1826, anothe new line was started to the city run by the "Proprietor" setting ou from the "Court Inn," site of the Monument House; down Monda and Thursday and up Tuesday and Saturday.

In 1829, an additional line to Philadelphia was put on, leavin Kohl's tavern Monday, Wednesday and Friday, at 8 a. m., via Mon gomery Square, North Wales Meeting House, Spring House, Ches nut Hill and Germantown, returning next day. Kohl was the Doyle town agent. The same year, in June, a new stage proprietor appear William Field, subsequently sheriff and otherwise prominent in the li of Doylestown. At this time he kept the "Green Tree" tavern, corner of Main and Broad streets. This line ran between Doylestown and New York, daily, via New Hope and New Brunswick, leaving here at 3.30 a. m. and reaching New York early in the afternoon, fare through $2.12½. This was Doylestown's first direct communication with New York. How long it lasted is not known. In 1830, a line of stages was established between New York and Pottsville via New Brunswick, New Hope Doylestown, Montgomeryville, &c.

This was a period of great activity in staging: new lines were frequently put on and opposition was rife. The tavern keepers did much to stimulate these enterprises as each new line brought custom to some one's hostelry. In 1832, William Field, then keeping the "Citizen's House," commenced running a line of "Post Coaches" between Doylestown and Philadelphia via Hartsville, fare $1.25, every other day.

The same year, in March, a new line was put on between Philadelphia and Easton, but not up the Easton road, giving Doylestown the go by. The proprietors were George Vogel, Philadelphia, who kept a tavern on Second street between Market and Arch, Melchior Horn, of Easton and Hugh Moyer and Co. They were daily "Post Coaches" and ran via Frankford, Holmesburg, Hulmeville, Newtown and Dolington, striking the River road at Brownsburg and continuing up it to their destination.

William Field embarks a second time in a staging enterprise, 1832, putting on a direct line to Philadelphia via, Newville, Hartsville, Hatboro, Willow Grove and Jenkintown, leaving Doylestown Monday, Wednesday and Friday at 8 a. m., reaching Philadelphia in time to dine. This shortened the time a little, showing there was progress. In February, 1833, one P. Luciani commenced running a line of post coaches from Doylestown to Philadelphia, via New Hope, Hartsville, Hatboro and Jenkintown, leaving Pettitt's tavern, now the Fountain House, and stopping at Mrs. Marple's sign of the Buck, Philadelphia. This was probably an opposition to Field's line of 1832.

In May, 1834, the "Pioneer and Metamora line of Post Coaches" commenced running from Stephen Brock's tavern, Doylestown, every Monday, Wednesday and Friday, leaving at 6 a. m., via Colonel Wilkinson's,[3] Pineville to Bristol, where the passengers took boat for

---

3 Centreville.

New York, via Trenton, and for Philadelphia. O. H. Cadwallader & Co. were proprietors.

In all these local lines not one of them penetrated the German townships—and their only stage connection with the county seat, at that day, was by the Easton stage. Post riders with cross mails subsequently went into that section of the country, carrying both newspapers and letters, and when the people wished to visit the county seat they came by their own conveyance.

On the completion of the railroad from Philadelphia to Norristown, 1835, a new line of stages was put on by William Field in an effort to shorten the time to the city. This was the first stage between Doylestown and Norristown, and called the "Citizen's Line," leaving here at 7.30 and reaching Philadelphia in time for dinner.

Probably the most famous stage line, between Doylestown and Philadelphia, was that known as the "High Grass Line," established by Benjamin F. Clark, in June 1837. It was an "Accomodation Line," if that means anything, and ran into the early Fifties and probably until the N. Penn. railroad was opened in 1856. Its original route was down the Easton road to Newville; then down the Bristol road to Hartsville and thence to the city via the York road. In after years it ran down and back on the Easton road. It left Doylestown on Mondays, Wednesdays and Fridays, and Gilbert's hotel, to return, on Tuesdays, Thursdays and Saturdays at 8 a. m. reaching Doylestown in time for dinner. At first the fare each way was $1.25, but reduced to 75c in 1845. This was probably the first stage that made the round trip to the city from Doylestown in a day, beginning August 1, 1839.

"Benny" Clark, as the proprietor and driver was familiarly called, was an interesting character and popular. The line got its name from Clark calling out to his horses, now and then, "Get out of the high Grass!" Clark, occasionally, unsettled the nerves of his female passengers by saying to his horses: "Now run away and kill another driver won't you?" He was then plied with questions to know when, how and where the awful catastrophy happened, and "Benny" had to explain to quiet the fears he had aroused. Recently we came into possession of a way bill of the "High Grass Line," of July 9, 1846, on its up trip. There were eleven passengers at 75c each, making $8.25, viz: Mrs. Philip Rich, Henry Sprick, Mrs.

Fox,[4] Mrs. Hulse, Miss Murray, Mrs. Davis, Mrs. Sharpless, Mrs. Shunk,[5] Miss Malone and Miss Shunk.[6] Clark is deceased many years.[7]

In 1840 a new stage was put on between Doylestown and Philadelphia by William Frazer, running via Newtown and Bristol, thence by boat, leaving Benjamin Morris' tavern site of Lenape building, Monday, Wednesday and Friday, reaching Philadelphia the next day. Fare $1.00.

On intermediate days the stage ran to New Hope and back. This line was short lived. In April, 1844, Shelmire[8] and Peters, the latter a celebrated stage proprietor, began running the "Citizens Line" from Doylestown to Philadelphia on the Easton road, the firm changing to Shelmire and Crawford the next spring. The same year, 1845, William Price put on a line to Philadelphia via Norristown and the railroad, starting from George H. Wyker's Court inn. The fare was 75c.

In 1848 Shelmire put on a new line of stages down the turnpike to Philadelphia, starting from the Citizen's House, Court and Pine streets, kept by A. R. Kram, and putting up at Marmaduke Watson's Barley Sheaf, Second below Vine. The following summer, William Price put on a coach between Lumberville and Philadelphia, via Doylestown and Norristown, and from the latter place, by rail. In June, 1851 D. W. C. Callender ran a stage between Doylestown and Lambertville, N. J. then by rail to Philadelphia. This line fell into the hands of John Weikel,[9] in July, who made a connection with Philadelphia and New York. The fare was reduced to 75c, and was never so low between these points before or since. There was one other stage that ran for several years between Doylestown and Phila-

---

4 Wife of Judge Fox.

5 and 6 Widow and daughter of the late Governor Shunk. Miss Sharpless lived in Doylestown.

7 Among the drivers of the local stage lines, between Doylestown and Philadelphia, was John Servis, a worthy man who lived here with his family. His son Harry, driver of the express wagon several years, died here.

8 Daniel Shelmire kept the hotel at Jenkintown for many years, removing there from the Black Bear, Richboro this county. He was an agreeable courteous man and very popular.

9 John Weikel lived several years, at that period at Doylestown, some of the time proprietor of a livery stable, and at one time keeping a tavern. He owned a handsome pair of gray match horses, which were much in favor with young men when they wished to take their "best girl" to a picnic.

delphia that should not be overlooked, that driven by "Joe" Lewis,[10] and we believe down to the opening of the North Penn railroad in the fall of 1856. He was an accommodating driver and well liked. He spent the last years of his life in Philadelphia and died there about 1890. The stages of "Benny" Clark and "Joe" Lewis were probably the last of the old coaches that carried passengers from Doylestown to Philadelphia, and were superseded by the railroad.

In the 40's, and probably earlier and later, the Easton stage came into Doylestown at the sound of the driver's horn, stopping at the Citizen's House for dinner. The driver threw his lines to the ground the moment he arrived, dismounted from his box, and himself and passengers went to the dining room. When the stage drove up the relay of horses stood ready to hitch to, and, as soon as the passengers had bolted their dinner, the driver remounted his seat, assumed the reins, cracked his whip, and went out of town as he came in, to the music of his horn. Coming down, the Easton stages entered the borough by North Main street, thence to Broad and along Broad to East Court and to the Citizen's House. Local travel has lost all its picturesqueness since the stage coach was relegated to history.

Doylestown was the changing place for horses and drivers and here a relay of each was kept. It was a custom, when a neighbor had a balky or kicking horse, to bring it to the stage stable and hitch it in a team as a wheel horse, a few trips always curing the animal's infirmity. It was the delight of the town boys to go with the horses to the Neshaminy to see them washed, and, on Sunday, a couple of coaches were filled with them and driven to the stream.

It may be charged we have given the old stages too much space, and gone into their history too minutely, but we do not think so. These stage lines have all passed away, never to return to this part of the country, and none but those who lived during that period can appreciate what an important factor they were in the life of the county capital. Staging, at that day, was an industry, and carried on with a vim hardly to be appreciated now in the days of rapid transit. Staging possessed a romance that belongs to neither electricity nor steam.

The post office and the stage are so closely associated in the

---

[10] Joseph Lewis was a descendant of Richard Backhouse, who owned the Durham Furnace many years, and the man who befriended Judge John Ross when struggling as a young man to make his way in the world. In after years Thomas Ross, not forgetting past favors done to his father, befriended Lewis in more ways than one, and was "Joe" Lewis' steadfast friend to the last. This was a credit to human nature.

THE STAGE AND THE MAILS.

transportation of the mails, there is no impropriety in grouping them in a single chapter.

In Colonial times, the mail facilities were "few and far between." Soon after Penn's arrival, the settlers of lower Bucks were enabled to send, and receive, letters by public conveyance, and passengers were conveyed in the same way. In the Fifth-month, 1683, William Penn established a post office at the Falls, and Henry Walby was authorized to hold one at Taconey, and to supply passengers with horses from Philadelphia to New Castle or the Falls. The rates of postage of letters, from the Falls to Philadelphia, were three pence, to Chester, five, to New Castle seven pence and to Maryland nine pence.

The first Post Office in Bucks county, after the establishment of the Federal government, was opened at Bristol, June 1, 1790, and Joseph Clun appointed Post Master, while that at Doylestown was opened January 1, 1802, and Charles Stuart the Post Master. He shortly resigned, when Enoch Harvey, his son-in-law, succeeded him, but we do not know the date of the change. The latter held the office until 1804, when Asher Miner, editor and proprietor of the *Correspondent*, succeeded him and had a long term. He kept the post office in his printing office, and, in many respects, it was of great convenience to him in a business way. The letters, remaining in the office uncalled for, were advertised for the first time in the *Correspondent* of October 1, 1804, and, in the issue of December 21, 1819, it was announced that:

"A letter box is now attached to the door of the P. O. into which all letters may be dropped intended for the mails, or communications for the *Correspondent* will be attended to." This was the first letter box at the Doylestown office, and probably in the county. Miner resigned March, 1821, after having held the office seventeen years.

In 1805 Congress established two mail routes in the county; one from Bristol to Quakertown, via Newtown and Doylestown, the other from New Hope, via Doylestown to Lancaster,[11] there and back once a week.[12] These routes appear to have been arranged to facilitate the

---

[11] At Buckwalter's tavern, two miles beyond Norristown, Sept. 7, 1825, Benjamin Hall, son of Isaac Hall, Doylestown in his twenty-fourth year. He was carrying the mail between Doylestown and Lancaster. He was a remarkably studious young man and was reading law with Mathias Morris at the time of his death.

[12] The records show that about March 1, 1805, a petition was presented in Congress for the establishment of a Postroad from Coryell's Ferry through Doylestown to Lancaster.

distribution of Asher Miner's newspaper; and the mail was carried over the latter of the two routes for several years, by the late John M'Intosh, of Doylestown. They belonged to the "Cross Mails" system, and at the present day are known as "Star Routes." Miner was succeeded in the post office by Charles E. DuBois, a young attorney recently admitted to the bar, who took charge April 1, 1821. The post office was then in a frame or stone building, on the west side of North Main street about opposite the Court House. Mr. DuBois had his law office in the same room probably on the site of the James' dwellings. He held the office but a short time, when William T. Rogers, who had recently purchased the *Doylestown Democrat*, was appointed in his stead. Among the announcements of the new P. M. was the following under date of February 24, 1824:

"In future no letters will be delivered out of the office without the cash, and persons wishing to avail themselves of a credit will be required to make a deposit in the office."

At that time the Southern mail arrived at Doylestown, from Philadelphia, every Monday, Wednesday and Friday morning at eleven, and closed at ten. There were but twenty-seven offices in the county. Rogers resigned November 23, 1829, and M. H. Snyder, who had recently established the *Bucks County Express* and purchased the *Democrat*, was appointed in his place. Snyder announced in the *Democrat* of April 27, 1830, that he will " publish every week, all the letters remaining in the post office of Doylestown received the preceding week." He stepped down and out of the post office, March 4, 1835, and Samuel A. Smith took the place. Doylestown had now had a post office thirty-one years, and, without including Smith, it had been held by six postmasters, of which three were printers, which shows the power of printer's ink. The post office was kept at the newspaper offices, and our county journalists, to some extent, "killed two birds with one stone." Now comes a change, the scepter of office, in handling the mails, passes from the type-setting fraternity to the craft that handles the yard stick, for General Smith was a store-keeper and moved the post office to his place of business.

There is nothing to be said of Smith's administration of the post office; he was allowed to remain but three years when Randall Maddock, a justice of the peace, was appointed. This was in 1838, sixty-five years ago and he opened the post office in the basement of what is now the Scheetz store house, northwest corner of Court and Pine streets. Maddock was an unique postmaster, and enjoyed the reputation of carrying the letter mail round town in the crown of his hat for distribution.[13] The travel, from Philadelphia to the "Forks of Delaware," was still up the Easton road, through Doylestown in Troy post coaches, carrying the mails. Land Admiral Reeside was proprietor, and his stages came into town at a spanking gallop, the driver tooting his long horn to arouse the drowsy burghers.

The author knew, personally, all the postmasters but the first three, Stewart, Harvey and Asher Miner, and he recalls them and the places where the office was kept. The former postmasters and the present have handled the mails at Doylestown for one hundred years. Maddock was succeeded by Charles H. Mann, who had recently moved from Danboro. His commission bore date, November 28, 1839, and the name of Amos Kendall was signed to it. Mann kept the office at his dwelling, corner of East State and Pine streets where Bernard McGinty lives. When Tyler stepped into Harrison's shoes Mann was removed, and Lester Rich supplanted him; and all the town went to his dwelling, on East State street, the site of Charles C. Cox's dwelling to get their letters, where Rich's pretty daughter waited on her customers with politeness and grace.

When James K. Polk came into power, 1845, the post office passed into the hands of Dr. George T. Harvey, and he kept it in his frame drug store on the site of the new Hart building.

The Doctor was a lucky man, and must have had some political witchery about him, that hypnotized three Presidents, Polk, Buchanan and Johnson, and induced them to trust him with handling the mails in this town of Doyle. What he didn't know of the tender correspondence going on between the young folks was hardly worth knowing. He made a good postmaster and kept the postal secrets locked up in his own bosom.

The Shearer family was as fortunate as the Harveys, for three postal commissions went to them. Enoch Harvey Shearer was postmaster under the Taylor-Filmore reign, 1849-'53; appointed by Lincoln in his first term, and, dying in office, 1865, his widow was commissioned for the remainder of the term. During this period the office was kept in the little frame, on the east side of North Main street, on the site of the Ziegler building. In it the husband

---

13 Postmaster Maddock was probably the pioneer of free delivery.

carried on harness making, and the daughter assisted to run the office.

When General Grant became President, Mrs. Prizer, widow of Enos Prizer, senior proprietor of the *Bucks County Intelligencer*, was appointed, and the office kept in a room of the Armstrong block west side of Court street, at intersection of Main; subsequently occupied as a drug store and now a cigar store. The accommodations here were better than for many years and it was thought superior quarters would never be needed.

Mrs. Prizer was succeeded by Thomas P. Miller in Grant's second term, and the office transferred to the little stone building where the Clerk of Quarter Sessions was housed for many years; then for a time, in what is the Sheriff's office in the new Court House, while that building was being completed. This was in 1878, and, the following spring, the post office was removed to the southwest room in Lenape Building. This becoming too small for the increasing business, the adjoining room, part of the former market house, was fitted up and occupied, 1894. Four postmasters handled the mails under the roof of Lenape; Thomas P. Miller,[14] Grant's second term, John G. Randall, Cleveland's first term, James Bartlett, under Harrison, John M. Purdy, an appointee of Cleveland, during his second term, and James Bartlett in both terms of McKinley. The latter was re-appointed by Roosevelt, February 20, 1902 for another term of four years.[15] The location of the post office was changed, in the winter of 1901, to the Armstrong building, northeast corner of Main street and Shewell avenue on Monument Place, in the heart of the borough.

Down to the introduction of railroads all the mail matter distributed from, and received at Doylestown was carried by horse back, sulkey and stage, the routes to and from the county seat, radiating in every direction. There was one trunk line of stages, that from Philadelphia up the Easton road to the Lehigh, with connections to all parts of the state, via the Susquehanna region and beyond. The others were "Cross Mails," crossing the county

---

14 Thomas P. Miller, is the son of Mahlon Miller, long the popular landlord of the Black Bear inn, Northampton township. He was named after Colonel Thomas Purdy Sheriff of the county, and, from boyhood, known as "Colonel" Miller. He served through the Civil war, and made a good record as Lieutenant of Infantry.

15 James W. Bartlett was born in Philadelphia, 1838, and came to Bucks county when a young man. He was elected Recorder of Deeds, 1878, and subsequently appointed Deputy Recorder.

in several directions. Sixty years ago four newspapers were published in Doylestown, almost their entire issue being distributed by post riders.

In 1826 the following "Cross Mails" carried the mail matter to different points in the county and some to places outside:

For Bristol, via Buckingham, Rockhill, Attleboro, Morrisville, Hulmeville, Dolington and New Hope, leaving at 7 a. m. every Tuesday morning, returning Thursday afternoon:

For Andalusia, via Lady Washington, Bustleton, Holmesburg and Warminister [16] every Tuesday morning, returning Wednesday at noon:

For Pottsgrove, via Hilltown, Sellersville, Trumbauerville, Sumneytown and Swamp Church every Tuesday, and returning Wednesday noon:

For New Hope, via Lumberville, every Tuesday morning at 7 o'clock, returning same evening:

For Durham, via Danboro, Plumstead, Erwinna and Monroe, every Tuesday morning, returning Thursday afternoon:

For Lancaster, via Montgomery Square, Centre Square, Norristown, Bell Tavern, Charleston, Pughtown, Morgantown, Churchtown, New Holland and Leacock, leaving every Wednesday morning at 7 o'clock, returning Saturday.

By 1830 the cross mail routes had been increased to nine; the Philadelphia and Easton mails were closed at 10 and 11 a. m. respectively, and the cross mails at 9 p. m. The latter mail routes were generally in the hands of the newspaper proprietors, and the papers were distributed by them.

The "Cross Mails" are kept up, and a large part of the correspondence with the county seat, and much of the newspaper mail, is carried by them. In 1897, seventy-one years after the first record of them, there were nine of these local mail routes, five making six trips a week, and four making twelve :

To Reiglesville, via Dyerstown, Danboro, Plumsteadville, Pipersville, Ottsville, Bucksville, Revere, Sundale, Kintnerville and Lehnenburg:

---

[16] This Warminister post office was on the street road just above Davisville, and Joseph Warner was postmaster. It was established in August, 1823, moved down to Davisville, 1827, and John Davis appointed postmaster, and it is still there.

To Ambler, via Tradesville, Eureka, Prospectville, Three Tuns, Jarrettown, Dreshertown, Maple Glen and Fitzwatertown :

To Levin;

To Wismer, via Point Pleasant, Gardenville and Tinicum:

To Willow Grove, via Edison, Warrington, Neshaminy, Davis Grove and Horsham:

To Bedminister, via Dublin and Fountainville:

To Buckingham, via Mechanics Valley, Buckingham Valley, Pineville, Penn's Park and Wrightstown. From Buckingham Valley the mail is distributed to several points by rail.

To Plumsteadville, via Danboro and Dyerstown:

To Mechanicsville, via Carversville. These mails are carried in vehicles adapted to the carrying of passengers, and are a convenience to many. In addition to the mails that arrive and leave the Doylestown office by stage, eight mails arrive and six depart by rail every day in the week, one only arriving on Sunday, in the evening.

In the hundred years since a post office was established at Doylestown, there have been sixteen postmasters and two postmistresses; two postmasters filling the office three times and another twice. Of the postmasters, most of them were men of prominence; one, Smith, represented the district in Congress, Rogers, served two terms in the State Senate, one term filling the Speaker's chair, Randall and Bartlett filled County offices, Mann and Purdy were High Sheriff, Harvey and Miller commissioned officers in the Union army in the Civil war, and Snyder an enlisted man. The increase, in the quantity of mail matter, handled at the Doylestown office, as compared with that at its beginning, and especially when the postmaster distributed the letter mail from the crown of his hat, has been enormous, but no greater than on other lines of progress. The weight of mails handled daily at the Doylestown post office, at the close of 1901, was as follows: First-class matter, which included letters and postal cards, etc., one hundred and twenty-five pounds, or about six thousand pieces, newspaper mail, nine hundred and fifty pounds, about 7,500 pieces and the weight of third and fourth-class matter handled daily is about thirty pounds. What better indication could there be of the spread of intelligence, and increase of business? The author is indebted to Postmaster Bartlett, for the figures giving the weight of mail matter.

Doylestown, Old and New.

XV
Our Public Inns.

The public inns, of city or town, are an interesting feature and much history is connected with them. A study of their signs is curious, often suggesting the method of thought and humors of their period. In the olden time, when few could read or write, the tavern played an important part and, not infrequently, the public inn was the first building erected on a street. Having given some account of the pioneer tavern of Doylestown, we purpose to write of others, old enough, to have a history. Of the six licensed houses, at Doylestown almost ninety years ago, four long since rendered their final account, with one other built twenty years later. We have formed them into two groups, for more convenient treating, and will take them up according to age. The first group, known in the past, as "The Three Taverns," the "Ship," the "Fox Chase" and the "Mansion House" stood on three of the four corners where State and Main streets cross, the "Fox Chase" being represented by the present Fountain House, its descendant.

The "Ship," at the southeast corner of State and Main streets, occupying the site of Lenape Building erected 1874, was the oldest of the group. There is some uncertainty when it was first licensed in the absence of documentary evidence. The property was owned by Samuel and James Flack, 1774-1791, and Mrs. Nathan Cornell, whose mother was a Doyle, told the author, many years ago, a tavern was kept there as early as 1778 by Samuel Flack. On May 1, of that year, a child of Mr. Flack was buried, from that house, at Neshaminy grave yard, the little funeral cortege consisting of two young men and two young women, all mounted. One of the young men carried the coffin, and, while the burial was taking place, the firing of the guns, at the battle of the Crooked Billet, was distinctly heard. One of the girls, who attended the burial, was Mary Doyle, mother of Mrs. Cornell. James Flack, Doylestown, a descendant of Samuel Flack, says it is a family tradition that the child was buried from the Ship tavern on the day mentioned, and that Samuel Flack kept the house. When the Ship tavern was torn down, 1874, for the erection of Lenape Building, there was evidence of great age, and tradition said it had rounded out a century as a licensed house. The east end, containing the long low parlor, was built first.

We next hear of the Ship in December, 1805, when George Stewart announced in the *Correspondent*, that he had "again commenced business in the village of Doylestown, a few doors southwest of the Two Taverns;" the two taverns being the Ship and the ancestor of the Fountain House, on diagonally opposite corners, the third of the group, the Mansion House, not being built until five years later. In 1806, Miner's paper speaks of "that noted tavern stand 'Sign of the Ship' in the tenure of Mathew Hare,[1] in Doylestown, fronting the Easton and New Hope roads." Hare was followed by landlords John Worman, Lott Carr, and Colonel Flack, the owner, and, in 1817, Jacob Kohl advertised his occupancy of the "Ship Inn" opposite the store of John Brock. Kohl was agent for a line of stages running to Philadelphia. In 1829, the "Ship"[2] was called the "Bucks County Hotel," and kept by Richard Leedom. A subsequent landlord was Benjamin Morris,[3] of Doyles-

---

[1] "At Doylestown, August 10, 1819, Mrs. Mary Evans, aged about 24 years, wife of David Evans and daughter of William Hair." We know but little of the "Hares," or "Haires," that throws light on the Doylestown branch. They are said to have come from England and settled in Bucks county prior to the Revolution. William Hare is the first of the name we have met with. George Hare went to New Jersey, was a Lieutenant in the Revolution and died, 1783. We hear of a Benjamin Thornton Hare, whose wife, Margaret, was a daughter of Jacob Krider, a soldier of the Revolution. One of the Hares, of Doylestown, was a Lieutenant in Captain Magill's rifle company, 1814.

[2] A deed book in the Recorder's office, Doylestown, contains the following record: John Worman, Inkeeper to Isaac Morris, Inkeeper, April 10, 1809: "beginning at a stone standing in cross-roads, being also a corner of William McGill and others, extending thence along the road leading to Coryell's Ferry." The lot is mentioned as being in Warwick. Isaac Morris was probably the father of Benjamin Morris, Sheriff of the county, who owned this property and kept the tavern.

[3] Benjamin Morris was elected Sheriff, 1830, and hung Mina the murderer of Dr. Chapman, 1832. Miss Mary LaRue, his step-daughter, was the first wife of Dr. George T. Harvey, and the mother of Judge Edward Harvey, of Allentown, Pa.

THE SHIP TAVERN, 1840.

town township, who kept it several years and died there. The "Ship" had a number of Commanders, after Benjamin Morris,[4] some of them owners of the property. It was purchased, 1874, by the Doylestown Improvement Company, which erected the Lenape Building on the site at the cost of $50,000. While the vote of Doylestown was cast at a single polling place, the elections were held at the Ship tavern until it was taken down.

The "Fox Chase," now the Fountain House, and the second of the group, has a record reaching back over a century under various names. It occupies part of the estate of Richard Swanwick, attainted of treason in the Revolution and his property confiscated. It was purchased by Samuel and Joseph Flack, who owned the "Ship," the state executing a deed to them June 8, 1780. Meanwhile Samuel Flack bought his brother's interest and sold the whole to John Shaw, innkeeper, Plumstead. It is thought Shaw built a house, obtained license and kept a tavern there; but, be that as it may, Shaw sold the property to Enoch Harvey, March 29, 1794, Harvey to Charles Stewart, his father-in-law, 1798, Stewart to Dr. Hugh Meredith, 1802, and Meredith back to Harvey, 1803, who now owned the property to his death.

The Stewarts were among the earliest Scotch-Irish settlers of Bucks county, John, of Northampton and Warwick, Robert of Warwick and Thomas of Tinicum. Charles Stewart, of Plumstead, 1738, was probably a son of John who first appears in Northampton, 1729. He bought 116 acres in Plumstead, of William Allen, April 1, 1757. His children were George, Charles and Rachel. This Charles Stewart is probably the same who removed to Lower Makefield, which a comparison of their signatures, 1738 to 1791 makes quite conclusive. Charles Stewart married Sarah, widow of David Lawell, Newtown, 1756-'57. At that time his residence is given as Plumstead. This was probably a second marriage, as John Harris married Lawell's daughter Hannah about that time. While it is thought she went to Kentucky for good, 1797, she appears to have been in Bucks county, 1803, when she acknowledged a letter of attorney to Robert Frazier, authorizing him to convey her interest in the "Mansion House" at Newtown, as the instrument was executed there. In a letter of attorney, dated June 30, 1797, which Hannah Harris and Mary Hunter executed, they are spoken of as "late

---

[4] At Doylestown, March 23, 1839, at the house of Benjamin Morris, Thomas Elton, a soldier of the Revolution, aged 87.

of Woodford in the state of Kentucky, but now of Bucks county. When Charles Stewart went to Upper Makefield we do not know but he was there February 5, 1773.

License was issued to Charles Stewart,[5] 1800, 1801 and 1802 and to Enoch Harvey from 1802 to 1808, and several years afterward In 1815 he rented the house to David D. Marple who subsequently went to Philadelphia, and died there, 1829. At this period the house was known as the "Doylestown Hotel" and the "Fox Chase," retaining the latter name in the 30's. In 1815 Harvey advertised the property for sale, but it did not sell, and the description is of interest after 86 years.[6] It was two stories high with the usual garret. We remember the "capacious" room spoken of and attended a militiary ball there over fifty years ago, where nodding plumes and glittering epaulets of the county militia officers made a brilliant scene The "capacious room" was formed by throwing three other rooms separated by moveable partitions into one and was known as the "ball room." Harvey made a second attempt to sell in 1830 with no better success, when he spoke of it as the "sign of the Fox Chase." Among the outhouses were two stone hay houses, carriage house, sheds and stabling for sixty horses, also a large stone blacksmith and good wheel wright shops.

The house changed owners several times in the next eight years Daniel Wierman in 1831; Stephen Brock in 1832, a famous landlord and James Meredith, 1835. Isaac W. James was the landlord 1836, under whom it was called the "Doylestown Hotel," an old name revived. It now had a double piazza and two-thirds of the building was three stories high. William Field kept the house 1837-38 and Elnathan Pettitt [7] bought it in the early spring of the latter year, taking possession April 1st. He sold out to Charles H. Mann 1849, who moved down from the Citizen's House.

From Mann's occupancy to the present day, 54 years, there have been but six owners and landlords; N. P. Brower, William Corson, Edward Yost, John T. Simpson, Daniel McLaughlin and

---

5 As Charles Stewart got license in 1800, either he or Shaw built a house there, if not built by the Flacks.

6 "The house is large and commodious, 76 feet in length and 30 wide containing six convenient rooms on the lower floor besides an entry, and two rooms on the second floor, one being sufficiently capacious to accommodate parties of business or pleasure. In front of the house is a porch, and contiguous to it, is a well of superior and lasting water with a good pump therein."

7 At Doylestown, October 3, 1832, Benjamin Pettitt, aged about twenty years, son of Elnathan Pettitt.

Joseph H. Fretz, 1900. During recent years the property has been much improved and is now the most imposing public inn of the county. The name was changed to "Fountain House" during the occupancy of Mr. Corson and retains it. One of the most interesting features, in the history of this inn, is its constant rise in value.

The following transfers of the Fountain House property, with the price at which it was sold, have taken place since 1776:

In 1776 William Doyle sold it to Daniel Hough and the same year Hough conveyed it to Richard Swanwick for $600. The property was confiscated, 1779 and sold to Samuel and Joseph Hough at public sale, 1792; Samuel Flack who had purchased Joseph's interest, to John Shaw, 1798; Shaw to Enoch Harvey; Harvey to Stewart, 1802; Stewart to Hugh Meredith, 1803; Meredith to Enoch Harvey, 1832; executors of Enoch Harvey to David Weirman, $1,976, 1833; Weirman to Stephen Brock, $3,500, 1835; Brock to James Meredith, $4,250, 1838; Meredith to Elnathan Pettitt, $8,000, 1849; Pettitt to C. H. Mann, $8,000, 1856; Mann to N. P. Brower, $6,000, 1868; Brower to Wm. Corson, $17,500, 1879; S. A. Firman, administrator of Corson, to Edward Yost, $22,300, 1880; Sheriff S. L. Ely, to Lydia Ann, wife of Edward Yost, 1883; Mrs. Yost to John T. Simpson, $23,000. During Simpson's ownership John M. Purdy kept the house and several improvements were made, including a Mansard roof; 189-, Robert Thompson,[8] executor of Simpson, to Daniel McLaughlin, $30,000, and, 1900, McLaughlin sold to Joseph H. Fretz, the present owner for $65,000.

The Mansion House, the third and last of this group, occupying the site of Keller's bakery, southwest corner of State and Main, was probably first built for a dwelling. Miss Laura Magill in a letter to the Author, under date of March 4, 1887, says: "While the Mansion House was being built, my grandfather lived on West State street opposite Green's property, with their children, Alfred and Arabella, born 1802 and 1804, while Louisa, their next child, was born in 1806 in the Mansion House, which, when built, was one story and a half or two stories high with finished basement."[9] This

---

[8] At Davisville, February 21, 1833, by Lemon Banes, Esq., David Robinson to Mary A. Reed, both of Davisville. The widow of the late Robert Thompson, of Doylestown, is the daughter of this marriage, and her grandfather was a warrant officer in the U. S. N. and served on board the frigate Brandywine, which carried General Lafayette home to France, 1825. A sister of Mrs. Thompson was the wife of the late Isaac G. Thomas, of Doylestown.

[9] Prior to living on State street, opposite Green's, the Magill family occupied a house on the premises.

confirms our belief that the house was enlarged in 1810, after the new county seat was fixed here, and changed to a tavern. This was done by William Magill, son of Robert.

After the county seat was removed to Doylestown, the house received a license and was kept several years by the Magills, father and son. In 1834, it fell into the possession of William Field a lessee, who was elected Sheriff that fall. He was a popular man an twice married.[10] His daughter Elizabeth, a sprightly, pretty girl and the toast of the town, married Rex Peters, son of the great stage proprietor, and they settled down on a farm in Chester county

Samuel E. Buck succeeded Field for a couple of years, and, in December, 1838, took charge of the Mount Vernon House, Philadelphia, where he died 1840. He was a dashing, handsome man and married one of Josiah Y. Shaw's pretty daughter, a runaway match[11] and created some sensation. He came to Doylestown, 1832 from Nockamixon, and began storekeeping with Daniel Wierman the latter dying, January 1834. Buck's widow married John Titus, member of the bar and, in future years, reached the chair of Chief Justice of Arizona. She was a lovely woman and of fine presence There were several other landlords at the Mansion House while continued in license, Zepp, of Philadelphia, succeeding Buck, then Charlie Tucker, a facetious fellow by nature and a tailor by trade who worked on the bench while he played the role of landlord, keeping the house three years.

Among the succeeding landlords were Thomas Sands from Solebury, and Daniel Wilson, 1853, the last, the Sheriff selling him out This house was Democratic headquarters for several years, and here the return riders assembled the night of election, and carried the news to distant parts of the county. At Samuel A. Bridge's first election to Congress, 1852, Dr. George T. Harvey and the author carried the result to him at Allentown, a drive of sixty miles there and back. In a room in this house, facing State street, the first telegraph instrument in the county was put up and experimented with about the first of January, 1846, which the author witnessed.

After the death of Alfred Magill, son of William and father

---

10 At Willow Grove, October 27, 1824, by George H. Pawling, Esq William Field to Miss Martha Dungan, both of Doylestown.

11 In Philadelphia, December 9, 1833, by John Swift, Esq., Mayo Samuel E. Buck, merchant, to Miss Martha E. Shaw, daughter of Josiah Y Shaw, both of Doylestown.

Charles H., 1853, the Mansion House was sold to William T. Eisenhart and Abraham L. Garron for $6,500. It subsequently fell into possession of James S. Mann, who converted it into a bakery and restaurant, Willoughy Shade being an intermediate owner and keeping a tin shop and stove store in it. Weinrebe bought it of Mann, and sold it to A. M. Keller in 1899, but bought it back in July, 1902, and is the present owner. Thus, two of the "Three Taverns," around which throbbed the pulse of the life and business of Doylestown three quarters of a century ago, have passed into history.

The Clear Spring, the last of the first group of our public inns, and licensed at the dawn of the nineteenth century, is at the "Germany" end of the village. At its birth it was surrounded by woods and fields, and named from the fine spring of water gushing up on the premises. The name was originally the "Spring House," its sign board bearing the inscription "Bucks County Farmer." John Worman kept it in 1806, probably the same who was a tailor in Doylestown prior to that time. On December 6, that year, he advertised his tavern "in Germany," the same name that end of the borough bears to-day, with 23 acres of land; "the house has two fronts, each 50x20 feet with good kitchen." As it did not sell, Worman continued to keep it until April 1, 1809, when he removed to Philadelphia to the sign of "The Drover," Third and Callowhill. The tannery, that formerly belonged to the premises, was not built in 1804, but probably erected by Dick, about 1810.

John Ledley Dick was the next owner buying it about 1810, and owning it to his death. He offered it for sale August 13, 1813, under the name of the "Spring House," sign of the "Bucks County Farmer;" the house "a new stone building with a living spring of water near its base in full view of the public buildings." Jacob Overholt, the landlord, shortly left, but, just before vacating the premises, advertised a "fox chase," to come off shortly in the following terms: "A handsome fox will be let out from the 'Bucks County Farmers' inn,' in Doylestown, when all who are fond of innocent sport are invited to attend with good dogs and fleet horses." We are not informed how the fox chase terminated or who took the brush. Dick died, 1815, and the tavern was sold to settle his estate. Valentine Opp,[12] Springfield township, being the purchaser.

Moving down in the spring of 1816, he took possession and began

---

[12] At Doylestown, June 10, 1833, Catharine Opp in her 61st year, wife of Valentine Opp, inn keeper. Buried at Hilltown church.

his long career as landlord. The tavern was in the Opp family until 1843, twenty-seven years, the son succeeding the father. It became quite a famous hostelry, and a noted stopping place for the upper end Germans, when visiting the county seat. Sergeant Peter Opp, who served though the Mexican war, and had a public reception on his return home, August, 1848, was a grandson of Valentine Opp,[13] and a son of Peter.[14] The last surviving members of the Opp family were Mrs. Catharine Constantine, who died at Doylestown, Oct. 7, 1896, in her 88th year and Mrs. Catharine Rickard, wife of Andrew B. Rickard, who died at the same place, Oct. 13, 1901, at the age of 81.

The Opps left the tavern in 1843, when it was occupied by Lewis Apple who kept it until 1846. He removed to the "Citizen's House," and was succeeded by Thomas Scotland and others down to the present time; among them being "Ad." Cleaver, many years the owner and keeper of the historic Brick Hotel, Newtown. The 23 acres, of land, belonging to the Clear Spring tavern when Worman owned it, 1806, were long since parted with. The house is in good condition, the present owner being Samuel K. Hager.

The "Indian Queen" the most famous of the old taverns of the second group, occupied the site of the new building of the Doylestown National Bank. It had three lives, so to speak, first a smith shop, next a public inn, and then, for nearly three quarters of a century, a private residence, known as the "Ross Mansion."[15]

The ground the Ross Mansion stood on, was originally part of the "Free Society of Traders tract," then to Jeremiah Langhorne, to Jonathan Kirkbride, to Joseph and Jesse Fell, who built a smith shop on it, and 1802 it came into possession of Nathaniel Shewell. When it became an assured fact—the seat of Justice would be removed to Doylestown, Shewell enlarged the ancient smithy into a two-story attic extending the southwest front to Main street. This was done,

---

13 Anna Catharine Opp, mother of Valentine Opp, died in Springfield township, 1828.

14 On Tuesday, July 7, 1818, by the Rev. Mr. Weiand, Mr. Peter Opp o Doylestown, to Miss Margaret Fries, of New Britain. Peter Opp died at his father's house, Doylestown, September 22, 1827, aged about 30 years.

15 The title, to the historic Ross Mansion for the past hundred and fifteen years, runs as follows : William Roberts, Sheriff, conveyed to Joseph Fell June 21, 1788; Fell's administrator to Nathaniel Shewell, April 1, 1802; Shewel to William Watts, April 14, 1818; Watts to John Ross, May 25, 1824; John Ross to son, Thomas Ross, 1834; and thence to son Henry P. Ross to George Ross and to the Doylestown National Bank, the present owner. John Ross was born in Solebury, February 24, 1770, settled in Easton, 1792, and died January 31, 1831.

1811, the year after Shewell sold the site for the public buildings to the county for one dollar.

The Indian Queen was a licensed house for eleven years, the first landlord being Frederick Nicholas, or Nicholaus, probably son of the early stage proprietor through Doylestown to Philadelphia. He took possession about April 1, 1813, kept it two years and was followed by Mathew Hare from the "Ship." In a newspaper notice of his change of location, Hare says he had "given up the Ship" and hoped, "by particular attention to the duties of a public house keeper, to reinlist a portion of his old shipmates." April 1, 1816, Stephen Brock assumed the baton of authority at the Indian Queen, his license being issued at the April sessions and renewed the following year. On taking possession, Mr. Brock made the following newspaper [16] announcement addressed to " Friends at a distance and neighbors near." "I have taken Shewell's convenient tavern stand in Doylestown, near the Court House, at the door of which the Indian Queen exhibits herself in all kinds of weather, her spirits neither depressed by *clouds* nor raised by *sunshine*. I have liquors of a good quality; I have made comfortable provision for the weary traveler, including provender for his horses, and having a disposition to live by the provision, I pledge myself to use every proper exertion to give satisfaction to those who may frequent the inn of

STEPHEN BROCK."

Mr. Brock was a picturesque person and not surpassed as an innkeeper. He was genial and popular, and an important factor in county politics. No man could play the role of candidate for office with greater success, and he knew how to enroll the mothers on his side. His strength among the voters was such, on two occasions, he ran as an independent candidate for sheriff against the field and was elected. In his first race, 1821, when returned by 983 majority, he announced his candidacy in a card, which starts off by saying: "I am no grandee, nor caucus man, nor political intriguer; but a plain man," and the people seem to have thought so, for they elected him. There was always a vein of humor about him. In the Spring of 1825 when he moved out to the Cross Keys, he announced, that instead of having "shifted his quarters to the Lake country, the Cherokee settlements, or any other outlandish region," he "had only removed

---

16 Pennsylvania Correspondent April 9, 1816.

to the sign of the Cross Keys, lately kept by Peter Adams, Esq., on the Easton road, one mile from Doylestown."

Mr. Brock left his "Indian Queen" April 1, 1818, and was succeeded by William McHenry, father of the late Charles McHenry of Doylestown. The new host came of a good Irish family, his father being the Rev. Francis Mc Henry, a prominent Presbyterian divine of the eighteenth century. Our new landlord was a watch and clock maker by trade and carried it on in the second story corner room of the inn. Mr. McHenry was followed by Abram Black, familiarly called "Walabocker," who was at the Indian Queen in 1821-22. Shewell had sold the property 1815, to William Watts, who came up from Newtown with the Courts and took out license in his own name. He kept the Queen 1823 and 1824 the latter year selling the building to John Ross, recently appointed to the Common Pleas Bench of the District. The house was a popular one, and, being in touch with the new county buildings, became the Court and political centre. During Mr. Watt's occupancy, November, 1823, the "Union Troop of Cavalry" was organized at a meeting held there. This was a famous military organization, and commanded several years by Joseph Archambault, one of the two "Archambault brothers" who belonged to the household of the great Napoleon, and were with him at St. Helena.

The "Court Inn," on the site of the present Monument House, across Main street from the "Indian Queen," came into life when the latter retired. It began as a small frame, and so remained a number of years. Wm. Watts commenced keeping it soon after selling the Queen to Judge Ross, 1824, and left it in November, 1826. He was then the owner, and may have erected the first building. His sale was held October, 1826, and, at it, was sold a pair of beautiful cream bays, known as the "Lafayette horses," quite a fad after the General's visit here, 1824, and were two of the six that drew the distinguished Frenchman through the streets of Philadelphia. William Field succeeded Watts November 4, 1826; Charles Morris kept the house, 1830 and Field was there again, 1832. In October of that year Field married Eliza Gordon for his second wife. Watts was still the owner of the Court Inn, in the spring of 1832, when William T. Rogers, as his agent, offered it for sale. The house was robbed, while Field occupied it, the night of April 15, 1830, and, among the articles stolen were a dozen silver spoons marked with the initial "D." belonging to his first wife. Here there is a break in the line of landlords

THE FOUNTAIN HOUSE, 1853.

and the Quarter Sessions records do not help us out. In this old inn was born Joseph H. Blackfan, many years "Superintendent of Foreign Mails," whose father, Crispin Blackfan, once kept the house, and was Prothonotary. John Weikel was the landlord 1842, and George H. Wyker, 1844. The latter advertised his removal in the *Intelligencer* of June 26, as follows:

"George H. Wyker, late from the Ladies', Gentlemen's Farmers' and ordinary Travelers' House of entertainment, two miles above the Willow Grove, on the Easton and Philadelphia State Road, begs leave to inform his friends, (if he be so fortunate as to have any) the rich as well as the poor, that he has absquatulated from the old stand, and has squatted down at Doylestown, at the 'Court Inn,' the original Stage House Hotel, where he will accommodate all who may see proper to accommodate him with their custom, 'according to the best of his ability, and with fidelity,' " as the lawyers say.

N. B. " A line of Stages for Norristown leaves this house every day, except Sundays, at 7 a. m., and returns at 7 p. m."

At the April term, 1846, license was granted to Joseph Strawn, "Pappy" Strawn as he was familiarly called. He kept the house twenty years, and developed a number of pecularities of character. He had a certain time for closing, and the rule was as rigid as the laws of the Medes and Persians. The hour was ten o'clock, and if guests were at the bar taking a "night cap" it made no difference, they had to go. He had great faith in the moon, and watched it closely, and, as age grew upon him, began to predict and prophesy. One of his pecularities was his dislike to negroes, and, with a single exception, none of this race was allowed to drink at his bar. The exception was Peter Jackson, a negro of the old school, tall and dignified, and a constant attendant upon the officers in the hey day of our county military. Strawn's only son, Clayton, after serving in the war of 1861-65, went to sea with a couple of his companions, and sailing the south seas over in different vessels, they met at Honolulu. The other two came home but Strawn remained; contracted leprosy, was sent to the island where such unfortunates are confined, and finally became its Governor. One of Strawn's daughters married William Beek, who built the first exhibition building on the Doylestown Fair Grounds, 1855; which was blown down that Fall, after a great fair at which Horace Greely and a baby exhibit were the drawing cards. Allen H. Heist succeeded Strawn at the Court Inn, 1866 and to him the house is indebted for modern improvements. He first erected the brick back building and then the front structure, the original frame, having to give way to the demands for better accomodations. The house subsequently passed out of the Heist family, being purchased by George Ott, the present owner. Just when it was given the name of the "Monument House" we cannot tell, but sometime after the monument was erected at the crossing of Main and Court streets, 1868.

The Green Tree, the third of the second group, at the northeast corner of Broad and Main streets, was built by Septimus Evans for a dwelling, about 1807, who lived there, following his trade as a clock and watch maker. In 1811, he married Catharine Houpt, of Durham, obtained a license and kept the house, 1813-'14 and '15, selling it to Daniel Woodruff, the fall of the latter year, who moved in the spring of 1816. Evans left Doylestown and was following his trade at Jenkintown,[17] 1821, and, at one time, lived in Delaware. He was the father of Henry S. Evans, many years proprietor and editor of the *Village Record*, West Chester, and served two terms in the State Senate. He was born in Doylestown, and, no doubt, drew his first breath under the roof of the Green Tree.

A new landlord took possession of the Green Tree the spring of 1817, a tailor named John Randall, the second of the name to play bonaface in the village. During his occupancy, a stranger, William Denison Burroughs, who stopped at the house over night on his return to his home, in the state of New York, died there of pleurisy. He had taken a raft down the Delaware to Philadelphia. Here there is a break in the landlords, but Margaret Kiple kept the house, 1822-23, leaving the first of April of the latter year.

Joseph Burrows, father of the "Citizens' House" of which more later on, bought the Green Tree in the Spring of '23 and moved in as Mrs. Kiple went out. Burrows, who was still there in 1826, announced that "Mineral water of the best quality, and ice cream equal to Philadelphia manufacture, can be had on Thursday and Saturday evenings," luxuries at that day. Mr. Burrows' wife, Sarah, died in Philadelphia, June 30, 1824. He left the tavern prior to 1828, and began keeping a flour and feed store in Doylestown, being succeeded at the Green Tree by Henry Carver, sub-

---

17 Septimus Evans offered the Green Tree and four other lots at public sale August 31, 1813, but it did not sell. The reason given, for wanting to sell, was because he wished to remove to the state of Delaware, where he had purchased property.

sequently elected Brigade Inspector; Carver was there in '28, and William Field from '29 to '31.

Thomas Purdy, of Southampton, father of ex-Sheriff John M. Purdy, was the next landlord to rule over the Green Tree, his administration beginning April 1, 1831; William Purdy, his father, having been recently appointed Prothonotary by Governor Wolf, father and son came to Doylestown and occupied the tavern. The license was taken out in the name of the son. The Purdys left the Green Tree in the Spring of 1833; the father removing to the house now occupied by Arthur Lehman, State street and Printers' alley, where he died 1834, the son going to the Black Bear, Northampton township, where he kept store a few years in the Stuckert storehouse, and then removed to his father's farm in Southampton. He died there in the Fall of 1844, two years after his election to the Sheriff's office.

Among the subsequent landlords were Benjamin Carver, the successor to Purdy; Kirk J. Price, who kept the house in 1836; Theodore Kinsey, who left the tavern to engage in the lightning rod business, and, striking it at the flood, it led on to fortune; Joel Vasey, who left the Green Tree in 1849, to give place to Abram R. Kram, the bartender for Lewis Apple at the Citizen's House; license was granted to both Apple and Vasey at the April Term, 1846. The Green Tree gave up the ghost as a licensed house sometime in the Spring of '54, and, since then, has been occupied as a residence by various persons. It belonged to the Chapman family many years. The present owner, Webster Grim has made handsome alterations and improvements to adapt it to two families. The improved house is in keeping with modern improvements, but we regret a photograph of the old building was not taken before its appearance was wholly changed.

The "Citizen's House," the last of the group, was on East Court street at the corner of Pine, built by Joseph Burrows, 1830-'31 for a temperance house and finished in March. One of the village newspapers announced in its issue of December 7, 1830: "The Citizen's House" is now ready for the reception of jurors, boarders and others, by the proprietor, Joseph Burrows." At that time there were no buildings on the south side of Court street between the Academy and Printers' alley, where Barton Stewart's log barn stood.

In 1835 the proprietor of the house had a collection of curios, which a "Subscriber" pays his compliments to in the issue of the

Intelligencer of May 13 : " Being at court last week, I had a curiosity to visit this establishment, and rarely have I spent a half hour more agreeably than in examining the collection of birds, minerals, sculpture and paintings, with which one of the rooms of the Inn is so tastefully decorated. The skill display in the arrangement of the specimens deserves praise, and the collection is highly creditable to the place." Kirk J. Price kept the house in 1836, removing hither from the Green Tree, and was there a year or two. He was succeeded by William Field, who probably obtained a license. The name was now changed to "Citizen's House," and Field remained there until the spring of 1841, when he removed to the Mount Vernon House, Philadelphia, the second Doylestown landlord who rounded out his occupation there as the keeper of a licensed house.

The next landlord was Stephen Brock, who moved in the spring Field moved out, and was there five years, removing to Cross Keys in 1846. When he took charge, he announced himself in the newspapers, as "Brock against the field," and it was literally so, while he kept the house, it was the centre of much of the social life of the village. Mr. Brock's two agreeable daughters, and three popular sons, were important factors in making it attractive during their father's administration. The Summer of 1845 was especially gay; the house was filled with boarders, among them several attractive girls from the city. Cotillion parties, in the large dining-room, were of almost nightly occurrence, and there were frequent picnics. Some hearts were touched, and, in after years, matches made by those who first met there. The author was then in Doylestown and joined in these innocent pleasures, and, subsequently when standing in that empty dining-room, and contemplating past delights, it seemed " like some banquet hall derserted."

Ex-Sheriff Charles H. Mann succeeded Mr. Brock in the Spring of 1846, and kept the house until he removed to the Fountain House 1849, which he bought of Pettitt. The landlords in rotation, from Mann, were Lewis Apple,[18] who moved from Opp's; J. Wilson Cowell, son of Joseph Cowell, of Point Pleasant, whose tavern was quite famous in its day, and where J. Wilson got his early training, whose eldest daughter married James Vanhorne, cashier of Hatboro National Bank; William C. Knight, Southampton, bought the house, 1863, kept it two years then returned to Southampton where he died 1877;

---

18 At Doylestown, November 1, 1844, Anna, wife of Lewis Apple, at the age of 27.

Thomas P. Miller, 1868, son of Mahlon Miller who kept the famous Black Bear many years, who made some valuable improvements, and was succeeded by ex-Sheriff Purdy in the Spring of 1878. Morgan Rufe bought the house of Purdy, 1883, and altered it for a general store. At his death it was bought by A. F. Scheetz, whose sons carry on the mercantile business there. Its glory hath departed, and no more will the music of the drivers horn be heard, as of old, when the Troy Post coaches, horses on a run, stopped before the house with the mail.

Of the nine taverns, we have discoursed about and, which during their best days, wielded great influence, six have been dropped from the rolls, and but three remain, the Fountain House, Monument, House and Clear Spring. As we call the roll of Doylestown landlords, a remarkable fact presents itself, eight of them, including one proprietor filled the office of High Sheriff of the county, one, Brock, being twice elected; William Field, Benjamin Morris, Thomas Purdy, Charles H. Mann, John M. Purdy, Allen H. Heist, John T. Simpson and Stephen Brock. Despite what is said of the increase of the liquor traffic and the growth of intemperance, Doylestown shows a different record. In the last sixty-five years only two new taverns have been erected and licensed in the borough, and it is a creditable fact, that in the last sixty years, while our population has largely increased the number of our public inns has decreased. When Doylestown had but 500 inhabitants there were seven licensed inns; now with a population of 3,500, it has only five, and has not had more in twenty-five years. With this record, Doylestown's increase in temperance and sobriety cannot be called in question.

In writing of the Doylestown taverns, it will hardly do to omit the Cross Keys on the Easton road, a short mile out of town. It was first licensed at the June term of Court, 1758, and has been in continued license one hundred and forty-five years. Alexander Brown, who received the first license, was a son of Thomas Brown, Plumstead township, stated, in his petition, that he "had settled by the side of the road that leads from the Great Swamp to Newtown, which crosses the road that leads from Durham to Philadelphia." Of the names signed to the petition are those of Henry Taylor, William Foulke, William Thomas, John Lester, Cephas Childs, John Childs, Isaac Childs, Henry Childs, William Yardley, Jonathan Foulke, Edward Thomas, Thomas Thomas, Samuel Shaw, Theophilus Foulke, John Thomas, Abel Roberts and Benjamin Chapmam, nearly all of them members of the Society of Friends. The sign is the "Cross Keys," the arms of the Papal See, and the emblem of Peter and his successors.

Of the Doylestown landlords in the past, two are claimed to have descended from distinguished ancestry. William Watts and Crispin Blackfin of the Monument House, the former from Sir Thomas Watts High Sheriff and Lord Mayor of London 1595-1600, and the latter from Sir William Crispin, who accompanied William the Conqueror to England, 1066, and was knighted on the field of Hastings.

Doylestown, Old and New.

XVI

The Bench and the Bar.

While it is not our purpose to write the history of the bench and bar, there is no reason the profession should not be accorded space in our volume, corresponding to their position in the community. Since Doylestown became the county seat, they have played an important part in its affairs, social, political, professional and otherwise, and "I'll not forget them now."[1]

Our county court was not presided over by a Judge, "learned in the law," prior to the early part of the last century. In 1806, Bird Wilson, whose father had been a member of the Federal constitutional convention, of 1787, and whom Washington considered the "father of the Constitution," was appointed President Judge of this district, composed of the counties of Bucks, Montgomery, Chester and Delaware. He took his seat in April, and, after serving twelve years, resigned to enter the church, 1818, and was succeeded by John Ross, John Fox, Thomas Burnside, David Krause, Daniel M. Smyser, Henry Chapman, Henry P. Ross, Stokes L. Roberts, Richard Watson, Harmon Yerkes, and Mahlon H. Stout, the present incumbent. In the meantime, Bucks county had been created a separate district, and the office of Associate Judge abolished. If we had more space to indulge in this direction, and it were not beyond the scope of our work, we should delight to enrich our volume with a more extended notice than a mere mention of names, for their memory is worthy of it.

In the twelve years, following the removal hither of the County

---

[1] The bench and bar are both referred to in a previous chapter, that relating to the removal of the county seat to Doylestown, but some repetition seemed unavoidable

seat, 1813-1825, there were fifteen admissions to the bar, only three of whom became prominent in the profession [2], Charles E. DuBois, admitted 1820, Eleazer T. McDowell, 1822 and Henry Chapman, 1825. Of the remainder there were several of highly respectable talent, but a thousand and one obstructions stood in their way of climbing the ladder that leads to fame in the legal profession; some have mistaken their calling discovering their error too late to remedy it; others lacked confidence in their own ability to cope with their seniors, forgetting the time would come when their seats would be vacant for their juniors to fill; while still others, becoming disgusted with the "law's delays" in bringing clients and fees sought new pursuits. Probably few, very few, realized the stubborn fact, that the law is a most jealous mistress, hardly second in this respect, to him who presides over the high court wherein the tender passion pleads at Cupid's bar. In the matter of legal success it seems to have been a case of the "survival of the fittest."

The three we name, as making the best showing of the fifteen, differed widely. DuBois, the eldest, had no gift nor taste for the forensic arena. He was more of a chamber lawyer than an advocate, and in his almost fifty years at the bar, skimmed the cream off the Orphan's Court practice, the most lucrative of the courts. At his death he had been several years Dean of the Bar Association. In all his long life, on two occasions only, did he become charmed enough in political office to step aside from his profession and relinquish the "Connings of Rush and the Maxims of Kent." He was the second Postmaster of Doylestown, and served one term as Clerk of the Orphan's Court. It was probably fortunate, for his professional success, that he early tested his likes and dislikes for political life. Had he left it later it might have wrecked his professional career with nothing to fall back on. Office never brings fortune unless prostituted to the greed of gain and then not always on honest lines.

Eleazer T. McDowell, the son of a Buckingham farmer, and the silver-tongued advocate of the Bucks County Bar, was a noted man of his period. He was admitted, 1822.[3] As an advocate he had no

---

2 At the February term, 1824 the following lawyers were present in the bar Abraham Chapman, John Fox, Robert Bethell, Jr., Alexander Moon, Jr., John Swift, Charles Meredith, George Grantham, Joseph Pickering, John Freedly, Levi Pawling, Albert Smith, Gilbert Rodman, Jr., Charles E. DuBois, Henry Chapman, George Smith, Thomas Morris, Jr., John Wilkinson, Thomas Stewart, Jr., Mathias Morris, Francis B. Shaw, Thomas L. Boileau, Eleazer T. Mc Dowell, and Charles Eastburn. Hon. John Ross was the presiding Judge.

3 At the residence of General Graciot, in Washington city, March 10, 1834 E. T. McDowell, Esq., to Miss Caroline Augustus Galvin, both of Doylestown, Pa.

ELEAZER T. McDOWELL, 1840.

equal, having the gift of eloquence in a remarkable degree, and his fine social qualities increased his popularity. The author heard him address a jury a few times, and it was a pleasure to listen to his persuasive eloquence. His graceful delivery, and liquid flow of words, added to his other charms as a public speaker. He possessed a genial personality and so much resembled Daniel Webster in appearance, that, on one occasion at a National Convention, the populace wished to take the horses from his carriage and draw him through the streets, believing him to be the great "Godlike," but he would not allow them to do it.

The location of McDowell's first office we cannot recall, but, in the spring of 1830, he removed to the frame that stood about opposite the Doylestown Trust Company building, on the east side of North Main street and remained there to his death. His dwelling, almost adjoining his office, was subsequently occupied by George Lear,[4] then by George Hart who erected the present stone building on its site. Now that modest frame is doing service as a Green Grocerie at the northeast corner of South Main and York streets.

Among McDowell's students was Emmet Quinn, a young man from one of the up river townships, admitted 1841. He had great fondness for mechanics, but the study of the law was distasteful, and he only yielded to his father's persuasion. Quinn was a graduate of Lafayette, and the family had means. He liked the practice of law no better than its study and so resolved,

"The Gordian knot of it he will unloose,"

by taking French leave. One morning, in August, 1843, Doylestown was startled by the rumor that Mr. Quinn had disappeared over night. This created a profound sensation, for the young man was popular. He was advertised, far and near, but nothing was heard of him, his father promising to give him a favorite mill property and set him up in business, would he but return. No response being made to these appeals, he was given up for dead. Several years elapsed and nothing was heard of the truant son, but finally he turned up in the United States Patent Office, Washington, where he was employed as a "special examiner." His aspirations had been partially gratified, at least, and he died in his favorite pursuit.[5]

Mr. McDowell was something of a poet as well as a lawyer, as

---

[4] From a card, dated December 11, 1844, and published in Frank Sellers' *Olive Branch*, Lear was then in the office recently occupied by the late E. T. McDowell, Esq., with whom he had read law.

[5] At Doylestown, Nov. 29, 1831. Albert Smith, a member of the bar, and late member of the State Legislature, in his thirty-ninth year.

the following ode will show. It was composed and recited by him on July 4, 1820, at a celebration at the "Sylvan Retreat," near Doylestown:

> Hark! Hark! the drum attends the fife,
>   In social union plighted;
> Freedom the cause—Freedom the life,
> Won by the patriots gory strife,
>   When foe-like clouds benighted.
>
> Mid angry scenes of warlike flood,
>   With freedom's sword inclining;
> Brave Washington undaunted stood,
> While o'er his brow the smiles of God
>   Were graciously reclining.
>
> Hail, spirit chief! to thee we owe,
>   To thee and thy attendants,
> The countless liberties that flow
> So envied by the jealous foe,
>   God shield thee, Independence!
>
> Hail to the day!—peace to the sires,
>   That wrought our happy Eden,
> Strike, strike again, the timbrel wires,
> To those who quelled the hostile fires
>   And lit the star of Freedom!
>
> Hail Independence! martial pride—
>   Thy bare, immortal sages;
> Borne on the surge of glory's tide,
> Thy royal stars majestic ride,
>   High o'er the rock of ages.
>
> When mad oppression stood to brave
>   The pride of Freedom's numbers,
> Thy beams a golden sceptre gave,
> That led the tyrant to his grave,
>   In death's eternal slumbers.
>
> See warmed by thy Creative ray,
>   The gest of native glory;
> Our thousand streams of commerce play,
> And Art usurps rude Nature's way,
>   The germs of future story.
>
> Proud Science with her bosom bare,
>   Unfurls her searing pinion;
> And where the Savage chill'd the air,
> The Virgin waves her golden hair
>   In triumph of her Union!
>
> Hail happy land!—home of the free!
>   To fragile mortals given;
> Blessed be thy seat—green be thy tree
> Thou are the soul, O, Liberty!
>   The choicest boon of Heaven!

While Mr. McDowell held pronounced political views, and was loyal to his party at the polls and elsewhere, he eschewed political office, and was never a candidate for any place with the exception of once being a Presidental elector, representing his party at National

Conventions, and a delegate to the Constitutional Convention of 1837-'38 to which he was elected, 1836, and occupied his seat to the end. He died March 12, 1845.[6] He left three daughters and one son, Edward Sayres McDowell, who was a Lieutenant in the 104th Pennsylvania regiment and fell in the Cival war, at the battle of Fair Oakes, in front of Richmond.

On the death of Mr. McDowell, the newspapers and bar paid proper respect to his memory. Of him the *Intelligencer* said:

"The deceased was a man of much more than ordinary capacity; his person cast in one of Nature's most perfect moulds, contained a mind fitted to its tenement, and a heart that ever throbbed with the purest emotions of an extended philanthropy. He was beloved by all who enjoyed the pleasure of his acquaintance; the enemy of no man; and we feel assured that no one could entertain for him anything approaching to a hostile feeling."

At a meeting of the bar, Abraham Chapman, Esq., presiding, the following, among other resolutions were adopted;

"That we entertain, with sentiments of deep emotion, the intelligence of the decease of E. T. McDowell, Esq., a dispensation of Divine Will, depriving our borough of a much respected citizen, our county of a talented and popular son and our bar of an honorable and eloquent member.

"That we cheerfully give this tribute of respect to the memory of one who largely enjoyed the esteem of his fellow citizens in the various capacities of an able jurist, a man of philanthropy, the kind neighbor, courteous gentleman and heart-warm friend."

A romance attaches to Mr. McDowell's career, that is worth the telling. About 1830, a lady, an entire stranger, brought her well-grown daughter to Doylestown and put her to school, taking board for her where the young attorney made his home. The mother shortly left but never returned. For a time remittances, to pay the young girl's expenses, came regularly and then ceased. The landlady explained the matter to Mr. McDowell, who agreed to be responsible for her bills, to save the young girl from mortification, if she were not let into the secret. Things went on as usual. The acquaintance of the young people ripened into love and from love to marriage. Sometime afterward, when Mr. and Mrs. McDowell were at a public ball in

---

6 Died, on Wednesday morning, the 12th, instant, (March, 1845) at his residence in the borough of Doylestown, after a painful and prolonged illness, E. T. McDowell, aged about 47 years.

Philadelphia, she complained to her husband that an elderly man, an entire stranger, had been looking at her constantly and she was much annoyed. Mr. McDowell asked for an explanation, which the stranger made by saying he believed the lady, he had been looking at, was "his long lost daughter." Further explanation followed and the truth was reached. The stranger and his wife were living in the city of Mexico, and the mother brought the daughter to New York for medical treatment. The physician recommended the girl be put to school in the country; an accident brought them to Doylestown. The mother is supposed to have been lost at sea, on her return home as she was never heard of. These facts were given to the author, many years ago, by an intimate friend of Mr. McDowell, who read law with him, and we believe them to be true.

Mr. Chapman, the third and last of our legal group, differed from his two compeers in mental fibre and other qualities. He was not only an able lawyer, and schooled in all the intricacies of the profession, but a scholarly man in general literature. As a speaker he was calm and deliberate but forcible, and, when fully aroused, was eloquent without making any pretense to it. He always had weight with the jury. On one occasion we heard him close his case to the jury for the plaintiff at twilight. The candles and lamps were brought into the old court room to throw a little light on the scene, but the Court and jury were half obscured by their uncertain flickering. Mr. Chapman was in his best mood; the plaintiff was a woman living in the borough, and the verdict rendered saved her character. Mr. Chapman made a powerful speech, the jury retired but soon returned. The room was as still as death while the Clerk was taking the verdict for the case had excited great interest, and, when the foreman said, "we find for the plaintiff, $1,000 and cost," the audience had their inning in spite of the Court's command for "Silence." Mr. Chapman was fond of politics, and his success was attested by a seat in the State Senate, for one term, and in the House of Representatives of the United States, for one Congress, declining re-election. He also received honors in his profession, being elected President Judge of the Chester-Delaware, and the Bucks-Montgomery districts, where he earned new legal laurels.

Among the young attorneys of this period, 1813-25, was Joseph Hough, admitted 1822, who met a violent death while hunting on the mountains near Mauch Chunk, December 9, 1826. Of this the *Democrat* gives the following account:

"Mr. Hough, with some of his friends, was in pursuit of deer.

While the dogs were in pursuit of one, another bounded up near him and he cried out 'a buck.' At this instant, a lad of about fifteen years, immediately in Mr. Hough's rear, hastily drew his rifle from his shoulder, and, from some unknown cause, it went off, and the ball, as well as the powder and wadding, entered the back of his head and blew it literally to pieces. He expired instantly."

In the following twenty-five years, 1825 to 1850, there were twenty-six admissions to the bar, ten of whom played prominent parts in life; Samuel A. Bridges,[7] 1828; Thomas Ross, 1829; Stokes L. Roberts and Gilbert R. Fox, 1832; Caleb E. Wright, 1833; John Titus, 1840; George Lear, 1844; Edward J. Fox and Elias Carver, 1845; Mahlon Yardley, Richard Watson, W. W. H. Davis, 1846; B. F. Fackenthall and Edward M. Paxson, 1850. Of this group, Roberts and Watson reached the Common Pleas Bench; Titus, bench U. S. District Court; Lear, Attorney-General, Pa.; Bridges removed to Allentown, and was elected to Congress; Ross[8] served two terms in Congress; Yardley one term in the State Senate; Elias Carver, District Attorney; W. W. H. Davis, U. S. District Attorney for New Mexico, filling other offices in that Territory and service in the army in the Mexican and Civil Wars. Of this group was Abel M. Griffith,[9] who served one term in the Legislature. In the next fifteen years there were nineteen admissions to the bar, of which N. C. James, 1851, filled the office of District Attorney two terms.

Henry P. Ross, 1859, Common Pleas bench of Bucks and Montgomery; B. F. Fisher, 1860, Chief Signal officer U. S. A., Civil war; B. F. Gilkeson, 1864, died 1903, Second Comptroller, U. S. Treasury; and State Bank Commissioner, George Ross, 1864, one term in State Senate; Harman Yerkes,[10] 1865, one term in State Senate, twice elected to the Common Pleas Bench, candidate for Supreme Court Bench in 1901. The Rosses are a race of lawyers.

Among the young attorneys admitted to this bar, 1832, and

---

7 In 1901, the Rev. S. A. Bridges Stopp, nephew of Samuel A. Bridges, Esq., was called to the pastorate of the Lutheran Church, Doylestown.

8 At Norristown, November 18, 1832, by the Rev. John Reynolds, Thomas Ross, Esq., of Doylestown, to Elizabeth, eldest daughter of Levi Paulding.

9 At New Britain, of consumption, September 10, 1846, Abel M. Griffith, in his 35th year.

10 Harman Yerkes is a descendant of Anthony Yerkes, an immigrant from Germany, who settled at Germantown about 1700, and removed to the Manor of Moreland, then in Philadelphia county, now Montgomery, in 1709. His father was Stephen Yerkes, and his mother, Amy Hart, daughter of the Rev. Thomas B. Montanye, a distinguished Baptist Clergyman of Southampton. Judge Yerkes was born in Warminster, where his father and mother lived and died.

thought of settling here, was William Strong, of Philadelphia. The motion for his admission was made by Charles Evans, of whom we know nothing. Mr. Strong subsequently settled at Lancaster and had a distinguished career, finally reaching the bench of the Supreme Court of the United States. Samuel A. Bridges came to Doylestown, from Connecticut and was admitted Dec. 9, 1828, on motion of James M. Porter. His card first appeared in the *Bucks County Intelligencer,* of Dec. 22, when he occupied the office of the late Mathias Morris, between Mr. Field's inn, (site of the Monument House) and Mr. Yardley's store (site of the Armstrong building). The office was probably in the Robert Thompson store house, torn down several years ago.

George R. Grantham, who was admitted February 17, 1821, practiced two years at Hulmeville, then removed to Doylestown, and subsequently went west, where he died.[11] Albert Smith, admitted to the bar in 1822, removed to Doylestown, 1826, and in his card, published in the newspapers, says he "solicits a share of the public patronage," and promises his best efforts "to prove deserving." His office was "on the Main street next door below Mr. Bush's watchmaker shop, opposite the residence of J. Y. Shaw, Esq." This was the John Donnelly house corner of south Main and Oakland streets. On December 23, 1823, Charles Eastburn, a student in the office of Abraham Chapman, and son of the late Thomas Eastburn, formerly of Bucks County, later of Wilmington, Del.; George W. Smith, son of General Samuel A. Smith, and John Wilkinson, son of Colonel Elisha Wilkinson students in the office of Mathias Morris, were admitted to the bar. Wilkinson died, 1832.

Stokes L. Roberts practiced at Newtown, his place of birth, from his admission, 1832 to 1841 when he removed to Doylestown, his office being on the block in front of the Court house. In 1844 Mr. Roberts built the double brick dwelling on East Court street, next door but one to Broad, was commissioned to the Common Pleas bench in December, 1872, but resigned the following January. Of the three sons of Judge Fox, Gilbert Rodman, the elder, settled in practice at Norristown, and Edward a younger brother, at Easton. Both reached distinguished places in the profession. Louis R., the youngest son of Judge Fox, after reading law and practicing a brief period, left the profession and entered the church, becoming a prominent Presbyterian

---

[11] At McDonnough Point, Ills., February 9, 1836, George R. Grantham, formerly Attorney at Law, Doylestown.

Clergyman. They are all dead. Mr. Wright, who came from Wilkesbarre, was a good speaker, and, in the latter years of his life, was licensed to preach. Judge Wilson, on his resignation, was succeeded by John Ross,[12] who, being shortly appointed to the Supreme bench on the death of Judge Todd, 1830, John Fox took his place the same year, serving until 1841. Thomas Burnside succeeded Fox, but the former being raised to the Supreme bench, 1845, David Krause, of Harrisburg, succeeded him as President Judge of the district. Our subsequent President Judges were elected under an amendment to the State Constitution.

Samuel D. Ingham was appointed Prothonotary of the County April, 1818 and removed with his family to Doylestown, but being appointed Secretary of the Commonwealth, the following year, qualified and took charge of the office, his family remaining here, his wife dying, 1819.[13] It will be remembered that Mr. Ingham was Secretary of the Treasury under General Jackson. For a part of this period Samuel Hart and Robert Smith were Associate Judges. Hart being appointed, 1814 and resigning 1818, when William Watts succeeded him.

Isaac Hall, father of the late Samuel Hall, was appointed Court Crier by Judge Wilson, and of him John D. James, his successor, told the following story in connection with the duties of that office. When Judge Fox was on the bench he did not like the way Mr. James opened and closed court, the latter by saying "May God bless the Commonwealth," the Judge telling him he should say "May God bless the Honorable Court." James then related to the Judge this anecdote of Hall, that, on one occasion, when disgruntled by something he concluded the opening of the Court by saying: "May God bless this damnable Court," ran out of the room and never returned. James said to Judge Fox if he made any change he was afraid he might fall into the same mistake as Hall, whereupon the Judge replied, "well, you had better keep on in the old way."

In 1830 Court officials, outside of the Judges, were, Prothon-

---

[12] Judge Ross received a portion of his education at the Southampton Classical School.

[13] At Doylestown, August 20, 1819 and, on the 18th anniversary of her marriage, Rebecca Ingham in the 40th year of her age, consort of Samuel D. Ingham, Secretary of the Commonwealth of Pennsylvania. Unwearied in her zeal, by precept and example and an extensive beneficence in promoting the cause of her Divine Lord; ardent, firm and consistent in her piety, she was an affectionate wife, a tender mother, a kind neighbor and an estimable friend. After a long and painful illness, which she supported with Christain patience and submission, she resigned her spirit into the hands of her Redeemer, in the full belief and hope of a glorious immortality through the merits of His atonement."

otary, William Purdy; Register, Andrew Heller; Recorder, Michael Desch and Clerk of Orphans Court, William Carr. Mr. Purdy,[14] the Prothonotary, dying in office was succeeded by Dr. Charles H. Mathews, and the *Doylestown Democrat* published the following obituary;

"It would seem almost superfluous, were it not for custom, to say anything of a man so universally known for more than a quarter of a century in the district in which he resided. He was a public man. He served for many years as a representative in the state Legislature, and was repeatedly a candidate of one of the great parties for higher offices. He took much interest in the great questions that have agitated our country; and was always firm in his opinions, and decided in his course; such was his unobtrusive gentleness, and regard for the feelings of others, that he died, we believe, even without a political enemy. In private life, the strict integrity and urbanity of his manners, endeared him to many friends, who, with his afflicted family, mourn this too early bereavement. He served in the "Whiskey Insurrection" and commanded a company of riflemen in Colonel Humphrey's regiment, in 1814".

Among the distinguished Attorneys of Philadelpia, practicing from time to time at the Doylestown bar, after the removal of the seat of Justice to Doylestown, were Nicholas Biddle and Horace Binney, both in 1822, the latter trying a case that year. At the February term, 1829, there was no criminal business before the Court, and not a single indictment to send to the grand jury. The bench, bar and Deputy Attorney General were ready, but no criminals. At the same court not a civil case was tried, and the jury was discharged without a verdict. Those virtuous times are passed and gone, never to return, we fear.

Edward M. Paxson, son of Thomas Paxson, Buckingham, read law with Judge Chapman, and was admitted to the bar, April 24, 1850. He opened an office and lived in what was known as the "Michener" house, East Court street, on the site of the Dr. Groff dwelling, and the next door but one to Pine street. After practicing here, for a few years, Mr. Paxson removed to Philadelphia where he was appointed, and afterwards elected, to the Common Pleas, and Supreme bench, reaching, in turn, the seat of Chief Justice.

In the recent past, the Doylestown bar has lost, by death, four of

---

14 "At Doylestown, on Friday, May 30, 1834, William Purdy, Esq., in the 65th year of his age, of pulmonary consumption, Prothonatary of the Court of Common Pleas of Bucks county."

JUDGE HENRY CHAPMAN.

its members, Paul H. Applebach, S. Ferdinand Long, Robert M. Yardley and B. F. Gilkyson, who enjoyed the reputation of being able lawyers, and were making their mark in their profession. Mr. Yardley and Gilkyson were active and influential in their party, and both were the recipients of important public trusts. Mr. Applebach was of Bucks county birth, while Mr. Long was a native of Wurtemburg, Germany, but came to this country when a child.

Almost half a century ago, the members of the bar effected an organization to which they gave the name of "The Association of the bar of Bucks County." The main object was to regulate the fees by making them uniform in amount and raising the Esprit de corps among the members. At the first recorded meeting, January 29, 1853, those present signed the agreement, and, on April 28, Charles E. DuBois was elected president, Mahlon Yardley secretary, and a committee, "of the senior members", Messrs. DuBois, Ross and Roberts, were appointed to revise the tariff of fees. The original members, whose names were enrolled on the minutes, were Charles E. DuBois, Thomas Ross, S. L. Roberts, John B. Pugh, C. E. Wright, George Hart, George H. Mitchener, George Lear, Elias Carver, Edward J. Fox, Mahlon Yardley, Richard Watson, W. W. H. Davis, E. Morris Lloyd, N. C. James, L. B. Thompson and James Gilkyson. The second annual meeting, was held at Kramer's Hotel, Doylestown, Monday evening, January 2, 1854, with the following attendence; DuBois, Pugh, James Gilkinson, Hart, Michener, Lear, Yardley, Watson, Lloyd and James. The organization is still maintained under the name of "The Legal Association" and is annually emphasized by a good dinner, going all the way to Philadelphia, on two or three occasions, to get it. In the lapse of almost half a century, since the society was organized, it has long since passed into new hands, but two of the original members surviving, Elias Carver and W. W. H. Davis. It has proved a benefit to the bar, at least from a professional standpoint if not otherwise. Elias Carver, the oldest surviving member of the Bucks county bar, is the Dean of the profession and still in practice.

If the personal, and professional, history of the bar of Doylestown in the past could be written, it would yield much that's interesting and entertaining. As we are about to close the chapter on our professional brethren, we pen a paragraph we hope may repay the reading, although but two are living who will appreciate it at its full value.

In the forties and early fifties, while Judges Krause and Smyser were on the bench, the Citizen's House was their headquarters while Court was in session. This made it the resort of the bar. After Court had adjourned for the day, it was not unusual to see almost the entire number of attorneys at this popular hostelry spending all, or part of the evening, talking politics, discussing points of law, and indulging in jokes, not infrequently seasoned with pungent wit. When the weather was mild enough to sit out, they gathered on the broad pavement in front of the house. The late Thomas Ross took great delight in these social-professional gatherings, and was the life of the assemblage. His gold snuff box played no mean part, for when that was taken out, the lid tapped and removed and passed around, it was equivalent to serving notice on the company there was fun ahead, and more than one fellow member was sure to suffer. If a brother possessed a weakness, it was sure to be punctured, and, by common consent, when wit began to sparkle each one had to lookout for himself. Evan the dignity of the judicial armour failed, at times, to ward off a thrust of the lance; whatever may have been the effect of a thrust at the victim, he had the good sense to laugh with the rest. Of that jolly crowd, all have rendered their final account with the exception of Elias Carver, Esq., and the author.[15]

The Attorneys, who graduated and were admitted, at Doylestown, have been fortunate in reaching the bench, at home and abroad, some achieving this honor in the most distant part of the Union. Among those, who reached the wool sack, was Henry W. Scott, of Newtown, who read law with E. Morris Lloyd, Esq., and admitted in 1867. He settled in practice at Easton, Pa., and, some years after, was elected to the bench, which he now worthily fills. Judge Scott's son was an officer in Admiral Dewey's fleet at the naval battle of Manilla. A full list of the attorneys, who studied here and were admitted to this bar, but afterward reached the bench elsewhere would make a long and honorable roll. Judge Harvey is mentioned elsewhere.

---

15 In Chapter XXX, on Historic Families, some of the members of the bar are spoken of at greater length, as it seemed a more befitting place.

Doylestown, Old and New.

XVII
Social Life in the Past.

While the Social life of Doylestown, in the past, differed in many respects from the present, there is a charm in calling it up. In rural communities, the world over, the recreations of a people, outside the domestic circle, are necessarily limited. With increased facilities, for going abroad, young and old rely less on home for their amusements and pleasures, and, as applied to Doylestown, they more frequently came here fifty years ago than at the present day. Now people go away from home to seek amusements; the trolley is rapidly becoming an important factor in revolutionizing social life; and public and private functions are more closely allied in the twentieth than in the nineteenth century. Not infrequently social, patriotic and political features are commingled in the same gathering. Our people, doubtless, get more fun out of life, but whether their manners and culture are improved is a question for others to answer. What the world calls "Society" has been revolutionized in the last half century.

The first amusement, of any kind, that we have heard of as coming to Doylestown to amuse and entertain its people, that is of record, was on Monday evening, August 13, 1804. According to Asher Miner's newspaper, then just established, one Rennie gave a "wonderful exhibition" at Mr. Harvey's tavern, and, among the performances, was that "wonderful manœuvre of breaking with a hammer twenty or thirty gold and silver watches." He also introduced an "Artificial Swan," and a "Philosophical Fish," with other attractions:

The first fourth of July celebration, at Doylestown, we have note of, was in 1806, held by the "Sons of Freedom." As the Union

Academy, built two years before, was the only suitable place for such occasion it was held there, and the president of the day was Samuel Fell. After the literary exercises were through with, the senior class of students, with a number of their friends, marched in procession to Worman's tavern, now the Clear Spring, and partook of an entertainment. Can the reader see, with his mind's eye, that little band of celebrants marching across lots, for there were no streets then, to the Easton road, and down the long slope of Lyman's hill, not a dwelling the whole distance, except the Russell, and Musgrave houses on the east side of North Main street, for such was the situation ninety eight years ago. The following is one of the toasts that has come down to us from that celebration;

"The fair of Bucks county; may they love merit, if they wish to merit love."

What festivities were held, meanwhile, we have no means of telling, until we come to 1817, fours years after Doylestown became the seat of justice, when we note another Fourth of July celebration. This was in the Court House; toasts were drunk in the "flowing bowl," and the Bucks County Rangers, under Captain William Magill, were present to lend zest and give a martial tinge to the occasion.

Among the organizations at Doylestown, in the long past, was the "Social Dozen" that came into life, 1820. The first meeting was held the evening of December 14, and it was in working order by the 28th, when the Constitution and By-Laws were adopted, and the following officers elected: President, Dr. James S. Rich; vice president, E. T. McDowell; secretary, L. Deffebach; and treasurer, A. Smith. The purpose of the society was for debating purposes and the number limited to twelve. The following named persons appear to have been the original members but the constitution was never signed by them; Robert Bethel, Charles E. DuBois, Henry Chapman, E. T. McDowell, Dr. James S. Rich, Lewis Deffebach, Edward Griffing, Albert Smith, Joseph Hough, Gilbert Rodman, Thomas Morris and Thomas Stewart. The first debate was on the evening of December 28, 1820; "Which is the most useless, or criminal character, the miser or the spendthrift?" The last entry in the Recorder's book was made April 17, 1823, when the "Social Twelve" probably wound up and passed into history.

On St. John's Day, 1824, the Benevolent Lodge of Masons honored the day, assisted by Lodges from Philadelphia and Montgomery county. The procession was led by the Doylestown band

under Captain Charles F. Beckel, the Chief Marshall being Joseph
Hough. An address was delivered by Mathias Morris, Esq. and
dinner served at Kohl's and Marple's taverns.

August 7, same year, Doylestown was stirred by an "Harvest
Home" celebration, possibly the first of the kind gotton up by the
citizens and military, and held on Baring's island in the Neshaminy
near Castle Valley bridge. A procession marched from Marple's
tavern, about 12 o'clock led by the Hatboro and Doylestown bands
in uniform, to the grove on the island. Refreshments were first
served and then Thomas Stewart, Esq. addressed the audience in an
"appropriate and interesting manner."

In 1826, the Fourth of July celebration was a little off color, as a
pure patriotic performance, for a dish of party politics was served up
with it. This was held at the Green Tree tavern, by the "Democratic-Republicans" of Doylestown, a combination that would not
pass muster at the opening of the twentieth century. John Pugh was
presiding officer, assisted by John S. Benezet, then Prothonotary.
Among the volunteer toasts was the following, by Charles E. DuBois,
Esq.: "George Wolf, our representative in Congress; a gentleman
entitled to our respect and esteen."

On the evenings of June 23 and 24, 1829, "A grand equestrian
performance," was given at the public house of Jacob Kohl, the whole
concluding with the two clowns, Messrs. Gallen and Hoofmaster.
Admission, 25 cents.

In the winter of 1832, the town was enlivened by a menagerie,
but how many had been at the County capital prior to this, we are not
informed. This one the author distinctly remembers; he was here a
boy at school, and it was the first time he had gazed upon so much
natural history in the wild animal line. As the king of beasts stood out
prominent in his sight, he made the lion the subject of a composition
the following Saturday, his first attempt. He is still in possession of
this master piece of school composition, and if the lion died young we
may know what to attribute it to.

In 1835 social life took a turn in a new direction, the "Doylestown Club" was organized. There may have been previous clubs for
a similar, different or kindred purpose, but this is the first record we
have fallen upon. It was for public debating purposes, and on Thursday evening, February 5, the following question was handled, presumably "without gloves:" "Is there more to be admired in the

northern and eastern cast of character than the southern?" We have no record of the disputants. The club had probably been annoyed by unruly boys for after that they were to be excluded from the room. This rule would argue that boys, sixty years ago, were no more angelic in their behavior than now. The club was still in existance in the winter of 1838, and had become a literary feature of the town. On Thursday evening, March 1, the members debated the following question, which had begun to disturb our national statesmen as well as those of Doylestown:

"Ought Texas to be admitted into the Union?"

At this time A. Dungan was secretary—probably the late Asher Dungan. On the following Fourth of July, the occasion was celebrated on the bank of the Neshaminy, by the "Wolf men of Doyletown and vicinity." The Declaration of Independence was read by John B. Pugh, Esq., and C. E. Wright, Esq., delivered the oration. In the afternoon a company of ladies and gentlemen met in a grove near the village, partook of refreshments and listened to excellent music by the band.

On Thursday, August 17, 1836, a Harvest Home celebration, of more than ordinary pretentions, was held at Doylestown. The ceremonies were initiated the afternoon before, by the arrival of the Union Fencibles from Philadelphia, in command Captain Robert M. Lee. They were met by the Doylestown Grays, Captain C. H. Mathews, accompanied by the Bethlehem band, half a mile below town and escorted to their quarters. In the evening the band gave a concert in the Court house, with songs in English and German. The following morning, the dwellings and public houses were handsomely decorated, and the people began coming into town early. Besides Captain Lee's company, and the Doylestown Grays, the military consisted of the Union Troop, Captain Wm. McHenry, Captain Gilbert's Company of Infantry, and a detachment of the First National Troop, Captain Miles, Philadelphia. The procession, under the escort of the military and led by General William T. Rogers, Chief Marshall, and Colonel Thomas Purdy and Captain John Robbarts, assistants, marched out to the grove. The address was delivered by E. T. McDowell, Esq., the Rev. Silas M. Andrews conducted the Religious exercises in English, and the Rev. William B. Kemmerer in German. After these were concluded the military gave an exhibition drill in an adjoining field, and then the procession marched back to town. The military dined at the taverns of Mrs. Buck and Mr. James and, shortly after, left town. The affair was a great success.

In 1840, Professor Wise, the celebrated Areonant, made a balloon ascension at Doylestown, probably the first one here.

In August, 1842, two Harvest Home celebrations were held in Doylestown, one on the 6th, the other on the 20th, the former being a temperance affair, attended by several temperance societies of the county. After marching through the village the company repaired to the Court house, where the Rev. Samuel Aaron, an elegant speaker, delivered the address. The second on Saturday, the 20th, was of the ordinary kind. The former we believe to have been the first time the County Temperance Societies united for such celebration. In 1845, August 22, the "Sons of Temperance" held a celebration in Riale's grove, marching there from the Court house where the procession was formed, led by the Doylestown Brass Band. The members of the societies were in regalia, that of Doylestown, called the "Olive Branch Division," carried a handsome banner painted by Samuel F. DuBois. One of the speakers was George Lear, Esq., of Doylestown, recently admitted to the bar.

In 1844, Independence day was celebrated with unusual eclat. The exercises were held in the Court house. Caleb N. Taylor reading the Declaration and the Honorable Samuel D. Ingham delivering the oration. He was the most distinguished man in the county and listened to with great interest. These exercises were followed by a dinner to the committee and guests at Brock's Citizens' House, and refreshments were served to the ladies and children in the Court house yard. An interesting feature of this occasion was the presence of Captain Alden Partridge's company of cadets under arms, from his mititary school at "China Retreat," near Bristol. They came up on the 3rd and returned on the 5th, marching the whole distance. They were accompanied by a baggage wagon, for the lame and halt, and the rations. Some of the boys were hardly more than twelve years old. They attracted great attention. The Doylestown Grays turned out to receive them and joined in the proeession. At the dinner toasts were read, after the cloth was removed, by Dr. Charles H. Mathews, toast master.

The following year, the Fourth of July programme was somewhat different. The day was ushered in by firing a salute from the brass 6 pounder of the Diller Artillerists, while the band played patriotic airs on the portico roof of the Court house. At 12 a national salute was fired from "Mount Timothy," an elevated piece of ground on the southwestern edge of the borough, now cut through by streets. In the afternoon there was a public picnic in Riale's Grove, on the northwest edge of the town, and the festivities of the day were concluded with dancing in the Court house in the evening. The *Democrat*, in speaking of the band playing on the Court house portico roof says: "It enlivened the morning with the soul-stirring strains of music as it broke forth in loud and heart-softening melodies, drowning all the feelings but those the most patriotic." The musical critic of the *Democrat* seems to have been very much affected, but doubtless survived it.

About this time the lecture fever broke out and continued, off and on, for several years. The first in it was David Paul Brown, Philadelphia, who lectured for the benefit of the Methodist Episcopal church, February 16, 1844; on Tuesday evening, October 21, 1845, the Rev. John Chambers, Philadelphia, in the Presbyterian church, subject, "The value of Scriptures and the value of circulating them;" Colonel John W. Forney, Philadelphia, Saturday evening, November 22, subject, "Our country and its people;" and Tuesday evening December 16, Morton McMichael, of Philadelphia, subject not mentioned. From this record, the Quaker City was quite largely drawn upon for the mental and social entertainment of Doylestown. The "Doylestown Scientific and Literary Institute" was in operation in 1846, but we do not know when it was organized nor how long it lived. On one evening, of that year, George Lear, Esq., lectured before it on the subject; "Which is the most dangerous to human conduct precipitation or procrastination?" On Friday evening, January 20th, Colonel Thomas W. Duffield, of Frankford, Philadelphia county, lectured at Doylestown but the subject has not come down to us. Colonel Duffield was a man of some considerable note in the social and political life of that period.

We now come to the era of picnics, a social function that afforded all who participated, and not unfrequently the lookers on, a deal of pleasure and amusement. They became the fashion in the early forties, and, by the middle of the decade had developed into affairs of social importance. If anything, Doylestown took the lead. The late John J. Brock was one of the leading spirits, probably the foremost, and no event gave more solid enjoyment to the young. One was held at Doylestown every year for several years. That of July 4, 1845, in Harvey's grove, the general place for holding them, was

SAMUEL F. DuBOIS.

a noted affair. Two hundred of both sexes were present; tables were spread with elegant refreshments; during the afternoon there was dancing in the grove, and, in the Court House in the evening, the Doylestown brass band furnishing the music.

The picnic held in Harvey's grove, August 6, 1847, the reporter of the *Bucks County Intelligencer* gives an elaborate account of, and, quoting from his report he said the following :

"The crowd of vehicles came from all points of the compass—dust flying, horses reeking, ribbons fluttering and happy hearts beating. From the shores of the Delaware to those of the Schuylkill, and as far north as the boundary of Penn's purchase, fixed by the Indian Walk, the gallantry and beauty of the land came pouring in. From the city, from Norristown, Bethlehem and every village along the Delaware, and town and borough of midland Bucks, there were delegates fair as the Causcasian mountains ever submitted to the polished mirror's face.

"At about ten in the morning, the guests began moving towards the grove, where a dancing floor of spacious dimentions had been laid down. From this time, until ten at night, the road was covered with vehicles of all descriptions, going and coming, racing and flying. Our two townsmen of the livery, Weikel and Booz, each with an omnibus (renowned sons of the ribbon and the whip!) performed prodigies that might have amazed the charioteers on the olympian plain. The dancing began—the waving and undulating of wreaths and gauzes and flounces, the glittering of sapphires, of bracelets, of strings of pearl, diamonds and emeralds, breastpins and cameos, garlands and buckels, silks, lawns and cambrics, laces vainly aiming to hide the alabaster underneath them, and embroidery creeping zig-zag mazes like gamble electricity in the cloud."

"A long table, canopied by the umbrageous boughs, presented a delectable spectacle to the undinnered multitude; and, when the signal came, most ample devotion was paid to the delicious collation. It were vain to attempt any description of the dulcet freight under which the table groaned; there was the whole family of cakes to the utmost generation, from the jumble to the mountain patriarch, thatched with evergreen, and cap'd like alpine summit with its glittering dome of snow. Then beef and tongue, ham and bacon, thrown in by way of substantial props amid the more fanciful and less stable viands. There was lemonade with mid-winter coldness, and ice-cream with a chill not unworthy the Arctic circle, and a flavor that would credit the Tropic of Capricorn.

"Then came night, and the grove turned into a Champs Elyses. The noble arch o'er head, formed by the towering oaks, became a firmament studded with lamps and torches. The way-lost wanderer, suddenly encountering the scene, might well have mistaken the spot for one of fabled enchantment, where nymphs and fairies were tripping to music made by kindred spirits of their magic realms. But before the meridian as some child of song has dubbed it, the noon of night came on, the threaders of the mazy dance had vanished, the lights were gone, the last neigh of the steed and footfall on the leafy turf, ceased to be heard."[1]

One of the features, of the Doylestown picnics of 1840-50, was that of the committe paying the entire expense, and they who attended were guests in reality, coming by card invitation. Similar social affairs were held in neighboring counties, but the ones at Doylestown were conceded to be the most enjoyable. On one occasion a delegation from Doylestown drove over to the Yellow Springs, Chester county. "Harvey's Grove," the place of holding picnics here, was the timber at present belonging to the Oakland property and fronting on West Court street.

The picnic period that had its birth in the forties, lasted, to some extent, through the fifties, and was revived at the close of the Civil War in the sixties, but gave up the ghost in the early seventies. Their life was prolonged, somewhat, by the erection of the large exhibition building, 1866, but the picnic, to those who knew, and enjoyed this social function from 1840 to 1852, now lives only in history and will never be revived. The erection of Doylestown Seminary spoiled Harvey's grove for picnic purposes, and the cutting down of Riale's woods did the same for that beautiful piece of timber. The last picnic at Doylestown, before the Civil War, was held September 5, 1860, of which a pretty full account was given in the papers of that day. It took place in Harvey's grove, and N. P. Brower, Edwin Fretz, Theodore P. Harvey, E. L. Rogers, J. W. Cowell, T. W. Robinson, E. W. Knight, George H. Rees, John Blair, J. S. Rhoads, Benjamin Cadwallader, M. S. Stewart, W. C. Warford, J. H. Harvey, M. O. Kulp and Henry L. DuBois were managers; and the floor managers,

---

[1] We hope the author survived this effusion, and, as his death notice is not found among our obituaries, we presume he did, but, was never heard from again in similar strains. It almost takes one's breath!

ex-Sheriff Joseph S. Ely, William DuBree and John Harman. For a period they were held annually, in the Exhibition building, and one of the last was on Thursday, August 15, 1872, when the building was lighted with old locomotive headlights, borrowed from the North Penn railroad, The music stand was in one wing of the building, and, right back of it, Connard Hahl furnished refreshments to the gay crowd. The picturesqueness, of the social gatherings, was spoiled when the invited guests came and returned by train. Among the masters of ceremonies, of these latter day picnics, were Charles H. Magill, H. H. Gilkeson, John Hart and Henry Lear, who live to recount their exploits to their children.

About the beginning of the fifties a coterie of our young people, some in their teens and others older, formed a social organization and, for want of a better name, called it the "Bob Narrative Society." It met once a week at different houses for social enjoyment, with a little fun and a trifle of literary culture thrown in. At that time a resident of the borough, and one of the brightest young men in the village, was in his prime, and wrote much for the papers. On one occasion he tried his caustic quill on the "Bob Narrative" and lammed the members in the columns of the *Doylestown Democrat.* This was resented, and the following shortly appeared in the *Bucks County Intelligencer,* in response:

"At a special meeting of the 'Bob Narrative Society,' held at the house of Mrs. Fuzzlegudgeon, 'Hannah Hateful' was called to the chair and 'Hypocritical Emily' appointed secretary, whereupon 'Crafty Abigail' arose and stated the object of the meeting. The chair now appointed 'Ruth Tattler,' 'Lucy Meddler' and 'Crafty Abigail' a committee to report a preamble and resolutions expressive of the sense of the society on the subject under consideration. The committee, having retired, returned in a few minutes and reported the following:

"Whereas   of this borough, the head and front of that modern school of literature, which '*always lives upon the perfumed breath of sympathy,*' or '*like a dark ringlet* resting upon a *green mantilla stretches out the turnpike,*' has been pleased to come down from his resting place, '*in brilliant gorgeousness amid the twinkling stars and gorgeous planets,*' and compliments the society of which we are members, we feel in duty bound to express our appreciation of the flattering notice. We assure this distinguished individual that we fully appreciate his intellectual effort in our behalf, and his pains-taking to spread the '*euphonious and intellectual designation*' of our society abroad among the people; and we are quite happy our honorable and ancient society has been the channel through which his over-charged intellect has been given vent, and his head prevented from bursting. It is so very seldom *such* among the literati condescend to dismount from their Pegassus and notice the dwellers on this poor, dull earth of ours, it is more necessary, on this occasion, to mete our award of praise. We take delight in doing impartial justice to his literary merit, and have no hesitancy in pronouncing him one of the greatest *ass*-piring geniuses of modern times; and his far fetched figures, and ' deep, glowing and untold erudition have added much to the wealth of the literary world. His acquirements, literary and other labors, have been so varied we can apply to him the following lines from Dryden:

> ' A man so various, that he seem'd to be
> Not one, but all mankind's epitome;
> Stiff in opinions, always in the wrong,
> Was everything by starts and nothing long:
> But in the course of one revolving moon
> Was chemist, fiddler, statesman and buffoon.'

"We are pleased the name of this society has given rise to a literary production that will be placed in the same category with ' Orphan Jane' and ' Time and its Home Faults,' which, though we are not able to appreciate them, are said to be, in regard to their beauties and merits, as '*varied as are the pumpkins in a corn field.* Therefore:

"*Resolved.* That being fully impressed with the literary merits of the Bard of Doylestown, he is hereby tendered the thanks of this society for his complimentary notice in the *Doylestown Democrat*, of the eighth inst. and that the said article be filed among the records of the society for future reference.

"*Resolved.* That the chair is ordered to have made and present to him a *leather medal* as a reward for the gallant manner in which he writes and speaks of the young ladies of this place.

"*Resolved.* That these proceedings be signed by the officers and published in the *Bucks County Intelligencer*. On motion the meeting adjourned."[2]

(Signed) "Hannah Hateful,"
"Hypocritical Emily," Secretary. President.

Doylestown has had but three organizations that approached Club

---

[2] The foregoing will be better understood by our saying the quotations, except that from Dryden, are from the writings of the assailant of the "Bob Narrative Society."

life, so called, and these were not strictly so, the "Social Dozen" in the early part of the century, the "T. O. S. Club" in the last quarter and the "Acorn Club," organized near its close, and the only one in existence. The first meeting of the latter was in December, 1893, when members of the committee, appointed to prepare rooms, met at the office of Robert M. Yardley. Henry O. Harris was called to the chair and John Yardley chosen secretary. On motion, the following committees were appointed: On furniture, paper and carpets, Frederick Tibbils, William C. Newell and Henry O. Harris; finance, George P. Brock, William C. Newell and John Yardley; janitor, George P. Brock and R. M. Yardley; name, Harman Yerkes, Henry O. Harris and R. M. Yardley. The next meeting was held at the same place, January 6, 1894, Mr. Harris acting as chairman and John Yardley, secretary. It was proposed to keep the list of charter members open for ten days; the committee on name reported in favor of "Acorn Club," with the motto, "Tall oaks from little acorns grow," which was adopted. The following officers were elected by ballot for the ensuing year: president, Harman Yerkes; vice president, Robert M. Yardley; treasurer, T. O. Atkinson; secretary, John Yardley; board of governors, Edward H. Buckman, Frederick Tibbils, George P. Brock, Henry O. Harris and Henry Lear. A Constitution, By-Laws and regulations were adopted, but when or where, the minutes do not mention. The object of the club was stated to be "for the purpose of providing entertainment and promoting social intercourse," the admission fee was fixed at ten dollars and annual dues twelve dollars. It has about fifty regular members. The first stated meeting was held the evening of February 10, 1894. The club occupies the same quarters it moved into upon its organization, the former Lloyd building, on the south side of East Court street.

One of the most pleasant social functions in Doylestown, of recent years, was the celebration of the fortieth anniversary of the marriage of the late John J. Brock and wife, on November 23, 1893. It gathered about them relatives and friends, including many of the leading people of the county's capital.

In a subsequent chapter will be found another feature of the social life of the county capital, wherin music played an important part.

Doylestown, Old and New.

XVIII
Mercantile Life.

In a previous Chapter we mentioned the pioneer storekeepers at Doylestown, embracing a period from 1790 to 1810, and, in the present Chapter, we purpose to complete the mercantile roll of those who have passed into history.

J. and C. Brock,[1] from Philadelphia, were an enterprising firm doing business here when the last century came in, and continued several years, but at what time they opened we are unable to say. In November, 1815, they added iron to their stock, and must have done an extensive trade from their advertising. In 1817 they advertised groceries, "Such as gunpowder, imperial young hyson and hyson skin teas." They closed out, March 1818, and returned to the city, but a John Brock [2] was keeping store here, 1835, but we do not know that he was the same person. On November 22, 1813, Thomas White[3] & Co. opened a store in a building formely occupied by the Messrs Reeds, "opposite the Doylestown Hotel," the present Fountain House. At this time Shaw & Morris appeared to have been leading storekeepers in the village, from the way they patronized printers' ink. They opened in June, 1813. The Shaw was probably

---

1 At Philadelphia, May 23, 1816, by the Rev. Philip F. Mayer, John Brock, of Doylestown, to Miss Catharine Eliza Egert, daughter of George Egert of the Northern Liberties, Philadelphia.

2 At Friends' meeting, October 11, 1827, Mark Wilson of Quakertown, to Mary Brock, daughter of John Brock of Doylestown.

3 On December 6, same year, 1813, Thomas White & Co. succeeded Messrs. Reeds in a general store oppositethe Doylestown hotel. This was on the east side of North Main street just above State.

Josiah Y. and his partner, Benjamin Morris. In 1817, Harvey & Dunlap were in the mercantile business in Doylestown, and Henry Scholl [4] in 1818.

Samuel Yardley was the leading storekeeper here seventy-five years ago, and was probably longer, continuously, in mercantile business than any one who preceded him. He and Benjamin W. Taylor, under the firm name of Yardley & Taylor, opened in 1820. They kept on the Armstrong corner, Yardley living in the adjoining dwelling, then, or subsequently, buying the property. The firm was dissolved, March 3, 1826, Yardley continuing in business.[5] Taylor was from the neighborhood of Dolington and the Yardleys born near Doylestown. Samuel's brother, Charles,[6] was with him as a salesman and clerk until 1826, when he opened a store in Newtown. Samuel Yardley owned and ran a grist mill at Spring Valley, burned down in the forties, probably the same that Ralph Sheelly afterward bought. It is said Yardley & Taylor first opened in the old frame on the site of Thompson's brick store, now the site of the Hellyer store.

Joseph Burrows was an early keeper of an iron store, being here in that business as early as 1825. He was the same who kept the "Green Tree," and afterwards built and kept the "Temperance House" before it was licensed. The same year, one John Allshouse kept a hat store " nearly opposite the residence of Mr. DuBois on the road leading to New Hope, having removed from the Main street." This was opposite the old DuBois dwelling, corner of Broad and State streets, and Allshouse occupied one of the frames opposite.

John H. Anderson [7] removed to Doylestown, 1831, and opened

---

4 At Arnwell, N. J., on Thursday, April 23, 1818, by the Rev. Mr. Kirkpatrick, Henry Scholl, merchant, to Miss Mary Kiple, both of Doylestown.

5 At Doylestown, October 15, 1844, Friends' ceremony, Joseph Mathers, of Montgomery county, to Lydia, daughter of Samuel Yardley of Doylestown.

6 At Doylestown, May 10, 1826, Charles Yardley to Miss Anne Jones, both of Doylestown. Mrs. Yardley survived her husband until March 23, 1897, dying at Bethlehem, Pa., in her 92nd year, retaining her faculties to a remarkable degree. Mrs. Yardley was the sister of the Miss Jones, who died at Judge Watts', Doylestown, of typhus fever, in February, 1815.

7 John H. Anderson was the son of Joshua Anderson, a farmer of Stockton, Hunterdon county, N. J., and born there. His grand-father, John Anderson, was a Captain of Militia in the Revolution. John H. began keeping store at Flemington, N. J., but, being boycotted for not selling liquor, he removed to Doylestown. He was twice married, his first wife being a daughter of Mahlon Hart, Flemington; his second a daughter of Thomas Alexander. He had several children, sons and daughters. His son, John A. was Superintendent of the Relief Department Pennsylvania Railroad, Edward L. several years Comptroller of New Jersey and recently Supervisor of the New Jersey state prison, and another son, Wm. L. is a civil engineer of Trenton. The daughters married and raised families.

in the old frame on site of the Thompson brick store, and now covered by the Hellyer block, next door south of Monument House. He announced in his adver, "My motto is cheap." He took Isaiah P. Smith as partner, the first of April, under the firm name of Anderson & Smith. In 1837 they fitted up a drug and medicine department, and dissolved, 1843, Smith going to Philadelphia and Anderson to Lambertville, N. J., where he passed the balance of his business life and died there 1877. Smith returned to Doylestown and opened store where he and Anderson had kept, but we do not know how long he remained. Anderson was a successful business man.

About the close of the thirties, John O. James, then keeping store in Hilltown, desiring a change of location thought of coming to Doylestown and occupying the Anderson & Smith property, but his attention being directed to Philadelphia, he established a successful house under the firm name of James, Kent & Santee, Isaiah P. Smith becoming a partner. In the spring of 1897, the Messrs. Hellyer & Son purchased the old Thompson property, where they erected a large brick store house and started bussiness on that popular site. The property had previously been sold to two parties, the National Bank, with a view of erecting a new banking house on it, and to Thomas H. Heist for the purpose of enlarging the Monument House of which he was then the owner. In 1830, there were but five retailers of foreign merchandise in Doylestown and four in the township. In July, 1834, Robert Magill opened a leather store on the Easton road below Field's and Petitt's taverns on South Main street.

Rutledge Thornton succeeded Anderson & Smith in the same building, the old frame on the site of the Thompson brick. Thornton, who was born in Buckingham township, was keeping store in New Hope, 1834, and, in his advertisement, calls that the "Village of Plenty." He moved thence to Kintnerville, Nockamixon township, where he kept store until 1839, when he was elected Sheriff. In 1844 Mrs. Johnson, his mother-in-law, bought the store property where Anderson & Smith had kept, and Thornton opened there the following spring. The brick store was built in 1853, and Thornton kept there until near the close of the fifties, living in the adjoining frame house. He subsequently bought the Harvey lot, corner of State and Church, on which he built a handsome frame where he resided to his death. The property is now owned and occupied by Louis Buckman.

The third occupant, of this historic store, was William Thomp-

HELLYER'S STORE, 1897.

son,[8] a descendant of Scotch-Irish ancestors, who came to this country at an early day, and established a home in Northampton township. The Thompsons, father and son, were prominent in the mercantile life of Doylestown. Mr. Thompson, the elder, removed to Doylestown about 1849, and followed his trade, that of a carpenter, until 1851, when he was elected Register of Wills. In 1856, he rented the Thornton store property and continued in business until his death, 1892, a portion of the time the firm being William Thompson & Son. Under this roof the Thompsons rounded out their business career, the son dying two years after the father. The son was executor of Mrs. Thornton, the widow of Rutledge, and purchased the property, 1890, subsequently selling it to Hellyer & Son, who erected the new store house now on it. Robert Thompson was born in Northampton township, 1825, came to Doylestown with his father, and, shortly after, entered the store of Thornton, later going into business with his father. He was a patriotic, public spirited citizen, served as a member of the borough council several years, and, during the Civil War, went out with the 128th Pa. regiment as sutler, and witnessed the stirring scenes at Antietam and Chancellorsville.

In 1835, Jonathan Brock opened a store at the old stand of Benjamin Morris, on the east side of South Main street, just below State, the latter quitting the store on being elected Sheriff, and never resuming the business. In April, 1839, Samuel A. Smith opened a general store in the same building, the late Cashier John J. Brock beginning his successful career as a salesman for ——— Smith. In 1844, Mr. Brock went into business with James Smith in the same building, but the venture was not a successful one. Smith subsequently went to Philadelphia and spent his life there with two or three large mercantile establishments, and John J. Brock shortly entered the Doylestown bank where he spent his life. Smith was the son of General Samuel A. Smith, of this county, a prominent figure in political and military life.

In 1841, John Clemens, son of Christian Clemens, of Doylestown township, opened an iron store at the junction of South Main and Green streets and kept there several years. After he closed out, the borough council took action to get the old building out of the way,

---

8 At Prospect Hill, November 24, 1831, by Parson Studdiford, William Thompson, of Northampton township, to Miss Isabella, daughter of James Simpson, of Buckingham.

it being an obstruction to the streets. This was in the seventies. In 1840, these were the following retailers of foreign merchandise in Doylestown: Samuel A. Smith, Samuel Yardley, Charles Harvey, Isaiah P. Smith, Samuel Nightingale and Moses and Robert Armstrong. The Armstrongs kept in the Kramer store, North Main street and Harvey on the corner where Randall keeps a hardware store.

The first lumber yard in Doylestown, that we have any note of, was that of Clemens & Timothy Smith, opened 1812. In their advertisement they pledged themselves to deliver all lumber bought at their yard, within a mile and half of the town, at the same price as at the yard. We have no knowledge how long they remained in business.

One would suppose Doylestown was not without a board yard after it became the County seat, but there are indications there was a longer, or shorter period when it was not thus equipped. How it was through the twenties we are not informed. One of the town papers in the thirties, in the enumeration of the different kinds of business carried on here, said: "It will soon be time to start a board yard," from which we may infer this business was not carried on here at that time. How soon after this a board-yard was opened we have no means of knowing; but as there was considerable building between thirty and forty the town was doubtless soon supplied with one.

Robert Bayard had a lumber yard in Doylestown, 1843, and perhaps earlier up in "Germany," North Main street, near the Cold Spring tavern. The Bayards were here ten years prior to that time to the knowledge of the author, as he and Robert Bayard, a son, were school mates at the Union Academy.

Samuel Solliday was proprietor of a board-yard in the forties but, at what time he went into business we do not know.[9] At one time he occupied the vacant lot between the dwelling of Mrs. McCoy and Mrs. N. C. James, North Main street, covering the site of the latter, and he may have been located elsewhere. At the same time he carried on clock and watch-making on the south side of East State street, about opposite Printers' Alley.

Toward the close of the fifties, John Clemens opened a board yard on what is now the Buckman property, west side of South Main street, and erected a large building on the site of Buckman's sash

---

[9] We have a memo that Samuel Solliday had a board-yard in 1826, but we have no knowledge whereat. It was hardly at Doylestown at that early day.

factory and planing mill. In the upper story was a large unfurnished room called "Clemens' Hall" used for social purposes. The 22nd of February, 1859, a civil and military dress ball was given there that was quite a swell affair, for the county volunteers and militia which, at that time were in high feather. In that same room Captain Davis drilled and disciplined the Doylestown Guards prior to taking the company into the field, in the Civil War, April, 1861.

Shortly after the war, Henry M. Twining, now of Philadelphia, carried on for a time, in this same building, pork-packing and sausage-making. Charles Wigton next purchased the property and opened a lumber and coal yard, but sold it to Charles Finney, 1870. Finney built the stack and carried on business there, Wigton & Trumbower opening business on the premises below.

In the meantime, Charles Shade and Charles Rotzel opened a board-yard in the early fifties on a vacant lot south side of East State street from about the Gaucher house, running east and bounded by York street on the south. Here their barn was burned in 1856 with two horses. About 1860 they removed to a vacant lot on the Magill property, south side of West State street two hundred feet from Main. Shade died while the firm was in business here, shortly after the close of the Civil War. The Magill property was now brought into the market, and Rotzel closed out the business.

Sometime in the seventies, Charles Finney [10] was sold out by the Sheriff, his property, on South Main street, going under the hammer to Charles Rotzel & Co., the "Company" being composed of John M. Purdy, Elias Hoagland and Lewis Buckman. They opened a lumber and coal yard and carried on a good business, but there were changes in the composition of the firm. The first change was to Rotzel and Buckman, 1878-84; then Lewis Buckman, 1884-90; next Buckman & Son, 1890-96, and finally to Edward H. Buckman & Co., the present proprietors. Shortly after Mr. Rotzel left the firm, he purchased a new site on the north side of West State street, beyond Clinton, where he carried on the lumber and coal business to his death, 1896. The business then passed into the hands of William Raike, a graduate of the *Democrat* office, and is still carried on by him. In 1832, there was neither a coal nor lumber yard, nor an apothecary in Doylestown, which had been the county seat for nineteen years.

Joseph J. Greir, connected with the business life of Doylestown

---

10 Charles Finney came to Doylestown from Northampton township, where he was a respectable farmer and doing well.

for twenty years, was the son of James Jefferson and Eliza Jones Greir, and born at Greir's Corner, Plumstead township, April 23, 1828. He assisted his father on the farm and in his store until 1849, when he came to Doylestown and took employment with Rutledge Thornton as clerk and salesman at the old Anderson stand, on the site of the Hellyer store, Monument place. In 1853, Thornton took him in as partner, and he remained with him until 1857, when Greir purchased the William T. Eisenhart store on the west side of Main street just below State, and went into business for himself. He continued here until, 1869 when he sold out to Silas Yerkes. In January 1870, Greir removed to Philadelphia, where he went into the manufacturing business at 505 Market Street, which he carried on until the summer of 1873, when, on account of failing health, he removed to Newtown. In 1875, he entered into partnership with William R. Carver, his brother-in-law, in the dry goods business which they carried on until the fall of 1889, when they sold out to Evan S. Worthington, after which Mr. Greir lived a retired life until his death, November 26, 1895. The Greirs are an old family in Bucks county, settling here with the influx of the Scotch-Irish Presbyterians in the first quarter of the eighteenth century.

Doylestown, Old and New.

XIX
Our Industries.

Having noticed the professional and mercantile life of our borough, and other agencies, that assisted to lift the cross roads hamlet to the beautiful town of the present, we take a snap shop at our industries. These embrace minor and major industries, including mechanical trades, workmen and dealers outside of the mercantile line, without which a modern town is illy prepared to make its way in the world.

Mechanism, fortunately, rests on a higher plane than in the past, and men, brought up to trades and are graduates of the workshop, are reaping honors in every walk of life. No doubt there were tradesmen, and other industrial callings at the site of Doylestown, as they were needed, from the opening of the two highways crossing each other, in the first quarter of the eighteenth century but, as we have no record of them, we can only deal with those we know of. If the industries, of Doylestown, do not occupy a leading place in our business affairs, it is because the site of our county's capital is off the leading lines of travel, and the absence of water power. The mechanical trades here, at an early day, only supplied the local demand.

Minor industries are the first to establish themselves at a new settlement, and we find Andrew Dennison, a shoemaker, here 1804, if not earlier. He was a long time in business and lived in or near the village about half a century. We may say of him, as Daniel Webster said of the Revolutionary veterans he addressed at the dedication of the Bunker Hill monument; "you have come down to us from a former generation," and truthfully, for Dennison saw service in the war for Independence. He was not only a shoemaker, but aimed at something higher, for he courted the Muse of poetry. How early, he indulged in this occcomplishment, we do not know, but when he advertised his occupation, 1827, he opened with the following stanza :

> " I've moved my shop from Elbow Square [1]
> Six doors right down the street,
> Where I do mean to carry on,
> And do my work complete."

In the spring of 1833, when Andrew Dennison moved out of Doylestown, he announced the change in one of the local papers in the following lines:

> "From Doylestown I have moved this Spring,
> In Middletown I dwell,
> Between Bridge Point and the Turk's Head,
> I make shoes to sell."

Andrew Dennison was still here in 1841, the year his wife died,[2] and some years longer, dying past ninety. Dennison had not only a rival in making and mending shoes, but also in writing poetry, and it would require a poet of the highest order to tell which excelled the other. His name was Joseph Mackey. He opened here, 1827, and appealed to printers' ink in the columns of the *Bucks County Patriot* in the following strains:

> " I and the Muses,
> Send you a pair of Shoeses,
> A tough rythme this
> Just like my leather."

It is to be hoped Joseph Mackey flourished—at least he deserved to, with such poetry to sustain him. We had always understood the shoemaker's trade was provocative of sentiment and we are now convinced of it.

Benjamin Vanluvanee was another old-time shoemaker, a veteran, he deserves to be called. He was born in what was then New Britain, now Doylestown township, May 19, 1789, married December 31, 1812, and died February 20, 1873, at the age of eighty-three years, nine months and one day. He began building a house 1812, probably

---

1 Can any of our readers enlighten us as to the location of " Elbow Square ?"

2 At Doylestown, November 2, 1841, Susanna Dennison, wife of Andrew Dennison, in her eightieth year. Her husband survived her at eighty-seven with two children out of a family of nine. They were married in 1781, and lived together sixty years six months and fifteen days." Andrew Dennison a soldier of the Rovolution and a pensioner, died at Doylestown, February 24, 1847, in his ninety-first year.

to celebrate his marriage, and, when finished, moved into it, following his trade there for fifty-seven years. This was the house where John Moyer lived for sometime on North Main street, nearly opposite the Kramer store property, with shop adjoining. A few years prior to his death, Vanluvanee sold the house to Henry Hough and moved into the township, but returned to the borough and died at the house of one of his sons. He was a good citizen and respected by his neighbors and friends. Two of his sons lived in the borough until recently, one following the trade of his father. One of them Henry, a soldier of the Union Army in the Civil War, died at Doylestown December 2, 1897, at the age of eighty-two, having been born May 3, 1815. Like his father, he was a shoemaker, and followed the trade until within a few years of his death. He was one of a family of nine children, the only survivor being his brother, A. Chapman Vanluvanee, who had lived continuously in Doylestown from his birth, June 1, 1824, to his death December 20, 1901, seventy-seven years and six months, and like his father and three brothers, was a shoemaker by trade. He followed it until ill health compelled him to retire, 1899. He married Mrs. Catharine Troxel, in early life, who lived less than a year. Two sisters survive him, Mrs. Clement Arment and Miss Jane Vanluvanee both living in West Philadelphia. Mr. Vanluvanee was buried by Odd Fellows' ceremony. Before Henry Vanluvanee's death, he was the oldest living person born in Doylestown, was twice married and left a widow of eighty-one. Next to Mr. Vanluvanee, Mrs. Andrew Rickard, who was an Opp, had lived the longest time in Doylestown, at her death, November 1901.

In 1820, Thomas B. Most was a maker and seller of boots in Doylestown, including "full dress boots, Cossacks, Wellington and Monroes," and this is all we know of him. Most's specialties, the fad of that day, have passed into history with their makers and sellers. The "Wellingtons," borrowed their name from the great English Duke who came off conqueror at Waterloo.

We have spoken of William Musgrave, in a previous chapter, who was doubtless the pioneer clock and watch maker at Doylestown, a Canadian who came here at the dawn of the nineteenth century. He married Mrs. Mary Kelley, widow of Rev. Erasmus Kelley, a distinguished Baptist divine and pastor of the First Baptist church, at Newport, Rhode Island. Musgrave removed from Doylestown to Harrisburg, where his wife died, February 10, 1817, at the age of sixty-four.

In 1813, James Lane, clock and watch maker, watch case

maker and fire gilder, removed from Philadelphia to Doylestown, but all trace of him is lost.

William McHenry was here in the trade as early as 1816,[3] at his old stand, next door to J. and C. Brock's store, "opposite the Doylestown Hotel." This would place him in the old frame on the east side of North Main street where the *Democrat* was burnt out, 1836. It will be remembered that McHenry was one of the landlords of the Indian Queen tavern, and, later in life, removed to Pike county where he died.

The Pennsylvania Correspondent, of September 15, 1823, says:

Charles T. Beckel, silversmith, clock and watch and musical instrument maker, has opened his shop near the tavern of Mr. Burrows." This was, doubtless, the same Beckel, who captained a brass band at this period, and met to practice at the Green Tree tavern, whence he dropped out and became

"Lost to memory dear."

The next to appear, of this trade, was Isaac W. Ely, whom we first encounter April 25, 1831, who "informs his friends and the public that he has removed to the house next door to Isaac B. Medary's tailor-shop, opposite to J. Y. Shaw, Esq., in Doylestown." This was the John Donnelly house, corner of Main and Centre streets subsequently named Oakland avenue. Ely was evidently here prior to 1831, as the occupancy of this house was only a "removal" from some other place in the village.

Charles Savage, the next to answer the clock and watch maker's roll-call, came in 1834. He, also, called himself a silversmith, and opened in the frame on the sight of the Stuckert building, North Main street, opposite the Fountain House. It will be remembered the *Democrat* was published in that building, 1835-36, and, in the winter of the latter year, the building was burned with its contents—press, types, etc., and Savage's clocks and watchs, and silverware all went up in smoke.

In the spring, of 1834, Samuel Solliday opened a clock and watch-making shop in Mrs. Thompson's stone house, west side of North Main street, between Hellyer's and the Armstrong block. From there he removed to the south side of East State street, site of Lehman's butcher shop, and subsequently to New Hope where he died. The

---

[3] At Painswick Hall, the residence of Nathaniel Shewell, Esq., March 6, 1817, by the Rev. Uriah DuBois, William McHenry, to Miss Margaret Fell, daughter of the late Joseph Fell, Esq.

FISHER'S OLD SMITH SHOP.

late Nathan C. James, Esq., many years president of the Bucks County Bar Association, was one of Solliday's apprentices, an example of what energy and talent may do for a young man.

Tradition, as well as record evidence, tells us that Joseph Fell was one of the earliest blacksmiths at Doylestown—at least prior to, and and at the time of, the Revolution. His shop was at the southwest corner of what afterward became the site of the "Ross Mansion." There were doubtless earlier blacksmiths at the cross roads, but Fell's name is the first to come down to us. Of Fell we have spoken generally in a previous chapter.

Anthony Miller was a blacksmith here in 1814, having recently begun business. He advertised, in Minor's *Correspondent*, "some unprincipled villain" for entering his smith shop and "with a knife or other instrument, had cut and nearly ruined his bellows;" speaking of himself as one "who is preparing to commence business in the place." There is no record of the length of his stay.

In May, 1821, Robert Ashton was on the Doylestown roll of blacksmiths, and offered a reward for a "second-hand leather apron," for the apprehension of a runaway apprentice. Whether Ashton recovered this valuable assistant to his bellow's blower and striker, is not recorded in the annals that have fallen under our notice.

Charles Wigton, whom the present generation remembers, began blacksmithing at Doylestown, April, 1832. The Wigtons were here early in the century, as we find two of them on Burges' map of 1810, "S. Wigton," on the east side of North Main street above Broad, and "J. Wigton" on the north side of East State street about where Maple avenue comes in. What relation, the subject of our notice, was to either or both, we do not know, but we believe Charles was born here. He carried on his trade for several years, but, subsequently, went into the coal and lumber business, became a land owner, built several houses and acquired a moderate competency. Charles Wigton spent his life here; was much respected, a man of influence, an active politician and, in 1860, was nominated for Register, but defeated at the polls with the ticket. His death, was a loss to the town. In his youth, Mr. Wigton lived in the Judge Watts' family. The Wigtons settled in this vicinity shortly after the middle of the eighteenth century, and the family was on the highlands, west of Doylestown, where the old mansion was built.

Joseph Derrickson, a coachmaker and wagon builder, was probably in Doylestown prior to 1811, for, in that year, he advertised for a journeyman. The prospect of the village becoming the county seat may have improved business, and created the necessity for more mechanics, but how long he remained we have no means of telling.

Smith & Kirk commenced coachmaking here in 1815, manufacturing every description of coaches, buggies, chairs, sulkeys and mail stages. In 1827, Jervis S. Smith and John Hess bought out Smith & Kirk; carried on business for a time, and were succeeded by Timothy Smith who built "coaches, razees, gigs, chairs, sulkeys and dearborn wagons." Smith continued in business a number of years, acquired considerable real estate, and died here. He was a prominent member of the community. His ownership of the elevated piece of ground on the southwestern borders of the village gave the name to "Mount Timothy." This was cut down to make way for a new street. Mr. Smith lived in the frame dwelling south side of East State street, opposite the foot of Printers' alley. The store house, on the same side of the street—in one half of which Thomas Gaucher lived and died, was Timothy Smith's barn but fitted it up for a dwelling in the early thirties.

In the Spring of 1831, a new worker in the wagon trade, John F. Purdy set up wheelwrighting here. He was a son of William Purdy, recently appointed Prothonotary, and lived in a frame on the site of the dwelling of the late John P. Rogers, east side of North Main street, and worked in a shop on the same premises. He remained there three or four years.

In November, 1840, there was an accession to the mechanical industries of Doylestown by the advent of Barzilla J. Gregg, a wheelwright and coachmaker. He lived in one of the brick dwellings on the south side of West State street for several years and had his work shop at various places about town. He was quite a character, well read on many subjects, and nothing delighted him more than to argue the questions of the day with anyone who came along. During such discussions, busidess was laid aside. Gregg's wheelwright shop, in one sense, was a free-lance debating club especially for those who loved talk better than work. A history of some of these discussions would make interesting reading. Mrs. Gregg, a most estimable woman and of much culture, kept school in the basement of their dwelling several years, and here a number of persons obtained the rudiments of their education. They both died there ; she at the close of the eighties, and he sometime in that decade. Mrs. Gregg was a descendant of the Gilberts, among the earliest settlers of Warminster township.

She was somethimg of an artist, and a production of her skill hangs in the museum of the Bucks County Historical Society, a painting, on velvet, of "A View of Fair Mount Water Works." The frame handsome and elaborate, is her own make.

On September 12, 1804, John Worman opened a tailor shop at the cross roads hamlet of "Doylestown." He may have had predecessors, but we have not met with them, and was probably the same John Worman who kept one of the taverns here at that period. In the *Pennsylvania Correspondent*, of September 18, 1804, Gooden Hall states, over his own signature, that "he had recommenced business (tailoring) at the house of John Worman in Doylestown, but, beyond this, there is nothing that throws light on the subject. When and where Hall first opened his business is entirely unknown. In so far as we are informed, either Worman or Hall is entitled to the honor of having been dean of the craft at that period. Gooden, or Goden, Hall, for the name was spelled both ways at that period, was a nephew of Isaac Hall, and his name appears on George Burges' map of Doylestown in 1810. His dwelling, and probably his shop, also, was on the north side of West State street, east of its junction with court. In April, 1813, Hall removed to Main street, "one hundred rods north of the Court House."

Isaac B. Medary,[4] a tailor by trade, was here prior to 1813, for, on the 15th of March of that year, the firm of "Medary & Heath, tailors," dissolved co-partnership. In Asher Miner's *correspondent* of December 16, 1814, Medary inserted an advertisement, in which he says; "Having returned from a tour of military duty. I will immediately resume the duties of the shop."[5] Medary continued in business, for many years, in the stone house at the northwest corner of Main street and Oakland avenue. He built the house, 1814, and probably moved into it in April, 1815. This is the same house in which Nathan Cornell lived and carried on his trade, also a tailor, for several years. As we recollect Isaac B. Medary, after the lapse of many years, he was a handsome, well-mannered man, much esteemed by all his acquaintances and prosperous in business. The last few years, of his life at Doylestown, he lived just out of town on the handsome farm on the right hand side of the New Hope Pike, and, in the

---

4 At Hatboro, March 9, 1815, Isaac B. Medary, Doylestown, to Miss Rebecca Childs of Hatboro.

5 He was a soldier in Captain Wm. Magill's rifle company, which served a tour of duty on the lower Delaware, 1814, in the war with England.

early forties, himself and family removed to Philadelphia. The son, Louis, who changed the spelling of his name to Mederie, preceded the father to the city and entered into business, becoming prominent in shipping circles, and died there in recent years.

In 1815, a woman, Mrs. Barclay, came to Doylestown and advertised that she proposes to devote her time to the business of "Tailoring and Mantau-making," in order to provide for a young family that had devolved upon her. In April, 1821, Timothy Mc Manus, a tailor, gives notice that he had removed to Doylestown, and taken the house, "on the east side of the stage road between Esq. Chapman's law office and Robert Armstrong's store." [6]

James Blackhurst, tailoring here, in 1829, removed next below Robert Armstrong's store, and advertised he had "just returned with the Paris Fall and Winter fashions for 1829," and all who favor him with their custom "may depend on not having their coats too long on the skirts of society." He removed to within a mile of Quakertown, in October, 1831. James Harl, who was tailoring here in 1826, commenced business in Nathan Cornell's house, formerly Isaac B. Medary's west side of South Main street, where Mrs. Randall carries on, in which the *Doylestown Democrat* was published more than half a century ago. Nathan Michener was a Mercer and Tailor at Doylestown in 1829-31. George A. Huntsmann had a tailor shop at his former residence on the Main street, a few doors below Mr. Ransey's iron foundry—"Country produce taken in exchange for work." In 1832 the roll of tailors was increased by the accession of Abraham Gray, who occupied a shop "between the Post Office and the Temperance House, in the most central part of the town." This was on the south side of East Court, between Main and Pine, the Post Office probably being in the Shearer frame, on the site of the Siegler building.

John Seitzinger was one of the best known tailors in Doylestown sixty-five years ago, commencing about the close of the twenties. He occupied the house of Mrs. Thomas Walton on the east side of South Main street living in the building. He was here many years, and active in the Episcopal church, assisting in its organization.

William T. Eisenhart, well-remembered by the present generation, came here and set up tailoring in 1849, over half a century ago,

---

6 This was in "Germany," on the east side of North Main street; Armstrongs store the same as that lately occupied by John Kramer, and the "house" one of the dwellings south of it.

carrying it on with varying success. His place of business, for several years, was on the west side of South Main street, in the brick block built about 1854-55. About 1850 he adopted the motto "No Fit No Pay," but whether this increased trade we are not informed. In his later years, he removed to a dwelling on Ashland, between Main and Clinton opposite the Agricultural works, where, in connection with his trade, he paid some attention to the cultivation of strawberries at which he was a success. On more than one occasion a friend of President Cleveland presented an invoice of Eisenhart's berries to the "First Lady of the Land;" for which courtesy, if European customs were followed, Mr. Eisenhart was entitled to a diploma as the "cultivator of strawberries to Her Excellenciess, the wife of the President." More than one polite note from the "First Lady" was evidence of her appreciation of the berries.

The next generation of tailors came near cleaning out that craft. In 1875, Burgoyne Rayton, an Englishman, came to Doylestown and set up in the business. At this time Gilbert Hay, William Hughes, Jacob Michener and one Euberoth plied the needle, but all have disappeared except Rayton. Euberoth came from about Bethlehem, whither he returned. His son was educated at the Annapolas Naval Academy, and entered the U. S. Cutter Service. The other tailor in Doylestown, who still carries on the business, is John Moyer, a German immigrant who came to this country in 1867, and to Doylestown, 1884. He found here Joseph Berger, now deceased, and another named Scheiley. Probably the oldest tailor, in years, in the county, is Philip H. Kepler, father-in-law of John Moyer, but Mr. Rayton is the Dean of the craft in Doylestown. The great clothing houses of the cities have driven nearly all the country tailors out of business, something much to be regretted.

The most pretentious industry Doylestown indulged in, manufacture of agricultural machinery, came at a later period. This was of considerable importance when carried on by Daniel Hulshizer. The business was started by Melick & Hulshizer, who came from Hunterdon county, New Jersey, to Doylestown in 1849. They began work in a small shop on "Oyster Shell Lane," which gradually grew and they turned out many horse powers and threshers. In 1851, they commenced the manufacture of agricultural implements, and were probably the first in the county to build "Wheeler's Patent Railway Chain Horse Power, Overshot Thresher, Feed Cutter and Clover Huller." During that summer while Mr. Hulshizer was walking through his stables, he was kicked by a strange horse and had two ribs broken. In 1859, the firm name was changed to Martin & Wetherill, and, 1865, they sold out to Daniel Hulshizer, who established a large plant on Ashland street near the railroad station, where Ruos carried on a branch of the same industry at a later period.

Mr. Hulshizer shortly enlarged the works and commenced the building of upright steam engines, the first one being constructed for the Doylestown Democrat office to run its Hoe power press and lasted several years, being the first engine built in the county of any kind. At this time the works gave employment to thirty or forty men. Mr. Hulshizer conducted the business, often with profit, until his death March 27, 1896. Meanwhile there had been two or three changes in the firm name, at one time Harry Larzelere being a member of it, but he removed to the Cumberland Valley and connected himself with an establishment there. During this period the firm supplied many creameries with machinery, and, while the boom was on, the demand was brisk.

Upon the death of Mr. Hulshizer, the Agricultural works fell into the hands of his son, W. Sharp Hulshizer, who owned them untill 1899, when he sold out to Henry D. Ruos, one of the proprietors of the Lenape Bicycle works, accepting the Bicycle works in part payment. The same evening, Mr. Hulshizer sold the Bicycle works to Ex-Sheriff Nicholas, who expected to re-establish there his Folding Box factory, recently destroyed by fire. The price paid was about $15,000, the sale including both plants. The property, subsequently, came into the possession of Ruos, Mills & Co., and is now employed in making and repairing agricultural machinery, having gone back to its "first love." The location of the works is on Ashland street near the Reading Railroad station, and is the oldest industrial establishment in Doylestown.

About 1850, Henry Druckenmiller came to Doylestown, from Lehigh county, and began wheelwrighting in Samuel Green's old shop at the intersection of Court and State streets, torn down many years ago, Craven's photographic gallery being built on the site. The business increased and gradually a good trade was built up with the south, whither a large number of light one horse buggies and carriages were shipped.

In 1857, Mr. Druckenmiller built a large brick shop on West Court street, opposite Harvey's grove, now Oakland, where he continued business, which prospered until the Civil War broke out.

This ruined him and he was obliged to close out. The property was subsequently sold by the Sheriff, the brick shop being purchased by Samnel Green. He utilized it for some time—but in after years it had two or three owners, one of them Samuel Geil; but was torn down in 1895 and a double brick dwelling erected on its site. If the past could be called up several first class ghost stories might be related, in connection with these premises, and others told not altogether ghostly.

When Wetherill and Martin 7 set up agricultural machinery works, at Doylestown, they opened in the old Fisher Smith shop West State street, north side near Main, but the building was torn down many years ago.

The bakers in Doylestown, first and last, have been almost legion, their number giving force to the adage that "bread is the staff of life." As it is impossible to call the roll of this necessary minor industry, we forego the attempt. In 1836, one John Barndollar was a baker here, and John Lyon 1840, but when they came, or how long they staid, we know not. In the recent past, many of our readers will remember Conrad Hahl as a baker, and especially his wife, who carried on the business after her husband's death and her remarriage to James S. Mann. She was a good business woman and well liked, and her ice cream was equally popular. The Hahls, for several years, carried on business on the west side of South Main street in a frame building, which was demolished when Oakland avenue was opened through to Main.

---

7 Joseph Martin, born in Stewartsville, Warren county, New Jersey, spent his business life in Doylestown, dying March 5, 1902. He came here in the sixties, and shortly connected himself with an agricultural implement factory, being for sometime with Daniel Hulshizer.

Doylestown, Old and New.

XX

More of Our Industries.

As our industries occupy more space than we anticipated, when we began writing them up, we make no apology for giving a second chapter to the same subject.

Samuel Kachline, prominent in his day, one of our earlier workers in wood, and a cabinet-maker by trade, was a descendant of John Peter Keichline, who settled in Bedminster township about 1740, and there Samuel was born. Of the pioneer's sons, Peter, Andrew and Charles, Peter commanded a company in Colonel Miles' regiment of riflemen in the Revolution, and was taken prisoner at the battle of Long Island. Lord Sterling wrote Washington, that the English General Grant was killed by some of Keichline's riflemen.

We do not know where Samuel Kachline learned his trade, but, the first we hear of him, was of his coming to Doylestown in 1812, and working on the public buildings then being erected. We now lose sight of him for a few years, but, in 1820, he set up in business here, and was married the following year.[1] He bought Timothy Smith's stock of tools and opened a shop on one of the corners of Garden alley and Pine street, then called "Shewell" street. This was probably at the northeast corner, where Judge Yerkes' tenant house stands. Here he carried on a successful business, as carpenter and nndertaker, for several years, until he was bought out by John P. Paul, who succeeded him. Subsequently to this, the date not known,

---

[1] By the Rev. Robert Boyd, September 16, 1821, Samuel Kachline, of Doylestown, to Miss Huldah Jones, daughter of John Jones of Buckingham.

OLD SPOKE FACTORY.

Samuel Kachline [2] went into the lumber business with Tobias L. Cressman and John Maugle, who had held public office here, opening a yard on the south side of East State street, occupying the Donaldson and Kochersperger's property, including the street between them. While here Mr. Kachline fell from a lumber pile which was the cause of his death. He survived his injuries ten weeks, and died October 29, 1853, at the age of sixty-two years and one month.

Mr. Kachline was a man well liked by his neighbors, and wielded considerable influence, serving one term of three years on the board of County Commissioners. Six children survived Samuel Kachline at his death, three sons and three daughters. Two of the sons, William and Samuel, following their patriotic instincts, and the example of their ancestors, enlisted in the Union Army at the outbreak of the Civil War. William joined the Doylestown Guards, the first company to leave this county, his name standing second on the roll, and served in the Shenandoah Valley campaign of 1861. Samuel enlisted in the Third New Jersey Cavalry for the war, and saw the end of it at Appomattox. Of Paul, who succeeded Mr. Kachline in cabinet-making, we know nothing beyond the fact he came here.

In 1827, George Luckenbach set up a cabinet-making shop, using dog power for turning his lathe. As this was probably the first time this was used in the county it attracted considerable attention. The *Intelligencer*, of June 29, 1827, mentions the editor's visit to Luckenbach's shop, where he saw a couple of dogs in a drum turning a lathe and speaks of it as "a new application of dog power." We do not know how long Luckenbach was here before calling dog power into requisition, nor when he left, but remember when the dogs were at work.

Lester Rich settled at Doylestown in January 1830, living on the "New Hope street," and, from that time, spent his life here. In 1840 his house, a frame, was on the site of Charles C. Cox's brick dwelling, north side of East State street four doors from Main, with shop on the same lot. Mr. Rich served one term as postmaster. His son, Silvester, read law, was admitted to the bar, practiced at Norristown, subsequently removed to Philadelphia where he died, 1893. Lester Rich had one daughter, a very pretty girl, who was her father's deputy while postmaster. In 1834, Daniel Tilton opened a cabinet

---

2 While the spelling of the name, by the first settlers, was *Keichline*, Samuel and family spelled it *Kachline*. We have used both ways.

wareroom in the village, and Theodore T. Kinsey in 1843-44; the latter in subsequent years going into the lightning rod business in Philadelphia, where he made a snug fortune at it and died there. He was a cabinet-maker by trade. At one time Mr. Kinsey kept the Green Tree tavern, corner of Broad and North Main streets, and, from there, moved into a private dwelling on East State street, and, while living here, began the lightning rod business.

In 1821, a new minor mechanical industry came to Doylestown, the trade of tin plate worker, and the person who set it up was William Maxwell. He opened his shop "on the Norristown road about twenty rods west of Harvey's store." As "Harvey's Store" was on the northeast corner of State and Main streets where William Randall keeps, this would bring the Maxwell place about Kolbe's tin shop on the north side of West State street. In 1832 Maxwell carried on business in the second story room in the old Shearer frame, on the site of the Seigler building, Court and North Main, the Post office occupying the first floor. The Maxwells remained here many years, removing to Philadelphia about 1850. The son John reached some prominence. He was a long time conductor on the Camden-Amboy railroad, and a member of the New Jersey Legislature one or two sessions. Maxwell was probably the first tin plate worker at the county seat.

The first foundry in Doylestown was established 1828, of which one of the town papers says:

"Among the improvements which are making in our pleasant village, we are pleased to notice that of our enterprising neighbors, Burrows and John McVickers. They have just gotten into operation a new foundry erected on the property of the senior partner, which from its novelty in this part of the country, has attracted the attention of our citizens, and drawn to their establishment a goodly number of spectators." The location is not given, but we believe it to have been on West State street, near Hamilton. Mr. Vickers died January 8, 1830 at the age of 25, and that winter John Ramsey bought the foundry, and began business. Francis Levering, a marble cutter in Doylestown, 1825, was set up in business by Yardley & Taylor, storekeepers, but, beyond this, nothing is known of him.

In 1825, Alexander Enochs, born in Philadelphia about where Girard College stands, came to Doylestown and opened a marble yard, having formerly carried on the business at Norristown. He remained here to his death, 1833 and was burried in the Presbyterian grave yard. His wife, was Elizabeth Bartle of Barren Hill, Montgomery county, and she conducted the business some time after her husband's death. His oldest son, Enoch, got the gold fever in 1849, and went to California as a pioneer, but returned after a brief stay and settled in Lousiana, where he established himself in business. In 1861, he returned to the North to await the issue of the Civil war, settling at Ardmore, Montgomery county. At the close of the war he went South again, retaining his home at Ardmore, whither he returned, and was appointed Postmaster by President Cleveland in his second term, and we believe is still living there. How many children Alexander Enochs had we do not know, nor when the widow died. The rest of the family removed to Philadelphia.

In so far as we have been able to learn, there have been but two book binderies in Doylestown. The first, of this useful trade to come among us, was John A. Haake, who went into business about the first of August, 1830. He had a stationery store connected with his bindery, "at the next door south of Charles Morris' tavern." As Morris kept what is now the Monument House, Haake must have occupied the frame on the site of Hellyer's new store house. Doylestown's second, book bindery was Joseph B. Steiner, who opened his place of business here, in January, 1901. He was born near Vienna, Austria, and learned the trade there. Steiner was succeeded by Eugene Laatz, who set up a bindery for himself in the *Democrat* office.

In 1830 the Misses M. and L. Sharpless, of Philadelphia, came to Doylestown accompanied by their mother, and opened a mantau-making establishment in their dwelling on South Main street, next door below Pettitt's tavern. They remained many years, their mother dying here. In the same period, Mary and Eleanor Austin,[3] daughters of William Austin, carried on the millinery business. One of them married a man named Higgins, the other, James McCoy, whose son, John, was a Lieutenant in the 104th regiment, in the Civil war. In 1846 the Misses Shewell, relatives of Nathaniel Shewell, possibly his sisters, were in the millinery business at Doylestown, but, how long they continued, we are not informed.

In 1831, Peter Adams was a "Vitualler" in Doylestown, the first of the occupation we have met with, and advertises for those indebted to him, "big and all" to pay up within ten days or they "will have the pleasure of settling with a magistrate." Norris Lee was an

---

[3] At Doylestown, March 10, 1836, Eleanor Austin, daughter of William Austin in the 25th year of her age.

oyster-man in 1836, and Nathaniel Hubbard keeping a restaurant in the basement of the frame on Main street, opposite the Fountain House, where he was burned out with the *Democrat* plant and other occupants of the building the same year.

Abraham Garron, who came here from Easton about 1841, to follow his trade, that of brick laying, did not follow it over a year before embarking in the restaurant business, probably the first to open such place in Doylestown. This was in 1842-43. He first kept in the little stone building at the south end of the Mansion house; from there he moved into the basement of the brick on Main street, opposite the Fountain House, and thence to the new brick he built, on the west side of South Main street one block from State, 1854-55. Prior to the Civil War, the price of the ordinary oyster stew was twelve and one-half cents, but it suddenly jumped up to twenty-five cents, other things in proportion and has kept there, Garron was without a competitor for years and did a successful business. His son succeeded him at his death, 1893, and conducted the business until 1895 when he sold out and engaged in rose culture in the township. In the meantime, by virtue of an order of Court, the saloon keepers were obliged to come up from the basements, whereby their places were much improved in appearance and otherwise.

In May, 1844, Mrs. White, wife of John White, opened a "New Fectory" at her residence, a two-story stone on the site of the Louis B. Thompson brick, recently owned by Joshua Tomlinson, south side of Court and Main. Here the author spent his spare pennies for candies, and other sweets in that line. Since the days we speak of, there have been a number of eating houses and restaurants in Doylestown, but none licensed to sell spirituous or vinous liquors.

A restaurant has been longer kept in the building on the south side of Court street at the junction of Main, than in any other place in Doylestown. The building was erected in 1848, by Samuel J. Paxson, for a printing office, but he sold it to Robert Evans, 1854, and moved into his new office next door above where the *Democrat* is still published. Evans kept the restaurant a short time and sold it to Samuel F. Ginsley [4] who was its owner several years. During his

---

[4] Samnel F. Ginsley was a resident of Doylestown over half a century, coming here in the fall of 1849, and dying February 4, 1901, at the age of eighty. He was born at Philadelphia, 1821, and his wife at Stuttgard, Germany, coming to America at the age of nine. Mr. Ginsley owned and lived in, three houses in Doylestown, dying in the dwelling he purchased of Dr. O. P. James, South Main street, at the close of the Civil War. Mr. and Mrs. Ginsley introduced the "Christmas Tree" into Doylestown and were the first to set one up in their own dwelling, and now an universal feature of Christmas holidays. Mrs. Ginsley died December 22, 1903.

ownership, a restaurant was kept in the basement, Charles Zenneck being the proprietor; Ginsley's barber shop was on the first floor and the rest of the building the owner occupied as a dwelling. Since the property passed out of Ginsley's hands there have been several owners. It again changed hands in the spring of 1901, being purchased by Harrold A. Hellyer and again in 1902 by Hugh Thompson, who sold it the following year. A restaurant has been kept in the building continuously since 1854, a period of forty-eight years. William Schooner owned the place several years, but sold out to Hellyer, and removed to New Jersey. It again changed hands in 1904 by Hugh Thompson selling out to A. V. Higgins, of Bordentown, N. J. several years in the railroad business. It long had a repute for its appetising dishes, and stewed terrapins and snappers are still specialties on the bill of fair.

Jacob Troxel, a hat manufacturer, was in Doylestown, 1811, and probably before, as the time of his beginning business is not known. He died five years afterward.[5] Nathan Cornell, the next in order in this calling, was here in 1819, and carried on for several years. He was still in business in 1841, when he advertised his stand as the "Doylestown 'O. K. Hat' manufactory." He did quite an extensive business, and died previous to 1844, leaving a widow, two sons and two daughters. The eldest son, Theophilus, is living in Philadelphia, and E. Mitchell Cornell, the younger son, is deceased. His eldest daughter was the first wife of George Hart, a member of the Bar and the younger, Fanny, married the Revd. John Tetlow, former rector of St. Paul's Protestant Episcopal Church, Doylestown, 1863-64, They went to Germany subsequently where both died.

In the meantime a new hat manufacturer, Thomas Hayes, came to town and set up business. He was born at Wilmington, Delaware, and married his wife at Line Lexington, Bucks county, coming here from West Chester about 1836. He moved into the Hargrave house, South Main street, and rented Shearer's old frame at North Main and Court for a place of business. In two years he moved to the Pugh Dungan house, West Court street, now owned by Wynne James and built a shop where the Hunt house stands. About 1840 he and O. P. Lunn went into busines together and carried on for several years. At first they made stiff hats and then silk, but the slouch

---

[5] In Doylestown, August 27, 1815, Jacob Troxel, hatter, in the thirty-second year of his age, leaving a widow and an infant daughter to lament the loss of an affectionate husband and parent.

broke up the silk hat business. Hayes was appointed a tipstave near the last of Judge Krause's time, and served under Smyser, Chapman Roberts and Watson. When James became disabled from old age, Hayes was appointed Acting Court Cryer, and served to James' death. Hayes died, 1872, at the age of sixty-seven, and Lunn, also, died here. They were the last hat makers at Doylestown.

Thomas Hayes was an ardent Democrat and active politician; a warm personal and political friend of Judge Chapman, and, withall, something of a wag. At that day politics was more picturesque than now, and greater attention paid to the role of by plays. One evening Hayes, his business partner, Lunn, and other friends of Chapman, met at what is now the Fountain House, and, warming up in their admiration of their political idol resolved to pay him a visit and bring him out for Governor. The Judge then lived in the house on North Main street now occupied by the family of the late O. P. James. Hayes led the delegation, and, knocking at the door, they were ushered into the parlor with due ceremony. The Judge soon made his appearance and gave proper welcome to his visitors. After the compliments of the season had passed, Hayes proceded to business by opening his nominating speech, which abounded in flattering allusion to the Judge's public and private career, concluding by pledging the support of himself and friends. Hayes reasserted his personal loyalty to the Judge, which he emphaized by saying; " for you I can jump up higher, dive down deeper, and come up dryer than any other man. You are my gallant Harry," and, suiting the action to the words, Hayes slapped the dignified Judge on the back. The delegation was now bowed out.

Samuel Hubbard, painter and glazier, was in Doylestown in 1813, and may have been here earlier, but we know nothing more of him. Nathaniel Hubbard, known to some of the present generation, of the same occupation as the former, not a relative so far as we know, was here in 1830. He added sign painting to the common branches of the trade, and, if our memory be not at fault, also made chairs. He dabbled in politics on the Democratic side, and, now and then, tasted of the sweets of office; was constable many years, and, altogether cut something of a figure in village life. At the breaking out of the Civil war, Hubbard enlisted in the 104th regiment, and served a three years enlistment. He had a son Joseph, who long since passed from view. Hubbard died here. In 1833 there was a painter, glazier and paper hanger in Doylestown named Joseph Scott, but this is all we know of him.

Edward Heston was here carrying on his trade, painter and glazier as early as 1840, and possibly before. He formed a partnership with George W. Firman which was dissolved April 1, 1841, each partner setting up for himself, Firman occupying the old shop, that of Lester Rich, on East State street. Heston followed the trade for several years, then opened a feed store on Pine street, occasionally doing a little at his trade. He lived on the northwest corner of Pine and York streets and died there in the nineties.

Conrad Shearer was an early harness maker at Doylestown, but what time he began business we are not informed. In the spring of 1838, he and his son, E. H. Shearer, were in partnership. The following year their shop was on the north side of West State street, a few doors west of the Fountain House. The son afterward carried on the trade for many years, and to his death. A considerable part of the time he occupied the little frame on the site of the Siegler building, corner of East Court and South Main streets, and in it kept the Post Office.

The Shearers were followed in harness making by Samuel P. Hamilton, who learned the trade with Conrad Shearer. He was the son of Benjamin Hamilton, and born in Solebury township, Bucks county. At what time he came here, or when he began busiuess, we do not know, but when Charles H. Mann quit the trade, 1843, Hamilton took his stand at the northwest corner of State and Pine streets, where he remained several years, and whence he removed to the brick block on the south side of West State street, erected soon after the close of the Civil War. He occupied the first house west of the Mansion House now included in Hotel Pollock. He died in 1885. Mr. Hamilton was a member of the Doylestown Greys, the crack military company of the county, and, at one time, the treasurer. He married Rebecca Divine, of Doylestown, one of the prettiest girls of the village, and had two or three sisters as pretty as herself. Mrs. Hamilton is still living.

In 1833, the tradesmen of the borough were increased by the arrival of Norris Lee, a "barber and perfumer," who not only shaved his customers, but sold to them, among other articles, " Milk of Roses, Chlorine Tooth Wash, Negro Head Tobacco and Orange Flower Water," and both bought and sold " second hand clothing." How long he staid, or whither he went, when we left we do not know.

In 1826, a man, named "Joe Bon," came to Doylestown and engaged in one of the minor industries advertising his calling in one of the town newspapers, as follows: "Joe Bon, informs the gentlemen of Doylestown, that he will engage to take boots in the evening and return them well polished the next morning at very reasonable terms." This is the first and last we know of "Joe" or whether his enterprise was a success or failure. Of him it cannot be said he is "known to fame." In 1830, Meredith and Raisner had 40,000, bricks for sale at their kilns, and, in 1833 Asher Cox was a stone mason and plasterer at the county capital.

Aden G. Hibbs was a chairmaker in Doylestown prior to 1830, in partnership with Pugh Dungan, but they dissolved in April, 1829. Their shop was on the "Easton Road" nearly opposite Squire Shaw's office. He removed to Hatboro, Montgomery county, and from there went west, settling near Columbus, Ohio. He accumulated a respectable competency of this world's goods, and died in 1900. The two Gaucher brothers, David and Thomae W. settled here about 1842. They were joiners and worked at it in partnership for a year or so, when they dissolved. John White purchased David's interest, and the latter now turned his attention to the carpenter trade, and built the large dwelling of Henry Chapman, 1844, at that time the finest house in the borough. David Gaucher soon left Doylestown, but Thomas W. passed his life here, following his trade a cabinet maker, working for several years in a frame shop on the south side of East State street, standing on the lot next to the dwelling of Dr. Hutchinson P. Yerkes, at the corner of the alley. Gaucher was not without talent, but was more fond of polemics than his trade.

Good horses being an early fad with the people of Doylestown, it led the proprietors of our livery stables to keeping fine stock in the past. Smith Price had a stable here in 1839, and John Weikel nine years later, 1848. The latter was smewhat sportive and picturesque. Among his horses was a pair of match grays the young men delighted to drive.

One of the most prosperous industries of Doylestown in recent years, was the Worstall & Carl Spoke and Wheel Co., incorporated, 1891. Their occupation was making wheels, spokes and felloes. It was founded thirty-seven years ago, and was of humble birth. In 1864, William Coheen, formerly in the wheelwright business, at Davisville and other places, came to Doylestown and began the manufacture of spokes, in the old building on the flatiron formed by the crossing of

West Court and State streets. At first, Dr. Evans, of Hatboro, was interested in the business, and subsequently William Goheen's son, J. Warner,[6] assisted his father. In 1872, Goheen sold his interest to Martin Jarrett, of Horsham, who carried on the business alone until 1877, when Carl and Worstall formed a partnership with Jarrett, who died about 1886. The property was now purchased by Carl & Worstall, who carried it on under the firm name of Worstall & Carl, and, in 1891, as we have already stated, they sold out to a corporation. They did quite an extensive business in both the home and foreign trade; shipping their goods to the middle and New England states, at home, and wheels to England and Ireland. The shipments to England, in a single year, averaged about eight hundred dollars a month and their business, reached is about twenty-five thousand dollars a year. On Monday evening, March 7, 1904, the establishment accidently took fire, and was totaly destroyed, with an estimate loss of thirty thousand dollars.

---

6 J. Warner Goheen, son of William Goheen was born at Davisville. After leaving his father's spoke factory, he read law with William Fell, Philadelphia; was admitted to the bar and rapidly grew into practice. In a few years he was elected to the Common Council where he made his mark in the municipal legislation of the city. In 1879, he married a daughter of the late John B. Pugh, Esq., Doylestown, and resided in Philadelphia to his death, in 1899. Had his life been spared he would undoubtedly have reached a prominent position.

Doylestown, Old and New.

XXI
Opening of Streets.

The streets of Doylestown were laid out and opened as they were needed, after the two main highways, connecting the Delaware with the Schuylkill, and Philadelphia with Easton, had been opened. This, however, was not done until a small hamlet had grown up about the cross-roads and received the name of "Doyle's Tavern," with changes that made the spelling the same as to-day. The first of these subsequent roads, or streets, was opened on the line between New Britain and Warwick townships, the present Court street, running east from the Easton road, now North Main street, to the Buckingham line.[1] This was in 1807, and then called the "Academy Lane" for many years, and a few of the "rude fore-fathers" still call it by this name. It was subsequently extended from Main street southwest, crossing West State street at what is now Clinton. Broad street was next opened, 1811, from East State street to North Main, then continuing into the country and known as "Dutch Lane."[2] There were no additional streets opened until after the village had became the county seat, 1813.

In the first movement for incorporating Doylestown into a

---

[1] The Buckingham line is still called the "Swamp Road," and, in the long ago, was the highway from Quakertown and the northwest section of the county to Newtown, the seat of Justice.

[2] Broad street was called "Dutch Lane," because it runs out to the "Dutch," or Mennonite meeting house after crossing Main street, and some people still call it by this name. Just what time York street was opened we are not informed, as we have never seen the official papers, but we believe about 1830.

194

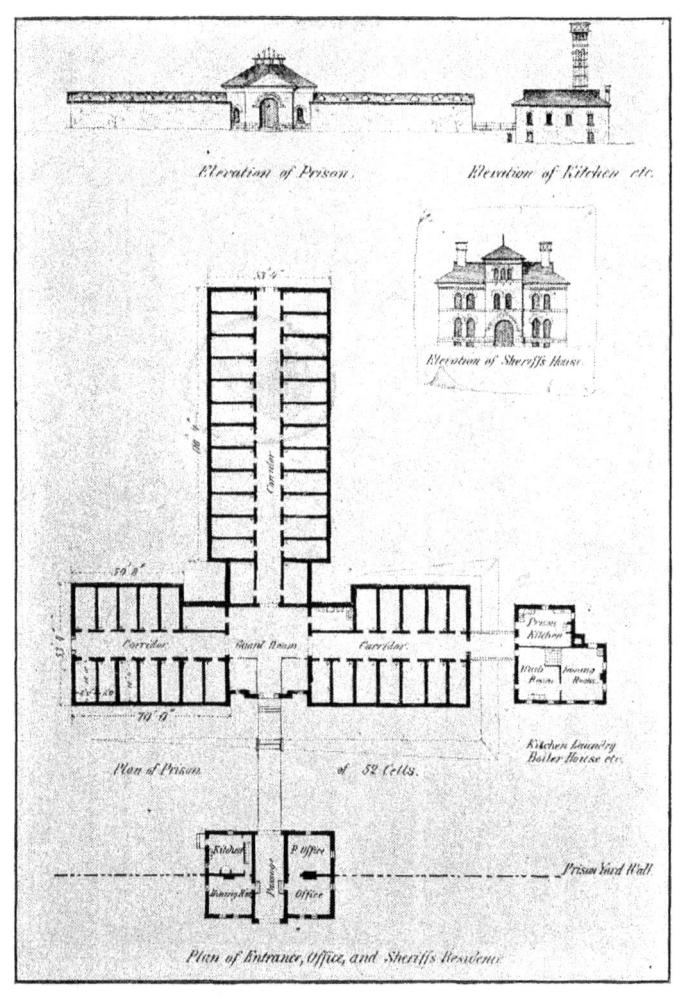

NEW JAIL, 1884.

borough, 1830, the jury, appointed to survey and lay out, returned two reports to the court, one giving the course and distance of the lines bounding it, the other the names of the streets, and, strange as it may seem, only one bore the name "street," the others "road" or "lane," a singular instance of modesty on the part of the jurors. The present Main street was the "Easton Road;" State street, the "New Hope Road;" Broad street, "Dutch Lane;" Court street, "Academy Lane;" and York street, "Front street." These were Doylestown's five public highways, in 1830, seventy-three years ago. Things were primitive at that day, for the seat of justice of the old and populous county of Bucks. The last of the old group of streets was York street running from South Main to the New Hope pike at the Catholic church. It was sometimes called Front street. Ashland street was opened about the time the North Penn R. R. entered the borough, 1856.

From this time forward, the opening of new portions of the borough for building purposes naturally suggested the laying out of streets, and the council was not slow in responding. In their order they were the eastern, southwestern and western suburbs. In the former the leading streets are Maple and Linden avenues. This was near the close of the sixties, and, in 1871 a subscription was solicited for the purpose of improving Maple avenue, then recently opened, and eighty-five dollars were subscribed. Andrew LaRue, instrumental in bringing this section into the market, and part owner of the land, was the heaviest subscriber, giving twenty-five dollars. This is a resident section, and Maple and Linden avenues are among the most pleasant streets in the borough. The Magill property, some thirty acres, in the triangle formed by South Main and West State streets, was put in the market soon after the close of the Civil war, streets opened and buildings erected.

As will be noticed, in another chapter, the Magills were among the early settlers of Doylestown, and they owned part of the borough site. Before the tract above mentioned was sold, the Magill family had opened three small streets contigious to West State and near South Main, named "Mary," "Arabella" and "Louisa" streets. In the deed of release, of the heirs of William Magill, of Doylestown, to Alfred Magill, a coheir of the said William Magill, it is provided that the three streets named "as laid down on the said draft are always to be kept open and free from incumbrance of any kind." It might be well for some of the owners of this tract to look to it that the condition of this deed of release is not violated. If this be overlooked trouble might be caused to the property.[3]

Our street system is the equal of most villages of its size and possibly better. The streets are well curbed, and paved and the road bed good. In addition, our location is such, on an elevated plateau, nearly six hundred feet above tidewater, and above the level of the country around us, that the streets act as conduits to carry off the water of a heavy rain.

Down to 1838, there was no outlet for the people of Doylestown except over the ordinary dirt roads, which, in winter, became almost impassible, a draw back to the prosperity of the county seat. Better roads were often talked about before final action was taken. The first movement for a turnpike, connecting with that at the Willow Grove, and leading to Philadelphia, was made at a meeting held at Field's tavern, 1828, and books were authorized to be kept open there and at Thomas Brunn's, Willow Grove, for six days, but it went no farther. Meanwhile, a new effort was made, and, by May 1, 1838, sufficient stock was subscribed to entitle the "Doylestown and Willow Grove Turnpike Company," to the state appropriation. Judge Fox became the first president, as well as an important factor in pushing the turnpike to completion, and Dr. Charles H. Mathews was secretary and treasurer.

The second turnpike, leading out of Doylestown, was the Doylestown and Buckingham, finished 1848. The first meeting was held at the public house of Isaac C. McCarty, Centreville, January 2, 1841, Colonel William Beans, chairman. The next we hear of this project was a meeting at Thatcher's tavern, Centreville, November 10, 1846; subscription books were opened December 1, and sufficient stock subscribed by January 20, '47; proposals for grading, stoning and building bridges were advertised May 6; the work was begun about June 1, and completed August 1, 1848. The road was opened for travel August 5, and twenty-one dollars and fifty cents received in toll on that day. It was a new thing. The president was William T. Rogers, Harvey Shaw, secretary and Edward Williams, treasurer. The turn-

---

[3] The following is the abstract of title of the said Magill property: Lawrence Growden and Langhorne Biles, executors of Jeremiah Langhorne, to William Scott, May 23, 1753; William Scott to Archibald Crawford, August 6, 1753; Archibald Crawford to Robert and Henry Magill, May 17, 1768, including the above ten acres; Henry Magill and wife to Robert Magill, March 2, 1776. Robert Magill died intestate leaving a widow Mary, and children Alfred, Louisa C., William D., Robert M. and Benjamin M. in whom the same vested in fee.

pikes from Doylestown to Plumsteadville and Dublin, and those from Centreville to New Hope and Newtown, giving the county seat good roads to those points, were subsequently built. Within recent years, a turnpike was projected from Doylestown, via New Britain, into Montgomery county and ultimately to reach Norristown, and stock subscribed, but some hitch prevented it being built.

At the session of the Legislature, of 1830-31, an act was passed authorizing a State Road from New Hope on the Delaware, via Doylestown, Norristown and West Chester, to the State line, and to be continued to Port Deposit, on the Susquehanna. This measure met with great opposition, and a meeting was called at Charles Morris' tavern, Doylestown, January 27, 1831 to take action against it and also against the State road from Easton to the Willow Grove.

At this meeting Dr. Charles H. Mathews, was chairman and John Lancaster, secretary. This was followed by a meeting of those opposed to a repeal of the act authorizing the laying out a State road from New Hope to Norristown, via Doylestown, held at Pettitt's tavern,[4] of which Josiah Y. Shaw was chairman, and James Kelley and C. E. DuBois, secretaries. These efforts for better lines of communication across this section of the peninsula, from the Delaware to the Schuylkill, resulted in what are known as the Upper and Lower State Roads, both running through Doylestown but diverging west of the town, one running through New Britain, and the other by Castle Valley. They were mainly laid on the old road beds.

We now come to the railroad period, and the craze, if such it may be called, which first struck this section as early as 1833. About the first of July a meeting was held at Henry Scholl's tavern,[5] of those friendly to a railroad from Lambertville on the Delaware, to Doylestown, of which Lester Rich was chairman and James Kelley, secretary. A committee, consisting of Philip Fretz, Wm. Fenton, Samuel Kachline, William Carr, and Joseph Moore, was appointed to procure a competent engineer to explore the proposed route and make a survey. In August, Samuel Hart, Doylestown, and Merrick Reeder, New Hope, took the levels and found the elevation, from the Delaware to Doylestown, to be overcome, was three hundred and sixty feet.

The project seems to have stopped here, but the idea of a railroad across our peninsula was not abandoned. At the session of

---

4 Present Fountain House.
5 Court Inn.

1835-36, a bill passed the Legislature, chartering a company to construct a railroad from Norristown, via Doylestown to New Hope. Engineers were put on the route, it was surveyed, and found to be entirely practicable, but the road was never located, railroad promoters having their attention attracted to more profitable fields. Subsequent attemps were made for a railroad from the Delaware to the Schuylkill but all of them proved abortive. Lewis S. Coryell, New Hope, was a leading man in the enterprise. The only thing like a favorable result from these efforts, is the railroad from Norristown to connect with the North Penn at Lansdale, which gives Doylestown, and this section, a continuous route of travel and traffic to the Schuylkill. The time will come, however, when there will be a trunk line between our two rivers and to New York, a new and direct outlet from the Schuylkill coal region to the commercial metropolis of America, recently become the second populous city of the world, with 4,000,000 inhabitants. The opening of the North Penn railroad, from Philadelphia to Bethlehem, 1856 with a connecting branch from Doylestown at Lansdale, completed our connections and put Bucks county's capital in touch with the outside world, so far as steam could make it, for the present.

Subsequently the trolley, so-called, comes along, and the subtle fluid, Franklin borrowed from the clouds, was converted into a motor that completed what the horse and steam had begun. The completion of the electric road to the Willow Grove, which affords a delightful, safe and convenient connection with the commercial centre of the Delaware-Schuylkill Peninsula, opens new possibilities for our county capital in the future. The first spike, in this trolley road, was driven Tuesday morning, November 30, 1897, by Daniel McLaughlin, Doylestown, and a bottle of wine broken at the track. The spike was afterward withdrawn and presented to Mr. McL. as a souvenir of the event. In 1901, the tracks of the Willow Grove trolley were extended from State street, its first terminus, along North Main to Church, the first trip, on the extension, being made with passenger cars on Sunday, July 21.

Since our trolley connection, with the Willow Grove and Philadelphia, has been such a success, it has stimulated lines in other directions, and the author's prediction that Doylestown was destined to become a great trolley centre, in the near future, seems almost within in sight. Following the Doylestown-Willow Grove trolley, was a line to Newtown, constructed in 1898-99, giving a continuous route to Bristol on the Delaware, and beyond, from Newtown, via Yardley to

Morrisville, and from that place to Bristol. Both of these roads have a connection with Trenton and New York by trolley. Shortly after, a line was surveyed from Doylestown to New Hope on the turnpike, and, later, another route was surveyed west of the pike between the same points, and, while nothing has yet been done to carry out this project, there is talk of a trolley line being constructed from New Hope, and it is said the right of way has been secured part of the distance to Norristown, via Doylestown. In the recent past, steps were taken to extend the trolley system from Doylestown into the upper end of the county in two directions, one on the Easton road to the Forks of the Delaware, the other in the direction of Perkaise, via Dublin, with possible extension to Quakertown. The latter is the plan of the Doylestown-Willow Grove trolley company, under an amended charter, while the former is the work of a new company, called the "Philadelphia & Easton Railway Company," and will be completed within the year. The cars are running between Doylestown and the Tohickon, and Riegelsville and Easton.

As these two roads will tap a rich and populous country, without trolley accommodations, we look for their completion in the near future. The trolley is not only the poor man's railway, but has come to stay. The steam roads have lost a considerable percentage of travel by antagonizing them at the beginning of their career, but what they may lose in the future is a problem to be solved.

The first spike, on the Doylestown-Easton trolley railway, was driven on Saturday morning, June 22, 1901, in the presence of a number of persons, who took a deep interest in the proceedings; among those present being Councilmen T. O. Atkinson and John G. Randall; Directors H. J. Shoemaker and Samuel A. Hellyer; Superintendent T. H. Connell, Construction Boss M. S. Shinn, Street Commissioner Andrew Rickard, C. E. Woodmansee *Wycombe Herald,* John Clemens, Wynne James, Esq., Nelson K. Leatherman, Daniel G. Fretz, James Shellenberger, Edward Newell and W. W. H. Davis. The spike was made at the foundry of the agricultural works of Ruos, and contained the following inscription :

D. & E.
1901
H. D. R.

This trolley railway, when completed, will put our county's capital in close touch with a rich and populous country, with which it has had, heretofore, no other communication than by the lumbering stage coach and wagon, on horse-back or afoot. It will become a trolley trunk line, and in the future, will be tapped by lateral trolley roads connecting with the North Pennsylvania and Belvidere-Delaware steam roads, on the east and the west. The rail trolley connection made, from and with Doylestown, was with New York, via Newtown, Yardley, Morrisville and Trenton.

The last group, of borough streets, was laid out and opened in Doylestown, in 1898. In the spring of that year James Pollock, a resident of the borough, made an addition, to the built-up portion of the town, by offering at public sale, one hundred and forty-two building lots, fifty by one hundred and fifty feet, northwest of Main street. Through this tract the council laid out five streets; Shewell and Harvey avenues, avenues A. and B. and Union street. Shewell avenue starts at Monument Place, the junction of Main and Court streets, and runs down into the valley of Pine Run. There was some opposition to opening Shewell avenue, but the matter was carried into the Court of Quarter Sessions where the trouble was straightened out. The sale of lots was held on May 5, but they were not all sold. Several nice dwellings have already been erected, and more are in prospect. This tract was a part of the Armstrong farm of which considerable has been said in this volume, and was owned by several persons, in the last century, including Dr. Hugh Meredith, Samuel Yardley and William Watts.

Crossing of Court & Main Streets.
1831.

THE OPENING OF STREETS.

Doylestown, Old and New.

XXII
A Group of Churches.

The fourth church, organized in Doylestown, was St Paul's Protestant Episcopal, which grew from seed planted in the spring of 1845 by the Rev. George P. Hopkins.

Living at Germantown, and occasionally preaching at neighboring towns and villages, Mr. Hopkins came to Doylestown May 7, with a letter to Thomas Ross, Esq., whose wife was the only church women here. Believing he saw his way clear before leaving, to establish a parish, Mr. Hopkins made an appointment to preach here on the 18th. Service was held in the hall of the Beneficial Institute building morning and evening, with a fair audience, and at Centreville in the afternoon. After this, service was held regularly by Mr. Hopkins, who continued to reside at Germantown the first two years, coming up by stage Saturday and returning Monday.

The first steps for organizing a parish, were taken at the house of Andrew Donaldson, Sunday evening, April 26, 1846. Several gentlemen were present, and Messrs. Donaldson, Henry J. C. Taylor, William Limeburner,[1] Richard M. Donaldson, James M. Kempton, Benjamin Jackson and Charles H. Mann were chosen vestrymen. Messrs. Limeburner and Mann were elected wardens, a charter was adopted, the title of "St. Paul's" being given the parish and Mr. Hopkins was elected rector. Of the original vestrymen all are dead. Steps were taken toward the erection of a church

---

[1] At Doylestown, February 27, 1846, John Limeburner, aged eighty-five years and eight months.

building at a vestry meeting held May 15, 1846, when a building committee was appointed, and a lot purchased of Captain Taylor, the same on which the church now stands, for $200, on condition he would subscribe $100 toward the building fund.

Ground was broken July 20, and the corner-stone laid September 6, by Bishop Potter, in the presence of a large audience. Work was discontinued on the approach of cold weather, but resumed in the spring. The size of the original building was sixty by thirty-seven feet, the architect John E. Carver, Philadelphia, and the style early English. The Court granted a charter February 8, 1848. While the building was being erected services were held in Beneficial Hall East State street, the last on Sunday, March 26, and the first service in the new church on April 23, 1848. Arrangements having been made, for payment of the debt on the building, it was dedicated May 30, 1850. There was a large turnout of clergy and laity, including Bishop Potter, and many persons of other denominations were present. The occasion was one of great interest to the community. The cost of the church, and furnishing, was $5,000. Mr. Hopkins, now feeling that he had finished his mission here, resigned the rectorship of the parish March 19, 1853, leaving with the blessings and regret of the congregation. Mr. Hopkins afterwards occupied parishes in Bradford county, Pa., where he died in recent years. He was an excellent man in every sense, music being one of his accomplishments, the flute his favorite instrument.

The church has had eleven rectors following Mr. Hopkins: The Reverends Reece C. Evans, William R. Gries [2] who resigned 1861 to accept a chaplaincy in the army where he served his country with the same zeal as his Divine Master, John Tetlow,[3] Byran McGann, Hurley Baldy, Thomas K. Coleman, V. Hummel Berghaus, Howard T. Widdemer, James F. Taunt, George N Eastman, and Edward M. Jeffreys who resigned in May, 1902, and the present rector, the Rev. John C. Gallaudet called in 1902.

The church building has been twice repaired and improved, 1870 at an expense of $3,200, and, 1896, at a cost of $4,000. On the latter occasion the interior finish was changed to the eleventh century style of church architecture, and exhibits good taste, the architect

---

2 Mr. Gries was chaplain of the 104th Pa. regiment, and served three years in the Civil War making a fine record.

3 Mr. Tetlow married Miss Fanny Cornell, of Doylestown. After his resignation they went to Germany and lived there until their death.

being Dr. H. P. Yerkes a member of the vestry. In its half century of life, St. Paul's parish has grown in number and strength, and its influence correspondingly increased. In 1895, the fiftieth anniversary of the church was celebrated, the Rev. Mr. Hopkins, the first rector being present, and W. W. H. Davis delivered the historical address. Among the church temporalties is a comfortable and convenient rectory.

St. Mary's Roman Catholic Church, otherwise called the church of "Our Lady of Mount Carmel," was the fifth religious organization in our borough, and belongs to the era of old Doylestown. The Rev. Father George was largely, if not wholly, entitled to the credit of founding it. He first came here as a missionery, 1850, and gathered the few catholics of the borough and vicinity together, and probably held service at private houses. Between the advent of Father George, and the fall of 1856, a church building was erected on the site of the present one, and dedicated November 23, by Bishop Newman, Philadelphia. It occupies one of the most eligible sites in the borough, on an elevated spot at the eastern entrance, overlooking a wide scope of hill and valley. They, who took the deepest interest in the organization of the parish of St. Mary's, and the most liberal contributors, were the Farren and Patterson families of Doylestown township.

Father George was pastor of the church until 1875, meanwhile building up a considerable congregation, when the Reverend Henry Stommel was called to the pastorate. Being a man of ability, possessing fine executive qualities and of popular manners, the parish soon felt the influence of his presence. The congregation increased in number and strength, and there was visible improvement on several lines, among them the enlargement of the building. On February 3, 1876, a parochial school was opened in an old barn, by the Sisters of St. Frances, which they fitted up; the corner stone was laid for the Sisters' House, May 14, the new school house dedicated by the pastor June 20, 1876, and the corner stone of the new steeple laid April 28, 1879. At the Silver Jubilee of the church, 1881, the sermon was delivered by the Rev. Igatius Huntsman, subsequently Bishop of Cleveland, Ohio. On June 11, 1879, the four new bells in the tower of the church, were blessed by the Rev. James F. Wood, Archbishop o Philadelphia; on July 6, the improvements of the church were blessed, and August 6, 1882, the new organ was opened for the first time for service, Augustus Siegler, the organist, presiding. On August 12, 1883 the altar was blessed.

During the pastorate of Father Stommel, at St. Mary's Church, two of the Missions attached to the congregation grew into parishes, St. Isidore at Lansdale, and St. Martin's at New Hope. The corner stone of St. Isidore, a brick church, was laid and blessed by Father Stommel on Easter Monday, April 26, 1886, and dedicated by him August 2, assisted by other priests, with sermons in English and German. The congregation of St. Martin's, was transferred to Stanislaus parish, Lambertville, September 1, 1886, free of debt, the Rev. James Winter the pastor. The corner stone, of St. Martin's new stone church, was laid and blessed May 3, 1885, by Father Bready, Lambertville, Father Stommel, the first baptism and bells blessed July 12, 1885, first Mass celebrated July 19, first wedding August 20, 1875, blessing of the Cemetery by the pastor, September 6, first funeral, September 7, and the church was dedicated by Archbishop Ryan, Philadelphia, assisted by eight priests, September 17, 1885. The first pastor was the Rev. Peter Quinn, who was installed Oct. 13, 1885.

In 1890 Father Stommel was called to a more important field in Philadelphia, but the fruit of his work is still seen and felt at St. Mary's. He was succeeded by the Rev. Hugh J. McManus, who had charge until his death in December, 1896. During his pastorate the temporalities of the church were improved, the interior being handsomely repaired and a new organ, the gift of Mrs. John Farren was put in. At his death, the Rev. J. F. Magin, of Downingtown took Father McManus's place, and the latter's place was filled by Father Cavenaugh in the winter of 1901. There have been but five pastors at St. Mary's church since Father George began his missionary work, 1850, including his pastorate. This speaks well for both priests and congregation. The church building is one of the handsomest in the borough and the congregation the largest but one.

The seed, from which the Reformed church of Doylestown grew, was planted when the Rev. Alexander Vaughan, a minister of this denomination who had a classical school here, 1858. He preached occasionally in the Methodist church of a Sunday afternoon, and gradually gathered a small congregation. In 1860, the Rev. W. R. Yearick was sent here by the Reformed Church Home Mission, to look after the little flock, and, on March 17, 1861, he succeeded in organizing a congregation of two hundred members. Services were held in what is now Masonic, then Benefical Hall until a church building could be erected, which they set about immediately.

A lot was shortly purchased of the Fox estate, on the south

side of East Court street; a committee, consisting of Leidy L. Gerheart, Michael Hoffman and Joseph L. Shelly, was appointed a board of trustees to have the congregation incorporated, and a charter was granted in September, 1864. Mr. Shelly is the only surviving charter member. The corner stone was laid October 16, 1864, and the building dedicated, 1865. Mr. Yearick continued pastor until the opening of 1868, when he was succeeded by the Rev. W. H. Heilman, who resigned in the fall. The Rev. Levi L. Sheip was now called. He began his pastorate December 1, 1868, and finished it only with his life. The church flourished under his pastorate. He labored faithfully and the result was most gratifying. His hopeful, cheerful disposition infused new energy in the congregation; the church debt was soon paid off and the number increased. Besides being a faithful pastor, Mr. Sheip was a public-spirited citizen, taking an interest in every movement calculated to benefit the community. He was a great friend of education and had charge of the public schools of Doylestown several years.

Feeling the necessity of a new church building, Mr. Sheip and the congregation took action in the spring of 1896; and at a congregational meeting, held in June, H. C. Beidler, Harvey Scheetz, Mrs. Abraham Barth, Mrs. Lizzie Fluck, Mrs. Morgan Rufe, and Ellwood Barnes, were appointed a committee to ascertain what amount of money could probably be raised for the purpose. The report being favorable, a subsequent congregational meeting decided to erect a new building, and the following committee was appointed: A. F. Scheetz, George G. Miles, H. J. Beidler, J. F. Long, Webster Grim, Franklin Garner, and William L. Hager. They proceeded at once with their work; a lot was purchased on the south side of Court street east of Church, an architect, A. O. Martin, of Doylestown, engaged to draw the plans and Mr. Overhalt, a master builder, employed. The corner stone was laid in September, the work pushed to completion and the building dedicated in 1897, with proper ceremonies.

In the meantime, the Rev. Mr. Sheip dying suddenly, after work had been commenced on the new building, February 17, 1897, the Rev. James R. Bergey, was called to succeed him and installed.

The Reformed new church building is a handsome stone structure of Gothic style of architecture, seventy-five by forty-eight feet and surmounted by a square tower at the northwest corner, seventy-six feet in height. The seating capacity of the auditorium is about five hundred, and it is adorned with stained glass windows. The central window over the altar, was the gift of a church organization known as "The King's Daughters," and memorial to their late pastor, the Rev Mr. Sheip. The building cost about $11,000.

In January, 1898, the Reformed Sunday School organized graded work for a course of Bible study, the first in the county to engage in it.

The Rev. Levi C. Sheip, late pastor of the Reformed church, and born in New Britain, December 30, 1833, was the son of John and Hannah Snyder Sheip. He was a pupil at the Doylestown Academy, at twelve, then taught school, fitted for college at the Frederick Institute, Montgomery, graduated at Franklin-Marshall college, 1861, and that year opened a school for boys in Temperance Hall, Doylestown. Selecting the ministry for his profession, Mr. Sheip entered the Reformed Theological Seminary at Mercersburg, where he graduated, and was licensed to preach in 1864. After a short pastorate of the Pennsburg church, he accepted a call from Bloomsburg where he remained two years, and, in 1868, accepted a call from the Salem Reformed Church, Doylestown, and remained here until his death. In 1869, he opened a school for girls in Masonic Hall, took charge of Linden Seminary in the early seventies, and was superintendent of Doylestown public schools from 1879 to 1890. In 1885, Mr. Sheip made an extended trip through Europe, visiting several of the leading institutions of learning. He took great interest in education, and advanced the cause of learning in Doylestown in every possible way. Mr. Sheip possessed an agreeable personality and had many friends.

St. Paul's Lutheran church, Doylestown, the fourth of our group, was founded, 1860. On the 25th of August, of that year, the Rev. F. Berkemeyer, pastor of the Hilltown Lutheran church, preached in the court house, by appointment, and from this beginning gathered the Germans of the vicinity and organized a congregation. Services were held in the court house for six months, when St. Paul's Protestant Episcopal church tendered the use of their building to the Lutherans. This courtesy was accepted, and enjoyed for a while, when the new congregation changed their place of worship to the Academy, where, it will be remembered, a room was reserved for religious services at its erection, by the donor of the lot.

As the Germans were usually members of either the Lutheran or Reformed church, and "union churches" everywhere the custom, it was at first proposed to adopt it at Doylestown. It was decided, however, in 1862, that no such union should be undertaken, and the little congregation assumed the responsibility of erecting a building of their own. This project received both encouragement and financial aid from the English churches, of Doylestown, which realized the need of religious ministration to the Germans in their own language.

About this time the Rev. Mr. Berkemeyer was succeeded in the pastorate by the Rev. George Heilig, who was followed by the Rev. R. M. Jacobs, and the church building was partially completed in 1867. Services were held at first in the basement, but, during this period, the congregation falling into financial trouble the building was sold by the contractors and bought for the church, for $2,600. The congregation now deciding to complete the building, a committee was appointed in April, 1875 to take subscriptions. This consisted of the Rev. J. H. Fretz, Morgan Rufe, Conrad Hahl, John L. Kramer and W. Shade. During the year, $800 were subscribed, but the work was deferred until the following spring. When it was resumed, the progress was slow, but the building was finally completed, and dedicated March 4, 1877. This was a day of rejoicing and rightfully so, after such a long struggle. In the meantime, on Ascension Day, May 6, 1875, at a congregational meeting; it was unanimously decided to use the Liturgy as prepared and recommended by the Ministerium of Pennsylvania, as almost all the members were provided with copies of the service book.

The Rev. G. Heileg was succeeded by the Rev. R. M. Jacobi, the length of time each served not being given, nor the time of their appointment. Following these, the pastors, from 1869 to 1885, were the Revs. George Miller Lazarus, W. R. Bruehler, who resigned, 1871, C. F. Welder, R. S. Wagner, 1873-75, J. H. Fritz, 1875-78, A. R, Horne, D. D, 1878-85, the well-known educator, E. L. Miller, 1885-88, and D. L. Coleman, 1888-90. The church was now without a pastor from September, 1890 to March 1891, being supplied for that period by students from the Lutheran Theological Seminary, Philadelphia. From 1891 to the present time, the church has had but two pastors, the Rev. J. R. Groff, and the incumbent, the Rev. Samuel A. Bridges Stopp, called June 16, 1901 and entered upon his pastorate July 1. He is an alumnus of Muhlenberg College, 1896, Princeton University, 1897, and the Lutheran Theological Seminary, Mount Airy, Philadelphia, 1901. Mr. Stopp is a nephew of the late Hon. Samuel A. Bridges, of Allentown, who represented the Bucks-Lehigh district in the House of Representatives of the United States, elected, 1852.

As early as 1874, the services were held alternately in English and German, but, since 1890, all the services have been in English. In 1875, the new constitution of the congregation was adopted, and the Sunday School organized in April of the same year. The Ladies' Aide Society did much toward finishing the church, and the capacious chancel, with its altar, reredos and windows, by Tiffany, were added in 1896.

The church is in a prosperous state. It has one hundred and seventy-five communicants; a Sunday School, whose future is encouraging; the fullest possible use is made of the Liturgy to the enrichment of the service, and the closest harmony with old Lutheran usages.

While a Baptist church was not erected in Doylestown until 1867, an attempt was made as early as 1846, by the Rev. Samuel Nightingale.[4] He was elected pastor, at New Britain, 1838, but resigned January 1846, having moved into Doylestown prior to that time. He bought a lot on the south side of East State street, near Church, sixty-four by one hundred and seventy-one feet and laid out a building forty by fifty-three, and, in the spring of 1850, began work but never got above the first floor. The expense incurred was $630, collections $519, cash subscription, unpaid $350, and in material and work $450. The money subscriptions were mostly in small amounts the two largest being that of John B. Pugh, $50, and Simon Callender, $30. Mr. Nightingale had not finally abandoned his church enterprise in 1865, when he received a subscription of $20 from a Philadelphian. The lot was subsequently sold and dwellings erected upon it.

The Rev. Samuel Nightingale was born in Burlington county, New Jersey, December 11, 1792, and died at Philadelpia, March 3, 1881. He married Emma Billington, of Philadelphia, June 8, 1814 and was the father of seven children. His eldest daughter, Anna, was twice married her first husband being Ex-Judge Richard Jones, Montgomery county, Pa., who was U. S Counsel General to Egypt. In his early years, Mr. Nightingale engaged in business in Baltimore and Philadelphia, which he left for the ministry. He was succeeded at New Britain by the Rev. Heman Lincoln, 1845. He now spent several years in Doylestown without a charge, occasionally preaching in the various churches. He was an unique person and an able preacher. One, who knew him well, and of the same faith and belief, called Mr. Nightingale the "Zachary Taylor of the Baptist ministry."

After the attempt of Mr. Nightingale, to organize a Baptist con-

---

4 At Doylestown, April 30, 1840, Matilda Nightingale, of consumption, daughter of the Rev. Samuel Nightingale, in her twentieth year.

SALEM REFORMED CHURCH, 1897.

gregation and erect a church building in Doylestown, a period of twenty-two years elapsed before a second effort was made. This was in 1867. From 1850, their pastors at New Britain preached occasionally in the Court House and Masonic Hall, and on the 14th of April, 1867, a Baptist Sunday School was organized in the Beneficial Hall. On the 11th of November, the Baptists of the vicinity met to consider the question of a church organization, the Rev. W. S. Wood in the chair. There were twenty-eight persons present, twenty-four from New Britain, three from Davisville and one from Philadelphia. The proposition was agreed to and, at a subsequent meeting, December 3, the First Baptist church, of Doylestown, was organized with forty-nine constituent members, thirty-six of whom brought letters of dismissal from New Britain. The New Hampshire confession of faith was adopted and the Rev. W. S. Wood chosen missionary pastor, one of the members guaranteeing his salary. The church organization was recognized January 16, 1868, at a council held in Beneficial Hall, composed of messengers from New Britain, Point Pleasant, First Philadelphia and Second Germantown churches, the Rev. George Dana Boardman preaching the sermon in the Presbyterian church in the evening.

The erection of a church building being the next thing in order, a lot was purchased May 26, for $1,200 on the southwest corner of West Court and Clinton streets, and a building erected at the cost of $23,000. The church was admitted into the North Philadelphia Association. The first pastor was the Rev. W. S. Wood, the same who was missionary pastor, but resigned in March 6, 1870. He was followed by the Revs. A. J. Hastings, 1870; John Miller, 1876; T. R. Howlett,[5] 1882; C. A. Hare, 1888; L. C. Leinback, 1893; N. C. Fetter, 1894 and the Rev. John H. Deming the present pastor.

The membership at different periods down to 1888, but have no return since, was as follows: 1876, 181; 1877, 227; 1879, 238; 1880, 215; 1882, 198 and 168 in 1888.

Two members of the Doylestown Baptist church entered the missionary field and have achieved success, William Edgar Geil and Franklin Pierce Lynch. The former, an evangelist, recently returned

---

[5] The Rev. Thomas Rosling Howlett, born in England, March 19, 1827, came to America at an early age, settled in Ohio, graduated in Divinity at Madison Seminary, 1858, and was first called to a Baptist church, at New Brunswick, N. J. In 1891, he met with an accident on the P. R. R. which caused the amputation of one of his legs. He died in Philadelphia, December 27, 1898. Mr. Howlett was an author of considerable note.

from a tour of the world, and, wherever he was heard, attracted great attention. Both entered life with adverse surroundings, but have overcome every obstacle and achieved success. This was especially the case with Mr. Lynch. He attracted attention when a boy, working in Mr. Dungan's bone factory, and became a scholar in the Baptist Sunday School. Here he developed an insatiate thirst for knowledge and a fixed purpose to gain an education. He became a ravenous reader, and the labors of the day were followed by reading and study in a barely furnished room, night after night. From the common school he entered Doylestown Seminary; thence to the Lewisburg Seminary where he graduated, 1884, the Yale Divinity school, and subsequent years at the Medical college of New York city, and in practice at Bridgeport, Conn. In 1893, the American Baptist Union sent Mr. Lynch to take charge of a sanitarium at the mouth of the Congo river, Africa, where he engaged in mission and hospital work, his hospital being equipped with instruments and medical supplies. He is not only a physician of high attainments, and a surgeon of great skill, but an impressive speaker. Despite flattering offers to establish himself in the United States, he declines to leave his work in Africa. The Rev. Mr. Lynch was born and brought up in Doylestown.

The latest church, built in Doylestown, was "The People's Colored church," so called, organized January 17, 1901, and erected on the site of the Colored Baptist church, destroyed by fire four years previous. The persons, most active in this movement, were George Gray, Annie Gray, Jane Ann Morris, Rev. John D. Mitchell, Emma Palmer, deceased, John Harris, James Harris, Dora Jackson, Lida Gould, Stephen Bowens, Cora Bowens and Mary Palmer. About this time, the Rev. Albert Price was called, and, for a time, insured a new spirit into the congregation and taught them the value of unity of action. A new church was shortly erected at a cost of $900, of which $300 were paid in cash, and an effort was made to pay the balance, but we do not know with what success. The working organizations, belonging to the congregation, are a "Young People's Christian Endeavor Society," "Look-Out Committee," "Pray Meeting Committee," a "Sunday School," with forty-five scholars, officers and teachers, and an "Anti-Swearing Society." Price, the pastor, left some time since.

Doylestown, Old and New.

XXIII
The Middle of the Century.

We have now reached the fifties and are at the middle of the century. Down through the decades, from the advent of the nineteenth century, there had been a gradual expansion and improvement, but everything still moved along conservative lines. All seemed to be waiting for some new development, for "something to turn up" as it were, and put the county capital in closer touch with the outside world. There were indications, and had been for some time, but nothing came to pass, until about the middle of the fifties, that looked like a fulfillment of the promise.

This "something" was the introduction of artificial light on the streets, in the dwellings and public buildings half a century ago. The first to make its appearance was rosin gas by John Simpson, of Philadelphia, who erected a plant, 1854, and put it in charge of Wayne Bartholomew. It fell shortly into the hands of Morris & Tasker, also of Philadelphia, who began the manufacture of gas from coal. In 1864, Morris & Tasker sold their works to Peter Munsiger, likewise of Philadelphia, but they passed into the hands of Morris & Tasker again between 1879 and 1882, and then to Charles Wheeler. On December 20, 1882, Wheeler sold the plant to Theodore P. Harvey and James Kane, who ran it until Harvey's death, April 1, 1886, Kane now had control of the gas works until the following November, when they were again sold, this time to Dumont & Wagner, other Philadelphians. The gas works again changed hands by their sale to James Kane, September 27, 1887, who retained possession and managed them until April 1, 1894, when he sold out to F. D. Zell, another Philadelphian, and Zell sold to the company which is the present owner. James Kane had more or less to do with all the gas companies down to the introduction of electricity, and was one of the pioneers in supplying our streets, and buildings with artificial light. Electricity came in 1892. The company was chartered January 26; the first meeting held at the office of Henry Lear, Esq., the 27th, and lights turned on May 30. The officers elected, for 1892, were Henry Lear, president, John Yardley, secretary and treasurer, and Alfred Paschall, Henry Lear, James Pollock, H. S. Murfit, J. D. James, W. H. Kirk, A. F. Sheetz and R. M. Yardley, directors.

The next thing, and the most important, destined to lift our town of Doyle out of its drowsy, quiet, was the charter of a railroad from Philadelphia, to tap the Lehigh and country beyond at South Bethlehem, with a promise of its completion in the near future. This would complete, by rail and steam, what the opening of the Bethlehem and Easton roads began, a century and quarter before.

As there was capital behind this project, work was begun forthwith and almost finished to Lansdale by the summer of 1856, where a branch tapped it from Doylestown. The last rails were laid on the branch October 1, that fall, and the approach of the iron horse is thus spoken of by the *Bucks County Intelligencer* of October 7:

"The scream of the locomotive had been very distinctly heard for some days, and, at length, it is at our doors. The road was yet in a very incomplete state, but the work was actively going on, and would soon be in good running order. To-day the cars will commence running over the entire distance, from Doylestown to Philadelphia, affording our citizens an opportunity to visit the exhibition of the National Agricultural Society at Powelton which is now open. The trains will run regularly twice every day, but, owing to the incompleteness of the road, the passage will be somewhat tedious. From Philadelphia to Doylestown, by the road, the distance is a little over thirty-two miles."

In speaking of the station houses on the road, the same article says, of the one to be built at Doylestown: "It will be situated on a large lot of land owned by the company, immediately at the southern entrance to the town, and will have a frame edifice fifty feet wide and one hundred and fifty long, suitably divided for the accommodation of passengers and of neat and ornamental workmanship." If this were ever promised, by the North Penn in relation to the station house to be erected at Doylestown, it reminds us of what Shakespeare put into the mouth of Macbeth, and was something

"That keep the word of promise to the ear,
And breaks it to the hope."

Another article, in the same issue of the *Intelligencer*, headed "Arrival of the cars; opening of the railroad," said:

"Yesterday afternoon a train, containing the directors and other officers of the North Pennsylvania Railroad, arrived in Doylestown. A large number of persons were in waiting to receive the visitors, and to witness the appearance of the iron horse in his professional capacity. The party took dinner at Kram's Hotel,[1] and in the afternoon, returned to the city. Hereafter we shall have communication with Philadelphia twice a day, by this route, morning and afternoon." Think of it!

Monday, October 6, was a red letter day for our county capital; it was put in touch with the commercial capital of the state by rail, "twice a day." Just think of it, after the lapse of forty-six years; Fifty years before, 1806, one of the inducements held out by the trustees of the newly-built Union Academy, for parents to send their children to it to school, was because "the Easton and Bethlehem stages run through the town twice a week," now in 1856, half a century later, the descendants of the same children can reach Philadelphia *twice* in one day. We repeat, "Just think of it!" The world does really move, we have stepped into new Doylestown, and our town will now leap along with its fellows, and bid farewell to the old. The name of the locomotive, that brought the first train of cars from Philadelphia to Doylestown, was an appropriate one, the "Civilizer," and the engineer John Gleason. Among the early locomotive engineers of that day that served on the North Penn for several years was John McDonald Laughlin, who deserted the throttle for the musket in 1861. He enlisted in the 104th regiment for the war, served over three years and returned with the rank of Major. McLaughlin's locomotive was the "Neshaminy" No. 5. In one of the early trains, of 1856, an excursion train, filled with children, ran off the track just below Fort Washington, by which many were killed or badly wounded. At this period there was an attempt to boom building lots out Court street, but was not a success.

The third local event, intended to push Doylestown ahead, and

---

[1] At that time Abram Kram kept the "Citizen's House," the same building, altered, in which the "Scheetz Sons" keep store, Pine and East Court.

would have done something toward it, had not misfortune overtaken the enterprise, was in the spring of 1855, when William Beek, an enterprising resident of the borough, purchased twenty-five acres in the southwest suburb for the purpose of putting on foot an exhibition of somewhat gigantic proportions. He enclosed it with a board fence, erected a large and attractive building, adapted to the purpose he had in view, and built extensive stabling to house the horses, cattle and lower animals that were to be placed on exhibition. The affair came off in August, and, according to the newspapers, and the consensus of public opinion, was a "howling success." And so it was at first blush. It was held under Beek's individual patronage, including a diversified display of stock, agricultural implements—products of house and farm, and last, though not least, a real baby show, the first of the kind ever seen in the county. This was a drawing card. How many of these babies ever got to congress or reached the White House, we are not informed. There was also competition among female equestrians, and many a young fellow sent his best girl to the ring. Horace Greeley delivered the address, and, as a drawing card, he was only second to the baby show. The attendance was very large and all pronounced it a most successful affair. But the aftermath spoiled all; that fall the building blew down in a gale of wind and was converted into kindling wood. The likeness, that accompanys the text, and probably the only one in existence, speaks well for it. The Beek enterprise deserved a better fate, and his misfortune received the sympathy of all.

Among the most conspicuous men, whose names were connected with the Beek exhibition of 1855, was that of the late Col. George G. Leiper, Delaware county, who was expected to preside as Chairman. His portrait was painted by Samuel F. DuBois, the noted Doylestown artist, and hung in the Art Department, but a death in his family preventing Colonel Leiper being present, the Hon. Charles Huffnagle, of New Hope, this county, Ex-U. S. Consul-General at Calcutta, was selected in his stead. When the exposition building was blown down, and Mr. Beek found himself financially ruined, he returned the portrait of Colonel Leiper to Mr. DuBois, the artist who painted it. On the latter's death, it came into possession of the family of the late Charles E. DuBois, Esq., where it remained until September, 1901, when it was presented to the Bucks County Historical Society.

The most valuable improvement to Doylestown, and gave the

borough the biggest boom it had received down to that period, and conduced to the health and comfort of the population, was the introduction of a plentiful supply of wholesome water for drinking and other domestic purposes. This has been so long enjoyed we fear the people fail to realize its importance. The late General William T. Rogers[2] is more entitled to the thanks of the people for this boon than any other one person living or dead. It was put on foot at the beginning of that decade, the first meeting being held on Tuesday evening, December 31, 1850, when a committee was appointed to consider the question, collect imformation, and report at a subsequent meeting. At this meeting an agreement was reached, among a few enterprising persons of the borough, that when the property, known as the "borough mill," came into the market it should be bought to secure the valuable water privileges it controlled, the only supply accessible. This consisted of several springs forming a mill dam, suitable for a pumping reservoir. The mill belonged to the estate of Sandham Stewart, and, when put up at public sale, was purchased by General Rogers. From this modest beginning, came the abundant water supply the town now enjoys, but it required eighteen years to carry out the plans of the projectors. During the session of the Legislature, of 1851-52, a bill was introduced and passed, authorizing the borough council to borrow money to erect water works. It was violently opposed at home, and, at the next spring election, an anti-water council was elected. This, for the present, put a stop to the enterprise but, in the meantime, the cemetery company had given permission to build the basin on their grounds and considerable work had been done. The question of the introduction of water now lay dormant for many years.

The railroad, from Philadelphia to the Lehigh, was partially completed in the spring of 1856, and the author, on his visit home from New Mexico in May of that year, rode up the North Penn railroad to Gwynedd, and then by stage across country to Doylestown. By the fall, the main line was finished to the Lehigh and also the branch to Doylestown. Down to this time, our county capital had passed through the various phazes of village life, from infancy to healthy boyhood, but now the old had passed away with many who had helped to make the town what it was, while a new generation stood ready to make history for themselves and the town they lived in. They, who

---

2 At Doylestown, January 8, 1822, by the Rev. John C. Murphy, William T. Rogers, editor of the *Democrat* and *Farmer's Gazette*, to Miss Sophia Pugh, daughter of John Pugh, Esq., of Doylestown.

are with us now, hardly realize, that down to 1856 all communication, with the outside world, was by horse and wagon in private conveyance, or the lumbering stage coach.

As we stand in the middle of the nineteenth century, let us turn our thoughts backward for a moment, and indulge in retrospect while we contemplate the cross roads hamlet, as we first knew it when the century came in. It then consisted of a few dwellings and a couple of road side inns. Four years later there was a newspaper and an Academy, and, by the end of the decade, the Legislature had decreed it should be the future county capital and its fortune was assured. From that time, down through the decades, improvements multiplied, and the population increased; churches were built, social, civic and educational organizations effected, town lots were brought into market and offered for sale, some changing owners without the erection of buildings; nevertheless it was a sign of effort to reach out on the lines of improvement and indicated a disposition to break away from the conservative fetters of the past.

As we quit the middle decade of the century, and draw the line between old and new Doylestown, we step into the sixties, and enter the Civil war period. It had a wonderful effect on the future of Doylestown, and, while the harvest was an evil one for the time being, the ultimate result was beneficial. We repeat here what we have said elsewhere, that the Civil war period stimulated everything, by making money plenty and cheap, and both the evil and good effect were seen and felt in Doylestown. At the close of the war, improvement set in; we may almost say it leaped forward. The first extension of the borough was in the direction of the southwest, by opening the Magill farm for building purposes; it was next extended on the east by the purchase of the DuBois fields, and subsequently the Riale tract on the northwest was taken hold of and brought into the market. These several tracts were laid out in building lots, streets opened through them and houses erected. By this time "New Doylestown" was able to speak for itself, and in a tone not to be misunderstood. A little time was required, to recover from the severe strain of the war, but, that done, our conservative interests were ready to go to work. While a portion of our new energy was expended in the sixties, the best of it was reserved for the seventies.

The effort, to introduce water into the borough, in 1851-52, and which failed for want of popular sympathy, was renewed in 1867. In that year an amendment to the borough charter was obtained, "which

DOYLESTOWN PUBLIC SCHOOL BUILDING

gave council power and authority to construct and maintain water works for the said borough," and the act also authorized the Town Council to borrow money not to exceed the sum of $35,000. The act was approved March 13. Since the first attempt to introduce water into Doylestown, the minds of the people had undergone a change, and an effort was made, at the spring election, 1869, to elect a borough council in favor of its introduction. The two tickets in the field were "water" and "anti-water," and, after a sharp contest, "water" carried the day; the following being the names of the new councilmen: John L. DuBois, Henry T. Darlington, W. W. H. Davis, George Deemer, Nathan P. Brower, Nathan C. James, Andrew J. Larue, Samuel Hall and Charles Rotzel. Of these, Brower, Larue and Deemer were new members.

The first practical step, looking to the erection of water works, was taken March 20, 1869, the day the new council met to organize. John L. DuBois was elected president and Benjamin Hough clerk, and, after the organization had been effected, W. W. H. Davis offered the following resolution:

Resolved, that the president appoint a committee of three to report at a special, or the next regular meeting, upon the practicability of introducing water into the borough; said report shall embody all the information obtained on the subject of supplying the town with water." After some discussion the resolution was adopted, whereupon the chair appointed the following special committee: W. W. H. Davis, Nathan C. James and Henry T. Darlington. The committee was appointed March 22, at a subsequent meeting, but whether a special or regular, the author does not remember nor is it material, as the committee was instructed to proceed with its work. It was authorized to employ a competent engineer, the choice falling on William E. Morris, Philadelphia, and W. W. H. Davis was chairman of the building committee.

Active operations were begun, without any unnecessary delay, and pushed as rapidly as possible. The opposition, however, was also active and appealed to the court to stop the work; but the water committee went ahead despite them, and, before an injunction could be obtained, the works were completed, and the water turned on in the fall. The cost was $32,000. When council came to put the water in the dwellings and places of business the men, who had so violently opposed its introduction, seemed almost to "tumble over each other," in their anxiety and haste to have it in their premises first. A number of springs were opened in the meadow above the mill dam, from which the water was pumped into a distributing basin in the cemetery, and thence conveyed in iron pipes over the borough. The water was raised, by a steam engine, placed in the mill, one hundred and fifty-seven feet in the distance of three thousand and two hundred feet and fire plugs were planted in the streets six hundred feet apart. Since water was introduced, the original system has been improved and the facilities increased. In recent years two artesian wells were sunk and the water supply largely added to, made necessary by the increased population and consumption. The enterprise was every way successful, and pays eight or ten per cent. on the investment.

As we turn out of old Doylestown, into the new, it seems a fitting opportunity to say something about the population of our county's capital down through the century and of which but little has yet been said.

The population of Doylestown was first taken by the census of 1840, two years after the borough was organized and twenty-seven after being made the county seat. Prior to 1840, we have to rely largely on tradition and heresay, never entirely reliable when dealing with figures. Going back to 1820, eighteen years prior to its organization as a borough, we are told the population was three hundred and sixty, and that it had grown to five hundred by 1829, an increase of one hundred and forty in nine years, but we have no evidence of its accuracy. In some periods of the same length, with a greater population to begin with, the increase under the census enumeration was not near so great. The *Bucks County Intelligencer*, of August 30, 1830, says of the population: The census have just been taken, and there are about eight hundred inhabitants within its limits. Several good houses are being built, two of which are of brick, being the first houses built of that kind of material in the place. The bricks are from the kiln of Dr. Charles Meredith within a few rods of the court house.

The census, taken of the village, must have been a very elastic one to give an increase of from five hundred to eight hundred in a single year. The enumerater would not be likely to make the population any less than it was, especially as the village had no "butts and bounds." On the authority of Wm. Buck, whom I esteem to be accurate in such matters, the number of dwellings in Doylestown, in 1832, was one hundred and two, and two hundred and seventy-nine in 1860. On the ordinary basis this would give five hundred and ten population for the former and thirteen hundred and ninety-five for the latter. The fact that the United States census, of 1840, gives Doylestown a population of but nine hundred and sixteen, the jump of three hundred from 1829 to 1830, was unreasonable and there were no conditions to warrant it. At the census, of 1840, there were four hundred and eight white males, four hundred and forty-one white females and forty-seven colored.

The late Thomas Brunner, Bridge Point, now Edison, told the author, that himself and the late Samuel Kachline counted the dwellings in Doylestown in 1821, and they numbered twenty-nine, including the Academy, in which a family lived. This would give the village a population of one hundred and forty-five at that time. We believe there is a mistake somewhere. There was some little increase each year, but it was not until in the thirties that the new county capital made solid advance in population. In one of the January issues of the *Intelligencer*, 1833, that paper says of Doylestown:

"The village now enumerates about one hundred and two dwelling houses of all sizes, which shows an average increase of nearly two houses annually since 1778, among which are seven houses for public entertainment." It would be an interesting fact to know how many dwellings were in Doylestown, in 1778, to begin the count on. In 1835 the borough and township had four hundred and seventy taxables, and, in 1842, the borough, alone, had two hundred and six taxables. By the census of 1850, there were nine hundred and seventy-four white and thirty-two colored, one thousand and six in all, the last of old Doylestown, the next, 1860, the first of new Doylestown. Drawing the line at 1856, the connecting of Doylestown with the outside world by rail, it is reasonable to base the increase in the previous decade to give it one half the increase from 1850 to 1860, four hundred and sixteen; one half being two hundred and eight which, added to that of 1850, would make the population twelve hundred and fourteen in 1856, when old Doylestown retires and new Doylestown comes to the front. The population, in 1860, was fourteen hundred and sixteen, 1870, one thousand six hundred and one, of which one hundred and thirty-nine were of foreign birth, in 1880, two thousand and seventy, 1890, two thousand five hundred and nineteen, and, in 1900, three thousand and thirty-four. These latter figures show an increase of two thousand and twenty-eight in population over 1850, and of two thousand one hundred and eighteen over the census of 1840. From 1840 to 1850, the increase in the population of Doylestown was but ninety, evidence the town needed something to give it a boom. The census returns do not show the entire population of the borough, for there are nearly five hundred persons living contiguous on the southwest, only separated by a street from the incorporated district. They enjoy some of our borough privileges, gas, electricity and water, but vote in the township. Practically the population of Doylestown is about three thousand and five hundred.

Among the strangers who came to Doylestown in the early fifties, were the Lawsons and Bazelys, two English families; both boarding at the Fountain House, but not at the same time. The Lawsons came first, about 1850, and had left before the Bazelys came. The family consisted of wife, daughter and two sons. The sons soon engaged in business, in Philadelphia, the others remaining. The daughter, Caroline, called "Caddy" for short, was a pretty, sprightly girl and a fine horsewoman. About the same time there came here from Philadelphia, a young man named William R. Brown, probably sent to sow his wild oats in the fertile soil of Bucks county. He also took board at the Fountain House. The young people naturally fell in love which resulted in marriage. In 1855, Brown built a dwelling about two miles from Doylestown, in Warrington township, in which himself and wife lived for a time, but it wrecked his fortune and they finally separated. He returned to Philadelphia, and the Lawsons removed to Norristown where father, mother and daughter died. The house that Brown built and was ruined by, and subsequently given the name of "Brown's Folly," is still standing and belongs to Mrs. Helen Larzelere. It is used as a summer boarding house, and has a little history of its own. The architect was Joseph D. Keacker, Philadelphia, and the plans and specifications were drawn in 1855. In 1895, they turned up among some papers of Edward Larkin, who died about 1899, and he sent them to the office of the Philadelphia-Wilmington and Baltimore R. R. Co., Wilmington, Del. Mr. Larkin was the engineer of the Susquehanna river bridge, Havre de Grace, where he died. In 1895, these papers were sent by Ralph Goodwin, assistant engineer, P. W. & B. R. R. Co. to postmaster Purdy, Doylestown, who presented them to the author. When the Civil War broke out, William R. Brown entered the army and reached the rank of captain. He was mustering officer at Philadelphia, 1864, and mustered out the 104th regiment, and then and there the author met him for the last time.

The Bazely family, mentioned in a previous page, came to Doylestown about 1852-53, John Bazely, the father, being an excellent type of an intelligent Englishman. The family consisted of the wife, and three children, Edward, Eliza and Harriet. They had previously lived at New Orleans, thence came to West Chester, boarding at the hotel where Judge Chapman stopped while holding court there. Upon Mr. Bazely inquiring of him for a pleasant place in the country to make their home, he recommended Doylestown. They came forthwith, and took board at what is now the Fountain House. They lived here some five years. The parents were cultivated people and the children young. Subsequently the family all died except the daughter, Eliza, who grew up to be a lovely women and now makes her home in Philadelphia. The son went into business, married and left children. The brother of John Bazely, the father, was Sir Thomas Bazely, the most extensive cotton spinner at Manchester, England, at that period, and a man of great wealth. Our Mr. Bazely was well informed on all public questions of that day, the tarriff being his especial hobby. He was a red hot free-trader, for an Englishman, and we listened many an hour to his discussion of the subject.

In 1859, or thereabouts, Jacob Hill came to Doylestown from Norristown and went into business here, renting what is now the Lehman house, at the northeast corner of East State street and Printers' alley. His family consisted of a single member, an unmarried daughter, Octavia C. Hill, who was a poetess of decided merit, and wrote under the nom de plume of "Annot Lyle." While the 104th regiment was being recruited and organized, several inspiring pieces in verse from her pen appeared in our newspapers, and, on its return from the field, her "Welcome Home" was not only appropriate, but much admired. Mr. Hill died here. His daughter married a Mr. Fahnstock, of Gettysburg, 1871, and died there in 1873, under very distressing circumstances.

In the early fifties, the period we have been writing about, the author was also a boarder at the Fountain House, and enjoyed the society of the two English families we have spoken of. They were agreeable people. About that time "table turning," some sort of necromancy with which electricity and galvanism had to do, made its appearance here. It was done by four persons sitting down to a small square table, and crossing hands on the top of it. When the chain of hands was thus completed, the table would slowly move round. On one occasion the author sat down, with three children at a small stand; presently the stand slowly moved round and when the current was broken it stopped. We then put several books on the top of the stand, renewed the current by crossing hands, and the table slowly moved. A good sized boy was next put on the stand, the current renewed and with the same result, the table or stand slowly turning round. This was practiced in many houses and became quite a fad. We hardly expect any one to believe it in this practical age, nor do we attempt to explain its "why's" and "wherefores," nevertheless we vouch for the truth of what we have written. Some old people will doubtless recall it.

We are now on the point of closing the happenings of the middle decade of the last century. On Washington's birthday night, February 22, 1859, the Doylestown Guards, the representative of the martial spirit of the county capital, gave a "Military and Citizen's Dress Ball." It took place at their Armory, in Clemens' Hall. There was a large attendance of the sons and daughters of old Bucks, and the affair was a great success.

> "And bright lamps shone o'er fair women and brave men,
>   A thousand hearts beat happily; and when
> Music arose with its voluptuous swell,
>   Soft eyes look'd love to eyes which spake again,
> And all went merry as a marriage bell."

Doylestown, Old and New.

XXIV
Doylestown in the Civil War.

Doylestown was as faithful to duty, in the great war for the Union, as it had been in previous wars, her sons being among the first in the state to enroll, and the *very first* in the county. News, of the firing on Sumter, reached Doylestown, Saturday, April 13, 1861, and, on Monday morning, before it was known the President had issued a call for troops, Captain Davis, of the Doylestown Guards, called a meeting of the company under the following notice;

"The members of the Doylestown Guards, and all other patriotic men, in favor of maintaining the honor of the Star Spangled Banner and the stability of the United States Government, are requested to meet in Clemens' Hall, on Thursday evening at eight o'clock, to take such measures as may be deemed necessary, in view of the critical condition of the country."[1]

April 15, 1861.   (Signed)   W. W. H. DAVIS, Captain.

On consulation with others, however, the time and place of holding the meeting was changed to the Court House, on Monday evening the 15th. In the meantime, the services of the company were offered

---

[1] Of the eighty officers and men, composing the company at the time it entered the service, before the war was over more than one half of the whole number bore commissions in the great armies of the United States. Two reached the rank of Brigadier-General by brevet, four were Colonels, one falling at the head of his regiment at Antietam, one Lieutenant-Colonel, four Majors, sixteen Captains, nine Lieutenants and two Surgeons; nearly all of them reaching their grade through regular promotion.

to Governor Curtin and accepted, and directed to "await orders." [2] These events made the borough aglow with excitement.

The meeting at the Court House was large and enthusiastic, the Honorable Henry Chapman presiding. On taking the chair, he made a patriotic address, and was followed by George Lear, Esq., Colonel John Blair, Nathan C. James and Enos Prizer. Captain Davis now arose with an enlistment roll in his hand, with his own name at the top, and called for recruits. The first person, to step forward and sign the roll, was William Kachline, of Doylestown, and it was almost filled before the meeting adjourned, men and women joining hands in fitting out the company for active service, while the captain drilled it day and night, and other-wise prepared it for the field. It received marching orders on the 26th, leaving the next morning, reaching Harrisburg that evening, where it was mustered into service. The company was now ordered to York, Pa., and thence to Washington in charge of the guns of the Ringgold battery, being the first body of armed men to pass through Baltimore—after the riot of the 19th of April. The company remained in Washington until June 25, when it marched with a battalion of the regiment, the 25th Pennsylvania, to join Colonel Stone's command near Edward's Ferry, opposite Leesburg, Va. The column marched up the left bank of the Potomac to Williamsport, where it forded the river and joined Patterson's army at Martinsburg. The Guards took part in the campaign in the Shenandoah Valley until its time was about to expire, when, with other troops, the company was sent to Harrisburg, mustered out and discharged, reaching Doylestown, July 29.

Through the brief campaign, the Doylestown Guards enjoyed the reputation of being one of the best drilled and disciplined companies in Patterson's army. A veteran officer, of the regular army, told the writer he had never seen a company superior to it in all his service. This is "a feather in the cap" of the first company, from Bucks county, to enter the military service in the war for the Union.

The following was the roll, of the Doylestown Guards, when the company left for Washington the morning of April 29, 1861, as printed in the newspapers of the next day :

---

[2] The following was the dispatch of Governor Curtin's acceptance of the Doylestown Guards :

HARRISBURG, April 18, 1861.
To Major W. W. H. Davis :
    Your company is accepted, and will await orders.
                                  (Signed)   R. C. HALL.

CAPTAIN,
W. W. H. DAVIS.

First Lieutenant, JACOB SWARTZLANDER.
Second Lieutenant, GEORGE T. HARVEY.

Drummer, JOHN HARGRAVE.   Fifer, WILLIAM K. SHEARER.

PRIVATES.

6. William Kachline,
7. William R. Stavely,
8. Michael E. Jenks,
9. Nathaniel Hubbard,
10. Samuel Croasdale,
11. James D. Hendrie,
12. Edwin Fretz,
13. Edward L. Rogers,
14. Edward S. Darling,
15. Juluis Kuster,
16. Ira F. Gensel,
17. Chris. K. Frankinfield,
18. Lawrence Frankinfield,
19. Charles Frankinfield,
20. Eleazer Beal,
21. Levi K. Markley,
22. William Follis,
23. Philip Hinkle,
24. Wm. Augustus Green,
25. Frederick Morley,
26. John H. Lewis,
27. Samuel C. Tussman,
28. David Firman,
29. Moses O. Kulp,
30. James Reed Orem,
31. Thomas Hart,
32. Enos P. Tomlinson,
33. Thomas F. Tomlinson,
34. Lazarus C. Andress,
35. A. Jackson Pierce,
36. Joseph H. Harvey,
37. John H. McCoy,
38. Thomas Brunner, Jr.,
39. Francis L. Coar,
40. Samuel N. Garron,
41. Theophilus Kephart,
42. George W. Emory,
43. John McD. Laughlin,
44. James M. Rogers,
45. Henry Hargrave,
46. Henry A. Widdiefield,
47. Eugene Magill,
48. Wm. H. Anglemeyer,
49. William Walker,
50. Henry W. Haney,
51. George A. Everheart,
52. Jacob W. Glase,
53. W. Warren Marple,
54. Lawrence Rush,
55. Edgar Kibby,
56. Washington G. Nugent,
57. James M. Carver,
58. Jacob Clemens,
59. George Hart,
60. Samuel Hart, Jr.,
61. Henry S. Service,
62. William Berkelbach,
63. Cephas W. Dyer,
64. Charles W. Hoffman,
65. John S. Hogeland,
66. Stephen Townsend,
67. Edward S. Mills,
68. Jacob Fries,
69. Wm. H. McDowell,
70. George W. Sunderland,
71. William McCarty,
72. William Peters,
73. William H. Jordon,
74. Emanuel K. Krauthamel,
75. William P. Heany,
76. George W. Garner,
77. William A. Shearer,
78. John Barndt,
79. John S. Hough,
80. J. Wilson Closson,
81. Eli Hofford,
82. Miles Williams,
83. Andrew Enders,
84. Abraham Maugle.

During the campaign the company lost but one man, Edgar Kibby who died of disease; and William Augustus Green died soon after reaching home.

Among the enlisted men, of the Guards, was Ira F. Gensel, deputy Prothonotary of the county, at the time he joined the Company. He was born at, or near Catawissa, Pa., but settled at Carversville, Pa., this county, shortly before the war, and followed his trade, a shoemaker. He was next at Doylestown, working at his trade for a time; then got clerical employment, and next entered the Prothonotary's office as deputy. He was one of the first to join the Guards, and, when organized, was appointed company clerk. Soon after reaching Washington, Captain Davis recommended Gensel for a Lieutenant's commission in the regular army, and obtained it. His military career was brief, being mortally wounded at the battle of Fredericksburg, and dying December 21, 1862. His remains were brought to Doylestown and buried in the cemetery. At the time of his death, Lieutenant Gensel was engaged to be married to a most estimable young lady of Doylestown.

While the Guards were in the field, the families of the enlisted men, which were not self-supporting with its head away, were taken care of by a borough committee, and another composed of citizens. That of the borough, organized May 9, 1861, was in operation two and one-half months, and disbursed $205.25, but this did not include the contributions of liberal citizens. The report, made by General William T. Rogers, who was active in the work, shows that only seven families were taken care of.

As there was no present prospect of the war coming to a close, Captain Davis took immediate steps to raise and organize a regiment of Infantry, to be placed in a camp of instruction near Doylestown, and, for this purpose, he went to Washington, August 21, and received the following authority from the Secretary of War:

WAR DEPARTMENT, August 22, 1861.
COLONEL W. W. H. DAVIS,
    Doylestown, Pennsylvania.

SIR :—" You are hereby authorized to raise a regiment of Infantry for the service of the United States, to serve for three years, or the war, to be armed, equipped and uniformed by the goverment.

"You are also authorized to form a camp of instruction, for the drilling and disciplining of your regiment, at a point convenient to the railroad, near Doylestown. When it shall be necessary, the quartermaster and commissary, at Philadelphia, upon the proper requisition and exhibition of this order, will furnish you with tents and rations and other necessary stores and transportation for the same.

"You are also authorized to raise and organize a battery of artillery to be attached to the regiment, subject to the approval of Lieutenant-General Scott. All necessary expenses, incurred in raising the regiment, will be paid by the United States, in accordance with general orders on that subject.

[SEAL]   (Signed) SIMON CAMERON, Secretary of War."

On Colonel Davis' return, from Washington, he made public announcement of his authority to raise a regiment, and called upon the young men of Bucks to "rally 'round the flag." The camp was located on the old exhibition ground, just west of the borough, and called "Camp Lacey," after General John Lacey, Bucks county's hero in the Revolution; requisitions were made for the necessary equippage and supplies, and tents pitched. Recruiting was so actively pushed that four hundred men were enrolled in ten days, and the first company mustered in September 6, in Clemens' Hall. This was known as the "Young Guard," and commanded by Captain Edward L. Rogers. By September 24, six hundred men were present, and, by the end of the month the whole ten companies were enrolled and mustered in. The camp was a model of neatness; the tents were floored and each company had a small frame kitchen. The men were fully armed and equipped by October 1, and their moral rapidly increased under the strict discipline enforced. When the regiment was full and ready for organization, Captain John W. Nields, of the First Pennsylvania Reserves, was appointed Lieutenat-Colonel, John M. Gries, Philadelphia, Major, Thompson D. Hart, Adjutant, and the Rev. William R. Gries, rector of St. Paul's Protestant Episcopal church, Doylestown, Chaplain. The band, of twenty-one pieces, came from Emaus, Lehigh county. The organization of the battery was turned over to Captain Durell, of Reading, an experienced artillery officer, and was detached from the regiment on reaching Washington. He commanded it the whole term of service, three years and ten months, and made a fine record.

While the regiment lay at Camp Lacey it made two excursions, the first to attend a union meeting, at Danboro, October 5, held in a woods nearby, the second to Hartsville on the 17th, where the ladies prepared a festival. On this occasion, the regiment appeared in all the "pomp, pride and circumstance of war," attracted great attention, and the officers and men received an ovation from the people of that patriotic community. While at the camp of instruction, the regiment was presented with two flags, the national and state, the former by the ladies, the latter by order of the Legislature. The presentation of both took place in camp, the first on October 21, the Rev. Jacob Belville representing the fair donors, the second, on the 31st, Governor Curtin appearing for the Commonwealth. Colonel Davis, on each occasion, received the flag for the regiment. The attendance was very large. In addition to these ceremonies, several officers had their maiden swords presented to them by friends, the ceremony taking place in the court house. Among these little affairs, the former members of the Doylestown Guards presented a Field Officer's sword to Colonel Davis, the late Edward J. Fox, Esq., of Easton, making an eloquent presentation speech. The number of the regiment, 104, was given the organization by the State authorities but the name assumed was the "Ringgold Regiment," which was beautifully wrought in silver on the national colors.

NORTH PENNSYLVANIA RAILROAD,
OFFICE OF GENERAL AGENT,
Front and Willow Streets,
PHILADELPHIA, November 5, 1861

Colonel W. W. H. Davis—Dear Sir:—A train of fifteen cars will be ready for your Regiment at Doylestown station to-morrow, (Wednesday) morning This allowing seventy-five men to a car, the usual number that we have carried on this road when moving large quantities, will carry your men, say one thousand and fifty. It is understood that you will be ready to move at eight a. m. for which hour our arrangements on the line of the road have been made.

It would be desirable, in order to expedite your transit through the city, that the stores and freight cars should precede the men, as they are to be hauled to Broad and Pine streets over the city track, upon which detentions often occur, that might interfere with your departure from the city, if we were allowed but a short time for their delivery. Either this evening's train or Wednesday morning train can take them if ready.

Very respectfully,

(Signed)　　　　　　　　ELLIS CLARK, General Agent

The regiment left camp the morning of November 6, reaching Washington the next afternoon, going into camp on an elevated spot back of Georgetown, overlooking the capital, and called "Meredian Hill." It bivouacked in the open air, and the weather was so severe water froze in the canteens. The strength of the regiment when it left Doylestown, was nine hundred, rank and file and the battery one hundred and fifty. The total casualties, during its service was five hundred and one. Of these, one hundred and six wounded returned to duty; fourteen officers were killed or wounded, and one hundred and forty-five men were discharged for disability. The heaviest loss, in a single action, was at Fair Oaks, May 31, 1862 whereof two hundred and ninety-three officers and men on the field the loss, killed and wounded, was fifty per cent.

The survivors of the regiment, except the re-enlisted veterens conscripts and substitutes recently joined, left Washington for Philadelphia September 23, 1864, and quartered over Sunday at the volunteer refreshment saloon. On Tuesday afternoon the city authorities gave the regiment a formal reception and escort through the principal streets. On Saturday they were mustered out and discharged, and that evening returned to Doylestown, where a befitting

LIEUT. E. S. McDOWELL,
KILLED AT FAIR OAKS.

reception awaited them. Through the influence of the ladies, a banquet was prepared in the court room, where their welcome home took place, Richard Watson, Esq.,[3] making the address. He opened his remarks by saying:

"Colonel Davis, officers and men of the 104th. On behalf of the committee, and those they represent, I bid you welcome home again.

" Three years ago this court house was the scene of the presentation of swords to several of your officers. They were conferred with the hope they might be worn with credit and honor, and the recipients promised the confidence of the donors should not be betrayed.

" Three years ago, on your old camp ground near by, your colors were given you. The one on behalf of the State by the Governor; the other, on behalf of the ladies of the county, by an elequent Divine whose heart was in the cause. They were given you, in confidence they would be borne wherever duty called you, and would be protected from every insult and danger, and that they would be returned unsullied by cowardice or shame. You promised to fullfil this trust. The hopes then expressed have been realized; the promises then made have been performed.

" You bring back these flags, pierced by ball and by shells, faded and torn by the wind, the sun and the rain, but on them are inscribed the names of the battle fields on which you have fought, and they are far more valuable now, thus faded and torn, than when presented to you glittering and new.

* . * * * * * * * *

" Your friends at home have eagerly watched your career; they have traced your marches, rejoiced over your successes, and mourned over your afflictions. They have heard with pride of your deeds of valor, and have had no reason to reproach you for disgrace.

* * * * * * * * * *

"Again I bid you welcome home, and ask you to accept the hospitalities of to-night, as a slight token of our regard for you and for your deeds."

In reply to Judge Watson's welcome home Col. Davis, said in part:

---

[3] The Rev. Dr. Andrews had been appointed to make the address, but was suddenly called from home.

"It is no new thing for soldiers returning from battle to be received with honors. It has been the custom for all nations and in all ages, when their armies returned to their homes to be welcomed with delight and pleasure. A sentiment of gratitude, alone, would dictate such reception, but to-night there is a stronger emotion that moves this assemblage to welcome home the defenders of their country ; it is not that you would honor those who have returned, but you thus show your thankfulness that they have returned at all in life and health.

* * * * *

"I need not speak to you, my friends, of the history of the 104th, your own regiment, which you have watched with such deep interest for three years, for its deeds have been written in blood. You do well to honor it.

* * * * *

Soldiers never faught in a better cause than that which called these men to the field. The rebellion, against the constituted authorities of the country, was both wicked and causeless. No man, in his right mind, would consent to a division of the Union; it would leave us a legacy of perpetual warfare to bequeath to our children, and our children's children.

* * * * *

"To you, my soldiers, is due the award of praise. Your courage, constancy and forbearance, amid all the vicissitudes of three years service, make you worthy soldiers of the Republic. The swamps of the Chickahominy, nor the trenches before Charleston interposed hardships your patriotism did not enable you to endure, and endure cheerfully; the battlefield had no terrors your courage did not meet and subdue. While you rejoice in your own happy return home, do not forget your comrades who fill a soldier's grave, nor fail to drop the tear of affection to their memory. The ashes of the brave smell sweet and blossom in the tomb!

* * * * * *

"Farewell officers and soldiers ! May the Almighty guide and direct you in all your ways, and make your future life as prosperous as the past has been glorious."

After the returning veterans had partaken of the feast the hand of affection had prepared, and exchanged congratulations with those from whom they had been so long separated, hosts and guests bade each other farewell, many carrying with them the following beautiful words of Annot Lyle:

> " And there are breaking hearts here in the crowd,
> And bitter thoughts around the banners cling,
> And sighs you hear not in the cheering loud,
> And aching smiles that passing leave a sting."

There was one thing about the organization of the 104th regiment that was unusual, in that Colonel Davis was the mustering officer of both himself and command. This was by the grace of his old friend General Cameron, then Secretary of War. He was instructed to apply for his own muster to the mustering officer at Philadelphia, Major Ruff, when his men were ready, and then muster his regiment. When the Colonel called on Major Ruff, he declined to recognize the Secretary's authority, whereupon the Colonel sent him to "thunder," saying he would go home, muster himself and then muster his regiment, and that it would "hold water." This he did despite the fact that it was very much off color, and it held water all the same. The case was not reached at the Adjutant General's office until 1863, when some correspondence took place, but the muster was recognized, and nothing more heard of it. It was a very unique proceeding.

No regiment, in the great war for the Union, did better service than the 104th, or made a more creditable record. The first year it served in the Army of the Potomac, taking part in the memorable campaign on the Peninsula. It led the Fourth corps from Yorktown to Harrison's Landing, bearing its full part in all that trying ordeal. It fired the first volley in front of Richmond, at the bloody battle of Fair Oaks, losing fifty per cent. of its men, in killed and wounded, of those engaged. It also participated in the "Seven Days' Battles." Going South, in the fall of 1862, the regiment saw the rest of its service in North and South Carolina and Florida, taking part in the long and arduous operations against the defences before Charleston. It afterward saw brief service in Virginia, on its way North to be mustered out, on the expiration of its term of enlistment.

When the regiment entered service its commander had other thoughts for the future, besides making his men good soldiers, one, the writing its history, the other, the erection of a monument to the memory of its dead; and both desires were long since carried out. The regimental history was written on Morris' Island, S. C., during the seige of Charleston, within sound of the enemy's guns, while the monument was manufactured in the fall of 1867, and erected the following spring at Doylestown. The important consideration, in the case of the monument, was the means wherewith to build it, but that was happily overcome. During the seige operations on Morris' Island the savings, from the regimental bakery, reached the generous sum of $2,000, but it could not be touched for this, or any other purpose, without consent of the Secretary of War and the enlisted men. I first approached the War Secretary with the query, whether the regimental Council of Admistration could appropriate $1,600 for a monument fund with the consent of the enlisted men, and, as the reader will see from the foot note below, ready assent was given.[4] Subsequent to this the men authorized the appropriation to be made and the money was placed in the Colonel's hands. This was the nest egg, which private subscriptions, a donation from Company E, and interest on the investment increased to about $3,000 in the next four years. The personal subscriptions were from one dollar up, the two largest being by General Henry M. Naglee, California, and J. Gillingham Fell, Philadelphia, one hundred dollars each.

In looking for a place, on which to erect the monument, the central plot, in the Doylestown cemetery, seeming the most desirable Col. Davis addressed a letter to the company, through its president, the late Rev. Silas M. Andrews, D. D., on January 30, 1867, on the subject, as follows:

DEAR SIR :—I have in my hands nearly $3,000, to be applied to building a monument, at Doylestown, to the memory of the officers and men of the 104th Pa. regiment who fell in the rebellion. The money was mainly the gift of the enlisted men, and I hold it as their trustee for this purpose only. It is contemplated to erect the monument the coming summer, and I desire to secure as eligible a location as practicable. With permission of the cemetery company, I would like to erect it on the central plot of the cemetery grounds at the head of the main avenue, and now unimproved. It would not occupy the entire plot, but should be placed in the centre. The monument will be built of white marble or granite, and will have a handsome iron railing around it. It is not

---

[4]   WAR DEPARTMENT, ADJUTANT GENERAL'S OFFICE,
            WASHINGTON, April 9, 1864.

Colonel W. W. H. Davis, 104th Pa. Volunteers Commanding Post at Morris Island, S. C.:

SIR:—I am directed to acknowledge the receipt of your communication of the twenty-fifth inst., desiring to know whether a regimental fund may be used for the erection of a monument to the memory of the deceased members of the regiment, the enlisted men consenting to the appropriation. In reply I am directed to say that there appears to be no objection to such appropriation on the condition named.

I am very respectfully, You Obedient Servant,
            (Signed)   E. D. TOWNSEND,
                        Assistant Adjutant General.

proposed to bury any of our dead under, or about it, as we already have a lot in your grounds for this purpose, given by the generosity of your company.

I need not observe that a structure of this kind will be an ornament to the cemetery grounds, and add greatly to their beauty. I am persuaded that it is only necessary to make a request for so patriotic a purpose to have it granted. An early reply is requested.

     Yours respectfully,
(Signed)   W. W. H. DAVIS, Late Colonel, 104th Pa. Regiment.

The records, of the Cemetery Company, show that the above letter of January 30, was not considered until May 23, when the request was unanimously granted, and Colonel Davis was notified on the 24th. In the meantime, however, the long delay having satisfied him, the proposition was not favorably received, he had secured the eligible site on which the monument stands, in the heart of the borough.

A contract was made with Struthers & Son, Philadelphia, for building the monument, July 17, 1867, the price to be $2,500, including the material, delivering the monument on the ground and putting it up. The specifications called for "white American marble, sound and free from flaw or other defect." The work on the monument was completed the same fall, but the weather was too cold and stormy to erect it before spring. The foundation was laid by home workmen in April 1868, in the most substantial manner, cement being used several feet under ground.

The shaft was set, as early in May, as the foundation was ready for it, Saturday, the 30th, being fixed for the dedication ceremonies. The day was fine and attendance large. Several hundred military were present from Philadelphia, with fine music, and a number of distinguished gentlemen in civil and military life. The procession was formed on State street, right resting on Main, and the line of march, directed by Chief Marshall Andrew Craven and his assistants, Benjamin Hough and William DeBree, was as follows: Up Main to Broad, Broad to Court, Court to Church, Church to State, State to Broad, Broad to Court and down Court to the monument, the bands playing delightful music on the march.

The exercises, at the stand, consisted of music, prayer by ex-Chaplain, Wm. R. Gries, of the 104th regiment; an ode, by George Lear, Esq.; music, address by Brevet Major-General Wm. H. Emory, U. S. A.; an appropriate dirge, by Miss Octavia Hill, sung by the choir, and closed with a benediction. The ode and dirge we insert in full, as we esteem them worthy of it; both written for the occasion:

ODE.

They have fallen, they have fallen,
    Where the battle tempest roared;
Where the blaze of strife was gleaming
    On each bayonet and sword.
They went down beneath the surging
    Of the tide of men and steeds,
And we raise this mausoleum,
    To commemorate their deeds.

They have fallen, they have fallen,
    In the battles of the free,
And their fame will be remembered
    In the ages yet to be;
And upon this shaft of marble,
    Reared by comrades in the fray,
Stands the record of their valor,
    Where it shall remain for aye.

They have fallen, they have fallen,
    In a high and holy cause,
Fighting for our starry banner,
    For our country and its laws;
For the glorious gift of freedom,
    For the land our fathers loved,
For the Right, which, 'spite of sceptres,
    Man proclaimed and God approved.

They have fallen, they have fallen,
    In the fierceness of the strife,
Leaving us to bear the battle,
    And the burden of this life,
While their disembodied spirits,
    Wing their way to realms above,
Where they sing their songs of triumph,
    Round the great white throne of love.

DIRGE.

[5] Let them rest, the fight is over,
    And the vict'ry bravely won,
Softly wrap their banner 'round them,
    Lay them low, their work is done.
        Rest in peace!
        Rest in Peace!
Rest in peace—the fight is over,
    And the vict'ry all is won.

Nevermore the roar of battle
    E'er shall break our comrade's sleep—
Safe the rest they've won, and o'er it
    Angel-sentries guardiance keep.
        Nevermore!
        Nevermore!
Nevermore shall foe surprise them,
    For the angels guardiance keep.

---

5 On May 30, 1898, when General Thomas J. Stewart delivered the Decoration Day address at Doylestown, he quoted the whole of this beautiful dirge because of its appropriateness to such occasion.

Many a flower this laughing May-time
    In a hero's heart hath root—
Sweet thy slumber 'neath the blossoms,
    Till their deeds have borne the fruit.
        Slumber on!
        Slumber on!
Slumber on beneath the blossoms,
    Till your deeds have borne the fruit.

Let the flags float out above them;
    Let the music fill the air;
In the hearts of those who love them
    It shall echo like a prayer.
        Free the flags!
        Free the flags!
That the stars they died defending
    Still may shine upon them there.

Leave we, now, our martyr-brothers.
    All to God and mem'ry then,
Till within the Great Hereafter
    Freedom's armies rise again.
        So, Farewell!
        Ah, Farewell!
Till within the Great Hereafter,
    Peace proclaimed, we meet again.

General Emory, the orator, of the day, under whom the regiment had served, paid it an high compliment, and, in opening his address, took occasion to say:

"The generous impulse, which suggested the erection of this structure, and the wise foresight and care which provided the means of doing it, cannot be too much commended. But, there is a monument still more enduring than the marble shaft around which we are assembled, to be found in the record of the regiment written by its chief. For truth, impartiality and clearness, it is altogether the most praiseworthy that has come under my notice, and had all the regiments, of our grand army, adopted the same idea and carried it out, what a complete record we should have had of the rebellion; a record from which the future historian could have collected the materials to write a true history of the war, and never failing and truthful guide would have been furnished for the Legislators and accounting officers of the Goverment, in adjusting the complicated and delicate questions of bounty, pension, and unclaimed pay. You are all doubtless so familiar with this history as to render it unnecessary for me to do more than glance at the principle incidents in the history of this regiment, some of which have fallen under my own observation."

The occasion was one of great interest to Doylestown, and all who participated. Many letters of regret, at not being able to be present, were received from distinguished civil and military gentlemen. The cannons were placed at the four corners of the base of the monument shortly after it was erected, and were the gift of the Hon. C. N. Taylor, our Representative in Congress, who got them of the War Department, and had them painted and shipped to Doylestown free of expense.

In addition to the commands and individuals, already named as entering the military service in defence of the union, from Doylestown, others deserve mention. Among these we recall General B. F. Fisher, who began his military career as first Lieutenant of Company H, Third Pa. Reserves, and, at its close, was Chief Signal Officer; Colonel Samuel C. Croasdale, 128th regiment, who fell at Antietam; Colonel James Gilkeson, 45th, a short term regiment, Captain George Hart, of an emergency regiment, Captain Christian Frankenfield, and Major Cephas Dyer, also 128th regiment, James S. Mann, captain of a company of cavelry, short term, and Richard Watson, private in emergency company. In addition a number enlisted in companies, whose names cannot be recalled. Fisher, Croasdale, Hart, Watson and Gilkeson were members of the bar.

We recall another, born in the immediate vicinity of Doylestown, who made his mark in the Civil War. This was General George B. Cadwallader, son of Dr. Peter and Hannah Magill Cadwallader, born October 20, 1830. He received his early education at the Union Academy, Doylestown while Silas H. Thompson was in charge, and, 1844, the family removed to Danville, Pa. The breaking out of the war found him engaged in the drug business, whence he enlisted in the 8th Pennsylvania Volunteers in which he served three months, when he was commissioned First Lieutenant in the 46th regiment, July 8, 1862, and appointed Assistant Quartermaster, army of the Potomac. He was ordered west, 1864, and accompanied Sherman in his march from Atlanta to the sea, in charge of the transportation of supplies. By Sherman's order he removed the obstructions from the mouth of the Savannah river, for which he received the Brevet rank of Brigadier-General. General Cadwallader lives at Sunbury.

The Civil war made its indellible impress on Doylestown, as on every other community, North and South. They were never the same afterward; it was a change from the Old to the New, view it from a national, state, business, political or social stand point. It drew lines as lasting as if drawn by the graver's tool.

Recurring to the collapse of the Beek Exhibition, 1855, ten years had passed before a similiar enterprise was attempted at Doylestown. This was in 1865, when a few farmers and others, interested in agriculture, caused a company to be incorporated under the name and little of the "Doylestown Agricultural and Mechanics' Institute." They purchased the Beek property and held an exhibition that fall under canvas, October 3, 4 and 5, which proved a success. It was largely attended, and the premiums amounted to $1,500. The president was Isaiah Michener, recording secretary, N. P. Brower and, corresponding secretary, James Lambert. Encouraged by the successful outcome of the new venture, the interested parties erected a handsome and convenient brick structure, the following year, in the shape of a cross, ninety-six feet each way, for the main exhibition building and made other improvements. The trotting track was half a mile round. The patronage increased from year to year until the exhibition became one of the most prosperous in the state. The attendance was very large for the first five years, being estimated at 40,000, and the display of farm and domestic products extensive and valuable. For several years people began coming into town to attend the exhibition very early in the morning, the streets being lined with vehicles before sunrise, while all the trains arrived crowded with passengers. The company paid a dividend on the stock for several years, and many thousands of dollars were awarded in premiums. The attendance gradually fell off in later years, the general public finding new, and more attractive resorts for a fall outing, and age and death among the officers reducing the efficiency of the management, the company wound up its affairs in the early nineties, after being in operation twenty-five years. It paid its debts and left a small dividend for the stockholders. In 1871, five years after the Society began business, the estimated value of its real estate was $35,573.17, and, for the same years, the receipts were $12,521.74, and expenditures $13,559.39. During the annual exhibition, Doylestown may be said to have been *en boom,* and it was a field day for several branches of local business. The real estate was sold to Robert Steel, of Philadelphia, who bought adjoining ground and established a stock farm on it and made extensive improvements.

Six years after the Agricultural and Mechanics' Institute was opened, a kindred society came into existence, the "Doylestown

Farmers' Club," but in no sense a rival. It was organized in James Gilkyson's office, North Main street opposite the Fountain House, January 2, 1871, when Thomas W. Trego was elected president, and Benjamin Cadwallader, secretary and treasurer. The general purpose, of this organization, was to stimulate farmers in the prosecution of this honorable calling. There were thirty-one members in all. In 1873, they met, occasionally, in the "Watson building," now the residence of the family of the late Judge Watson, west side of North Main street opposite the Court house grounds. At that time Davis E. Brower was secretary and treasurer. The Society also met at times in Lenape Building, not having any fixed place of meeting. Various questions were discussed in which farmers were interested, and papers read on kindred subjects. The last meeting was held in Lenape Building, March 15, 1876, with but three members present, Thomas W. Trego, the president, Dr. A. M. Dickey and Davis E. Brower. After discussing the subject of "Fertilizers," in an informal way, the club adjourned, subject to the call of the president, a call that was never made. The balance of funds, in the hands of the treasurer, was $11.31. Since the last meeting several of the members have died, Dr. Dickey meeting a violent death by his horse running away.

In 1869, two young German immigrants came to Doylestown, and opened a watch and clock making establishment on the northeast corner of Main and State streets. Their names were Louis H. Spellier and Abraham Yeakel. The latter, shortly went to Perkasie and established himself in business, the former remaining here several years. Spellier was an ingenious man, and, while occupying what was Joseph Harvey's front parlor northeast corner of Main and State streets, opposite the Fountain House, he invented a "Time Clock," as he called it, run by a galvanic battery. The battery was in a closet in his shop from which was run a wire to Mr. Gilkyson's office clock next door, thus completing the connection and setting the telegraph time piece going. He fixed a large dial to one of his shop windows, on which this simple, though ingenous, clock told the time with the greatest accuracy. Mr. Spellier made the works in Philadelphia. The invention gained him considerable notoriety and attracted the attention of the scientists of this country and Europe. The invention was perfected at Doylestown, 1876, while Spellier was occupying the Harvey parlor but was subsequently improved. The Iconographic Encyclopedia, a magazine of applied Mechanics published at Leipzig, Germany, called this invention the "Electromagnetic escapement," and said it "removed noted defects of electric clocks." In 1884, Spellier added to his inventions and discoveries, on this line, by devising means by which the electric circuit could be made and broken at pleasure, and, by the escape-wheel of the master clock, developed sufficient energy for a firm contact. Mr. Spellier's ingenuity did away with the most serious evil presented in the proper action of the electric clock. He died at Philadelphia, August 22, 1891, and was buried in the Doylestown Cemetery.

Doylestown, Old and New.

XXV
Our Schools.

In writing of our schools, some will doubtless be overlooked, their stay, among us, being so brief they were forgotten almost before the end of the generation they had served. Some of the earlier schools left no record behind them. As this vicinity was settled a century and three-quarters ago, a country school was no doubt opened at, or near, the cross roads as soon as there were children to send to it. Everywhere in the country west of the Delaware, the school house closely followed the church, and, in some instances, preceded it. Such was the case at Doylestown. The earliest school here, of which we have any record, was kept in the Union Academy by the Rev. Uriah DuBois, and opened in June, 1804.[1] An advertisement appeared in Asher Miner's paper, of July 2 the same year, announcing that "a Seminary for the instruction of youth, is now opened at Doylestown, under the superintendence of the Rev. Uriah DuBois." This was signed by Hugh Meredith. Nathl. Shewell and Josiah Y. Shaw "Acting Committee." The Rev. Jacob Lazelere, pastor of the Dutch Reformed church, of North and Southampton, was advertised to deliver an address in the Academy on Sunday afternoon, July 29, at 3.30, at which a collection was to be taken up, the amount to be appropriated towards "finishing the building." How much was

---

[1] About this time a man, named McGreggor, a Scotchman, opened a classical and mathematical school at Bridge Point, a mile below Doylestown, the father teaching the dead languages, and the daughters mathematics. It became quite famous, and, among the pupils, was the late Judge Chapman. The McGreggors disappeared mysteriously, and were never heard of again.

PUBLIC SCHOOL BOARD, 1897.

collected is not mentioned in the paper, nor does it contain any notice of the proceedings at the meeting.

At the death of Mr. DuBois, 1821, the trustees employed Eleazar Smith,[2] of Connecticut, and a graduate of Yale, to take charge of the Academy. He resigned, 1828, and removed to a farm in Warwick township, where he died, 1829. For the next five years the Academy was in charge of Samuel Aaron,[3] the brilliant son of a New Britain farmer, and Robert P. DuBois, son of the Rev. Uriah. They maintained the reputation Mr. DuBois the elder earned for the school, and the attendance was increased.

Shortly after the removal of the county seat from Newtown to Doylestown, but it is impossible to give the exact date, Alfred Magill, father of Charles H. Magill, of our borough, opened a school here and kept it several years. Later he built a stone school house for his urchins and taught there, but how long we cannot say. The quaint-looking building with its gable to the street is still standing on the west side of South Main street below State. It has been occupied as a dwelling for nearly three quarters of a century, and its unique phiz assists to illustrate this chapter.

In 1835, the Rev. Silas M. Andrews, recently called to the pastorate of the Presbyterian church, took charge of the Academy, with Joseph Patterson as assistant, but relinquished it at the end of two years, to open a classical and English school in his own dwelling at the northwest corner of State and Broad streets. It became a noted school, and Mr. Andrews kept it several years. He was succeeded at the Academy by John Robinson, who opened a classical and mathematical Institute in the building. He was a fine scholar and good teacher, and his reputation has survived him. He taught there several years. Down to this time, over forty years ago, the school had a high reputation, and young men and boys came to it from a considerable distance to be educated, but, after Mr. Robinson left, the institution lost its prestige and influence as an educator. From this time forward the schools kept in the Academy were day schools. A female department was opened about 1823, with a Mrs. Jones in charge, who was followed by Mrs. May Jarvis, 1826; Maria McGlauphlen, 1827; Sarah M. Kuhn, 1830 and subsequently Sarah Dunlap and others.

The male teachers, who taught in the Academy as principal or

---

[2] While Mr. Smith was in charge of the Academy, George Murray taught the English department.

[3] Mr. Aaron was partially educated at the Academy, and, in 1808, was a member of the senior class and delivered the Fourth of July oration.

assistant, besides those already named, make a long roll, but their names cannot be recalled except those mentioned below:

Henry Ufford, 1807; Thomas Gibson, 1810; George Seigfried 1814, in charge of the English Department; Mr. Kulp, 1817; E. F. Griffith, 1821; Alfred Magill, 1830; Jacob Price, 1833; Nelson Phillips, 1834; John G. Michener, 1836-'37; Rev. Jacob P. Reed, Jacob F. Burns, George Winslow, principal of French Department, and brother of Daniel, 1841; Rev. Samuel Nightingale, Stephen Phelps, 1842; Elias Carver, 1842-'43; Lewis B. Thompson, Silas H. Thompson, 1844-'46, Solomon Wright, 1846; Thomas McReynolds, William Stuckert, Stephen Kirk, afterward County Superintendent and died in California; Henry M. Hough, William Walker, Allen J. Flitcraft, Eugene Smith, Jonathan Fly, ——— Stultz, killed in the Civil War, Hause and others, whose names are forgotten. A few of these taught in the public school, while it occupied the Academy. The late William J. Buck, an accurate historian, and pupil, estimates that 4,000 received all, or a part of their education at the Union Academy. If a full list could be procured, of the pupils of this historic seat of learning, what an interesting roll it would be. They would be found in every walk of life, and some of them made a mark on their generation.

The author, a boy of twelve, was a pupil at the Academy 1832-'33, but there are few survivors of that period. Among the scholars, we remember Franklin Taylor, son of Anthony Taylor, Bristol township, who spent the greater part of his life in Philadelphia. We had not met him since our school days, until May, 1895, a period of sixty-two years, when he called on us at Doylestown. We renewed old acquaintance and talked of our school mates in the long past. Among those alive in Doylestown, at that time, who had filled the benches with us, was only cashier John J. Brock, but, since then, he has crossed the dark river. My meeting with Mr. Taylor was a very pleasant episode. At that day the block bounded by Broad, Court, Pine street and Garden Alley, had no buildings on it, and the boys used it for playing shinny. The first house was built on it, 1833. In 1889, the Academy [4] was torn down, to make way for the new

---

4 The following is related of a pupil at the Academy: For a public entertainment, the lad had learned a piece that was illustrated with the picture of a monkey at the top, and, underneath, was the inscription: "Did you ever see an ape or monkey? If not here is one." The young orator came upon the stage, and, making a bow, opened by repeating, "Did you ever see an ape or monkey, if not, here is one." The lad's debut brought down the house; he said no more, but left the stage amid a roar of laughter. Smaller incidents have made the actor famous on the stage of life.

public school building, and passed into history. At what time the public school was opened in it we are not informed.

The next most important school, in Doylestown, for the period, was George Murray's boarding school, for boys, opened 1829 or '30 in the stone house south side of East State street recently owned by Alfred H. Barber. Murray was a Scotchman, born in the parish of Keith, 1781; graduated at New Aberdeen and came to America, 1804. After teaching near Morristown, N. J., in Bensalem, Hatboro, Hulmeville and elsewhere, he came to Doylestown, 1821, and taught at the Academy, under DuBois and Smith, until 1829, when he opened a "Select Boarding School for Boys," called "Inverary," probably after his birth place. He continued the school in Doylestown until 1842, when he removed it to his farm in the township, where he kept it up until 1850. It was a noted school and always full. He was a strict disciplinarian, and none of his pupils were ruined by "sparing the rod." The pranks of "Murray's boys," while the school was in the town, were numerous, and the history of some of them still lingers in the air. He taught fifty-five years in all, probably longer than any other teacher in the county. He lived to be almost an hundred, and was hale and hearty at ninety-five.

In March, 1834, Mary L. Cox opened the "Doylestown Boarding School For Girls'," but, beyond this slender knowledge, we know nothing. It doubtless had a short existence, and left not a ripple on the great sea of education. A German boarding school was opened at Doylestown, April 1, 1836, by Frederick N. Lauener, probably in the Academy, who likewise gave instruction in the French, Latin and Greek languages. In August, 1838, L. Hawley and wife opened a "Select Ladies' School," called "Doylestown Female Seminary," and also a boys' school in connection with it, but was soon abandoned. The Hawley educational venture lasted longer than some of the others and gave satisfaction. At this period Miss Sarah Kuhn, from Philadelphia, aunt of the late Richard K. Kuhn, opened a private school, April 1, 1840, called "Greenfield Seminary." She taught in Doylestown several years, and died here. These sporadic efforts at school teaching were evidence Doylestown was thought to be missionary ground, for those interested in the cause of education, but nothing was accomplished of a permanent character.

In 1837, a few prominent people of the county, feeling the necessity of better facilities for the education of girls at the county seat, procured a charter for the "Ingham Female Seminary," named after the Hon.

Samuel D. Ingham. It was intended for a boarding and day school, and received a small annual appropriation from tne state. Dr. C. Soule Cartee, a graduate of Brown University, and wife were engaged to take charge of the new school, which they opened in the fall of 1838, in the house on the southeast corner of Court and Pine Streets, where Mrs. John L. DuBois lives.[5] It was started with flattering prospects. The second year it was opened September 2, 1839, in a school building erected at the corner of Broad and Mechanics street, on the lot now occupied by the Presbyterian Manse. It was a frame building with the gable end to Broad street, and, over the door in black letters, was the name of the school, "Ingham Female Seminary," in a semi-circular form. Dr. Cartee and family, while here, boarded part of the time with Charles H. Mann, subsequently elected Sheriff, on the corner of State and Pine streets. Dr. Cartee having a taste for history, thought of collecting material to write the History of Bucks county, and opened correspondence with several persons to obtain information;[6] but, beyond this, nothing was done. He did not realize the world of vexation he escaped by giving up the project.

The school not proving a success, Dr. Cartee left in the spring of 1843, and returned to Boston, and no further effort was made to maintain a boarding school in the building. He shortly settled in Charlestown, Mass., and was subsequently appointed librarian of the city library. There he spent the remainder of his life, dying a few years ago from the effects of a fall while in the discharge of his duties in the library. Dr. Cartee was a scholarly man, quite a musician, and much esteemed by those who knew him. When the author was a student at Harvard, after Dr. and Mrs. Cartee had settled at Charlestown, their house was a second home to us, and many a courtesy was extended to the old acquaintance. The presence of their sprightly daughter, Elizabeth, did not distract from the attractions of the household. In June, 1843, the trustees announced they had secured Miss Christiana A. Murry as principal of the school, but how long she taught we are not imformed. The organization of the Seminary was probably kept up until 1847. Judge Fox was president of the

---

[5] Samuel D. Ingham was president of the board of trustees, with the following members: Rev. S. M. Andrews, Hon. John Fox, General Wm. S. Rogers, Dr. C. H. Mathews, C. E. DuBois, John H. Anderson and John B. Pugh.

[6] We learn this from a communication in the *Bucks County Intelligencer* of September 16, 1840.

board of trustees. In 1848, Rev. Silas M. Andrews taught school in the Seminary building.

During the greater part of the subsequent life of the little "Seminary" building, it was used as a school room for small children, and several persons taught in it, principally women. It was occasionally used for social purposes, and the author remembers that about the close of the forties or beginning of the fifties our musicians practiced in it, and, on two or three occasions, select concerts were given in it. The little frame, dignified with the name of Jackson's first Secretary of the Treasury, was taken down, 1885-'86, to make way for the Presbyterian Manse, the proceeds, arising from its sale, being given to the Linden Seminary, established 1871. The cost of the Manse was $8,200. Something more than a great man's name is required to make a school a success.[7]

One of the most noted teachers of Doylestown, of the period, was Thomas Hughes, many years a resident of the borough, and one of the oldest educators in the state at his death. He was born at Dundee, Scotland, 1791, and, when a youth, learned the trade of cabinet maker. He now gave his attention to books and became a good scholar. Himself and wife came to America, 1819, and, settling in Philadelphia, took charge of one of the most prominent boarding schools in the city. About 1841-'42, they removed to near Doylestown, purchasing the Stuart farm on the highlands, northwest of the the village, where Mr. Hughes opened a boarding school. Their next move was into the borough, where they taught as long as age permitted. At first they opened a school in what was afterwards Gaucher's shop, on the north side of East State street, where Mr. Cox's dwelling stands; next in a frame on the south side of East State street, about opposite the old DuBois house, corner of Broad and State. Mr. Hughes next assisted his daughter, Mrs. Taylor, in a school she kept in the Ingham Seminary building. He was now appointed librarian of the town library, which place he occupied to about his death, dying at Doylestown, September 14, 1887, at the age of 86. Mrs. Hughes, who died several years prior to her husband, turned her attention to literature in her latter years, and wrote a number of popular books

Next, in order of date, were the schools established in Doylestown

---

7 In 1841, a Doylestown newspaper gives the following list of boarding and select schools in the borough: "Family Boarding School, Rev. S. M. Andrews; Ingham Female Seminary, Dr. C. Soule Cartee; Classical and Mathematical School, John Robinson. If we add to these the Academy, it will be conceded that Doylestown, with a population of 700, was fairly well supplied with schools.

under the public school system of the state, Doylestown accepted the school law about 1850, and, by this time, the Academy, as a school, had deteriorated to such extent, the trustees allowed the directors to use it for public school purposes. These schools were kept in the building several years until better occommodations could be provided. In the meanwhile there were a number of private, and a couple of public schools established, which had their day, and passed away, a few with a history but more without it. Among these was a girls' school opened in the summer of 1858, by a Mr. Vaughan and wife, in a frame building on the north side of York street, east of Main. They gave satisfaction, but in the fall, or following spring, removed to North Carolina. The majority of these schools have been forgotten, but the most noted of the group was the boarding and day school of the Rev. Silas M. Andrews, in his dwelling at the northwest corner of Broad and East State streets. He built a frame school house in his yard, where he instilled the dead languages into his pupils by precept and example. The Doctor was a fine linguist and, for several years, it was one of the most noted private schools at the county seat. He fitted several young men for college who made their mark on public affairs, among them the late Judge Henry Ross. Mrs. Gregg, wife of Barzilla Gregg, kept a private school in her own dwelling a number of years, on West State street, where she instructed the children of many families.

In the fall of 1861, the Rev. Levi Sheip, on his graduation from Franklin-Marshall College, came to Doylestown and opened a school for boys in the basement of Temperance Hall, north side of East State street, between Broad and Church. The following year he gave it up to attend the Reformed Seminary, Mercersburg, but on graduating from there 1863, and prior to ordination, he returned to Doylestown and re-opened the school. At the end of the term, Mr. Sheip gave up the school to his assistant, Levi M. Koons, of Frederick, Pa. The school was prosperous. In 1865, Mr. Sheip again returned to Doylestown, this time as pastor of Salem Reformed church, and, in 1869, opened a girls' school in the basement of Masonic Hall.

This proving a success, and better accommodations being needed, a lot was purchased at the southeast corner of Maple avenue and East street, whereon a suitable building was erected, 1871, a charter obtained and the pupils transferred from the Masonic Hall in the spring of 1872. It was called "Linden Seminary," and had an exceptionally fine view to the southwest. The scholars numbered eighty-four for the scholastic year, ending July 2, 1874. At that time the Rev. Silas M. Andrews, D. D., was president of the board of trustees, the members being Dr. O. P. James, Hon. Richard Watson, N. C. James, George Lear, Moritz Loeb, Louis Worthington, Andrew Scott and Samuel Trumbower, all now deceased. The catalogue of 1874, the only one that has fallen into our hands, shows that fifty-one of the pupils were from Doylestown, and, of the remainder, only eleven came from outside the county. The school year was forty weeks, and the necessary expenses $265.

The faculty consisted of six teachers, who instructed the pupils in the higher branches. The school prospered for a few years and the building then came into the possession of Miss Amanda Morris and Mrs. Cathers, who are still the owners. Mr. Sheip dying suddenly, February 17, 1897, Mr. Hough took charge. He taught for several years when he resigned and was appointed to a situation in the Pension Bureau, Washington, and died there in June, 1902. The drawing of the building, which accompanies this chapter, was taken from the catalogue of 1874.

The Doylestown Seminary was established about the same period on the southwest edge of the borough with an equally fine outlook. The wing was erected in 1867, the main building, 1869, and the entire cost of the buildings was about $30,000, the amount being subscribed by the people of Doylestown and vicinity interested in education. Sometime in 1867, Benjamin Smith, son of Jonathan Smith, of Solebury, who opened a school in the basement of Masonic Hall, moved into the wing when that was finished. He now set up a school of higher grade including the classics. The course of study embraced preparatory, literary, classical, and musical branches with all others essential to a liberal education. The expense was $250 a year. The records show there were four graduates in 1870, twelve in 1871, nine in 1872 and ten in 1873. In 1884, with a graduating class of five, the students numbered fifty males and forty-three females. While Mr. Smith was at the head of the institution, he had a large school, the greatest number, in 1872-'73, reaching two hundred boarders and day scholars. The failure of Jay Cook effected the attendance as the parents, who lost money by it, could not so well afford to send their children to a pay school. Smith left the school in August, 1876.[8]

Mr. Smith was succeeded by the Rev. M. L. Hofford, 1876, where

---

[8] When Mr. Smith left the Doylestown Seminary, he went to a Friends' School in New York, and remained there about nine years, then to Swarthmore some six or eight years, next opened a private school in New York, and then to Friends' School in Philadelphia, 1895-'96.

he remained about a year. He was followed at the Seminary by
Prof. M. E. Scheibner, 1877, a Russian and a graduate of the University of Warsaw. He was a fine scholar, speaking several European
languages, and was an equally good English scholar. He was a
soldier in our Civil War and wounded. Being in Paris he came here
expecting to get a commission, but failing, enlisted. On one occasion
Scheibner was invited to dine at my house; during the dinner he
asked my wife if she had a raw beef steak; she answered in the
affirmative, it was brought to him and he ate it. When he left the
Seminary, 1881, he went to Reading, Pa., where he had charge of
the High school for several years.

From this time, those in charge of Doylestown Seminary for a
period were A. C. Winters, Dr. John Gosman and George Wheeler,
who probably came from Schuylkill county, Pa. Winters went to Florida
and engaged in orange culture, but, not being successful, took charge
of a school in Georgia, where he died in '84 or '85. In its day
Doylestown Seminary was a flourishing school for a few years, but
getting into financial trouble, the property was sold to private parties
of which three were Henry T. Darlington, the main factor in its
erection, Thomas Trego and W. W. H. Davis. They owned it but
a short time, when they sold it to Prof. A. C. Winters for $16,000,
and he to Dr. Gosman, 1882. In 1890, they leased the property to
George Wheeler. The next year Wheeler removed the school to
the Shellenberger house on north side of East Court street, and called
it the "Doylestown Seminary." He was there two years and failed,
and is now 1902, principal of a school in Philadelphia. In May, 1891,
Dr. John Gosman sold the school property to Frank Hart for $16,000,
and is now a popular summer resort, and largely patronized. The
public school system has driven from the field every private school in
Doylestown, and enjoys a monopoly of organized education.

The necessity for better quarters for the public schools, and the
means of properly developing their usefulness, led to the demolition
of the Union Academy, which had played so important a part in the
cause of education. The question, of increased accommodations, was
frequently discussed, but no conclusion reached until 1883, when the
directors determined to erect a new building on the Academy lot, if
the property could be obtained. This was accomplished, through the
action of the trustees and the court, and the conveyance was made
to the directors, January 28, 1889. Steps were now taken to erect a

building the coming season; an architect employed, and contracts made.

Prior to taking down the Academy, memorial exercises were held in it by its friends, patrons and former pupils. This took place on Tuesday afternoon, May 6, 1889, and the public were assembled by the ringing of the bell, which had called the pupils together for eighty-five years. It was like bidding farewell to an old friend and a shade of sadness pervaded the audience. The services consisted of a prayer, by the Rev. Willian A. Patton, of the Presbyterian church; vocal and instrumental music, in charge of J. Freeman Hendricks, Esq., Miss Annie Hill presiding at the organ; opening remarks by the Rev. Levi L. Sheip, principal of the public schools; Historical address by W. W. H. Davis, who had "come to bury Cæsar not to praise him;" short addresses by John L. DuBois and Elias Carver, Esqs., and John P. Rogers and William J. Buck, all pupils but one and he a teacher. The choir now sang, "Nearer My God to Thee," all joining in the Doxology, and the exercises were concluded by the Rev. D. Levin Coleman pronouncing a benediction. The old seminary of learning was now relegated to history, and its walls turned over to the merciless hands of the despoiler. Principal Sheip, of the public schools, with his corps of teachers, Isaiah K. Clymer, Julia VanHorn, Nellie Wetherill, Alma B. Shelly, Lillie A. Martin and Florence B. Kephard were all present.

The last board of trustees of the Academy, and the one that transferred the property to the school board, consisted of Alfred Fackenthal, president; Robert S. Garner, secretary; Whittingham J. Livezey, W. W. H. Davis, J. Monroe Shellenberger, Henry Lear, James Barrett, John M. Purdy and John Yardley.

The school board, on whom devolved the work of taking down the old building, and replacing it with a new structure, were Howard Templin, president; Henry P. Sands, secretary; Henry D. Livezey, M. K. Dungan, Louis H. James and George McReynolds. Before the work was begun, Livezey and James resigned, and their places filled by A. F. Scheetz and Rev. D. Levin Coleman. The new building, finished and occupied in the spring of 1890, the total cost being $28,239, is one of the handsomest school buildings in the state, and very attractive. It faces one hundred and one feet on Broad street and sixty-five on Court, three stories high and surmounted by a belfry. It is built of Bucks county stone, the facing Norristown granite, and the trimmings Wyoming blue stone. Milton B. Bean, of Lansdale, was the Architect, Henry D. Livezey, contractor, and the builders Henry D. Livezey and James Flack, of Doylestown.

About 1854-'55, a Mrs. Mathews an elderly woman of Doylestown, with two daughters, opened a school for boys and girls in her own residence. This was afterwards the Lewis Worthington dwelling, north side of East State street, second house from Broad, now owned and occupied by Edward Buckman and family. She probably taught there a couple of years but we have learned little of the school. Among the pupils were Mary Andrews, daughter of the Rev. Silas M. Andrews, L. L. D., "Tilley" Hall, daughter of Samuel Hall, and the two sons of the late John S. Brown, then proprietor and editor of the *Bucks County Intelligencer.* One of the prizes, awarded for good behavior, was a doll baby, and one of the Brown boys got it. A former pupil, a lady of Doylestown, informs us that one amusement of the girls was riding sticks for horses, and one of the young equestrians was given a penny for quitting the practice. Whether this cavalry school turned out any " Rough Riders" during the Civil War, we are not informed. We presume, without knowing it to be the fact, that Mrs. Mathews was of the New Britain family of this name.

Mr. Jacob Byrnes, of Philadelphia, partly educated at Doylestown Academy, seventy-two years ago, and a school mate of the author, in writing to us about the schools of that period says in relation to them:

"Doylestown had its Academy, with its classical department, its school for boys, in what were taught the elements of a plain English education, and schools for girls. The first had its apartment in the second story and the other two on the lower floor. A school for small children was taught by Miss Kuhn, near the Presbyterian church. This school was one of the institutions of the town, and the teacher a well known and highly esteemed member of the community. There was another school for older girls in the second story of the printing office of the *Bucks County Intelligencer,* taught by a Miss Haley, if I have the correct name, but not maintained for any great length of time. I remember a Christmas entertainment held in this school room, the year having escaped my memory."

" Mr. Murray, a Scotchman, kept a boarding school for boys, at the extreme end of the town, on the New Hope street or road; his house adjoined the school lot on the west. I think this school was mainly supported by scholars from a distance, some from Philadelphia; my recollection is that few of the boys living in the town attended. Mr. Murray's personality was pronounced; broadly Scotch in accent, his person heavy, with strongly marked Scotch features. He was the ideal of the strict, stern school master of 'ye ancient days.' He was an agreeable, pleasant man with an amiable family. The above I believe included all our schools at the time of which I write."

"At this time, the classical department of the Academy was conducted by the Rev. Samuel Aaron, an unique character in every respect, and a man of mark at any time. His early years, if I am correctly informed, were those of cares and sorrows, and they marked, and may have stamped, his after-life with some of its strong features. Mentally he was a strong man; nor was he less a man of strong convictions and passions, the latter held in check by a still stronger will. His modes of punishment of big boys was not always after the approved manner of the school room, and this became generally understood by them. As a young fellow, in his early teens, I had a wholesome fear of him, though I was never punished by him. He had a full school when I attended. As a teacher he was remarkably able and efficient. He had a peculiarly fine voice and, as a reader, had few equals. I remember some of his striking corrections in pronunciation in the reading class. As a forcible and eloquent public speaker, he always commanded marked attention. Out of the strict line of my subject, but in keeping with the character of the man, let me say, three years after he taught in the Academy, a group of some of the boys of the town, at the instance of John Titus, Esq., then an attorney of Doylestown, walked to the New Britain Baptist Church, three miles on three successive evenings, to hear Mr. Aaron lecture on temperance. We had a double interest in his subject, one from a public and one from a personal standpoint. His preaching and his denunciations were made with an eloquence that was intense to painfulness. Years afterward I heard him speak in the cause of anti-slavery in the hall at Wilmington, Delaware. He was in a place not in accord with the sentiments he uttered, for Delaware, at the time, was a slave state and therefore pro-slavery in sentiment. His oration was as fervid as fearless, his metalic voice rung through the house like a note from a clarion. He was a man who had no sense of personal fear. His invective was terrible, and in invective he dealt more than in words of pursuasion."

Libraries, as co-educators, naturally take their place with schools. In so far as we are informed, there have been only two public libraries in Doylestown, the "Society Library" and the "Doylestown Library," but there is a difference of opinion as to the time the former was established. One authority says it was incorporated by an Act of Assembly, December, 1799, another 1832, but there is an agreement as to the time it wound up its affairs, 1845-'46.

An old document, recently found in the Orphans' Court office at Doylestown, headed, "List of Members of the 'Society Library Company,'" gives the following "Signers of the Constitution, July 1804:" David Evans, Hugh Meredith, Thomas M. Meredith, Ellis Pugh, Meshach Michener, Joseph Harvey, John Fell, Joseph Shepherd, Samuel Mason, Christian Clemens, John Riale, James Thomas, Lewis Thomas, Benjamin Mathews, Jr., Rachel Dungan, Thomas Stewart, Benjamin Comly, Edward Fell, Rachel Large, Benjamin Watson, Nathaniel Shewell, Jonathan Large, John Moore, Jonathan Fell, Samuel Currie, George Burges, John Jamison, William White, James Watson, Robert Jamison and John Hough.

Another record of the "Society Library," recently presented to the Bucks County Historical Society by Miss DuBois, of Doylestown, throws additional light on the time of its founding. In the company's account book I find this entry, "1800, paid to 1830, January 1, George Burgess' widow, Dr. to annuity for 1831, $1; January 8, Cr. by Cash in full, $1. Mrs. Burgess accounts until 1835, when she died. There is a similar account in the names of Christian Clemens, Samuel Curry, Elizabeth Large, Benjamin Mathews, et al. Other accounts were opened later, John Fox, 1816, the year he was married, Charles E. DuBois, 1821, Nathan Cornell, 1816. The accounts are all computed to 1830, when new accounts were opened. This is evidence the library was reorganized about 1830. Seventeen of the members paid to 1840.

The location of the library was in a small frame building on the Academy lot facing Broad street, and about opposite Garden alley. The catalogue called for seven hundred volumes, doubless the best current literature of the period, but the number fell short from loss. The books, with stove, desk and other fixtures, were sold at public sale, November 20, 1846, Stephen Brock, auctioneer, the committee, to attend the sale, being William T. Rogers, Caleb E. Wright and Alfred Magill.

Ten years now elapsed before a new library was organized at Doylestown, to take the place of the old one, which a few public spirited men and women made a success. The outcome of this effort was the Doylestown Library Company, chartered by the Court, 1856, and put on record.

The petition was signed by Silas M. Andrews, George Hart,

William R. Gries, Henry T. Darlington, Enos Prizer, Richard Watson, M. Yardley, C. E. DuBois, George Lear, Edwin Fretz, J. Brown, James Gilkyson and Henry Chapman, all deceased.

When we came to look up the record of the Doylestown Library Company, in order to tell our readers something of its history, we found the charter and a book entitled "Account of the Treasurer of the Doylestown Library Company." The first entry of any kind with the exception of the money accounts, is of the date of May 8, 1886, entitled "An Election held for Officers," when the following were chosen directors: Henry Lear, Alfred Paschall and Thomas W. Gaucher; Purchasing Committee, Lewis P. Worthington and Henry C. Michener; Treasurer, Elias Carver. When and how, the previous officers were elected is not stated, or may we presume there were no officers elected between 1856 and 1886? While we were not able to find any entry purporting to be a roll of members, seventy-two persons paid the admission fee and annual dues the first year, who may be accepted as the original members. So far as that book is concerned, and we were told it is the only record of the Society, annual meetings have been held regularly down to the present time. The collection of books have increased until the number of volumes on the shelves has reached 3,400, made up of history and current literature of the day. As an educator of the borough, the use of its books assists to cultivate a taste for reading. Thomas Hughes was librarian of this library for some time. Each of our churches has a library, books of a religious character predominating, and a few persons, in our borough, have private collections of books of sufficient number to entitle them to be called a library, and, among them are some valuable publications. This is a very commendable ambition. The inhabitants of Doylestown are a reading people and always have been, and are equally well equipped in music.

Doylestown, Old and New.

XXVI

Art in Doylestown.

The difficulty of writing of art in Doylestown, in the past, and we refer particularly to music and painting, will be apparent when the reader reflects that the county capital was only a modest hamlet in 1800, and without a church until sixteen years later. The best we can do will be to present a brief view of these two civilizing influences as we knew them.

As to music, there is no doubt it was cultivated to some extent, from the earliest settlement, for the Welsh Baptists and Scotch-Irish Presbyterians were a religious people, and practiced singing in the family circle, in the church and elsewhere. Their music may have been of a crude character, but better than none at all, for every cultivation of the "harmony of sweet sounds" elevates the social standard. Music, as an accomplishment, was not cultivated in Doylestown until a much later period. Prior to 1830, there were not more than two pianos in Doylestown and one of these was in the house of Judge Fox. At that time there were no organs here in church or dwelling; this favorite reed instrument had not yet made its appearance, and pipe organs were rarely heard in the country. The melodian, which preceded the reed organ, was introduced into this county about 1840, when country singing schools were much in vogue. There may have been a spinet here and there, the forerunner of the piano, but they were very few. At the period of which we write, the Doylestown Presbyterian Church introduced a melodian to assist the choir in singing, and was the first in this section. It was placed in the left

SAMUEL DuBOIS, Musician.

hand gallery of the old church building of 1845, a copy of which helps to illustrate our text. As this was the oldest church organization in the village, it was meet and proper this congregation should lead off in the introduction of music in their place of worship. Some denominations tabooed musical instruments altogether, believing they gave rise to too much levity.

The first musical organization, we have met with, in Doylestown, was a brass band in 1824, though it may have had a predecessor. Its leader was Charles F. Beckel, and it was still in existence in 1830. The same year, Charles Gibson was "Captain of the Doylestown band," which was ordered to meet in uniform at the Cross Keys, Saturday, August 27, at ten o'clock. It is possible they were one and the same band. On Saturday evening, March 4, 1835, the "Doylestown Band" held a meeting at Andrew Mayer's Green Tree tavern, to decide whether it should continue its organization another year, but the decision reached is not known. It is probable this was the Beckel band under another leader. We may safely say, that from this time, for the next forty years, Doylestown was seldom without a brass band.

For the following decade there was something of a boom in music. In 1840, Dr. Cartee, in charge of the "Ingham Female Seminary," opened a singing school at Doylestown, and a few nearby places, teaching what was known as the "Pestalozzian system," but how long it was continued we do not know. In November, 1842, a "Social Club" was organized "for the purpose of mutual improvement in literary and musical pursuits," the leaders in the movement being Dr. Cartee and Edward J. Fox. The Doctor was appointed leader of the musical department, Mr. Fox, Secretary, and the meetings were held on Friday evening. We have no farther information of this organization. One of the best instrumental players of the period was Preston Jones,[1] uncle of the late John J. Brock, and leader of the Doylestown band in the 40's, his favorite instrument being the Kent bugle, B-flat. He was more than an ordinary musician, and on his death, Samuel Frankenfield took charge of the band.

On the evening of March 26, 1845, the Doylestown Brass Band

---

[1] Preston Jones was a native of Buckingham, and brother-in-law of Stephen Brock. He died at Doylestown, January 5, 1849, of typhoid fever, and was buried according to the rites of the Odd Fellows of which he was an active and esteemed member.

gave a "Grand Concert" of instrumental music at the Beneficial Hall, with the following "Program:"

PART I.
1. Walsh's Concerto by . . . . J. K. Walsh
2. Goshen Rondo . . . . J. Marsh
3. Blue Quick Step . . . . J. Halloway
4. Sweet Home, with variations . . . . ——
5. Harmonic, Trio with Violins . . . . J. M.
6. Jackson's March, Trio and Full Band . . . . Auber
7. Albany Quick Step . . . . J. M.
8. Gaucher's March . . . . "
9. Concerted Waltz, Trio with Violin . . . . "
10. Quadrille Waltz . . . . "
11. Battle, Full Band . . . . "
12. Chase the Devil, Etc. . . . . "

PART II.
1. Grand Entre . . . . J. K. Walsh
2. Chromatic Quick Step . . . . J. M.
3. Guard's Quick Step, Violin . . . . Walsh
4. Violin Solo, an Overture . . . . J. M.
5. Chapman's Quick Step, Full Band . . . . "
6. Kite March . . . . "
7. Gun . . . . "
8. German Waltz, Violins . . . . "
9. Mount Hope Quick Step . . . . "
10. Fireman's Quick Step . . . . "
11. Irishman's Washer . . . . "
12. Hail Columbia, Chief and Yankee Doodle, Good Bye . . . . "

Doors open at 6½ o'clock. Admittance, 12½ cents; children half price.

One of the Doylestown papers, in speaking of the preparations for the concert says: "The Beneficial Hall is about being completed, and is greatly improved for the accomodation of assemblages such as it may be used for. An ample number of comfortable seats with backs are now finished and fit for use, and likewise a neat stand or pulpit is erected for public speakers. The spacious hall can now be brilliantly illuminated, having suspended, from the centre of the ceiling a splendid chandelier containing six globe lamps, with gothic shades, and elegantly gilded, and ornamented with drops and spangles reflecting all the colors of the rainbow. Besides these are four solar lamps of elegant finish and appearance on the pulpit. All of these are constructed for lard, and, when lighted, will present a splendid appearance as well as produce a dazzling and beautiful light. As the band, on this occasion, will use the Hall for the first time since its completion, it may be some inducement for attendants to know that comfort and taste will be amply provided for in addition to the rich and rare treat of music." [2]

In the summer of 1845, Edward Perkins, professor of music at

---

[2] This building is the same now owned and occupied by the Masonic Lodge.

Captain Partridge's Military Institute, near Bristol, came to Doylestown and opened a school for instruction in instrumental music, but it did not last long. He was a fine performer on the E-flat bugle; was professor of music several years at the Norwich University, Vt., and subsequently at Captain Partridge's Military School at Harrisburg. In the early winter, 1847, an association of young men, musically inclined, and calling themselves "The Orphean Society," was organized at Doylestown, giving their first public concert in Beneficial Hall, on Christmas night, in the presence of a large audience. It is not known who were the leaders in this movement, but we have no doubt George McIntosh and Henry C. Nightingale were members. They played for the Episcopal fairs in 1848 and 1849.

Doylestown was probably more musical in the 40's and early 50's, than at any previous, or subsequent period. Mrs. Stokes L. Roberts, who came here to reside on her marriage, 1844, was the leading vocalist among the ladies, and Edward J. Fox among the gentlemen. The Misses Chapman, daughters of Judge Chapman, Miss Morris, a niece, all of Doylestown, and Miss McIntosh, Miss Brunner, and Miss Shell, of Bridge Point, all sang well and bore their part. Samuel F. DuBois excelled as a violinist, few amateurs equalling him, while George McIntosh was a good tenor. Their music contributed much to the social pleasures of society.

Near the close of the 40's, the four best male singers, Edward J. Fox, George McIntosh, Samuel F. DuBois and Abel H. James, a recent comer, organized a quartett that lasted several years. They were excellent singers with a good knowledge of music. Mr. DuBois played the violin when needed. Some of the present generation remember Mr. Fox, son of the late Judge Fox. He was a graduate of Princeton, read law in his father's office, and, shortly after his admission, settled at Easton, became a prominent lawyer, suddenly dying there in 1889. Mr. DuBois, a son of the Rev. Uriah DuBois, was a portrait painter, and Mr. McIntosh was a son of Jonathan McIntosh; all were born at Doylestown, and two of them died here. Mr. James, the fourth member of this somewhat famous quartett, the son of Colonel Isaiah James, of New Britain, was brought up in his uncle's counting room, Philadelphia, but came to Doylestown, 1848, soon after his father was elected Prothonotary, to take charge of the office. He was an accomplished musician, playing on several instruments, his favorite being the "flutina" just introduced. He died at his father's house, in New Britain, September 20, 1850, mourned by a large circle of friends. This was the best male quartette Doylestown ever had.

Mrs. James W. Mercur, of Towanda, Pa., a poetess of ability, wrote a Monody on the death of Mr. James, of which we print the following stanzas:

    And thou art gone! Dust is upon thy brow,
        Thy faded lip the seal of silence wears,
    Thy cherished form as Parian marble now
        Lies cold and still beyond earth's joys and cares.

    Yea thou art gone! Within the silent tomb,
        In the full pride of manhood thou wert laid,
    For thee no more our summer flow'rs shall bloom,
        Nor autum's glow with tints of light and shade.

    Earth will put on her myriad glories still,
        And every season deck her form anew,
    And regal grandeur every crevice fill
        Which lies beneath God's masonry of blue.

    But never more, Oh! Never more thine eye,
        Can gaze enchanted on our smiling earth,
    Can trace the splendors of our starry sky,
        Or greet the voice of music or of mirth.

       *   *   *   *   *   *

    Lone are the hearts which ye were won't to cheer,
        Oh thou! whose smile from our cold earth is riven,
    And we no more shall great thy virtues here,
        Which ever rose as incense unto Heaven.

       *   *   *   *   *   *

    But thy free'd spirit rose beyond the sky,
        And roams in realms where sorrow is unknown,
    Where fadeless glory meets the tranquil eye,
        And bliss is deathless round His Heavenly Throne.

It was the custom of the quartette to serenade twice or thrice a week, and, when they were abroad, the streets were "vocal with sweet sounds." Mr. DuBois generally took his violin along, and sometimes a flutist was pressed into service. The quartette frequently met at private houses; Judge Chapman's, Judge Fox's, Mr. Roberts' Mrs. Morris' and Charles E. DuBois', where delightful evenings were passed. On a few occassions a semi-public concert was given in the building of the "Ingham Female Seminary," to which the friends of the performers were admitted by card.

The dwelling of Mr. Roberts, on Court street, because of his wife's musical accomplishments, was headquarters and frequent meetings were held there for practice. Miss Morris was the best pianist in town at that day, and long maintained her supremacy. Mr. Fox's voice was a cultivated tenor, and when he sang his two favorite pieces,

Crouch's "Kathleen Mavourneen," and "I'm Sitting on the Stile, Mary," he was sure to receive encores. Mr. DuBois, who was esteemed Doylestown's Paganini, played delightfully and it was a treat to listen to him, when in his best mood. Mr. McIntosh and Mr. James led the Presbyterian and Episcopal choirs, respectively, and, when the latter died, his place in the quartette was filled by William P. Seymour, a young printer who had recently came to Doylestown from Buffalo, N. Y. He had a good voice and sang well, and, as he was a gentleman in his manners, was admitted into the musical circle.

As the author looks back on the musical life of Doylestown, in the forties and early fifties, he fully realizes what pleasant, happy days they were. A small coterie of congenial young men and women fond of music and song, met from house to house and indulged in their hobbie. The occasions were always of the most agreeable character. Although the author was *with* them he was hardly *of* them, for he neither played nor sang, except *very* occasionally touched the keys of a flute. Of the ladies it is not known that more than two of them are deceased, Miss Morris, widow of the late John Lyman, and Miss McIntosh, while all the young men are dead unless the writer be counted, and then he is the only survivor. Among the musical features were frequent serenades by the young men, when the streets were fairly made vocal with the songs they sang, and the accompanying music from the violin, flute and flutina.

A new brass band was organized in 1853, with John L. DuBois, leader, and Prof. Rowbotham, of Philadelphia, instructor. It lasted three years, taking the name of the "Doylestown Brass Band." The instructor played on every instrument in use, and it was thought to have been the best band the town ever had. Its services were in frequent demand, for parades, concerts, political meetings, etc. The uniform was blue and white, and it made a fine appearance on the street. There were sixteen members: John L. DuBois, leader, James M. Rogers, Stewart Addis, George E. Donaldson, Ira F. Gensel, Harvey Shearer, George C. Worrell, Daniel S. Hulshizer, Richard K. Kuhn, William P. Seymour, William Cox, John Hulshizer, Samuel F. DuBois, William Frankenfield, Nathan C. James and Thomas Kachline. Of the whole number but three are living, Addis, Worrell and Cox. It was the custom, after a wedding, and the return of the parties from the honey moon trip, for the band to serenade them, accepting refreshments in pay. On one occasion, during this period, Samuel Johnson Paxson, editor and proprietor of the *Democrat,* wishing to dilate on music, compressed his opinion into a brief sentence:

> "Music hath charms to soothe the savage,
> Break a rock and split a cabbage."

No one pretended to question his criticism.

From the time the band of 1853 dissolved, 1856, the balance of the decade and through the war period, there was a lull in the public culture of music, but it was revived in the seventies. One of the first organizations after the war was a cornet band, whose instructor was Rowbotham, with Silas Selser, quite a musician, for leader, but it lasted only a few years. Its original members, were Augustus Seigler, first E-flat cornet; Aaron Frankenfield, second; Frank H. Barndt; third; Adam Frankenfield, first B-flat; Howard Twining, second B-flat; Wallace Gilkyson, piccola; Conrad Hahl, E-flat clarionet; J. M. Vandegrift, B-flat claironet; Lewis H. Clemens, first alto; H. J. Booz, second; S. A. Selser, third; R. M. Eisenhart, first tenor, Isaac C. Roberts, second; Thomas P. Otter, baritone; John Cassell, first basso; Tom J. Smith, second; H. C. McIntosh, L. V. Garron, tenor drum; Tom Lukens, bass; and Walter C. Corson, symballs. Edgar Ruth was leader of the Selser band, after the latter gave it up, but it did not last long.

At the Teachers' Institute, in the fall, of 1870, the entire musical programme consisted of selections on a mouth organ by a Doylestown barber, who was introduced to the audience as "Professor H." While he acquitted himself with credit, it was evident music, as a social feature of the Institute, had reached a pretty low ebb, but better times for music, were near at hand, and, during the decade, very considerable progress was made.

Late in the fall of that year, 1870, the "Doylestown Musical Association" was organized, the first meeting being held the evening of December 19, in the Presbyterian lecture room, southeast corner of the grave yard. The Rev. A. J. Hastings, was elected president; W. W. H. Davis, secretary; Milton J. Sheetz, treasurer; and Miss Addie Brower, musical director, with an executive committee of which the Rev. Silas M. Andrews was chairman. The regular meetings, for instruction and practice, were first held Monday evenings in the council chamber, then in the Watson building, North Main street, but afterward changed to the lecture room of the Baptist church. A piano was purchased, and the members went to work vigorously.

The association kept together for three years, practicing through the winter, with a musical convention of four days each year, and closing with a public concert. It then adjourned until fall. Professor Henry Harding, of Trenton, had charge one or more of the conventions. The first concert yielded $59.40; the second, $65.03; and the third, $67.29. The last meeting was held December 9, 1872. The membership reached seventy-five, and numbered forty-two when it dissolved. The association assisted in the improvement of vocal music.

We are now in the period when Doylestown's most noted musical organization came into existence. This was "Brock's Orchestra," organized in 1875, the Godfather being George P. Brock, a great lover of music, and their instructor Prof. Keller, of Philadelphia. It soon became the musical feature of the town, and bore a leading part in entertainments, social, benefical and otherwise. The honors of the quartett of thirty years before naturally descended upon it. In a few years it had scarcely an equal, and no superior as an amateur orchestra.

Its repertoire contained classical music, the rendering of which was much admired, and chaste. For a considerable time Professor Schaumberg presided at the piano. Within this organization grew up another, the "Horn Quartette," consisting of Messrs. Selser, Hulshizer, Ruth and Yardley.

The original members of the orchesta were George P. Brock, leader and founder; William K. Black, Silas A. Selser. Benjamin Doan, Martin Hulshizer, Clarence White, Harvey Scheetz, Alfred W. Walton, John Yardley, W. Sharp Hulshizer, Theodore Schaumberg, Edward Ruth, John Hellerman and W. Harry Cadwallader; of the above, Black, Doan, White and Scheetz were not long members, having left Doylestown. In recent years there was little change in its personnel. In 1883, the members with the instruments they played were: Geo. Brock, first violin, leader; John Hellermam, second violin; Edward Ruth, bass; Silas Selser, cornet; W. S. Hulshizer, second cornet; John Yardley, trombone; Martin Hulshizer, clarionet; and Harvey F. Scheetz, flute.

Saying the orchestra was one of the leading social features of Doylestown, hardly expresses the place it held in the community. It not only responded to social calls, but local charities, and religious functions never appealed to it in vain. It had numerous calls from home, and, wherever it played, encores were showered upon it. While the orchestra was in existence it played yearly at the County Teacher's Institute, and was one of its most enjoyable features. For such occasions, two or three additional musicians were engaged from the city, a harpist being one of them. Doylestown is under many obligations to Mr. Brock and his orchestra, for their delightful music. We hope it may be reorganized in the near future.

Near the close of the seventies, Professor John L. Field organized the "Bucks County Music Association," with singing societies at Doylestown, Sellersville, Valley Park and Nockamixon, with about fifty voices each. The Association was in existence two or three years, and gave annual concerts in the large building on the exhibition grounds just outside the borough on its south-western border. The first was in August, 1879, with an attendance of four thousand, the second in the same building, August 25, 1880, with an attendance of three thousand, the weather being unfavorable. The grand chorus, sung by two hundred voices, fairly made the building shake. In addition to the presence of the singing societies on this occasion, the Richlandtown, Pa., and the Woodbury, N. J., bands and Brock's Orchestra were present, and took part. Colonel John W. Forney, Philadelphia, delivered an address on the "Progress of Music," and Miss Ella Heist sang two solos. The affair was a success. In the evening there was a concert in Lenape Hall, a complimentary benefit for Brock's Orchestra, in acknowledgement of the many favors extended the people of Doylestown. The Richlandtown band assisted and the Doylestown Singing Society did the choral work. The concert in the evening was thought superior to that of the afternoon. The rendering of "Star of Descending Night," by the Doylestown Society, was especially commended. The following were the programmes in the afternoon and evening respectively:

AFTERNOON.
PART I.
SELECTION . . . . Richlandtown Cornet Band
CHORUS . . . . To Thee, O Country
SELECTION . . . . Brock's Amateur Orchestra
I LOVE THE MERRY SUNSHINE . . . . Valley Park Singing Society
SOLO . . . . Ocean, Thou Mighty Monster—Miss Ella Heist
SELECTION . . . . Richlandtown Cornet Band
SEMI-CHORUS . . . . . . Star of Descending Night—Doylestown Singing Society
CHORUS . . . . Festival Hymn
ADDRESS . . . . Colonel John W. Forney

PART II.
SELECTION . . . . Richlandtown Cornet Band
CHORUS . . . . Adestes Fideles
SELECTION . . . . Brock's Amateur Orchestra

SEMI-CHORUS . . . . Nockamixon Singing Society
SOLO . . . . Night's Shade No Longer.   (Selected)—Miss Ella Heist
CHORUS . . . . Angel of Peace
SELECTION . . . . Richlandtown Cornet Band
SEMI-CHORUS . . . . (Selected)—Sellersville Singing Society
CHORUS . . . . Whittier's Hymn

MUSICAL DIRECTOR—Prof. John L. Field.
PIANIST—Prof. C. R. Hoffman.

EVENING.
PART I.

1. CHORUS—"Adestes Fideles." . . . . Novello
2. SELECTION—"Boccaccio March."—Orchestra . . . . Suppe
3. VOCAL SOLO—"Stacatto Polka."—Miss Ella Heist . . . . R. Mulder
4. VIOLIN SOLO.
5. CHORUS—"Angel of Peace." . . . . Keller
6. TRIO—"O Restless Sea." . . . . C. A. White
   Miss Ella Heist and Messrs. Field and Siegler.
7. OVERTURE—"Fatinitza."—Orchestra . . . . Suppe
8. CHORUS—"Festival Hymn." . . . . D. Buck

PART II.

1. SELECTION—"Sounds from the North."—Orchestra . . . . Zikoff
2. CHORUS—"To Thee, O Country." . . . . J. Eichberg
3. CLARIONET SOLO—Mr. L. Seal.
4. VOCAL SOLO—"The Future Shines Still Brightly." . . . . Lucia
   Miss Ella Heist.
5. CHORUS—"Star of Descending Night." . . . . L. O. Emerson
6. DUETT—"Only Thee." . . . . C. A. White
   Miss Ella Heist and Prof. J. L. Field
7. OVERTURE—"Crown of Gold."—Orchestra . . . . Hermann
8. CHORUS—"Whittier's Hymn." . . . . Paine

PROF. J. L. FIELD,   PROF. C. P. HOFFMAN,
    Conductor.   Pianist.

On the 12th of September, 1880, the "Amateur Band Association" of Bucks and Montgomery counties, gave a Concert Tournament on the exhibition grounds, the first effort of the kind in either of the counties, and proved a great success. Two bands, with about one hundred instruments were present; the attendance was large and the music appreciated.

In the summer of 1887, a new feature was introduced into the musical life of Doylestown, evening open air concerts. The suggestion met public approbation, and, in a short time, money was collected for the first season, the expense being $300. The music was furnished by Brock's Orchestra, and a handsome pavillion, lighted with gas, was erected on the Court House park. The first concert, Tuesday evening, July 15, was a great success, with large attendance from town and country. There was one concert a week. Everybody appreciated the music, and, during the performance, the people occupied seats on the lawn, or promenaded the adjoining streets. It was a novel entertainment and thoroughly enjoyed.

The following was the programme the first evening:

1. GRAND MARCH—Knights of Pythias . . . . *John Wilgard*
2. OVERTURE—The Bridal Rose . . . . *C. Lavallee*
3. WALTZES—Souvenir de Baden Bader . . . . *N. Bousquet*
4. SELECTION—Jollification Medley . . . . *George Wilgard*
5. FLUTE SOLO—Theme and Variation—Mr. Thompson . . . . . . *Thornton*
6. POLKA—Irresistable . . . . *William Welker*

INTERMISSION.

1. SELECTION—Medley of Latest Song . . . . *E. Boetkger*
2. WATZES—"Haunting Eyes"—C. F. J. Keller . . . . . . *Theodore Toban*
3. GAVATTE—Brock's Amateur Orchestra . . . . . . *Theodore Schaumberg*
4. GALOP VINEA . . . . *Cale Trichner*

The concerts were repeated the following year, 1888, with the eclat of the first season, brass music being introduced with the Orchestra, some thinking it an improvement, as it could be heard a greater distance. The last open air concert was given in 1891, but with increased cost of about $400. After this they were not resumed; their discontinuance being generally regretted. They were one of the most enjoyable features of our town's social life, and, being free, gave them great popularity. One of the most musical families of Doylestown, in the past, was the Frankenfields, seven sons all delighting in music. They had good voices and sang in church choirs and elsewhere. Two of them became instrumental teachers of considerable note, Samuel and Harry. Samuel began his musical life by playing in one of the Doylestown bands, and, in the 40's, was the leader of a band here, but afterward went to Philadelphia and devoted himself to teaching instrumental music. He organized the "Philadelphia Band," one of the best in the city. He is since deceased. Harry's first experience was beating the tenor drum for the Doylestown Guards, and sometimes playing the fife. He also went to Philadelphia, and, after the Civil War, in which he served, made music his profession—composing band music and instructing bands. In all he taught over two hundred bands, north and south. William, another member of the family, led the Methodist Episcopal church choir several years, and to his last illness.

When the Doylestown Guards was reorganized at the firing on Fort Sumter, April, 1861, three of the young Frankenfields joined the company and served in the Three Months' Campaign. While fording the Potomac, at Williamsport, the Frankenfield brothers began singing the Methodist hymn beginning, "I'm in the stream a drinking," and, when about half way across, the whole company joined in the chorus, and it was kept up until we stepped on the Virginia bank. The southern shore was lined with people, who seemed pleased and encored the singing.

On the evening of July 1, 1883, D. Baumann, Leonard Bute, Joseph Schurle, Christian Esser, Fred Wendt, Fred Bechlein, Albert Golle, Ernest Weaver, Ed. Carl, Jr., Enos Weiss, George Schroth, Dr. Charles Siegler and William Schoner, all Germans, living at Doylestown, met at Christian Esser's tavern and organized a singing society. Ed. Carl, was elected president; Fred. Bechlein, secretary; Dr. Siegler, treasurer; and Augutus Siegler appointed teacher. The organization, called the "Mænnerchoir," was conducted purely as a singing society until July 1, 1884, when the beneficial feature was engrafted on it, the dues being fixed at fifty cents a month, benefits four dollars, during sickness; seventy-five dollars at death of member and forty dollars at death of wife. The combined societies were incorporated March 17, 1887, with the title of "Doylestown Mænnerchoir," the second article of the Constitution specifying its object to be the "Cultivation and elevation of the German song and music, and to assist the members in case of sickness and death." The first of April, 1889, the social feature was added to the society, and were its full history rehearsed, many enjoyable balls and picnics would occupy a prominent place in it. For the present the society met at various places, in McGinty's building, Kane's hall, Tomlinson's building, and in the Fountain House hall. In June, 1894, the society bought a lot of the Taylor estate, corner of York and Donaldson streets, and erected a building at the cost of one thousand nine hundred and seventeen dollars, on which subsequent improvements were made at the additional expense of one thousand dollars. The society moved into its new quarters July 13, 1894. The present membership is eighty, dues sixty cents a month. The building is paid for, and a three hundred dollar surplus. The officers are president, vice president, treasurer and secretary. The meeting night is Thursday. This combination, music, social pleasures and the beneficial feature, makes a desirable organization.

The youngest musical organization, of Doylestown, grew out of a meeting held in the public school building, Friday evening, March 9, 1900, by those "who believe vocal music can be fostered and aided best by united work and endeavor." About forty were present.

Hugh B. Eastburn called the meeting to order and suggested the name of Rev. J. R. Groff as temporary chairman and C. D. Hotchkiss secretary. A Constitution and By-Laws were adopted and the name of "Doylestown Choral" fixed upon. It has two classes of members, "Active and Associate," and its affairs are managed by the following committees: Executive, Music and Admissions, and Professor William B. Godfrey, Philadelphia, was chosen leader. The permanent organization was effected at the second meeting, Friday evening, March 16, when twenty-eight signed the agreement to become active members: John A. Groff, C. D. Hotchkiss, Eugene S. Shuman, Kate Shuman, L. F. Harris, Mary F. C. Paschall, Helen Buckman, F. M. VanLaverall, Blanche Hill, Alice Wodock, Lillian Yeager, Sara A. Hotchkiss, Ruth H. Perkins, Margaret D. Patterson, Eleanor H. Davis, Elizabeth A. Price, Lucy Switzer, L. J. Keeler, Reba N. E. Trego, Henry A. James, George MacReynolds, Frank J. Gerlitzki, Madeleine M. James, Mary H. S. Gerlitzki, Albertine W. Hotchkiss, Calvin S. Boyer, Jane Watson and Sophia P. Eastburn. After reading the minutes of the preliminary meeting, the report of the committee for nominating officers, reported the following: President, Rev. J. R. Groff; Vice President, Hugh B. Eastburn; Secretary, Miss Louisa E. Butler; Treasurer, Miss Jane Watson. The president appointed the permanent committees, the active members signed the Constitution and By-Laws, and the permanent organization was completed.

The first public concert of the Choral was given in Lenape Hall, Friday evening, June 8, 1900, assisted by Brock's Orchestra; Conductor, Prof. Wm. B. Godfrey; Pianist, Mrs. Madeleine Mai James, and George P. Brock leader of the Orchestra; and the following was the programme:

PART I.

1. CHORUS—"The Belfry Tower." . . . . *Hatton*
2. "Greetings to the Doylestown Choral Union." . . . . *Kohler*
   Selection by the Orchestra.
3. CHORUS—"How Lovely are the Messengers." . . . . *Mendelsohn*
4. Waltzes from "The Singing Girl." . . . . *Langey*
5. CHORUS—"The Miller's Wooing." . . . . *Faning*
6. SOPRANO SOLO—"Barque of Dreams."—Mrs. Ella Heist-Bitting . *Gray*
7. MALE CHORUS—March "Onward." . . . . *Geibel*
8. MEDLEY OVERTURES—"The Hummer." . . . . *Machil*

PART II.

9. CHORUS—"Gloria" from "Twelfth Mass." . . . . *Mozart*
10. ENTRE ACT—"Visians of the Ballet." . . . . *Mark*

11. BASS SOLO—"Son of Hyorias the Cretan."—Prof. Wm. B. Godfrey . *Eliot*
12. CHORUSES—{ a. "Madeleine." . . . . *Roeckel*
    { b. "Dream, Baby Dream." . . . . *Smart*
13. PIANO DUET, SUITE OF DANCES—{ a. Spanish Dance . . . . . . *Nerz*
    { b. Norwegian Dance . . . . *Grieg*
    { c. Hungarian Dance . . . . . *Woeff*
    Madeleine Mai James.
    Mary Nields Buckman.
14. "THE SPINNING CHORUS."—from "Flying Dutchman." . . . . *Wagner*
    Ladies Voices.
15. MARCH—from "The Rounders." . . . . *Englanier*
16. "BRIDAL CHORUS."—from "Rose Maiden." . . . . *Cowen*

The choral continues its practice with an annual concert in April, in Lenape Hall. The quality of the music improves, from year to year, and an increased audience welcomes the concert. The membership has grown to two hundred and fifty, of which one hundred and twenty-five are on the active list. At the annual concert, Brock's Orchestra sustains its part with its usual spirit.

Doylestown has lost none of its taste for music in the immediate past, or present. Constant attention is paid to it in the home circle and churches, and we are never without vocal and instrumental teachers. Very few dwellings, that can afford them, are without a piano or organ, some having both. Every church has an organ, some of them, costing several thousand dollars, with choirs of more or less training, the Protestant Episcopal having introduced the processional with pleasing and beneficial effect. Vocal music is also taught in the public schools. Doylestown is not behind other towns of its size in musical culture.

The early days of the kindred art, painting are as much obscured in Doylestown as music, few of its sons and daughters having worshipped at this shrine. In our research, we find that a portrait painter located here as early as 1804, one Daniel Farley, who, when he had nothing better to do, turned his hand to sign painting, glazing and hanging paper, "Coming from two cities," as he advertised, he should have been a success.

Our most conspicuous artist was the late Samuel F. DuBois, son of Rev. Uriah DuBois, born here, 1805, and died, October 20, 1889. He passed the greater part of his long life in his native village, and did much to encourage art. His specialty was portrait painting at which he excelled. He exhibited such talent for this in his youth, his family sent him to Sulley to take lessons. A portrait he painted of himself, 1830, at the age of twenty-five, now hangs in the DuBois homestead, at Doylestown, the coloring apparently as fresh as when the brush was first applied to the canvas. He had an attack of California fever, 1849, and his trunk was packed for the trip, but, the night before he was to leave his mother said to him on retiring, "Samuel, I would sleep better if you were not going away," whereupon the warm hearted son unpacked his trunk and staid at home. He became noted as a portrait painter and many of his portraits are in possession of the old families of Bucks and adjoining counties. He is said to have painted all the portraits that hung on the walls of the United States Mint, Philadelphia. In a local paper, of February 11, 1835, he announced that he had "taken a room in the house belonging to S. Aaron, which he intends to occupy as a painting room for a few months." This was the house of his brother-in-law, the Rev. Samuel Aaron, on the northwest corner of State and Broad streets, now occupied by Miss Emma Smith. Mr. DuBois was also a musician of more than local celebrity and devoted many of his leisure hours to Paginini's favorite instrument. Doylestown owes much to his memory for his labors in behalf of music and painting. A correspondent, of the *Bucks County Intelligencer*, of September 1, 1857, writing of Mr. DuBois, as an artist, said:

"It may be doubted if the Commonwealth, in which we live, has three artists superior to our townsman. His portraits are nature itself, standing forth in light and shade, in expression and feature. The coloring is excellent—the proportion exact. When fame shall take him in hand, and, under sanction of her nod, commend him to the world's admiration, he will not paint better—indeed there will be no need of it then, and he may not paint so well."

For several years Mr. DuBois divided his time between Doylestown and Wilkesbarre, but, for the last twenty-five years of his life, lived continuously at Doylestown, occupying a small brick studio on Pine street between State and York. It is said his residence, at Wilkesbarre, was shortened by an unfortunate affair of the heart. He never married. Mr. DuBois introduced the Daguerreotype art into Doylestown, producing the likeness of many pretty girls and customers of more mature years. When this was succeeded by photography, he gave a portion of his time to it, and many of his productions are yet in possession of his friends. Not the least interesting piece of art, from the brush of Mr. DuBois, still in Doylestown, is that of "Mac," the Mexican pony the author rode in the Civil War. It it true to nature, and, as one looks at the canvas in its frame, the good natured animal seems to invite its master to mount.

In 1844, Mr. DuBois had a rival in portrait painting, where-from we know not, of the name of Mason. He took rooms adjoining Vasey's Green Tree tavern. How long he remained, or whither he went when he left, is not known.

The coming of Thomas P. Otter, to Doylestown, in the eighties, did much for art in this community; but his talent and labors were not appreciated at their full value until after he was dead. He studied at the Philadelphia Academy, where his pictures were exhibited at the annual exhibition, one year a painting from his brush taking a premium. He was a man of undoubted genius, and some of his productions, would not discredit any artist. His fort was probably landscape painting, but he worked on several lines of art, was excellent in ink, and no mean carver in wood. He was a native of Montgomery county, but spent several years in Philadelphia. Mr. Otter returned to his native county in later years, and then came across into Bucks, settling at Vauxtown, almost a suburb of Doylestown, and subsequently moved into the borough, residing here to his death, 1891. His talent was versatile, and his brush and pencil were ever ready to aid any worthy local enterprise. He did a great deal to encourage art at the county seat and vicinity, and its refining influences is still with us. His two sons and two daughters are artists in wood and oil, but neither of them follow it professionally. Had Mr. Otter possessed ambition and energy, equal to his talent, he would have made his mark in the art world. It is a misfortune, the same man is not always equipped with both genius and ambition.

At various times somebody, given to art in some one line, has pitched his tent with us, and, on more than one occasion, the home of the artist was literally a "tent" and, for a time, plied his calling here. There has been no period of any length, in many years, when our borough did not have an artist in it, who could take a phiz, a la Daguerre, or by the photo art, and amateurs, likewise, are always with us. Edward A. Trego, son of the late Thomas W. Trego, deceased, is an artist of very considerable merit, although he does not follow it as a profession, and his son, a youth of twelve, gives promise of making his mark in art. There is a great deal of art in the Trego family, a brother, of Thomas W., being a distinguished portrait painter, while a son of the latter is a noted military painter, having studied in Paris and is not excelled, if equalled in America.

Summers A. Smith was one of the pioneers in the Daguerrian art at Doylestown. He opened a studio, about the close of the forties, or beginning of the fifties, in the second story of the Stuckert building, east side of North Main street. We do not know how long he remained there, but he moved thence up to "Germany," to a small frame on the lot whereon he subsequently built a brick dwelling. This was his home for several years, and here he carried on business. When photography took the place of Daguerr's process, Mr. Smith took it up but we do not know how long he continued it in Doylestown. He subsequently established himself in the business in Philadelphia, and we learn from an issue of the *Doylestown Democrat,* of February 8, 1859, that he had, at that time, a studio in the city.

Mr. Smith was an enterprising man, and, while living at Doylestown, imported the first Holstein cattle seen in this part of the country, making a trip to Holland for them, but the investment did not prove a success. At the same period Smith took Daguerreotypes in Doylestown, a man, named John Young, was here engaged in the same occupation.

About 1850, a young artist from New York, named Louis Lang, who had already made some reputation, spent part of a summer at Doylestown. Being quite a musician as well, he was introduced to a few of our musical families for whom he played. He was never here afterwards so far as I know, but I met him once in N. Y., 1863, at the Century Club in company with Leutze, Thomas Hicks and Kensette, all distinguished artists, Mr. Hicks was born at Newtown, this county.

Doylestown, Old and New.

XXVII
Our Military History.

While Doylestown makes no pretension to anything, entitled to be called "military history," the author flatters himself, he will be able to group a few paragraphs on the subject, that will repay the reading. Our military history, as we understand it, in this connection, embraces the movement of troops from abroad in our immediate vicinity, the volunteer militia that belong here, in peace or war, including our sem-military patriotic societies.

In a previous chapter, we briefly narrated the modest part our village played in the war for independence; how General Lacey made it his headquarters in the winter of 1778, while keeping watch and ward over the Delaware-Schuylkill peninsula to prevent the British Light horse raiding the loyal farmers, and prohibiting those of tory proclivities, taking their marketing to the English troops in Philadelphia, and exchanging it for gold and silver; and the passing of the Continental army, under Washington, through "Doyle Town," on the march from Valley Forge to strike the enemy at Monmouth, New Jersey, a part of the force, stopping here over Sunday.

More recently, we have learned, from Baker's Itinerary of General Washington, what throws additional light on the march of the Continental army from Valley Forge, via Doylestown to New Jersey. This we copy verbatim, and the reader will find it highly interesting. Of this event Washington writes:

THURSDAY, JUNE 18.

"At Valley Forge, Headquarters. Half after eleven, a. m., 18 June, I have the pleasure to inform Congress that I was this minute advised by Mr.

Roberts that the enemy evacuated the city early this morning. I have put six brigades in motion, and the rest of the army are preparing to follow with all possible dispatches. We shall proceed towards Jersey and govern ourselves according to circumstances." Washington to the President of Congress.

JUNE 18.

This day we learned the enemy had left Philadelphia. About 12 o'clock Ceneral Poor's, Varnons (Varnums) and Huntington's Brigades (under General Lee) marched off. At three o'clock the 2d Pennsylvania and another Southern Brigade marched off; and we had orders with the rest of the whole army to march to-morrow morning at 5 o'clock. Journal of Ebenezer Wild.

FRIDAY, JUNE 19.

Leaves Valley Forge. "The enemy evacuated Philadelphia, on the 18th instant. At ten o'clock that day I got intelligence of it, and by two o'clock, or soon after, had six brigades on their march for the Jerseys, and followed with the whole army next morning." Washington to John Augustine Washington, July 4, 1778.

SATURDAY, JUNE 20.

At Doylestown, Pennsylvania: "I am now with the main body of the army within ten miles of Coryell's Ferry. General Lee is advanced with six brigades, and will cross (the Delaware) to-night or to-morrow morning. I shall enter the Jerseys to-morrow. Washington to General Gates.

"The Doylestown of 1778 was a cross-roads hamlet, about ten miles from Coryell's Ferry on the Delaware (now New Hope,) consisting of a tavern kept by William Doyle, and several small houses, Washington pitched his tent near the dwelling of Jonathan Fell, late John G. Mann's farm house, just east of the present borough. The Doylestown of 1892, the county seat of Bucks county, Pennsylvania, is a town of three thousand inhabitants."

SUNDAY, JUNE 21.

At Doylestown: "The whole army is advancing to the Delaware. We have been much impeded by rain. The troops with General Lee crossed the river last night." Washington to General Arnold.

MONDAY, JUNE 22.

"At Coryell's Ferry," (now Lambertville,) New Jersey: "I have the honor to inform you that I am now in New Jersey, and that the troops are passing the river at Coryell's, and are mostly over. We have been a good deal impeded in our march by rainy weather. As soon as we have cleaned the arms, and can get matters in train, we propose moving towards Princeton." Washington to the President of Congress.

JUNE 22.

"The whole army encamped near the meeting house; having got word the enemy were moving towards Trenton, the army marched next morning toward them, and encamped at Hopewell, the enemy having altered their route wards Monmouth " Diary of Joseph Clark.

No other movement, of a military character, at or near Doylestown, took place for the third of a century, until the difficulty between the United States and Great Britain broke out and led to the war of 1812-'15. A public meeting was then called at the tavern of Enoch Harvey to organize an Artillery company, but nothing came of the sporadic effort of patriotism. After Congress had declared war, another meeting was held at Magill's tavern the evening of July 12, 1812, and a second effort was made to organize an Artillery company. "Men of spirit and enterprise" were invited to come forward, enrol their names, study the art of war, and resolve to live as freemen, or die in defence of the liberties of the country," but there is no evidence that any body "come forward." The second effort was likewise abortive.

Even after war had been declared by the United States, against Great Britain, some time elapsed before any active steps were taken in this community to sustain the goverment in its war policy. The first meeting at Doylestown, was held in the Court house, July 4, 1814, to "give forth some expression of public opinion concerning the situation of the country." After prayer, by the Rev. Thomas B. Montanye, who came up from Southampton to be present, John Pugh was called to the chair and John Fox appointed secretary. The meeting being organized, the following exercises followed: Willian Watts read the Declaration of Independence, the Rev. Uriah DuBois, the President's Message to Congress, of June 1, 1812, Mathias Morris delivered an oration, and the Hon. Samuel D. Ingham submitted a preamble and resolutions, expressive of the sense of the meeting touching the recent declaration of war, the situation of the country, and the obligation of the people to defend it.

In the meantime, a reminder, that war actually existed, came home to the people of the county seat. On March 22, 1814, twenty-five British officers, prisoners of war, passed through Doylestown on their way to Philadelphia to be confined in the Penitentiary. They were in charge of a detachment of Light Dragoons and Infantry, under Major Asa B. Sizer. The prisoners came from Pittsfield, Mass., and, among them, were Colonel Clench, of the militia, and Major Valette of De Watteville's regiment.

After the burning of the capitol, and other public buildings at Washington, by the British in 1814, and their threatened attack on Philadelphia, Doylestown's patriotism was fully aroused; the war was coming too near home to be treated with indifference. The news reached Doylestown on the Monday morning of September court, and, when court opened, John Fox, Deputy-Attorney General, made a brief address and moved the court do adjourn. The judge on the bench, Bird Wilson, would not assent to this and the business went on, but Fox, and William W. Hart, another young Attorney, uncle of the author, threw down their briefs, abandoned their profession and entered the military service; the former as Aid-de-camp on the staff of General Worrell, the latter as Adjutant of Colonel Thomas Humphrey's regiment of Riflemen.

By this time the patriotic spirit of Doylestown was touched in a tender spot; the war was coming too near home to be longer neglected. William Magill now stepped forward and organized a company of volunteer riflemen, called the "Bucks County Rangers," for a three months campaign on the lower Delaware. They left Doylestown on Wednesday morning, September 21, in full uniform, sixty-six strong for camp Dupont, near Wilmington, Delaware. The *Pennsylvania Correspondent*, of Doylestown, of the 26th, gives the following account of the departure of the company: "The preceding day the ladies of the village, married and single, with a cheerfulness and alacrity and spirit that entitle them to the highest praise, assembled at the Court House to finish lacing the clothing of their friends, whose zeal had induced the association. When paraded, they marched in single file to the Court House, separating to the right and left as they entered the court room. In the presence of a numerous audience, the Rev. U. DuBois delivered an address, concluding with an invocation of the "blessings of Heaven on the enterprise."

The following is a copy of the company's roll after it was mustered in: Captain, William Magill; First Lieutenant, William W. Hart; Second Lieutenant, —— Hare; Ensign, —— Eder.

James Robinson, Isaac Stelle, Arcturus Todd, Joseph Mathews, David Evans, Benjamin Robinson, William Harrar, John Heath, John M. Kinney, Joseph Anderson, John Bear, Robert Barclay, Paul Brunner, Nicholas Cisler, John Dennisson, John W. Doyle, William Dennisson, Isaac Dunlap, Joseph Engles, John Everit, Christian Fritzinger, Joseph Fries, David Fell, Jacob Fries, Gooden G. Hall, Benjamin Hare, Septemus Harrar, Samuel Hughes, Samuel Hubbert, Benjamin James, Mason James, Joseph James, Andrew Kirkpatrick, Jesse Lacey, Ephraim Lewis, William Marshall, Daniel McIntosh, Sem Moyers, Nathan Makinstry, Benjamin S. Mann, Isaac B. Medary, John Morris, Daniel Markley, William Megoken, William E. Patterson, James Picker, Christian Ruth, Anthony Rich, Samuel Rodman. Job Simpson, Samuel Smith, John W. Stover, John Swartzlander, Morgan N. Thomas, William Thomas, John Toy, Philip Trumbower, Mark Tanner, John Williams, Jonathan Wood, Joseph Pool, John Whittenham, Robert Roberts, Samuel Horn, William Horn, John F. Daniels, Joseph Hunter and Robert Patterson.

Captain Magill's company, at the close of the campaign, reached

THE HARVEY HOUSE, 1812.

home about the middle of December, and was discharged, but did not receive their pay. There was a hitch in the payment of the troops, and the company met in the Court House to see what steps should be taken, to accelerate it, Colonel Louis Bache being chairman, and Major Thomas G. Kenneday, secretary. The meeting found the fault lay with the Paymaster-General of the Army, for non-payment, and Colonel Bache, Major Wm. Watts and Major John Fox were appointed a committee to address a memorial to the President, setting forth their grievances, and asking for redress. The troops were paid in October, some of them at Doylestown, including the company of Phineas Kelley, at the Mansion House.

The war of 1812-'15 stimulated the organization of volunteer companies and the military spirit increased throughout the county. Captain Magill's Bucks County Rangers was in commission several years, but he probably resigned, meanwhile, as we find William T. Rogers in command, in 1823. After Captain Magill left the Rangers, he organized a company of "Volunteer Artillerists" at Doylestown, which he commanded to his death, 1824, when the arms were called in and delivered to his widow, October 17, 1828, and the company disbanded.

In 1822, Doylestown had a company of volunteers called "Independent Artillerists" organized the preceding fall and winter. It met at the Court House, January 24, was inspected by Brigade Inspector Samuel A. Smith, and officers elected: Captain, Joseph Hair; first Lieutenant, Anthony Rich, and second Lieutenant, Peter Opp. The uniform was adopted at a meeting held at Jacob Kohl's tavern, Doylestown, March 6, 1822, consisting of a blue "round-about" jacket, single breasted, three rows of guilt bullet buttons in front, trimmed with yellow cord, plain blue pantaloons, black leather stock and black leather cap, comforming to the pattern worn by the United States Army, each member to furnish his own uniform.[1]

The 4th of July, 1822, was observed at Doylestown by a military celebration in the Court House. Major Francis B. Shaw was the orator, and a dinner provided in the woods east of the Presbyterian church, the tables being furnished with necessary viands and liquors. A newspaper of the town, in speaking of the occasion, says:

"The welcome morning was ushered in by the ringing of the bells,

---

[1] What became of this company? Was it the one whose arms were turned in at the Mansion House? Magill was captain of the "Doylestown Artillerists" in 1824, the year of his death, when they celebrated the 4th of July at Opp's tavern, now the Clear Spring hotel. These two companies of the long ago may have gotten mixed.

and thunder from the cannon. The county hall, (Court House), the afternoon previous, had been decorated in a style the most enchanting for rural scenery and displaying in point of effect admirably appropriate to the occasion. The interior was darkened with the tall green forest of spruce, and laurels most beautifully disposed. The large folding doors, at the entrance of the hall, were thrown wide and the citizens passed in under wreathed arches of laurals. Every window in the hall was ornamented in the same manner. The large semi-circular recess, occupied by the Judge's bench, was adorned in the most imposing style. The back ground presented a thick forest, showing, in some degree, the mist of distances, over which was seen towering in bolder approach a grand arch about twenty-one feet, from point to point, in its base and about ten feet to its centre, formed of the richest foliage by the laurel, and upon which was displayed, at the equal distance, the thirteen stars, with radiance of seven inches, representing the thirteen states that united in that *Declaration of Independence*, Pennsylvania being the key and centre, and, immediately under the centre, in large letters and figures appeared, "July the Fourth, '76."

For many years Doylestown was the military centre of the county; there was great activity in military circles, new companies were organized, old ones drilled and numerous meetings held to stimulate the movement. On November 17, 1821, the commissioned officers, of the volunteers and militia of the county, met at Doylestown to take action toward forming a "Military Society," to assemble once or twice a year to improve the members in military tactics. The meeting was held at what is now the Fountain House, then kept by David D. Marple, the chairman being Captain John Davis, Southampton.

The first step, toward organizing the "Union Troop of Cavalry," one of the finest companys of horse in the state, was taken at a public meeting held at the "Indian Queen" tavern, later the "Ross Mansion," June 20, 1822, John Robbarts was chairman and William Field, secretary. It was resolved to form a company to be called the "Doylestown Cavalry." The meeting adjourned to meet at the public house of Francis Gurney Lukens, Newville, Warrington township, August 17. Officers were elected prior to November 7, for, on that day, the company met at the Cross Keys, a mile above Doylestown, "fully uniformed and equipped," probably the company's first appearance in martial array. John Robbarts was the first captain. The name of the company was changed to "Union Troop of Cavalry" about 1824, this name first appearing in the advertisement for the May training of that spring. On a card attached to the old flag of the Union Troop, presented to the Bucks County Historical Society, by the executor of Major James S. Mann, its last captain, is the following: "Organized October 8, 1823." This is an error in date. George H. Pawling was elected captain to succeed Robbarts, May, 1831. Among the captains, of this troop, were Joseph Archambault, who succeeded Pawling, Lambert Lashley and James S. Mann, the last, Archambault was a Frenchman, a member of Napoleon's household, was with him at Waterloo, and left for dead on the field. He went with the Emperor to St. Helena, and was the officer who broke his sword across his knee throwing the pieces into the sea, rather than give them to the English. He subsequently came to this country, spending most of his life in Bucks county, and dying in Philadelphia. The troop was disbanded in the Civil War period.

John Robbarts died at New Britain, December 28, 1844, aged about seventy. Some mystery hangs over his memory. He was an Englishman, and followed the sea when a boy; deserted that service for the American; became a trustworty sea captain, and long commanded one of Stephen Girard's vessels. In 1813, during our second war with England, he commanded a private armed ship called the "Jacob Jones" of sixteen guns and seventy-four men, and sailed out of Boston. He took a number of prizes. He settled in New Britain in 1819, and spent the rest of his life there.

About 1820, three or four companies of volunteers, of Doylestown and vicinity, were organized into a battalion, and Stephen Brock elected Major. It was subsequently known as the "Centre Union Battalion," and, in September, 1824, took part in the reception of Lafayette at Philadelphia. It rendezvoused at Willow Grove, proceeding thence to Frankford, where it joined the escort to the city. The Bucks County Rangers belonged to this battalion. Washington's birthday, 1824, was celebrated at Doylestown on Saturday, February 21, by the Union troop, Captain Robbarts. The members, and invited guests, sat down to a banquet at Marple's tavern, Captain Robbarts presiding, assisted by Lieutenants George W. Pawling and William McHenry, Cornet William VanHorn and Trumpeter John Smith. The Doylestown band was present.

Among the military from Northampton county, which participated in the welcome, and reception of Lafayette at Philadelphia, September 24, 1824, were four companies from Easton, those of Captains David D. Wagener, A. H. Reeder, the "Citizen Volunteers," Captain

Jacob Weyandt, and one other. They went down the Delaware in Durham boats, marching home up the Easton road, and stopping over night at Doylestown. The present Fountain House was made headquarters, the officers and men being quartered there and at private houses. Captain Reeder became prominent as a lawyer and politician. The battalion was accompanied by a wagon, loaded with "creature comforts" for the home trip, and, with it, was a boy, named Abraham Garron, who afterward settled at Doylestown, and spent his life here, dying 1892.

At a military election held July 7, 1828, for Major-General of the division, John Fox, of Doylestown, was elected over Mahlon Dungan, Fox polling twenty-four votes and Dungan eleven. Fox did not qualify and never held an office outside of his profession.

In the period of which we write, there was much visiting among military companies, and many excursions made. In June, 1830, the State Fencibles, a crack company of Philadelphia, Captain James Page, made an excursion to Easton and Bethlehem, accompained by Frank Johnson's celebrated negro band. They marched up the Easton road, reaching Doylestown the morning of the 22d, the people of the village entertaining them at breakfast at Field's tavern. That through with, the company reformed and marched through the streets leaving for Easton at eight o'clock. They returned home down the Delaware in a Durham boat. George Dorff, a member of the company, died at Easton from the effect of drinking cold water when overheated. On August 29, 1822, the field and company officers, of the Bucks County Brigade, met at Doylestown, were drilled by Colonel John Davis, for which he was given a vote of thanks. In 1830, Doylestown had a company of infantry called "Union Cadets," Stephen Brock, captain, which met at the Court Inn, kept by Charles Morris, but was so short lived it left no record behind, except this brief mention. At this time Doylestown could boast of a military band, of which David E. Gibson was captain, and, two years after, Joseph H. Purdy was treasurer.

The execution of Mina, June 21, 1832, for the murder of Dr. William Chapman, of Bensalem, brought out a finer display of military than Doylestown had ever seen, before or since. The occasion was made a gala day, the long procession of citizens and soldiers escorting the culprit to the gallows, on the Alms House farm, as if he were a conquering hero, instead of a miserable criminal. The military force consisted of twelve or fifteen hundred handsomely equipped Volunteers, six companies of Cavalry and fourteen of Infantry.

The issue of the *Democrat* of November 1, 1833, makes the following mention of a visiting troop :

" A handsome troop of cavalry, from the neighborhood of Philadelphia, arrived in our village on Monday evening last, and early next morning set off for Easton, escorted by a number of our citizens on horseback. They were under command of Captain Franklin Vansant, made a handsome and imposing appearance, and seemed to be well-versed in military tactics. They visited Bethlehem and Allentown, returning by way of Quakertown, to Doylestown, and left Saturday morning for their homes, well pleased with the excursion."

Saturday, September 6, 1834, Doylestown had a visit from the military company of New Hope, the "Independent Volunteers," Captain George Merrick. They paraded through the streets, forenoon and afternoon, and quartered at Field's Mansion House. *The Intelligencer* said of them:

"The uniform of the company is very neat; their accoutrements in excellent order; and they displayed a knowledge of military exercise that reflected credit upon them and their drill officers."

In 1836 an effort was made to organize a troop of cavalry in Doylestown, and Thomas Ross was chairman of a meeting held for that purpose, but the movement was not successful.

This was the period of crack companies for the girls to date on, and men and women to be proud of, and the county capital had her's in the "Doylestown Grays." It was organized in 1835, the first meeting being held at the Green Tree Tavern, Saturday evening, September 12. The original officers were Captain Charles H. Mathews, first Lieutenant, Pugh Dungan and second Lieutenant, Asher Cox. The company made its first appearance in uniform October 1 in a street parade at home, presenting a handsome appearance. The uniform was gray cloth; the cap, glazed leather; the men wore leather stocks to keep the head up and straps under their boots to keep the trousers down. Think of marching to glory thus hampered at the present day!

The Grays played its alloted part and played it reasonable well; parading the streets of the borough, visiting military trainings and encampments, including camps Washington and Jefferson in this county, 1837 and 1838, and camp Cadwallader, Easton, 1842. On the latter occasion the company went up the Delaware canal in a passenger boat, returning the same way, Abraham Garron, the sutler driving the baggage wagon up the Easton road loaded with camp luxuries. The author remembers, when a boy, of seeing the Grays at the trainings down county, and he has not forgotten with what awe he looked upon the company. The Grays and the Union Troop paraded the streets of Doylestown, on Washington's birth day, 1838, and supped at Field's in the evening. *The Intelligencer* in speaking of the appearance of the company, says:

"The Grays, on this occasion, manifested their usual neatness and military spirit. Their captain, Henry Chapman, Esq., appeared for the first time in uniform, and took command of the company. His military '*contour*' showed that he duly appreciated the honor the company had conferred on him in selecting him for their commander; and while it had 'stuck a feather in his cap' we observed the other officers, Dungan and Brock likewise, had one placed in theirs."

When the call was made for volunteers, at the out-break of the Mexican War, 1846, the Grays offered their services, but was not accepted, the offers far exceeding the number authorized. Charles H. Mann was then captain and under him the company's name was changed to "Doylestown Guards," and a regulation uniform adopted. In 1858, W. W. H. Davis was elected captain, and in command when the Civil War broke out, 1861. It was the first company in the county that offered its services, was accepted, and served through the three months' campaign in the Shenandoah Valley. To meet this emergency, the ranks were filled up and it was reorganized. On its return home the company was disbanded, but furnished forty of its rank and file for commissioned officers of other commands during the great war that followed.[2]

A company of artillery was organized at Doylestown, 1844; at first called "Keystone Artillerists," the name afterward changed to "Diller Artillerists," and Abel M. Griffith, a member of the bar, elected captain. It was armed with a brass six-pounder and muskets. On the death of Griffith, Peter Opp, Doylestown, succeeded him as captain, August 7th.

He had just returned from the Mexican War, having served in

---

[2] The services of the company were offered to Governor Curtin, April 15th, and accepted on the 18th, as per following despatch: "Harrisburg, April 18, 1861. To Major W. W. H. Davis: Your company is accepted, and will await orders." (Signed) "R. C. HALE."

Colonel Wynkoop's 1st Pa. regiment. The Doylestown Grays escorted him into town, Dr. Charles H. Mathews welcoming him in a speech from the porch of the Mansion House.[3] W. W. H. Davis was next elected captain of the company, but it was soon disbanded and the arms turned into the state arsenal.

Camp Jackson, at Doylestown, August, 1843, was one of the best military displays ever made in the county in time of peace. The tents were pitched on part of the Exhibition Grounds on the Lower State road; commanded by Major-General John Davis, and the force under arms—about eight hundred. Captain Alden Partridge was military instructor, and delivered a lecture each evening. The camp lasted four days. The attendance of spectators, on a single day, was estimated at twenty thousand.

The last military display at Doylestown, under the old volunteer militia regime, was on September 1, 1846. This was the fall parade of the "Centre Union Battalion," with some visiting companies. The following were present: The Union Troop, Captain Joseph Archambault; Lafayette Blues, Captain Williams; Lambertville Cadets, Captain Kohl; Independent Rifle Greens, Captain Swartzlander; Nockamixon Infantry, Captain Rutledge Thornton; Diller Artillerists, Captain Abel Griffith, and Doylestown Grays, Captain Charles H. Mann. Major Charles H. Mathews commanded the Battalion and W. W. H. Davis acted as Adjutant. The line was formed on East Court street, the right resting on Pine, and facing south, whence they marched to a field out of town on the State Road, where the Battalion was reviewed by Brigadier-General John S. Bryan.

During the railroad riots, several years ago, a new company was organized under the name of "The Naglee Rifles" to assist in quelling the disturbance, but was not called upon. It subsequently entered the state National Guard, and is still in this service, known as Company G, 6th Regiment, and was recently commanded by Captain John O. J. Shellenberger, Doylestown; and has been represented in active service; in peace and war, and always with credit.

During the century, just closed, Doylestown had eight volunteer

---

[3] On the 5th of August, 1848, General Robert Patterson, Colonel Francis M. Wynkoop and Lieutentant-Colonel Black, of the First Pennsylvania, and Captain Davis, of the Massachusetts regiment, all just returned from the Mexican War, visited Doylestown. A Democratic mass meeting had been called, and they were invited to attend it. The speakers' platform was erected on the Court House grounds, in front of the old jail, from which the returned officers addressed the audience.

companies, belonging to the village, and local organizations in every sense; the Bucks County Rangers, Volunteer Artillerists, Independent Artillerists, Union Troop of Cavalry, Union Cadets, Doylestown Grays-Guards, Diller Artillerists and Company G, 6th Regiment, the survivor of the group. The war of 1812-'15, with England, stimulated volunteer organizations, and, within the next ten years, the county had over twenty uniformed, and equipped companies, organized in two regiments and two Battalions, and were maintained with spirit for over a quarter of a century. In 1830 there were thirty-four volunteer companies in the county, and when the Civil War broke out there were still ten organized volunteer companies in the county, of which only two reorganized and entered the military service, the Doylestown Guards, and the company of Joseph Thomas, Applebachville. The war killed the remainder, and no attempt has been made to revive the volunteer system. In its place, the state has a National Guard organization, a compact, well-officered and well disciplined body of eight thousand men, which responds, with alacrity, to every call. The change is probably better for both offensive and defensive purposes, but it does little, if anything, to encourage the military spirit of the state, and seemingly calls in question, indirectly, if not directly, the right of the people to "bear arms," as is guaranteed in the Federal Constitution.

The last occasian, the goverment called for volunteers to sustain the flag, was in the Spanish-American war, 1898, when Doylestown furnished the Naglee Rifles, the officers of the company being B. Frank Atler, Captain; C. A. Vandegrift, First Lieutenant, and William Black, Second Lieutenant. They served a few months at a camp of instruction in Virginia, and, when no longer required, were sent home and mustered out. For the same war, two young men, of Doylestown, enlisted in the First Regiment U. S. Volunteer Engineers, Abel MacReynolds and John Ely. They saw service in Porto Rico, where young Ely contracted a fever from exposure, of which he died after his return home, October 11, 1898, in his twenty-second year.[4]

The last military display in Doylestown, by home troops, not of the borough, was the encampment of a couple of regiments of Pennsylvania Sons of Veterans, opened on Saturday, June, 14, 1902, and broke up the following Friday, the 20th. The number under canvas was about seven hundred, and their drilling and discipline highly

---

[4] John Ely was the son of the late Sheriff Samuel L. Ely, and grandson of General John Ely, Colonel Twenty-Third Pa. Regiment in the Civil War. He was an excellent young man, and much respected.

creditable. On Thursday they paraded the streets of the borough and presented a handsome appearance. The force consisted of Cavalry and Infantry and four light brass field pieces. The order held a convention, in Lenape Hall, Tuesday Morning and in the evening, gathered there about a camp fire, with vocal and instrumental music and addresses. They pitched their tents in what was known as "Taylor's Field," now the south edge of the borough, near the jail, and called it Camp Alexandra, after their Commander-in-Chief. Colonel R. M. J. Reed was in command, assisted by Lieutenant-Colonel E. Kochersperger, Major George W. Fritz, Major Charles E. Stover, Major R. T. Hart and a numerous staff. During the stay of the Sons of Veterans, the public and many private buildings were handsomely decorated, and the attractions brought many strangers to town. The order, organized from the first on a military bases, was started in Philadelphia, 1879. The number of Posts in the state is upward of two hundred, and their object to keep green the memory of their fathers, sacrificed for the preservation of the Union, and to cultivate the spirit of patriotism. The flag and the Union are their two objective points and watch words and, on these lines, the Sons of Veterans are doing good.

Doylestown, Old and New.

XXVIII
Beneficial Societies.

Next to the church and school beneficial and kindred societies challenge support from a community. The assistance they render the sick and afflicted, and the good they do their members on other lines, can hardly be estimated by the frequency of their ministrations, or computed by figures. In this respect, Doylestown has kept abreast with other boroughs of the same size, and doubtless ahead of many. We have been blest with such societies from an early day, all treading the same path and gaining laurels by alleviating distress.

The first, and oldest of these societies, making their home in Doylestown, was the Benevolent Lodge [1] of Masons, No. 188, organized 1819. Their place of meeting was the grand jury room in the old Court House, and Lewis Deffebach, editor of the *Democrat*, was secretary. Of its history we know but little, its record never having fallen into our hands. It was in working order until some time in the 30's of the last century, when the excitement, attending the "Anti Masonic period," caused the lodge to be turned out of its quarters in the Court House. This led to its dissolution, and it was never reorganized.

On July 24, 1820, the Benevolent Lodge with members of neighboring lodges, had a celebration at Doylestown that was numerously attended. Forming in procession, and led by the Southampton band

---

[1] While the Masonic order is not considered, a beneficial society, strictly speaking, we have so classed it here because its charities and beneficence are generous and far reaching; and administered, so quietly and unostentatiously, they never reach the public ear.

of music, with Mathias Morris, Chief Marshall, they marched round the public grounds, and then to the Presbyterian church. After religious services, the Rev. William B. Ashton, officiating, the meeting closed with prayer and singing the 33d Psalm. The procession now returned to the Court House, where a couple of short addresses were delivered, and the affair was over.

The successor and descendant, of the Benevolent Lodge, was the Doylestown Lodge, F. & A. M., 245, organized, 1850. A warrant was granted for its institution, August 27, to William Carr, Stephen Brock, Abraham Morris, Josiah Rich, John McIntosh, John D. James, William Fry, John S. Bryan, Caleb E. Wright and Jonas Ott. The warrant, for Benevolent Lodge, was lost for many years, but found, quite recently, among some family papers of the late Stephen Brock. The first stated meeting, under the new warrant, was held September 16, 1850, and the following the first officers elected: John William Fry, Worshipful Master; Josiah Rich, Senior Warden; Caleb E. Wright, Junior Warden; Stephen Brock, Treasurer; and William Carr, Secretary. The first person elected a member of this lodge, after its organization, was the late Dr. O. P. James, of Doylestown, the subsequent accession of members being quite rapid, and, on its fifteenth anniversary, the membership had reached one hundred and sixty-eight, and, in this time, there had been fifty-one Worshipful Masters. Among other officers was the late Hiram Lukens who filled the office of secretary of the lodge from December 27, 1858 to November 20, 1897. Mr. Lukens was one of the most devoted members of the lodge, and was never absent from a meeting if it could be avoided. In this regard he set an example it would be well for others to follow. In the list of members, were twenty-two whose descendants became Masons. The total receipts, in fifty years, reached the sum of $39,096.84, almost entirely from payment of fees and dues of members.

Although the Benevolent Lodge was not a benevolent organization, the Doylestown Lodge has found many ways of exercising charity and relieving distress. Since the lodge was instituted, it has had but two homes. In the beginning it held meetings in the old " Temperance Hall on the north side of East State street, now occupied by Francis Brothers, and in Beneficial Hall," its present quarters purchased 1857, for $2,500. Since that time it has expended $1,500 in improvements and refurnishing. The late Dr. O. P. James was treasurer from December 27, 1863, to February 19, 1894, and was the first to be initiated. When Doylestown Lodge was founded, the only other Masonic Lodge in the county was at Bristol, but, since that time, lodges have been organized at Newtown, Quakertown and Sellersville, in this county, and at Hatboro and Lansdale near neighbors in Montgomery. John McIntosh, who had been a member and officer of the Benevolent, was buried from the former lodge room in the old Court House, while the Masonic Hall was being repaired. Among those in attendance, was Dr. James S. Rich, also a former member of the Benevolent, who is reported to have said when all were assembled, "This reminds me of old times."

In the past sixty years, three lodges of Odd Fellows, of which two are in working order, have been organized in Doylestown. The oldest of these, the Doylestown Lodge, No. 94, was instituted March 30, 1844, at a special meeting of the Grand Lodge of Pennsylvania, held in the Court House, in the absence of any other proper place. The following officers and members of the Grand Lodge were present and officiated at the ceremony: John C. Yeager, grand master, occupied the chair, and was assisted by charter members, P. G. Enoch, H. Shearer, John G. Michener, William Limeburner, William Bryan, Rutledge Thornton and David H. Gaucher. After the organization of the new lodge had been effected, the following officers and members were elected at the same meeting: N. G., David H. Gaucher; V. G., Rutledge Thornton; Secretary, John G. Michener; Assistant Secretary, Enoch H. Shearer; Treasurer, William Limeburner; and members, Charles Wigton, O. G. Lunn, Robert A. Bayard, William Kachline, Jacob Shade, Levi L. Closson, Joseph Young, Samuel Solliday and Robert Stoneback. These were duly initiated to membership, and Daniel Thomas of Franklin Lodge, Frankford, No. 5, was chosen the representative to the Grand Lodge of Pennsylvania. The same night the following persons were proposed for membership: George H. Michener, taylor; Elijah Cox, John D. Brunner and Charles Massey. They now adjourned until Monday evening, April 15, to meet in the Academy. The lodge paid no benefits the first year.

Among the members of this lodge was William S. Black, a native of this county, a printer, who learned his trade in the *Democrat* office, under John S. Bryan, and was probably an apprentice when initiated. When last heard from he was living at Harrisburg. A meeting, held June 3d, was adjourned to hold the next stated meeting on the 10th, "in the new lodge room." The minutes of this meeting were headed,

"New Lodge Room," and while its location is not given, it was in the attic of the "Limeburner building," on the east side of South Main street, next door to Mrs. Walton's, lately occupied by Mrs. Stone. On June 24, the lodge was visited by Grand Master John C. Yeager accompanied by several brothers, from Philadelphia, and, at the request of the lodge, brother William H. Wittee delivered an "able and deeply interesting address, setting forth the advantages arising from the order, its benign and healthful influence on society, and the moral and religious effect upon its members." As Mr. Wittee was one of the best public speakers in the state, no doubt the address was a very fine one. The thanks of the lodge were tendered him. At the meeting held September 14, about forty members were present. Down to this time the lodge had expended in furniture, &c., &c., some $250, and, besides this outlay, had given a mortgage on their hall for $600. Where this hall was located seems not to be known.

After the Aquetong Lodge had fitted up the attic of the Academy, in the winter of 1848, the Doylestown Lodge, No. 94, rented the priviledge of meeting in the same room, paying a rental of $30. A dispensation, to change their quarters to the Academy, was received at a meeting held March 18, and, at the same meeting, Thomas W. Gaucher, of 193, was elected outside janitor. The Doylestown Lodge moved into their new quarters about April 1. From that time the lodges continued to occupy these quarters, until the Academy was torn down to make room for the handsome new school building erected on the lot, when they removed to their new quarters in Lenape Building. This was July 1, 1875, in order that mechanics might go to work in taking down the Academy.

The new lodge room in the Academy was opened for public inspection the afternoon of March 21, a large number of visitors being present. The *Bucks County Intelligencer* of the next day, in speaking of the new lodge room said:

"At one end, a fine painting, illustrating a scriptural subject from the tasteful brush of Mr. DuBois, decorated the wall half concealed by a scarlet curtain, in front of which a golden eagle spreads his wings, and, holding in his beak, two pendants of the same brilliant metal. At the other extreme, another curtain drooped in festoons of a blue color, ornamented with rosettes, whose centre sparkled with silver stars. The wall exhibited several charters, each bearing the chirographs of the magnates of the order, no doubt, and loaded with divers colored ribbons. Pedestals were standing on platforms at each end, having on them blocks of marble of the size of a brick and little mallets, the use of which we are (alas for our ignorance) unable to determine. A gorgeous carpet covered the floor; good enough both in texture and coloring to be trodden by the Great Mogul himself. Then there were some closets, with locked doors, around the apartment, into which we were not invited to look, and here, it was hinted, was kept—nobody knows what.''

In June, 1848, Frank Ferguson, of New Jersey, an Odd Fellow, brought the dead body of his daughter to Doylestown for interment. Accommodations being refused him at the hotels, the lodge room was thrown open, the funeral services held there, and the body taken hence to the grave yard. The Rev. Silas M. Andrews officiated, preaching an eloquent discourse. In 1858, the Doylestown, Aquetong and St. Tammany Lodges occupied the same room in the Academy. On February 22, 1860, Schuyler Colfax, then a member of Congress from Indiana, subsequently Vice President of the United States, delivered a lecture before the assembled lodges in the Presbyterian church, under the auspices of the Aquetong. On January 8, 1898, the lodge celebrated its fiftieth anniversary, at the lodge room, in Lenape building, Past Grand, Elias Carver delivering the address. He had been fifty-three years an Odd Fellow, and one of the oldest Past Grands in the state. The second Lodge of Odd Fellows, in order of date, to be organized in Doylestown, was the Aquetong, No. 193, in 1846. Our readers have already been informed that this lodge shared the quarters of the Doylestown in the attic of the Academy, from about April 1, 1848 to 1875, when they removed to Lenape building. When this new lodge was organized, a little scandal was indulged embracing the reason for this movement, but whether true or false, we do not know. It was alleged that politics had crept into the management of the Doylestown Lodge, at which the Democrats took great umbrage. A new lodge was suggested as the proper remedy, and Aquetong was organized in the lodge room of No. 94, at a special meeting held the evening of June 8, 1846, in obedience to authority granted by the Grand Lodge of Pennsylvania. The first regular meeting was held on the evening of July 8, with Caleb E. Wright in the chair and William Limeburner acting as Vice Grand. The following officers were elected: N. G., George H. Michener; V. G., William Kachline; Secretary, Isaac Lippencott; Assistant Secretary, O. P. Zink, and Treasurer,

OFFICE OF JUDGE FOX.

John G. Michener. Among those elected members, at this meeting, were Dr. William S. Hendre, Josiah Rich, Richard Watson, Daniel T. Moore, Robert Winder, Pierson Gilbert and Robert B. Flores. The same evening the subordinate lodge officers, and committees to manage the details of business, were appointed, and the new lodge started upon its career of sweet charity.

The lodge gained members at every meeting, and soon was a strong organization, among the accessions in the near future being George Lear. At the second meeting a board of Trustees was elected, consisting of William S. Hendrie, Josiah Rich, and Richard Watson, and John G. Michener was elected representative to Grand Lodge of Pennsylvania.

For the first ten years of its existence, and, in fact, down to the time of its occupancy of its new quarters in Lenape Building, there was want of life and activity among the members, who failed to exhibit the needed vigor, but, after they removed into the new lodge room, there was a marked improvement. During this formative period Richard Watson, Dr. William S. Hendrie and Thomas W. Gaucher were the mainstay of the lodge, the first named becoming one of the most active workers in the order in the state.

From the institution of the Aquetong down to its fiftieth anniversary, seventy-six persons occupied the principal chairs, all men of character and standing, some of especial prominence in the community. With the active assistance of the secretaries, they had much to do in making the life of the lodge a success. During these fifty years, its members numbered five hundred and sixty-three; it possessed $9,800 of invested funds, and the value of furniture was estimated at $700. The usefulness of the lodge can be best estimated by the statement, that for the same period, $23,000 were spent in assisting the sick and afflicted, burying the dead and caring for the orphan, a service worthy of all praise. The benevolance of Odd Fellowship is broad and far-reaching, and, as it is administered through the regular channels of the order, there is little, if any, danger of its benefactions being applied to unworthy purposes.

In Odd Fellowship, as in kindred organizations, the labors of a few men make the lodge a success. With the Aquetong, Richard Watson and Dr. William S. Hendrie are entitled to a large measure of credit. Thomas W. Gaucher was another devoted member, and Henry D. Livezey, Benjamin Cadwallader, Isaac R. VanHorn and Hugh Kintner are spoken of as among the early members, who gave great service to the lodge, all of whom have gone to their reward. On July 8, 1896, Alfred Paschall, long a member, delivered the semi-centennial address in the lodge room, embracing a carefully prepared sketch of the lodge's history.

The St. Tammany Lodge, No. 257, was chartered April 16, 1847, and instituted the 30th of August, same year, by C. E. Wright, D. D. of M. Where the ceremony took place we are not informed, but possibly in the lodge room of one of the other lodges. From the first, the meetings were held in the upper room of the building on East State street where Francis Brothers carry on business. This is on the north side of State street, adjoining what was the Murfit property for many years, recently purchased by Judge Yerkes. The author was a member of St. Tammany Lodge while meeting in this room, and we have no knowledge of its meeting elsewhere. Just when St. Tammany gave up the ghost we do not know, but sometime in the 50's, subsequent to 1853. The building alluded to, as the home of St. Tammany Lodge, was known as "Temperance Hall." After St. Tammany surrendered its charter as Mount Horeb Lodge, it was re-instituted at Freeland, Luzerne county, Pa., November 25, 1886, by Past Grand Sire Nicholson. When the lodge closed, Abiah J. Riale was the treasurer with $400 in cash on hand. On the Secretary of Mount Moriah Lodge being written to for information, he replied he could find no records of St. Tammany but the cash, order, ledger and receipt books. A search was made for the minute book, but none could be found. General John S. Bryan was one of the leaders in organizing St. Tammany Lodge, and there was no love lost between it and the Doylestown Lodge, on account of past political friction. On Friday evening, March 21, 1851, V. L. Bradford, Esq., a distinguished lawyer of Philadelphia, lectured before St. Tammany Lodge, but the subject we cannot recall. The committee were C. H. Mann, N. C. James and John S. Bryan. Among the societies, kindred to those spoken of, was the Olive Branch Division, Sons of Temperance. They had a celebration August 22, 1845, and, after parading the streets of the borough, adjourned to a grove out of town where speeches were made. One of the speakers was Judge Conard, Philadelphia, who, with his family, was boarding here at the time. Frank Sellers, who was active in running this Society, published the *Olive Branch* newspaper.

The German Aid Society, the next youngest of the beneficial societies, of Doylestown, was organized June 24, 1866. The preliminary meeting was held at the private residence of John Bauer, who lived on North Main street, in that part of the borough then called "Germany." The temporary officers elected were: Frederick Constantine, president; George Kraft, vice president; Mathias Siegler, treasurer; Dominic Baumann, secretary; and John Bauer, Augustus Siegler and Conard Hall were choosen to draft a constitution and by-laws. These were adopted July 8, and signed by the following persons, who were the original members:

Frederick Constantine, Dominic Baumann, John Bauer, Augustus Siegler, Conard Hahl, Dr. Charles Siegler, Christian Miller, W. F. Orbann, Jacob Long, John Koch, F. X. C. Fuss, Jacob Constantine, John Moyer, Johannes Brown, Christian M. Esser, Louis Spellier, Herman Schmutz, Frederick Long, Martin Hahl, Levi Nace, John Miller, Francis Fluck, Peter Haubert, William Lightcap, A. B. Birkert, Frederick Schrag, Michael Roth, Charles Fritsche, Samuel Durstine, Moritz Lœb, Dr. F. Mierson and Isaac Transue. Of these thirty-two original members, of the German Aid Society, twenty-five have deceased since they signed their names to the constitution and by-laws, leaving but seven survivors. The society was incorporated, by the Court of Common Pleas of Bucks county, May 3, 1867, and immediately began its good work which it has continued. The present membership is ninety-five.

The object of the German Aid Society, as set forth in the second Article of the Constitution, is "to aid its members in cases of sickness or death," and the membership is limited to "healthy males, possessing a good character, citizens of Pennsylvania and speaking the German language." From the first, the dues of the members have been ten cents a week. The sick benefits are $5 per week during the entire sickness of the member, and the funeral benefits $75 for a member and $50 for a member's wife. The funeral benefits were paid out of the treasury until 1898, but are now paid by assessments, each member paying one dollar, when a member dies and fifty cents on the death of the wife. The society's capital, at present, is $3,000, and running expenses $50 a year. The officers, in 1902, were President, Ernest Werner; Vice President, George Schroth; Treasurer, Jonas Kern; Secretary, John C. Copple, and Trustees, Charles F. Myers, Dr. Charles Siegler and Edward Carl.

The first member, of the society to die, was Julius Kuster, born of German parents, and spent most of his life in Doylestown. His father lived and died in Warsaw, Poland. Julius learned the printing trade in the *Democrat* office and subsequently worked on the *Standard*. When the Civil War broke out he enlisted in the Doylestown Guards and served three months, participating in the Shenandoah Valley campaign, reaching the grade of corporal. Mr. Kuster was an excellent man and very popular.

The next beneficial society in our borough, in the order of age, is that of the United American Mechanics, organized 1868. The preliminary meeting was held the evening of August 12, in Brower's Hall, on the Fountain House property. T. N. Myers was called to the chair, and stated the object of the meeting. A committee was appointed to wait on one of the Societies of Odd Fellows, and ask permission to make use of its room, but this being refused, quarters were obtained of Lewis B. Thompson. After the necessary preliminary business had been transacted, the meeting adjourned.

The next meeting was held September 2, in their permanent quarters, and the chapter members were constituted the Doylestown Council, "No. 166, of U. A. M." Representatives from the Jefferson Council, No. 75, performed the ceremonies. The following members were initiated: A. H. Heany, Lewis Heller, H. S. Sigafus, David Firman, William Fluck, E. R. J. Uberoth, James H. Clark, William Lightcap, John P. Kinny, Wilson D. James, A. C. Large, D. S. Willard, James A. Martin, A. B. Rickard, Theodore P. Harvey, and Oliver H. Smith. From these the following officers were elected: Myers, V. C.; Martin, R. S.; Heany, A. R. S.; Firman, F. S.; Clark, I.; Funk, Ex.; James, I. P.; Sigafus, O. P., and Theodore P. Harvey, William C. Knight, William Fluck, and John Kenney, Trustees. After the installation of officers and the State charter presented, the council was declared to be in working order. At this meeting, steps were taken to procure the necessary regalia and other articles required to fully equip the new organization. From the date of the Council's institution, it has been active in the discharge of its functions. The membership of the Society is one hundred, the initiation fee from three to eight dollars, according to age of the applicant, sick allowance five dollars a week, funeral benefit one hundred dollars for a member and fifty dollars for the wife. The present meeting place is Seigler's Hall.[2]

In additon to the beneficial societies named, there are several

---

[2] The Doylestown Council of American Mechanics celebrated its thirtieth anniversary, in Lenape Hall, Saturday evening, July 10, 1898. The hall was handsomely decorated with flags, and the attendance large. Several other orders were represented.

others in Doylestown, organized for this and kindred purposes. These we group, giving name and object, as far as our information warrants it. The first is the Knights of the Golden Eagle, a strong and popular organization, whose mission is beneficial and the cultivation of the social virtues; Knights and Ladies of Honor, beneficial; True Blue, accident and sick benefits; Improved Order Heptasophs, life insurance; Royal Arcanum, life insurance and beneficial; St. Joseph's, beneficial; the Red Men; the Senior and Junior Order of American Mechanics, both beneficial, and the Daughters of Liberty, Doylestown Council, No. 40, also beneficial. This latter society was organized in 1897. A committee of six men, three from the Senior American Mechanics and three from the Junior, who would be eligible to membership in the Daughters of Liberty, met to ascertain if it were possible to organize such lodge. After it was determined to make the attempt, and the actual work of organization had begun, the members of the committee dropped out until but two were left, Parke B. Summers and Ellwood B. Myers, members of the Junior Order of U. A. M. They proceeded with the work, but Mr. Summers being suddenly called away, the work of organization, institution, etc., devolved on Mr. Myers. The effort was successful, and, he and Mr. Summers are still members of the order. It has proved a successful organization, and is growing stronger. In the first four years, the receipts reached $2,343.09, and $2,000 were paid out for sick benefits. On Saturday evening, October 12, 1901, the council presented the School Board an American flag, the presentation speech being made by Lieutenant .Charles A. Cuffel, and received by Robert Yardley, Esq. The presentation was preceded by a short literary programme and followed by refreshments. The presence of this number of beneficial societies, in a town of the size of Doylestown, shows how closely mankind, outside of the family circle, is united in the common purpose of doing good to each other.[3]

As stated above the Daughters of Liberty was organized October 9, 1897, with forty-five charter members, forty-one females and four males. The following composed the sub-ordinate officers: Councillor, Mrs. Lucy Switzer; Associate Councillor, Miss Elizabeth B. Hoffman; Vice Councillor, Miss Hannah E. McIntosh; Assistant Vice Councillor, Miss Georgia M. Shinn; Recording Secretary, Miss Virginia Balles; Assistant Recording Secretary, Miss Emma Fuss;

---

[3] A few of our local societies have been omitted, because we were not able to get the necessary data.

First Secretary, Elwood B. Myers; Treasurer, Miss Lucy Dyer; Guide, Miss M. Ida Gross; Junior Ex-Councillor, Miss Laura Fretz; Associate Junior Ex-Councillor, Parker Summers; Trustees, Parker Summers, Miss Fannie Eisenhart, Mrs. Ida M. Keuler; Representative, Parker Summers; Deputy Representative, J. Bailey Harvey, Philadelphia, member of John E. Armstrong Council. The present membership is sixty-nine females and five males, suspended ten and lost by death two. Since the organization the council has paid out for sick and death benefits, over $1,000, and the value of the council is $900. The place of meeting is in Siegler's Hall, every Monday evening. On Sunday evening, November 24, 1902, the Daughters of Liberty attended St. Paul's Lutheran church, where the Rev. S. A. Bridges Stopp preached a special sermon for the occasion and the choir rendered appropriate music.

Of the patriotic societies, of Doylestown, and semi-military in character, the Grand Army of the Republic was the earliest organized. The first attempt was in 1867, and Thomas P. Miller, 68th Pa., Charles A. Cuffel, Durell's Battery, and Burt Schurz, regiment unknown, were the most active. It survived about a year, and its early death is said to have been caused by one of the local newspapers charging it with an object not thought of. About this time, the graves of the soldiers, who fell in the Civil War, and were buried at Doylestown, were first decorated with flowers, Miller and Cuffel being leaders in this movement. This was continued for several years, and led legitimately to the organization of a Grand Army Post here. This was in 1883, and called the General Robert L. Bodine Post, No. 306.

The formal muster in, of the members composing the organization, was on January 23, by Post No. 2, of Philadelphia, which the Department Commander detailed for the purpose. The ceremonies took place in Lenape Hall, and attracted no little attention. The following were the names of the charter members:

Charles A. Cuffel, Isaiah J. Sellers, Robert Conard, James Bissey, Durell's Battery; C. K. Frankenfield, J. F. Atkinson, 128th P. V.; John Townsend, 29 P. V.; Thomas P. Miller, 68th P. V.; John Hargrave, Andrew Connard, James Garis, Miles Williams, William S. Radcliff, Evan Stover, Samuel Silvey, 104 P. V.; Dr. Frank Swartzlander, Assistant Surgeon; Joseph M. Fulton, 174 P. M.; Lewis K. Bryan, Berdans Sharpshooters and 174 P. M.; D. W. C. Callender, 8th Pa. Cavalry; Samuel S. Ely, 215 Pa.; V. Rudolph Meyer, 3 Battery V. R. C.; James Gilkyson, 31st Pa. M.; Joseph S.

Hawk, 3d Pa. Artillery; C. Howard Magill, John Flack, 196 Pa. V.; Jacob Clemens, 25 Pa. V.; Patrick Harford, 11 N. J. C.; Richard Watson, Pa. M.

The first regular meeting of the Post was held in the room of the Doylestown Public Library, Lenape Building, and, for a year or more, in a large room in the third story of James S. Mann's bakery at the southwest corner of Main and State streets. The headquarters of the Post was next moved to the second story of James Kane's building on Donaldson street, where it remained for several years, and thence to the Thompson building on Main street. Subsequently the Post moved its quarters back to the Kane building and then to their present quarters in Mannerchoir Hall. On Memorial Day, May 30th, the Post turns out to do honor to the memory of their dead comrades, by holding a public meeting in the Court House, the exercises consisting in a recital of the ritual, reading orders, an address, music and religious services. A procession is then formed and marches to the cemetery, where the soldiers' graves are decorated, additional religious services held, followed by firing a volley. On such occasions the attendance is large, the day almost an holiday.

In December, 1901, a meeting was held at the dwelling of Captain Charles A. Vandegrift for the purpose of organizing a camp of the "National Association of Veterans of the Spanish-American war." It was given the name of Doylestown Camp, No. 228, and the following officers elected and subsequently installed: Commander, Captain F. B. Atler; Senior Vice Commander, Sergeant A. F. Lear; Junior do, Joseph R. Wood; Adjutant, C. F. Kratz; Quartermaster, Sergeant Edward Maulsbury; Chaplain, Captain W. H. Black, Officer of the Guard, August Kurtz, and, officer of the Day, Robert McIntosh. The charter members elected, were Captains, F. B. Atler, C. A. Vandegrift, and Wm. H. Black; Sergeants, Edward Maulsbury, A. F. Lear and George W. Kohl; Corporal, Henry W. Bryan, and privates, C. F. Kratz, Joseph R. Wood, Robert McIntosh, August Kurtz and Oscar Bice. The first subsequent meeting was held in the Tomlinson building, January 23, 1902, and the regular meetings the last Saturday evening of each month.

Doylestown, Old and New.

XXIX
Our Medical Life.

The medical life, of a community, is a matter of interest, whether the practioner makes use of the knife, in a case demanding the most consummate skill to save the life of the patient, administers curatives or renders other professional services to amend

> "The heartaches and the thousand natural shocks
> That flesh is heir to."

No other profession holds such confidential relations with the human family, and, to reach our purpose, we treat the physicians, druggists and dentists, who have lived and practiced in Doylestown, in a single group. In doing this, however, we shall deal only with the eldest, the Dean of each branch of the profession, making him the examplar of his brethren.

The first physician, we have knowledge of, in practice at Doylestown and vicinity, was Dr. Hugh Meredith,[1] although there may have been earlier ones, whose names have not come down to us. The Merediths were early settlers in Doylestown township, then part of New Britain, James Meredith,[2] the Bucks county ancestor, settling in the vicinity of Castle Valley about 1730, coming over from Chester county. He was the father of Dr. Hugh, who studied medicine, married Mary Todd and lived and died in Doylestown. Just at what time he came is a little uncertain, though tradition says he was

---

[1] Dr. Hugh Meredith's name is among those on the roll of the New Britain Associators, 1776.

[2] Near Doylestown, April 18, 1819, Hannah Meredith, aged 87 years.

DR. CHARLES H. MATHEWS.

practicing here as early as 1778. He had two sons, Thomas [3] and Charles,[4] and a daughter Elizabeth who married Abraham Chapman, and was the mother of the late Hon. Henry Chapman. Dr. Hugh Meredith's dwelling was on, or near, what is known as "Armstrong's Corner," where he is said to have built a dwelling, 1789. He died July 15, 1815, and was succeeded in practice by his son Charles, who died in 1831.[5 and 6] Father and son are both highly spoken of. Dr. Charles Meredith, the son, was born 1774.[7] On the death of Dr. Charles Meredith he was succeeded in his practice by Dr. Charles H. Mathews, his brother-in-law, who had married his sister. Dr. Mathews was born at Roxborough, Philadelphia county, November 5, 1805, and graduated from the Medical Department of the University of Pennsylvania, 1827. While his life was devoted to his profession, he took an interest in public affairs, giving some of his time to politics, and was interested in the volunteer militia. He held the office of Prothonotary of the Courts for one term, was Captain of the Doylestown Grays, the crack company of the county, Major of the Centre Union Battalion, and elected and Commissioned Major-General of the second division, Pennsylvnnia Militia, composed of Bucks and Montgomery counties. He was chosen to this office while upon his death bed, and the author had the meloncholy satisfaction of presenting him the certificate of his election, a day or two before he died. He had a delightful personality, was successful in the practice of his profession and popular with all classes. . Dr. Mathews was twice married, his first wife being a daughter of Dr. Hugh Meredith, and his second a daughter of Gilbert Rodman, Bensalem, and a sister of Mrs. John Fox. He died July 25, 1849.

Dr. James S. Rich was probably in practice, at Doylestown, prior

---

3 On the 26th ult. April, 1826, by Conrad Myers, Esq., Mr. Charles Buck, Jr., of Tinicum, to Miss Mary Matilda, daughter of Dr. Thomas N. Meredith, of Nockamixon, and grand-daughter of Dr. Charles Meredith, Doylestown.

4 Dr. Charles Meredith received part of his education at the classical school, at Southampton Baptist church.

5 At Doylestown, July 27, 1831, Dr. Charles Meredith, in his 57th year. "If universal benevolence, it charity and kindness to the poor, if incorruptible integrity be claims to consideration, he richly deserved it; while his medical experience, exerted through a long and extensive practice, has called forth the gratitude of numbers for their experience of its benefits. 6 At Philadelphia, February 7, 1832, Mrs. Isabella, relict of the late Dr. Charles Meredith, of Doylestown.

7 Wishing to know whether the two Dr. Merediths had graduated from the Medical Department of Pennsylvania University, we wrote that institution, and received the reply: "We are sorry to state that these honored doctors were not from this school."

to the death of Dr. Charles Meredith, and succeeded him to the Dean's chair, but of this we are not certain. He was a native of Doylestown township, a son of Anthony Rich, and may have settled here as soon as he graduated from the Medical School. He continued in practice until 1841, but Dr. C. B. Ferguson from Philadelphia, coming here, meanwhile, Dr. Rich removed to Churchville to take the practice of Dr. Baker, and spent the remainder of his life there. This made Dr. Mathews the Dean of the profession at Doylestown. Dr. Ferguson moved into Dr. Rich's house, April 1, 1841, on East State street, the same now owned and occupied by Postmaster James Bartlett, and was in practice here until the summer of 1849, when he died of Asiatic cholera contracted at the Alms House. Dr. William S. Hendrie, who had previously settled in Hilltown, removing hither from Springtown, doubtless having an eye on the relinquished practice of Dr. Rich, came down to Doylestown in the spring of 1841. He subsequently purchased the Dr. Rich house and spent his life in it. Dr. Hendrie was Dean of the profession, at Doylestown, until his death in 1875, and was succeeded by Dr. Gilbert R. McCoy, the next in succession.

At the death of Dr. Mathews, 1849, Dr. McCoy, came to Doylestown and took his practice. He was a son of Anthony McCoy, of Easton, a relative of the family by marriage, and, being the oldest in practice, became the Dean. He was a graduate of the University Medical School and having the piece of parchment that stamps the owner as qualified to practice medicine, he settled in Chester county. Upon learning of the death of Dr. Mathews, Dr. McCoy came here living in the Meredith house on North Main street, opposite the Court House. Through these four physicians, the two Meredith's, Mathews and McCoy, ran the blood of relationship, and the fourth in line was as acceptable to his generation as the other three had been to theirs. During Dr. McCoy's practice of forty years, he gathered a clientage about him that appreciated his gentle manners and professional skill. He died in 1882, and his wife since followed him to the grave.

In the meantime, Dr. Frank Swartzlander, son of Joseph Swartzlander, Lower Makefield, and a graduate of the Pennsylvania University School, had settled at Doylestown, and began practice January 1, 1866. By seniority he became the Dean on the death of Dr. McCoy and still wears his honors. Dr. Swartzlander has had an unusual experience, serving through the Civil War, as Assistant Surgeon, having charge of a hospital on the field at Gettysburg, and participated in the siege of Charleston, the most noted of modern times. To the historian of the future we leave the medical Dean of 1902.

The next physician to settle in Doylestown, in the order of time, was Dr. Andrew J. Hines, who removed here in 1870. He was a descendant of Matthew Hines, born in Ireland, came to America, 1740, and settled in Whitemarsh township, then Philadelphia county, now Montgomery. He married Mrs. Ann Simpson. Dr. Hines was born in Warrington township, Bucks county, August 5, 1826, brought up on his father's farm, received a classical education, read medicine with Dr. O. P. James, Doylestown, and graduated from the Jefferson Medical School, 1853. He began practice at Leidytown, Hilltown township, remaining there seventeen years before coming to Doylestown, having previously married Anna M. Armstrong, daughter of Jesse Armstrong. He was widely known in Bucks and Montgomery counties; was a member of the Bucks County Medical Society, and a Trustee of the Doylestown Baptist Church.

Since the time of which we write the science of medicine has broadened, and the knowledge and skill, that wait on its practice, have wonderfully grown. There are more physicians in Doylestown, at present, than ever before at any one time, and of a greater number of schools.[8]

The druggist, the second in our group of the Medical life of Doylestown, according to our arrangement, come later than the physician, and the harmony, between these two branches of the profession, shows how essential they are to each other. The first "Drug and Medicine store" in Doylestown, was opened 1818, and, as strange as it may seem, the proprietor of it was Frances B. Shaw, a member of the bar. He was probably the first in this business at the county seat.[9] The location is not definitely known but was probably in the old Shaw stone dwelling that stood on the east side of North Main street, almost opposite the Doylestown Trust Company. How the two professions got along together, without clashing, is a question law and medicine, both would like to have answered. In the early fall of 1837, John H. Anderson, who was keeping a general store, here on the west side

---

8 With increase in practice, and growth of skill, it is quite natural the Medical fee bill has kept pace. The author has, in his possession, the bill of Dr. John Wilson, for "Medical attendance" on Judge Watts' family, for February and March, 1815, while the epidemic of typhus fever prevailed here and amounts to but $27. There were five patients and all died.

9 Dr. Mathew Otto was the first regular apothecary in the county, opening his drug shop at Bethlehem, about 1745. We find he was called to attend the sick at Durham furnace, May, 1746, and his bill was £3-5 S.

of what is now "Monument Place," fitted up a "Drug and Medicine Department," and we suppose he kept it until he went to Lambertville, where he died, In 1838, Dr. John Pettitt, son of Elnathan, opened a drug store "in the new building, opposite the Doylestown Hotel." The building was the same now owned by William Stuckert, opposite the Fountain House, and was *new* in 1838, having been lately rebuilt, after the fire of 1836, which destroyed the *Democrat* building on that site. While the foregoing were pioneers in the drug business, they did not take it up professionally, but one came shortly, to stay, making it his life work. This was the late Dr. George T. Harvey.

Dr. Harvey, the son of Enoch Harvey, was born in Doylestown, 1813, and educated at the school at Bridge Point, then kept by Samuel Aaron and at the Union Academy, and, at twenty, began the study of medicine with Dr. Abraham Stout, Bethlehem. He attended lectures at the University of Pennsylvania, where he graduated, 1835. He now went to Missouri, where he practiced medicine and tried to "grow up with the country," until 1840, when he returned home and settled down in the drug business, erecting a building on the west side of North Main street, between the Doylestown bank and the Harvey dwelling, on the site of the present Hart building. This was the only drug store in Doylestown for many years, and possibly in the county, and here Dr. Harvey kept for well nigh half a century. He became a prominent and public spirited citizen; was three times postmaster, a member of council, 1869, that introduced water into the borough, and held the commissions of Lieutenant and Captain in the Civil War, first in the three months army, and subsequently three years in the 104th Regiment. Dr. Harvey was twice married, his first wife being Mary LaRue, of Doylestown, by whom he had one child, a son, Judge Edward Harvey, of Allentown. After the death of his wife he married Mary Rex, of Norristown, 1856, and two daughters were born to them. Doctor Harvey was the Dean of the druggists. The Harvey drug building was quite historic, and, when taken down, was one of the oldest frames in the borough. The upper story had been used for various purposes. In the fall of 1848, the author opened his law office on the lower floor moving up stairs the following spring, reaching his quarters by an outside pair of steps; the "T. O. S. Club," a social organization of young men, had its quarters there several years, whence it removed to Lenape Building, and dissolved about 1890, when most of the members went out into the world to make a living and earn fame. Doylestown of the present

DR. GEORGE T. HARVEY.

day, is equipped with drug stores that will compare favorably with city establishments in the same profession, and Mr. Hulshizer is the Dean.

A. M. Freeman was an early dentist, if not the first in Doylestown, September 1, 1823, and could be seen "at the house of Mrs. Anderson, first door north of Asher Miner's printing office." He announced that the public "need have no occasion to dread his operations, as they are attended with very little pain or uneasiness." He was probably one of the traveling tooth pullers, who went about the country relieving men and women of troublesome molars. At that day there were no professional dentists, the calling not being known as a profession. In 1834, the newspapers of Doylestown announced that Dr. W. F. De La Mater "a surgeon dentist, lately from New York," had opened an office in the Green Tree Tavern, then kept by Andrew Meyer. His specialty was "setting porcelain incorruptible teeth." He was followed by Dr. Henry C. Lloyd who opened a dentistry office in Doylestown, July 1846, remained for a time and then went to Texas, where he had an uncle living, and married there. The degree of M. D. being conferred upon him, July 2, 1848, he subsequently returned to Bucks county, settling at Yardley where he practiced medicine to his death, about 1890. He was a brother of E. Morris Lloyd, Esq., a member of this bar; both were sons of the late John Lloyd, and grandsons of Enos Morris, Esq., a prominent lawyer prior, and subsequent, to the removal of the county seat.

Dr. Parsons, a dentist from Wilkesbarre, settled here in the practice of his profession, 1848, but went to California the following year, when the gold fever became epidemic. It carried him off in January, 1849. He sailed in the Gray Eagle from Philadelphia, accompanied by Charles McHenry, of Doylestown, and J. Neeley Thompson, of Solebury, while Asher Cox followed them in a few months. McHenry and Cox returned in a few years, Parsons remaining permanently, dying there. Thompson made California his home for several years, being fortunate in his ventures; then returned to New York, subsequently going to the city of Mexico where he died.

Dr. Parsons was succeeded in professional dentistry, at Doylestown, by Dr. A. J. Yerkes, Jr., son of Andrew Yerkes, of Warminster township, where he was born, 1826. He came here, November, 1851, and, in the *Democrat* of the 18th, advertised himself as a "Surgical and Mechanical Dentist, office opposite Mann's Hotel," and that he will be, on Monday next, the 24th, "at his father's house one mile above Hatborough to remain one week." He located in what is now the Stuckert building, opposite the Fountain House, North Main street. He learned his profession with Dr. Charles Sloan, of Philadelphia. Dr. Yerkes had his office in three other localities before getting into his own dwelling, which he erected in 1855; in the Joshua Beans house, on the north side of East State street, three doors from Main, the Nightingale house, southeast corner of East State and Pine, and in the McGinty building, northeast corner of the same streets. Being a skillful dentist, Dr. Yerkes drew a large patronage. He was assisted in this by purchasing, of the patentee, the right to manufacture mineral teeth and make vitrous oxide. In 1860, Dr. Yerkes' brother, Hutchinson P. came to learn the profession with him, and, on concluding his studies, located at Norristown. He remained there until 1865, when he returned to Doylestown to assist his brother, then in failing health. Dr. Andrew J. Yerkes died here in 1868 in his forty-second year, when Dr. Hutchinson P. succeeded him, and is still in practice. Dr. Andrew, being the eldest dentist in practic, became the Dean and held it to his death.

In the meantime, after Dr. Yerkes, the elder, had settled at Doylestown, a new dentist made his appearance, Dr. John S. Rhoads. Whence he came has escaped our memory, but he married Miss Sophia Evans, sister of Judson Evans, then well known in this section. We are not able to find the exact time when Dr. Rhoads came here, but the first mention of him is in the *Doylestown Democrat,* of November 8, 1859, when he was in partnership with J. M. Childs, and they advertise as "Surgical and Mechanical Dentists." The office was on Main street, first door above W. T. Eisenhart's clothing store. On April 19, 1859, Childs was in partnership with Dr. R. Yost, at which date they advertise they have "located themselves permanently in Doylestown." After these dates, they appear to have dropped out, and we know nothing more of either of them.

Dr. Rhoads purchased the McDowell residence east side of North Main below Court, then owned by George Hart, April 15, 1865, and continued practice there to his death, his will being dated October 1, 1868, and proved June 6, 1882. His widow married Dr. Joseph Hart, but, as they did not live in harmony, they separated, and she and her daughter are now living in California, A dentist, named William Lewis, was in practice here in March, 1859. Dr. Rhoads became Dean of the profession, on the death of Dr. A. J.

Yerkes, by virtue of seniority in practice, but, on his decease, the honors passed to Dr. Hutchinson P. Yerkes, who still wears them worthily. He resides in the dwelling built by his brother Andrew, 1853, which has been his home since he succeeded him in practice, on the south side of East State street, second door west of Pine.

Doylestown, Old and New.

XXX
Historic Families.

Great interest attaches to the pioneer settlers the world over, for they are the true nation makers. In previous chapters we made mention of the oldest families which settled here, or in the immediate vicinity, who made their mark on the life and history of Doylestown; in this, we shall speak of them more at length, at the risk of being charged with telling "an oft told tale."

The "Free Society of Traders,"[1] followed by Jeremiah Langhorne and Joseph Kirkbride, were the original proprietors of the land the county seat stands upon, and for a considerable distance around it. The Langhornes were immigrants from Westmoreland, England, Thomas Langhorne, the ancestor, settling in Middletown, 1682, and dying there, 1687. He took up 800 acres in that township, and the family increased their holdings largely by purchase. His son, Jeremiah, became a man of mark and held many places of public trust; Justice of the Peace, 1715-'19; commissioned to build the jail at Newtown, 1724; Speaker of the Provincial Council, Justice of the Supreme Court, 1726-'39, and Chief Justice, 1739, dying in 1742.

The Kirkbrides came from Cumberland, Joseph, the ancestor, arriving in the Welcome, 1682, and settling in Falls township; an indentured apprentice, he ran away from his master at the age of nine-

---

[1] Penn's largest and oldest grant in the county was made to the "Free Society of Traders," in London, the 22d and 23rd of March, 1682, and covered 20,000 acres. The object of the company, mostly composed of gentlemen of London, was to carry on trading operations on an extensive scale, but its provisions were never carried out.

JUDGE JOHN FOX.

teen, starting for the new world with a little wallet of clothing and a
flail. He was first employed at Pennsbury, but removed to West
Jersey and there married a daughter of Randall Blackshaw, 1688. He
became influential and wealthy, and a leading minister among friends,
dying 1738, at the age of seventy-five. From his son Mahlon have
descended all that bear the name, and a numerous posterity in the
female line. Mahlon Kirkbride married Mary, daughter of John and
Mary Sotcher, favorites of William Penn.

Walter Shewell, an early settler in that part of New Britain that
fell into Doylestown township, was an immigrant from Gloucestershire,
England, arriving in 1732. Landing at Philadelphia, he made his
way to Bucks county and took up a tract, on the State Road two
miles from Doylestown. Here he built a handsome dwelling, 1769,
and called it "Painswick Hall" after his birth place in England. He
married Mary Kimmer, of Maryland, and raised a family of sons and
daughters. Robert, the youngest son, born January 27, 1740, and
married Mary Sallows, January 15, 1764, became a prominent merchant of Philadelphia, but, retiring early to Painswick, spent the remainder of his life there, dying December 28, 1823. Of his eight
children, five sons became merchants in Philadelphia, Thomas, the
youngest, and the most noted, being three years in a merchantile
house in London. Betsy Shewell, a daughter of this family, married
Benjamin West the celebrated painter, and, while Thomas Shewell was
in London, he spent his Sunday evenings at West's house. He returned home, 1799, resumed business in Philadelphia, and died there
1848. He was thrice married. Nathaniel Shewell, of whom more
will be said elsewhere, a descendant of Walter Shewell, played a leading part here in his day.

The Merediths, early settlers in New Britain, took up land on
the Neshaminy, near Castle Valley bridge. James Meredith, who
arrived about 1730, descended from Chester county ancestry, whence
he came to Bucks, and his descendants are numerous in this and
neighboring counties. William Meredith, a partner of Benjamin
Franklin about 1725, and the late Hon. Wm. M. Meredith, were
both of the same family, while James, said to have been a brother of
Franklin's partner, was the immediate ancestor of the Bucks county
branch of the family. It is a tradition that Thomas Meredith, a son
of Thomas, being crazed with over-much study, and the inheritor of
considerable land about Castle Valley, was sent from Philadelphia to
spend his life there, accompanied by his brother James to look after

him. The harmless young man planned a castle on the right bank of Neshaminy, near the Alms House road, carried thither a great quantity of stones which he piled up in a circle, cut down trees and had the logs hauled to the site. His whims were not interfered with, and, after his death, the logs and stones were used to build the first bridge across the stream. Thomas Meredith's castle building gave the name to the locility. The land fell to his cousin James, embracing several farms, including that of the late Monroe Buckman, subsequently Sheridan T. Patterson. James Meredith had four sons, Simon, John, Thomas and Hugh. Simon, born 1740, married Hannah Hough, 1766, a daughter of Joseph, and grandaughter of Richard Hough who settled on the Delaware, 1682. Dr. Hugh Meredith,[2] a son of James, became a physician, settled at Doylestown about the breaking out of the Revolution, erected a stone dwelling on or near the Armstrong corner and married Mary Todd.[3] They had two sons, Charles and Thomas, both physicians and one daughter, Elizabeth, who married Abraham Chapman. Charles Meredith married Isabella Dick, sister of John L. Dick,[4] and their daughter [5] was the first wife of Dr. Charles H. Mathews, and Susan the wife of a Mr. Garth, of Hannible, Mo., whither she removed.

When Dr. Charles H. Mathews married, he moved into what was the McDowell house, on the east side of North Main street, below Court. The wife was a beautiful but a delicate woman, and there she and her child both died.

Dr. Thomas Meredith married a Miss Burson, and their daughter, Matilda, married Nicholas Buck, Jr., Nockamixon, and afterwards went west. Dr. Charles Meredith had sons, Hamilton, Richard, and Campbell, who left Doylestown, for the west, many years ago. Dr. Charles Meredith died here, 1831. The elder branches of the Meredith family intermarried with the Fells, Mathews, Foulks, et al, the two former familes living near neighbors. Dr. Hugh Meredith, the elder, at one

---

2 At Doylestown, July 15, 1815, Dr. Hugh Meredith in the 72d year of his age. He had been successful in the practice of physic ; was extensively known and much respected.

3 At Doylestown, October 28, 1822, in the eightieth year of her age. Mrs. Mary Meredith, late of this village, widow of Dr. Hugh.

4 At Doylestown, on Saturday, February 18, 1815, at the house of his brother-in-law, Dr. Charles Meredith, John L. Dick, aged 27 years.

5 At Doylestown, April 13, 1830, by the Rev. Samuel Aaron, Dr. Charles H. Mathews to Mary E., eldest daughter of Dr. Charles Meredith, of Doylestown.

time lived in the old Thomas Stephens house, on the Upper State Road, a mile west of Doylestown.

Benjamin Snodgrass, ancestor of those bearing this name in Bucks county, and in other parts of the country, was an Irish immigrant of 1730. During the long voyage, all of his family, except his daughter Mary and himself, perished at sea of hunger. He settled in what was then New Britain, now Doylestown township, married Jane Borland, a widow, and, by her, had five children, Benjamin, born 1730, James, 1734, Rebecca, Margaret and Jane. Mary, the daughter, who survived the voyage, married Robert Stewart, and had one daughter, Jane, who married John Greir, father of the late John Stewart Greir. Benjamin Snodgrass died 1778. His oldest son, by the second wife, married Mary McFarland, born 1731, and died 1818, had three sons and one daughter. While on his way to visit his son James, a Presbyterian minister at New Hanover, Dauphin county, Pa., July 1, 1804, he was thrown from his gig, and died from the effects of it, in a few days. Benjamin, son of the second Benjamin, a soldier of the Revolution, was at the battle of Trenton. His youngest sister, Mary, born 1772, married John Mann and died in 1803. James Snodgrass, son, and youngest child of Benjamin, the elder, and born October 21, 1780, married Mary McKinstry, and died at Doylestown, April, 1870. The daughters married into the families of Pool, Harrar, Todd, Rich, Greir, and Armstrong. Benjamin S. Rich, Buckingham, was a descendant of James, the elder, and Jefferson Greir, a descendant of Sarah Snodgrass. The Rev. Wm. D. Snodgrass, Goshen, New York, was a son of Rev. James Snodgrass, New Hanover, Dauphin county, Pa., and died 1846. The late Dr. James S. Rich, Churchville, was the son of Mary Snodgrass, and grandaughter of James the second.

The James family, numerous and influential in their day, were near neighbors to the cross-roads before Doyles' Tavern was christened "in the flowing bowel," 1745. They came from Wales and settled in the edge of Montgomery county, 1711, and, about 1720, John James and his two sons, Thomas and William, came over the line into Bucks and took up 1,000 acres on Pine run and North branch in New Britain. We learn nothing more of John James after 1726, as he probably died about that time, but William and Thomas added to their holdings and became large land owners. Thomas lived to be a very old man, dying about the time of the Revolution. John James left a numerous offspring in the male and female lines, which have continued to increase and multiply, and have been in every walk of life, in the profession, the church, politics and the halls of legislation. Four of the James' signed the petition for New Britain township to be laid out. Of the James family, Dr. O. P. James, of New Britain, who lived in Doylestown the latter years of his life and practiced his profession, served one term in the State Senate; and Nathan C., a member of the bar, was twice elected to the office of District Attorney, and his father, John D., was fifty years cryer of the Courts.

The Riale family were among the earliest settlers in New Britain, subsequently fell into Doylestown township, but we have not the date of their coming here. The tomb stone of John Riale, the first settler is in New Britain grave yard with a legible inscription. He died in 1748 at the age of sixty, which carries his birth back to 1688. He was the great grandfather of the late David Riale. One of the Riale homesteads was within the borough limits.

The Stewarts were among the first to settle in, or near, the present limits of the borough, whose first representative, Charles Stewart, came from Scotland between 1720 and 1730, and bought a farm. He was a young man of culture and some means, and served in the French and Indian Wars with the rank of Captain. His wife was a Mrs. Finney, whose sister was the mother of Mrs. Hugh Meredith. George Stewart, son of Charles, whose wife was Parthena Barton, was the father of Barton Stewart,[6] a well-known inhabitant of Doylestown in his day. Barton Stewart's log wheelwright shop stood on the site of the *Intelligencer* office—monument place.[7]

The Harveys are descended from Thomas Harvey of Long Island, who settled in Upper Makefield about 1750, and died there 1779. He left two sons, of which one was Joseph, the father of Enoch Harvey, born 1769, and settled at Doylestown, about 1790. He married a daughter of Charles Stewart, then living here on the Warwick side of the line. He had several children, of which two were the late Joseph[8] and Dr. George T. Harvey,[9] the latter being the father of Judge Edward Harvey, Allentown, and the former, the

---

6 At Doylestown, February 27, 1818, Margaret Stewart, wife of Barton Stewart, aged about 32 years.

7 At Doylestown, February 1, 1842, Thomas J. Stewart, in his fortieth year.

8 At Philadelphia, May 6, 1830, by the Rev. Robert B. Belville, Joseph Harvey, of Doylestown, to Miss Anna Horner of that city.

9 At Doylestown, June 27, 1842, by the Rev. John McDowell, Dr. George T. Harvey, of Doylestown, to Miss Mary K. LaRue, of Philadelphia.

only descendant in the county bearing the grandfather's surname. Enoch Harvey [10] has several descendants, in the female line, who lived at Doylestown.

About the close of the eighteenth century three brothers, McIntosh, John, Jonathan [11] and Daniel,[12] came from Martinsburg, Virginia, where they were born, and settled at this, then cross-roads hamlet. They all died at an advanced age, within the memory of persons now living, and left numerous descendants. They were farmers and mechanics, and, some of the members, took to the "Art preservation of all arts."

The Halls were descendants of Jacob and Mary Hall, of Macclesfield, Cheshire, England, who sailed from Liverpool in the Friendship, 1684, and arrived in Maryland, Twelfth-month 3d, 1684. Thence, with their children, Jacob and Mary, they came to the Province of Pennsylvania, Third-month 23d, 1685, and settled on a tract of five hundred acres, which Jacob Hall, purchased of William Penn, before leaving England. Jacob Hall and family soon after removed to Taconey, Philadelphia county, where two sons were born to them, viz, Jacob and Solomon. Theodorus Hall, son of Joseph and grandson of Jacob, Sr., removed from Moreland, in Philadelphia, to Southampton in Bucks county in 1753, and from thence to Kingwood, Hunterdon county, New Jersey, 1754.

Theodorus Hall, son of Joseph and grandson of Jacob, Sr., who removed to Hunterdon county, New Jersey, had a son Samuel, the father of Isaac Hall, who came to Doylestown, about 1800, married and purchased a lot on the present East State street, just west of Broad, and, at that time, included within the township of New Britain. When this lot was purchased, 1803, it belonged to Josiah Y. Shaw. Hall built a house on it in 1804, and, in it, the late Samuel Hall was born October 17, 1811, the youngest son of Isaac Hall. The house, in which Samuel Hall lived, and where he died, in 1896, was the same his father built soon after coming here, has never been out of the family. Charles Hall, a member of the Bucks County Bar, is the only representative of the family living here.[13]

Uriah DuBois, ancestor of the family of this name at Doyles-

---

10 At Doylestown, July 15, 1831, Enoch Harvey in the sixty-fifth year of his age. At Doylestown, February 16, 1847, in the 74th year of her age, Sarah, widow of Enoch Harvey.

11 At Philadelphia, by Rev. William M. White, Jonathan McIntosh, of Doylestown, to Miss Sarah Fryer, of Philadelphia.

12 At Doylestown, May 26, 1808, by the Rev. Uriah DuBois, Daniel McIntosh, to Miss Sallie Hair, daughter of William Hair.

13 At Doylestown, December, 1829, by the Rev. Samuel Aaron, John Hodgson, printer, to Miss Mary Hall, both of Doylestown.

town, was the descendant of a French Hugonaut immigrant, Louis, the son of Peter, and Ann DuBois, who came to America about 1660, and settled at Kingston on the Hudson. Uriah DuBois was born in Salem county, New Jersey, 1768, graduated at the University of Pennsylvania, 1790, and licensed to preach 1796. He married Martha Patterson, and took up his residence at the village of Dublin, Bedminister township, when called to the Deep Run Presbyterian church, 1798. He came to Doylestown, 1804, to take charge of the Union Academy, and died here 1821. He was a power in this community, and the founder of the Doylestown Presbyterian church.

The Chapmans immigrated from Stannah, Yorkshire, England, John with his wife Jane and three children, landing 1684, and settling in Wrightstown. He is said to have been the first white settler north of Newtown. Abraham Chapman, the first of the family to settle in Doylestown, was born in Wrightstown, married Elizabeth Meredith[14] and read law with John Ross at West Chester. In the office with him were Daniel Stroud and a Darlington. He was admitted to the Bucks county bar, 1790, and practiced at Newtown until the removal of the county seat to Doylestown, 1813, and died here, 1855. Seth Chapman, another member of the family, while in practice at Newtown, 1811, was appointed President Judge of the Eighth Judicial District. The late Judge Henry Chapman, son of Abraham, born in Wrightstown, 1804, and the most distinguished member of the family, received his early education at the Union Academy, Doylestown, and Duncan McGregor's classical school, Bridge Point, finishing at Samuel Gummere's school, Burlington, N. J. He read law with his father, and was admitted to the bar, 1825. He was one of the committee to receive Samuel D. Ingham, Jackson's Secretary of the Treasury, on his return home after his resignation, and also made the Welcome Home address. Judge Chapman was twice married, his first wife being a daughter of Thomas Stewart, Doylestown, the second Nancy Findley, daughter of Governor Shunk, and grand-daughter of Governor Findley, of Pennsylvania. The daughters of two of our Governors came brides into Bucks county, the other being the wife of Dr. Phineas Jenks, Newtown, a daughter of Governor Snyder. Judge Chapman in the course of his public career, was President Judge of the Judical Districts of Bucks and Montgomery, and Chester county, and was elected to the State Senate and the Congress of the United States.

The Rosses, likewise English Friends, are descendants of Thomas

---

14 At Doylestown, October 12, 1812, Elizabeth Chapman, daughter of Dr. Hugh Meredith and wife of Abraham Chapman.

Ross, County Tyrone, Ireland, and born of Episcopal parents, 1708. Himself and sister settled in Upper Makefield, at the age of twenty, joining Wrightstown Friends' Meeting the following year. He soon became an accepted minister, and married Kesiah Wilkinson, daughter of a prominent county family, 1731. Thomas Ross went to England on a visit, 1784, and, being taken sick, died at the house of Lindley Murray, near York, 1786, in his seventy-eighth year. The Ross family has produced several able men, prominent in politics and the law. Three reached the bench, one of them the Supreme Court, and one branch gave to the profession four generations of lawyers. The late Thomas Ross served four years in the House of Representatives of the United States. Henry Ross, a son of Thomas, and one of the ablest members of the family, was a graduate of Princeton and admitted to the bar, 1859. He soon had a large practice and was recognized as a brilliant lawyer. He was District Attorney, 1862-'65; Additional Law Judge, 1869; President Judge of Montgomery, 1871; re-elected 1881, and died 1882. He possessed many fine traits of character, and had a charm of manners that gave him great personal popularity. George Ross, a younger son of Thomas, was almost as distinguished as his elder brother. He was born at Doylestown, August 21, 1841, graduated at Princeton in the class of 1861; read law with his fater, admitted to the bar, 1864; member of the Constitutional Convention, 1873; elected to the State Senate, 1886, re-elected, 1890; was caucus candidate for U. S. Senate, 1893; twice nominated for Congress in the Bucks-Montgomery district, but defeated at the polls. He died November 19, 1894.

The ancestor of the Fox family was not a native of Bucks county, Edward Fox, the father of Judge John Fox, being an Englishman by descent, born in Ireland. He came to this country when young and settled in Philadelphia, marrying a sister of Jonathan Dickinson Sergeant, and aunt of John and Thomas Sergeant. He was a merchant for many years, and afterward held a responsible office under the State Government, that of Auditor General, which, at that day, paid a salary of $1,700. With whom Judge Fox read law, we are not informed, but probably in Philadelphia, and, upon admission to the bar, 1807, settled at Newtown then the county seat and commenced practice. He came to Doylestown with the removal of the county seat, 1813, made this his home, and, in 1876, married a daughter of Gilbert Rodman, Bensalem. He never left his profession for the sake of political office, but in that he was Deputy-Attorney General, and President

Judge of the Common Pleas of the county for the term of ten years, 1830-'40. In addition to these honors, he was elected Major-General of Militia but never took out his commission. He was an astute political leader, and, had he been disposed to enter that field, would have reached a high position. His three sons, Gilbert, Rodman, Edward J. and Lewis R., were all trained to their father's profession and admitted to the bar. The first two named made it their life calling, and became distinguished lawyers, while the third entered the church as a Presbyterian clergyman. In the war of 1812-'15, Judge Fox, left his profession to serve his country in the field. He was a very able lawyer, the peer of any at this bar during his generation, and an agreeable man. The author, who read law in Judge Fox's office, has a very keen recollection of his universal kindness and courtesy. The Fox house, at Broad aud Court streets, now the property of George P. Brock, and built by Rev. Uriah DuBois, 1807, was the home in recent years of the Fox family until the death of Mrs. Fox, when it passed into the possession of Caleb E. Wright, Esq., and from him to its present owner.

Judge Fox was a politician in the best sense of that word, never entering into a squabble for office and always ready to show his party friends how to "set a squadron in the field." His acquaintance with the statesmen of the country was extensive and confidential. To his house came Samuel D. Ingham, at the Zenith of his fame, and, after his retirement from public life, he made that his stopping place to discuss county, state and national politics and talk of the days of Auld Lang Syne. The author frequently saw the horse, of the Ex-Secretary of the Treasury, hitched to the fence across the street. When Mr. Ingham was appointed Prothonotary of the county, 1817, he removed with his family to Doylestown, and, becoming a neighbor to Mr. Fox, served to cement their friendship closer. He also made Doylestown his home for some time after being appointed Secretary of the Commonwealth, 1819.[15] Mr. Fox was the main factor in having Mr. Ingham selected for the portfolio of the Treasury in Jackson's first Cabinet, through the southern wing of the Democratic party, with whose leaders he held close relations. When Mr. Ingham returned home, after leaving the Cabinet, Mr. Fox was one of the committee to welcome him.

Mathias Morris a native of Hilltown, and born 1787, was a great grandson of Morris Morris, the first of the name to settle

---

[15] Mrs. Ingham subsequently died at Doylestown.

in Bucks county. He read law, was admitted to this bar, at Newtown and practiced in Philadelphia [16] until 1819, when he established himself at Doylestown, and spent the rest of his life here, dying 1839. His wife was a daughter of Abraham Chapman.[17] He was admitted to practice in the Supreme Court of the U. S., February 22, 1833. Mr. Morris was Deputy Attorney General of the county, and served one term, each, in the State Senate and in Congress.

The Rogers family, of Connecticut descent, settled in Philadelphia, where William T. Rogers, the son of William C., was born 1799, the family removing subsequently to Warrington township, this county. The son learned the printing trade with Asher Miner, in the *Correspondent* office, and, after his time was out, purchased the *Democrat* which he owned and edited until 1829. He became prominent in politics, serving two terms, eight years in the State Senate, four of them in the Speaker's chair, and was afterward collector of canal tolls at Bristol. Mr. Rogers, having a taste for military affairs, joined the Volunteer Militia passing through the grades of Captain, Brigade Inspector, with the rank of Major, and Major-General of the Division of Bucks and Montgomery. He married a daughter of John Pugh, and was the father of a family of children all sons and all dead. One of his sons, Edward L. inheriting his father's taste for the military, served an enlistment of three months in the Doylestown Guards at the opening of the Civil War, and a subsequent term of three years in the 104th regiment, holding the commissions of Captain and Major. He was an excellent officer. General Rogers died in 1867, his wife preceding him to the grave. He left two monuments behind him, evidence of the interest he felt in Doylestown, the cemetery and water works, and, but for his thoughtfulness, we doubt if either had been built.

John P. Rogers, the oldest son and child of General Rogers, reached considerable local prominence. He was naturally a brilliant man, but lack of proper training and discipline, in his youth, marred his success in life. He was born at Doylestown, August 10, 1825; was educated at the Union Academy and other home schools, read law with Eleazar T. McDowell, the brilliant lawyer, but never applied

---

16 Mathias Morris, Attorney at Law, has opened an office at 113 North Fifth street, between Race and Vine. He will continue to attend his practice in Bucks county and may be found during the sitting of the Courts at James Thompson's tavern in Doylestown. Correspondent November 1, 1813.

17 At Philadelphia, 1829, Mathias Morris to Wilhelmina Chapman, daughter of Abraham Chapman, all of Doylestown.

for admission to the bar. He subsequently learned the printing trade in the office of the *Lancaster Intelligencer* under Colonel John W. Forney, was then, for a brief period, editor of the *Inland Daily,* the first daily newspaper published at Lancaster. He now returned to Doylestown and was connected, for many years, with the *Democrat* and *Intelligencer,* in charge of their local department. He was a prolific newspaper writer, possessed a vein of romance and was a fine conversationalist. Mr. Rogers had many excellent traits of character, was true to his friends, but hated his enemies with great cordiality. His most pretentious and popular contribution, to our local literature, was the "History of the Doanes," the celebrated outlaws of Bucks county in the Revolutionary period, which is still read with interest. At the breaking out of the Civil War, Rogers at once took the side of the union, and enlisted in the 104th regiment, but, when the army took the field, he was honorably discharged, as he was not robust enough for a soldier's life. He was twice married, leaving a son named after Roscoe Conkling, the father's ideal of a statesman. John P. Rogers died November 27, 1894, in his seventieth year.

Dr. William S. Hendrie, though of a later generation than the families we are writing of, occupied a prominent place in Doylestown from the time of settling here. He was born in Sussex county, New Jersey, 1798, his father, a Scotchman and a graduate of the University of Edinburg, coming to America early in life. The son read medicine with Dr. Wilson, of Buckingham, and, on being admitted to practice, settled at Springtown, this county. After practicing there and in Hilltown, for a few years, he came to Doylestown, 1841, and took the practice of Dr. James S. Rich, who removed to Churchville, and also purchased his dwelling on the south side of East State street near Broad, where he died, 1875. While living in Hilltown Dr. Hendrie assisted in the capture of the Spaniard, Mina, the murderer of Dr. William Chapman, who broke jail while waiting trial. This gave him considerable notoriety. Dr. Hendrie occupied the Common Pleas bench of Bucks county, for a term of five years as Associate Judge. He had two sons and two daughters. The sons both graduated in medicine, and served in the Civil War, James D. as Quarter Master of the 104th regiment, and Scott, the younger, Assistant Surgeon, James was badly wounded at the battle of Fair Oaks. One of the daughters, Julia H. married E. Morris Lloyd, a member of the Bucks county bar, and died at St. Louis, Mo., 1892. James D.

GEORGE LEAR, AT 60.

Hendrie, the elder of the two sons, died at Chicago, December 27, 1900 at the age of seventy years.

The Lears are a Warwick family of Celtic origin, George Lear, the father, being born there in 1818. He was brought up on a farm, and had no opportunity for acquiring an education except at the common schools of the period, much inferior to the present day, as all will testify, who graduated from them.

After leaving school, Mr. Lear did his share of work on the farm, etc. As it is now well settled, that all men, who would make their mark on their generation, must climb upward from the bottom rung of the ladder, young Lear had the good sense to begin at the right place. When approaching manhood he was, in turn, a school teacher, and clerk in a store, in his leisure picking up quite a fund of knowledge by reading. He also took a hand in the debating schools of the period, the poor boys Parliament. Meanwhile, he paid Court to Blackstone and other text books of the legal profession, and, early in 1844, entered his name with McDowell as a student of law and was admitted to the bar in November of that year. He immediately opened an office and began practice. Mr. Lear was married soon after his admission and went to house keeping in a brick dwelling on East York street, the oldest brick in the borough. He was successful at the bar from the beginning, being a good speaker and popular, and took the stump, in the Polk and Dallas campaign, 1844, and won laurels.

In 1848, he was appointed Deputy Attorney-General for Bucks, and served until 1850. He gradually worked his way to the head of the bar and was clothed with other honors, including that of member of the Constitutional Convention of 1872-'73, taking a leading part in the proceedings, and, in 1875, was appointed Attorney-General of Pennsylvania by Governor Hartranft, serving four years. After his term had expired Mr. Lear persued his profession to his death, 1885, at the age of 67.

The Brocks came to this county early, but it is not known whether the Doylestown family are descended from John Brock, of Stockport, County of Chester, England, who settled in Lower Makefield about 1682. The *Bucks County Intelligencer* of February 7, 1844, in its obituary notice of John Brock, gandfather of the late John J. Brock, of Doylestown, said:

"In Philadelphia, January 30, 1848, at the residence of his son, after a protracted affliction, which he endured with the resignation and fortitude which ever illumines the approaching exit of those who are rich in the hope of a happy immorality, John Brock, Jr., in the eighty-second year of his age. The deceased was a member of the Society of Friends, and was eminently distinguished and esteemed for his piety, benevolence and great excellence of heart. The last few years of his life were spent in Philadelphia in the family of his son, where he died. In youth he displayed a taste for military life and stood guard at the battle of Trenton. At a later period he held a commission of Justice of the Peace under Governor McKean for several years, in Northampton county, the duties of which he discharged with a scrupulous regard to justice. On Fifth day, the 1st instance, his remains were brought from the city to the house of his son, Stephen Brock, in Doylestown and thence taken, followed by numerous relations and friends, to the burying ground at Buckingham.

From the obituary we learn that John Brock, was born, 1762. He was one of the Commissioners of the county, 1800, and built the handsome stone bridge that year that still spans the Neshaminy at Bridge Point.[18] Stephen Brock, the son of John mentioned above, was a prominent figure in the political and business life of Doylestown and the county to his death, in the 40's. His wife was a Miss Jones,[19] and a family of children, sons and daughters were born to them.[20] As a successful politician, Stephen Brock had no superior in the county, his personal popularity carrying him twice into the Sheriff's office as an independent candidate against the field. He was also connected with the county military and, in 1824, commanded the Centre Union Battalion, which formed part of the escort of Lafayette when he entered Philadelphia.[21]

The late John J. Brock, almost half a century cashier of the Doylestown State and National Bank, was born, and educated, at Doylestown. His first business venture was store keeping in partnership with James B. Smith, son of General Samuel A. Smith, 1844. He

---

18 Some years ago, the late General George B. McClellan while visiting friends near Doylestown, was taken to see the Bridge Point bridge of which he spoke in the highest terms. This was a compliment coming from such a distinguished engineer.

19 At Buckingham, February 7, 1815, by J. Kooker, Esq., Stephen Brock to Miss Mary Jones.

20 At Doylestown, November 23, 1839, Mary Brock youngest daughter of Stephen Brock.

21 At Doylestown, November 24, 1842, by the Rev. Samuel Nightingale, Josiah Hart to Sarah Brock, daughter of Stephen Brock, of Doylestown.

sold out to Smith, 1846; was shortly appointed clerk in the bank, and elected cashier, 1847, which office he held to his death, 1895. As a bank officer he enjoyed an high reputation. He was intimately associated with the social and business life of his native town, and active in politics. His wife was Miss Philler, of Philadelphia, to whom he was married November 23, 1853. Their death, within a few hours of each other, was a sad ending to a happy married life.

Caleb E. Wright, born at Plymouth, Luzerne county, Pennsylvania, and admitted to the bar at Wilkesbarre, August 6, 1833, settled in practice at Doylestown the following September. The family were early settlers in the Wyoming Valley, coming from New England. The son Caleb married Phœbe Ann, daughter of William Fell, Buckingham. Mr. Wright was president of the first borough council of Doylestown, 1838, and appointed Deputy-Attorney General for Bucks, 1839. In 1853, he returned to Wilkesbarre where he continued in practice until 1876, when he came back to Doylestown to spend the remainder of his life. During his second residence at Wilkesbarre, he was appointed to the office of United States Collector of Internal Revenue for the counties of Luzerne and Susquehannah, 1866-'69, and, was elected a member of the constitutional convention of 1872-'73. Mr. Wright, for a number of years, was a local preacher in the Methodist Episcopal church. He relinquished the practice of the law after his return to Doylestown, devoting his time to literary pursuits, and church work. Mr. Wright possessed fine literary attainments, and the books he wrote and published were popular. He was the son of Joseph and Ellen Hendrick Wright, born February 4, 1810 and died December 2, 1889.

Charles H. Mann, a conspicuous figure of the county, in political and military life, for several years, was born at Philadelphia and educated there, but spent his boyhood in Plumstead township. A harness maker by trade, he settled at Danborough, four miles above Doylestown, in 1837, where he followed his trade until 1843, when he moved down to the county seat, occupying the dwelling on the northwest corner of State and Pine streets. A man of popular manners, he made many friends and gained confidence. He held several places of public trust, was appointed Postmaster by VanBuren, 1839, but removed, 1841, when Tyler succeeded Harrison; Deputy Sheriff, 1842-'44; Sheriff, 1845-'48; captain of the Doylestown Grays-Guards, 1845-'49; Major, Center-Union Battalion, 1849; and was landlord of the Fountain House, 1849-'56. He also kept the Jones House at

Harrisburg, several years, and lived at Towsontown, Md., 1863-69; passing his declining years at Washington, D. C., with his son Charles, who held the office of Assistant Doorkeeper of the United States Senate, and was buried at Doylestown, dying there, 1892, at the age of eighty-three. He also had two daughters, the elder, Kate, an accomplished women; the younger, Elizabeth, becoming the wife of George C. Ripley, a nephew of the late Governor Buckingham, of Connecticut, a member of the Minneapolis bar. He served on the staff of Major-General Casey, Civil War, and gained the rank of Lieutenant Colonel.[22] When Major Mann's old Company, the Doylestown Grays-Guards, on its way to Washington at the out-break of the Civil War, passed through Baltimore, he rode on one of the gun carriages of the Battery it was escorting.

Stokes L. Roberts, a member of the bar, a genial and agreeable figure in the social and professional life of Doylestown, was the son of David Roberts, of Newtown, and a descendant of Edward and Mary Roberts, who settled in Richland township, 1716. He was admitted to the bar, 1832, began practice at Newtown, but removed to Doylestown in a few years where he died. He was elected to the House of Representatives, 1838, and Associate Law Judge of the district, 1872. Mrs. Roberts still makes her home at Doylestown, but spends some of her time in traveling. The residence of Mr. and Mrs. Roberts was the musical centre of our borough over fifty years ago, and this accomplished couple dispensed a delightful hospitality at their Court street home. All were made welcome who entered its portals.

Had we the space to spare, we would add the names of a number of others who deserve to be placed on our list, among them Timothy Smith,[23] a carpenter by trade, who came from Wrightstown about 1820, whose wife was Rachel Stokes, aunt of General John S. Bryan. He was an active business man, owned "Mount Timothy," but is said to have refused to sell it because the would-be buyer was a Democrat. Smith built the first hay scale in town, about the site of Lehman's butcher shop, East State street, near which his dwelling is still standing; Samuel Kachline, who appears elsewhere, Charles Wigton, the descendant of one of the earliest settlers on the slopes of

---

22 At Broodmoor, Colorado Springs, May 2, 1890, of pleuro-pneumonia, Eleanor Buckingham Ripley, aged twenty-one years, daughter of George Coit and Elizabeth Cartee Ripley, of Minneapolis, Minnesota, and grand daughter of the late Ex-Sheriff, Charles H. Mann, of Doylestown, Pa.

23 At Doylestown, April 20, 1841, Elizabeth Smith, daughter of Timothy Smith, to Robert Williams, of Montgomery county.

the neighboring highlands, where the old homestead is still in the flesh et al.

Samuel A. Smith,[24] merchant, politician and General in the volunteer militia, was an important factor in the affairs of life when in his prime, and made his influence felt. He was the son of James Smith and born on the Durham road near Bucksville, Nockamixon township, about 1796, and removed to Doylestown when appointed Register of Wills, 1824. He held several important offices; Brigade Inspector and Major-General of the Militia, Associate Judge of the county, served one term in the State Senate, and three years in the House of Representatives of the United States, 1829-'32, including the unexpired term of Samuel D. Ingham when the latter was appointed to Jackson's Cabinet. He was defeated in the Bucks-Northampton district for Congress, 1830, but at the following election was returned by a handsome majority. General Smith, and household were fortunate in the possession of a most lovely daughter, excelled by none. She was the toast of the town and merited all the pleasant things that were said to her. She died shortly after coming to womanhood, and the *Democrat,* in noticing her death, said:

"At Doylestown, 1846, Amanda Smith, daughter of General Samuel A. Smith, at the age of twenty-two. A large concourse followed to the tomb, one, who, grown up in our midst, had from earliest years shared much of the public esteem. We have traced her progress from the artless child to the lady of matured loveliness; adorned with matchless charms, the circle that the purity of her life enriched. Duty called her to act in no situation that her sympathetic and virtuous impulses did not exalt. But the flower then blooming to the sun which universal love hung over, the destroyer has snatched from all others to himself. Yet he, whose hand comes marshalled with so many terrors touched in relenting gentleness the form he would not mar, for, saving that the pulse was dead the watchers knew not but the victim slept. The pangs of disease, for so many months insiduously wasted the springs of life, were born with the spirit of a christian martyr, and to the close of this trial, none looked with more composure than herself. Let the mourners be consoled, for in this transition, to the happier world, there is much to sweeten the parents

---

24 In Doylestown, the 23rd of May, 1818, by the Rev. Uriah DuBois, Samuel A. Smith, Esq., to Miss Elizabeth Bloom, daughter of Colonel Christopher Bloom, all of Rockhill township.

tears, relieve the sister's anguish, and disrobe the general mind of gloom."

The Shaws came to this section from the lower end of the county, first settling in Southampton and Northampton townships. John Shaw, the elder, was in Plumstead, in 1748, and later appointed a tax collector for the crown in that township, where his son, an inkeeper, was born. In 1792 the latter bought a messuage and three tracts of land in Warwick township, now in Doylestown borough, "at the crossing of the roads to Well's ferry and the Dyer's Mill Road," the present State and Main streets. The first tract of two acres, was in Warwick, the other one in New Britain, northwest of Court street. On first coming to Doylestown, John Shaw opened a store on the Warwick tract, but subsequently purchased, of Enoch Harvey, the tavern property formerly Flack's, now the site of Lenape Building. In 1795, he bought the Robinson[25] tavern property, and removed thither, but, 1799, he sold the property to his son John. In June, 1798, John Shaw, the elder, was Justice of the Peace for the district of Bedminster, but removed to New Britain on the Mercer tract, where he died. The following obituary notice appeared in one of the village newspapers at Mr. Shaw's death:

"At his residence in New Britain, May 18, 1818, after a confinement of nearly four months, John Shaw, Esq., aged seventy-four years, for many years a respected magistrate of Bucks county. He was the oldest magistrate in the county but one, being commissioned by Governor Mifflin. He removed from Bedminster to New Britain, in 1802. He was a Whig in the Revolution, and, while enthusiastic in the great cause, he did not forget the tender treatment that was due to his neighbors, who differed in sentiment from him. Before his death, he selected two appropriate Psalms, one, the sixty-first, beginning,

"When overwhelmed with grief,
My heart within me dies."

John Shaw, the elder, was the father of seven children, John, Josiah Y.,[26] who passed his life in Doylestown and died here, Francis B., member of the Doylestown bar, Martha, Mary, William a physi-

---

25 There is a question whether this tavern was at Dublin or Pipersville.

26 Josiah Y. Shaw was a Justice of the Peace, and Brigade Inspector of Militia, 1809.

BEEK'S EXHIBITION BUILDING, 185

cian of Philadelphia, and Thompson D. Shaw,[27] who entered the U. S. Navy, as a Midshipman and died a Commodore.[28] The late James Shaw was a son of Josiah Y. The name is sometimes spelled Shawe.[29]

Jerome Buck, a descendant of John Shaw, was one of the most brilliant men born in Doylestown. His mother was a daughter of Josiah Y. Shaw, and his father, Samuel E. Buck, a descendant of Nicholas Buck, who came of an ancient family of Lorain, and settled in this county, 1752. Jerome was born May 18, 1835; educated in the Philadelphia schools and at Tremont Seminary, Norristown, read law with John Titus, the second husband of his mother, was a member of the Doylestown bar, and subsequently Chief Justice of Arizona. Mr. Buck practiced law in New York and died there, 1900. He was an eloquent speaker, and brilliant conversationlist, and some of his addresses were master pieces of English. In his leisure he entered the field of literature, and was prominent in the Masonic order.

The Pughs were long settled at Doylestown, but are older in the county. The ancestor, Hugh Pugh, a Welsh immigrant, settled in Chester county about 1725. There he married Mary Harris, whose family gave the name to Harrisburg our State Capital. From Chester county they removed to the east bank of the Schuylkill, near Norristown, whence the son Daniel, born January 17, 1730, came to Hilltown, Bucks county, about 1750, married a daughter of the Rev. William B. Thomas, and died, 1813. He was the ancestor of the Bucks county family of the name, and John, his eldest son, born in Hilltown, June 2, 1761, was the progenitor of the Doylestown branch. He was twice married, his first wife being Rachel Bates, the second, Elizabeth Owen, both of Hilltown. John Pugh became a prominent man in county, state and national politics, serving four consecutive years in the State Legislature, two terms in the House of Representatives of the United States, fourteen years Register and Recorder of Deeds of the county, rounding out his official life by holding the

---

27 At Burlington, N. J., September 2, 1824, Midshipman Thompson D. Shaw, U. S. N., of Doylestown, to Miss Louisa C. Sprogell, youngest daughter of the late Edward Sprogell, Esq., of Philadelphia.

28 The naval record of Commodore Shaw shows that he was appointed a Midshipman May 1820; reported for duty on board the Constellation, May 30, 1820; ordered from Philadelphia to Boston to Constitution, March 17, 1821; commissioned Lieutenant, March 31, 1829, to take rank from May 18, 1828; commissioned a commander on the active list, January 6, 1859, to take rank from August 7, 1850; commissioned a Commodore on the retired list, October 4, 1867; died at Germantown, Pa., July 26, 1874.

29 In Doylestown, January 1, 1832, after a long illness, Mrs. Agnes Shaw, widow of the late John Shaw, Esq., in the ninetieth year of her age.

commission of Justice of the Peace for twenty-five years. He came to Doylestown with the removal of the county seat, from Newtown, 1813, and died here 1842 at the age of eighty-one. John Pugh had two children, the late John B. Pugh, Esq., and a daughter who married General William T. Rogers. The son, John B. Pugh, born May 20, 1809, was educated at a Baptist College at Georgetown, D. C., and the University of Pennsylvania, read law with Mathias Morris, and admitted to the bar, 1830. The practice of law being distasteful to him, he soon relinquished it. Governor Porter appointed him Prothonotary of the County, 1839, and he held the office of Justice of the Peace for forty-five years. Being fond of military affairs, he assisted to recruit and organize the Doylestown Grays, and served as First Lieutenant and Captain. In 1845, Mr. Pugh married Elizabeth L., daughter of Judge John Fox, who died, 1885, and he May 28, 1898, five children surviving them, three sons and two daughters. Mr. Pugh was one of the most scholarly members of the bar. The late Edward L. Rogers, Major of the 104th Pa. Regiment, Civil War, was a grandson of John Pugh, the elder.[30]

One of the most prominent families, in the immediate vicinity of Doylestown in the past, was that of Dr. Samuel Moore, who was born in West Jersey. He married a daughter of Dr. Robert Patterson, the first Director of the United States Mint at Philadelphia, and settled at Bridge Point, a mile below Doylestown. Soon after being admitted to practice, and married, 1798; Dr. Moore located at the village of Dublin, Bedminster township, but subsequently removed to Trenton. Delicate health drove him from his profession, and he spent the next nine years trading to the East Indies. Returning to Bucks county, 1808, he purchased the grist and oil mills at Bridge Point, where he erected a saw mill, with shops and dwellings, store and school house and, afterward, a woolen factory. On an elevated site he erected a beautiful dwelling for himself, now owned by Thomas Hadden, and long the home of Aaron Fries, of Philadelphia. Dr. Moore resided there several years and carried on a prosperous business. He was one of the most active in the erection of the first Presbyterian church at Doylestown, and the heaviest contributor, giving two hundred dollars. He was elected to congress, 1818 to fill the vacancy caused by the resignation of Mr. Ingham, and was twice re-elected. In 1824, Dr. Moore was appointed Director of the Mint at

---

[30] Some of the families, noticed in this chapter, are briefly mentioned elsewhere, but it could not well be avoided in making the text complete.

Philadelphia to succeed Dr. Patterson, his father-in-law, but retired from office, 1835, and devoted the rest of his life to private affairs. His eldest daughter, Emily P. born March 9, 1799, was married April 16, 1828, to John Beatty, a son of Dr. Reading Beatty, of this county, and grandson of the distinguished Rev. Charles Beatty, a graduate of the Log College. She died at her father's house, in Philadelphia, July 17, 1829. Mr. Beatty married, for a second wife, Miss Mary Asheton, of Evansburg, Pa.; spent many years of his life in Doylestown, and both himself and wife died here. He was a conspicuous figure, and active in the church.

Doylestown, Old and New.

XXXI
A Building Period.

The decade, from 1870 to 1880, was probably the most prosperous Doylestown ever experienced, especially in the erection of costly buildings. The first step was the organization of the "Doylestown Building and Loan Association," in 1870, Henry T. Darlington, president, and John J. Brock, treasurer.

At the first annual meeting, of this new enterprise, held April 29, 1871, the following figures exhibited its condition: During the year seven loans, of $200 had been sold at a premium of $35 and the earnings for the same time were reported, as follows: Dues, interest and fines $11,805.10; advanced by treasurer, $74.10; orders drawn, 72 loans, $11,549.75; expenses and interest refunded, $329.35, making $11,879.10. Assets; mortgages, $14,400; due from stockholders, $70.50-$14,470.50; less due treasurer, $74; net assets, $14,396.50; profits, premiums, $2,850.25; inst. and fines, $495.50, $2,325.35; less expenses and interest refunded, $329.35; net profits, $2,996.50; present value of one share, $17.99 9-16; amount paid on each share, $14.25; gain in fourteen months, each share, $3.74 9-16. The association ran its alloted time fixed by the charter, when it was wound up, each one receiving a dividend according to the number of shares he held. It was well managed, and to the interest of each investor.

Following the "Building and Loan Association," was the opening of an office for the purchase and sale of real estate.

Offices, for handling real estate and conveyancing, had been opened many years before, but a small success met the effort. The first of either was a real estate office opened by the late General William T. Rogers, 1831, but it is not known how long he continued. The following year Joseph H. Purdy, son of William Purdy, the Prothonotary, opened an office for conveyancing, but it was short lived. He was a fine penman and should have succeeded, but he shortly removed to Trenton, married a daughter of the Rev. E. F. Cooley, of Ewing, N. J., and died there June 12, 1842, in his twenty-eighth year. The next, to venture, in this line of business, was Randall Maddock, the same who was previously Postmaster at Doylestown, and established a rural free delivery of letters from the crown of his hat; but real estate had no charm for him, and he soon quit it. At a later period, George Hart, Esq., a member of the bar, opened a conveyancing office in the McDowell dwelling, east side of North Main street, and continued it several years, to his death. He was a good penman and wrote many mortgages, and other legal documents. They were not printed in blank then, as now, but the whole instrument had to be written out, generally on parchment. This was the case with the Sheriff's deeds, not infrequently given to a young attorney to write. At that day there were no printed blanks in use for any purpose.

The heaviest real estate transactions, in Doylestown, was by the firm of T. O. Atkinson & Co. Mr. Atkinson, who had been a storekeeper for several years at Penn's Park, Wrightstown township, came to Doylestown, January 1, 1871, and entered into the real estate business with A. J. Larue, under the firm name of A. J. Larue & Co., and they continued together for over a year. In the spring of 1872, Samuel A. Firman, likewise a country store-keeper, at Carversville, and other places, including a years' experience with Stoddard & Brother, Philadelphia, came to Doylestown, and shortly he and Atkinson entered into the real estate and general agency business under the firm name of T. O. Atkinson & Co. They remained together several years, their business growing to large proportions, greater than ever before in the county in that line, their transactions, some years, amounting to half a million dollars. They struck it at "flood tide," and it led on to fortune. There was a boon in real estate, at this period, and as the firm were liberal advertisers, printers' ink was an excellent agency in pushing their business. They dissolved in 1881, by Mr. Firman withdrawing and going into business alone, including the buying and selling of real estate.

Mr. Atkinson, meanwhile, continued the business until 1886,

when, upon the organization of the Bucks County Trust Company, he connected himself with that corporation as trust officer, closing out his real estate transactions, except such as were in the interest of the company, and of which he took charge. He is still with the Trust Company, but Mr. Firman, his old partner, is deceased, dying December 2, 1897 at the age of seventy-one. Mr. Atkinson has been very useful to the borough, in his handling of real estate during his connection with the Trust Company; being the means of bringing several parcels of land into the market, and adding to the improved parts of the borough. He took charge of Samuel Green's real estate at his death, cut it up into building lots, offered it at public sale, disposing of it at fair prices. The most of it has since been built upon. In the same period, 1886-'90, Mr. Atkinson handled the real estate of Lewis B. Thompson, deceased, in the northeast section of the borough. It was likewise cut up into building lots and sold at public sale, and, many of these lots have been built upon. The last transaction of the kind that Mr. Atkinson had charge of, for the Bucks County Trust Company, was in 1894, when he brought into the market the eligibly situated real estate of Captain H. J. C. Taylor, deceased, the Trust Company being guardian for the minor children. The tract was bounded by South Main, York, Pine and Ashland streets; the sale taking place the afternoon of June 16. It was cut up into twenty-three building lots; all were sold at fair prices, and, since the sale, many of the lots have been built upon.

The first building operation of any consequence, in the decade of 70-'80, was the erection of a new Presbyterian church, 1871-'72, on the site of the original, built 1815-'16, and the remodeled old one of 1845. The architect was Addison Hutton, Philadelphia, whose plans and specifications were delivered early in April, and the work put under contract.

The building is "a basement church," with the audience room on the next floor above, ninety feet in length and sixty in breadth, capable of seating six hundred and fifty persons. A tower, with a spire 150 feet high, stands at the southwest angle; the pulpit is recessed, and the basement contains a lecture room with seats for about one hundred and fifty, and a class room for Sunday School. It is built of brown stone, from Charles Rotzell's quarry, and is a handsome and imposing structure facing Court street instead of Church, as was the case with the old building. The stone work, of the tower proper, is seventy-four feet high, strengthened by buttresses at the corners and angles, with ornamented dormers where the spire sets upon it. The main entrance is on the ground floor through a large double door into a vestibule twelve feet wide. There are three blocks of pews, in the audience room, which has an open ceiling, sixteen feet to the square. The walls are two feet thick, except the front and rear walls of the first story, which are two feet six inches. The audience room is lighted by five windows on each side and three large tripple windows, one over the pulpit, and another in the opposite end over a gallery running the whole width of the building.

The corner stone was laid on June 21, in the presence of a considerable number of persons, members of the church and congregation and others attracted by the ceremonies. The services were simple but impressive, Dr. Andrews opening them with some apt remarks touching the occasion, and the circumstances that had brought them together. He said the old church had stood fifty-five years and its walls had been taken down to be built up in the new structure, concluding with a brief invocation to the Deity to direct the work to be done. After reading a few appropriate selections, from the Bible, he introduced the Rev. Dr. Mutchmore, of Philadelphia, who made the address of the occasion, and then formally laid the corner stone. In the box, inserted in the cavity cut in the stone and the whole hermetically sealed, were deposited a number of articles, including the history of the church. The corner stone, the gift of Mathew Gibney, was dressed and lettered by Thomas Hargrave and put in place by Francis Adleman, all of Doylestown, and long since deceased. The box was now lowered into its resting place and the audience quietly dispersed.

The new building was not finished until the following May, 1872, when the services of dedication occupied portions of three days, the 16th, 17th and 18th, with a large and interested audience. They were opened by the Rev. Dr. Andrews, at eleven o'clock, Thursday morning, delivering an appropriate prayer, followed by the choir, singing an anthem, Martin Hulshizer playing the organ. Dr. Andrews next delivered an address, taking for his text, the eighth chapter of the first book of Kings, which refers to the building of the Temple of Jerusalem. In his comments he said, among other things, that we have in scripture ample authority for dedicating houses to God's service. This was followed by a prayer from the Rev. Robert P. DuBois, the audience rising. The choir now sang a dedicatory hymn, opening:

> "And will the great eternal God,
> On earth establish his abode?
> And will He from His radiant throne,
> Accept our temple for His own?

Dr. Andrews next announced that the house "has been dedicated to the worship of Almighty God," etc. He was followed by the Rev. Dr. R. H. Allen, Philadelphia, in a discourse from the sixteenth chapter of Mark, thirty-sixth and fortieth verses, the choir singing a Psalm, of which the first verse reads:

> "I love his kingdom, Lord,
> The house of thine abode;
> The church of blest Redeemer saved
> With His own precious blood.

The greater part of the rest of the morning was consumed in the pastor's statement touching the cost of the new edifice, saying that only $4,000 are needed to liquidate the balance of the indebtedness. A collection was then taken but the amount received was not given; remarks followed by the Rev. Mr. Jewett, of New Brunswick, New Jersey, and the congregation was dismissed. In the afternoon the Rev. Dr. Beadle, Philadelphia, preached a sermon. On Friday morning the number in attendance was greater and listened to a sermon from the Rev. Dr. Bread, Philadelphia. On Saturday, the Rev. Louis R. Fox preached in the morning, and the Rev. Robert P. DuBois on Sunday morning. An interesting incident, of the services on the Sabbath, was the baptism of Mary Andrews Thompson, granddaughter of the pastor of the church. The collections, during the dedicatory services, were $700.[1]

The erection of "Lenape Building," following the Presbyterian church, was the greatest building improvement in Doylestown, on private capital, before or since. This was in 1874. The late Henry T. Darlington, then editor and proprietor of the *Bucks County Intelligencer*, in common with other citizens, appreciating the necessity of a public hall at the county seat, had previously obtained from the Legislature an Act incorporating the "Doylestown Improvement Com-

---

[1] Joseph Updegrove, born in this county, June 20, 1821, and died at Doylestown, 1896, was sexton of the church thirty years. He was descended from Herman Opdem Græff, who was a delegate from Crefeld to the Mennonite Council at Dordrecht, 1682. Three brothers, Herman, Dirck Isaacs and Abraham Upden Græff, came to America in October, 1688, and shared with Pastorious the honor of founding Germantown.

pany." In the early spring of 1874, a few energetic persons, who took an interest in the proposed building, began canvassing for stock subscriptions, and, meeting with success, other steps were taken. Stock, to the amount of $25,000, was subscribed in all, the balance of the money needed being left for a mortgage. The company was now organized, with Mr. Darlington for President of the board of trustees, and W. W. H. Davis chairman of the building committee. The next thing to be done, was the selection of a proper site for the building, the choice falling upon the lot at the southeast corner of Main and State streets. It was then occupied as a public inn, the oldest inn in the borough, known as the "Ship Tavern" in the long ago, but, in later years, called by the name of its proprietor. It was purchased of the trustees of Mrs. Abigail Barndt, widow of Aaron Barndt, for $12,000 and conveyed to the Improvement Company, April 15, 1874. The next thing was to consult an architect and get his views as to the kind of building that should be erected on the site. The choice fell on Hutton and Cernea, Philadelphia, the latter being the son of the late Dr. Cernea, Buckingham township, this county. They were employed, the drawings and working plans soon completed and accepted, mechanics secured, the old building torn down and the new one put under contract.

This was a notable corner, in Doylestown, and one of the most accessible for its purpose, at the crossing of the two great highways that first cut this section, one leading from Philadelphia to Easton, the other from Coryell's Ferry on the Delaware to the Schuylkill. A noted inn had stood on this corner for about a century, and the following were its owners for eighty years prior to its conveyance to the Improvement Company:

In 1794, Christian Wertz conveyed it to John Shaw; 1801, John Shaw to Josiah Shaw; 1801, Josiah Shaw to John Shaw, Jr.; 1804, John Shaw, Jr., to John Worman; 1808, John Worman to Isaac Morris; 1812, Isaac Morris to Adam Shearer; 1813, Adam Shearer to John Hough and Timothy Smith; 1814, John Hough to Samuel Flack; 1818, Samuel Flack to Jacob Kohl; 1830, Jacob Kohl to Elnathan Pettit; 1837, Elnathan Pettit to Stephen Brock; 1837, Stephen Brock to Richard Leedom, Richard Leedom to Benjamin Morris; 1851, James Gilkyson, Administrator, of Benjamin Morris, to Pearson W. Hyde; 1852, Pearson W. Hyde to A. H. Barber;

1858, A. H. Barber [2] to Aaron Barndt, and April 1, 1874, the trustee of Abagail Barndt, widow of Aaron Barndt, conveyed it to the Doylestown Improvement Company. Among these landlords, two reached the office of High Sheriff of the county, Brock and Morris, and one, Leedom, was noted for playing the violin.

Lenape Building was finished by the middle of November, and the Hall dedicated on the evening of the 17th. The ceremonies were imposing and the attendance very large, the number present being estimated at eight hundred, probably the largest audience ever seated under one roof in Doylestown, since John B. Gough lectured in the exhibition building. The Rev. Silas M. Andrews delivered an address both unique and entertaining. The music for the occasion was in charge of Thomas E. Harkens, of Philadelphia, and was said to have been better than any previously heard in Doylestown. The erection of the building, which cost $50,000, and the most imposing in the county, was quite an achievement under the circumstances. It fronts ninety feet on State street, seventy-four feet six inches on Main, and is three stories high with cellar underneath. It is built of pressed brick, on Main and State streets, laid in dark mortar, the fronts trimmed and ornamented with belt courses of Wilwaukie brick, Cleaveland and brown stone with brick panels. The first story is divided into three stores on State street and two on Main, the hall, on the second story, seats eight hundred people, with a gallery, has a stage thirty-nine feet eight inches long by twenty-six feet six inches wide with a drop curtain, and is well lighted with side brackets and foot lights. On the third floor are two handsome Lodge rooms. The drop curtain to the stage, one of the most inviting features of Lenape Hall, was painted by Thomas P. Otter, the artist. The scene represents a market day in Luino, one of the many towns that fringe the beautiful lake of Maggiora, Italy. At the angle of State and Main streets, a corner is cut off twelve feet across and carried to full height in which is a clock, a present from a lady of Doylestown.

Among the features of Lenape Building, was a market house on the ground floor, south side under the hall. A few years prior, bor-

---

2 A. H. Barber was born at Oakdale, N. J., March 27, 1809; came to this county when a boy; began life in a store at Lumberville; next kept a general store at Lower Black's Eddy and came to Doylestown, 1851. He was a useful citizen and a mainstay of the Doylestown Agricultural and Mechanics' Institute; a member of Council and held other borough offices; was Census Enumerator for Bucks county, 1850, member of Lodge No. 94, I. O. O. F. He died August 12, 1898, and his wife, nee Asenath Carver, died 1885.

NEW PRESBYTERIAN CHURCH, 1871-2.

ough council established a street market, farmers' wagons standing on Main and State streets, and it was so well patronized, the Improvement Company felt justified in putting market accommodations in Lenape. It was equipped with stalls and other conveniences, and was well attended by farmers and customers at first, but they gradually fell off. The market was then closed and fitted up for other purposes, the post office being there for several years.

The erection of a new Court House that had been agitated several years without success, many reasons being urged against it, among others the great cost. While the old building answered every purpose when built and for many years after, the business of the courts had outgrown the accommodations. It lacked every modern convenience. The question was brought before the Grand Jury, court after court, and year after year, with the same result. It required the endorsement of two consecutive Grand Juries, but this was hard to get. There was no difficulty in getting the approval of one Grand Jury, but, when the second was asked for, political and other interests prevented its approval. The politicians, of the lower end of the county, had a lingering hope of having the county divided, and it took a long time to disabuse their minds. They had sometimes come very near it. At the April term of court, 1877, the efforts, of the advocates of a new Court House, were crowned with success, a second Grand Jury approving it. The two main factors, in the effort for a new Court House, were the *Doylestown Democrat* and *Bucks County Intelligencer*, and their editors, who advocated it persistently.

In the report of the Grand Jury, to the Court of Quarter Sessions, touching the erection of a new Court House, that body made the following recommendation:

"Having viewed the Court House and public offices, we find them inadequate for the purpose used, and, after an earnest consideration of the subject, in all its bearings, recommend the erection of a new Court House on the site of the present one, at a cost, we think, that should not exceed one hundred thousand dollars." The report was sighed, "J. S. Williams, Foreman" and dated April 26, 1877. The same day the court approved and signed the report, as follows:

"The within, report and recommendation therein, approved. The clerk is directed to furnished a certified copy, and of the approval, to the County Commissioners."

By the Court, April 26, 1877.

(Signed) RICHARD WATSON, P. J.
JOSEPH MORRISON, A. J.

This completed the struggle for a new Court House at Doylestown, and the Board of County Commissioners now became responsible for carrying out the recommendation of the Grand Jury and the Court.

The Commissioners, being authorized to demolish the old building and replace it with a new one, "did not stand on the order" of their getting to work. They employed Addison Hutton as architect, one of the same, who made the drawings for Lenape Building; he took the matter in hand at once, and, on Saturday, June 16, the plans were on exhibition in the old Court room; they were accepted, and proposals, for the erection of the new building, advertised for. The contract was awarded to James Doyle, of Philadelphia. Preparatory to taking down the old building, the books and papers of the offices were transferred to Lenape, and the Courts were held in the hall of that building while the new Court House was being built, and made ready for occupancy. The new Court House does not occupy the exact site of the old one, as its increased size compelled its location a few feet farther west to avoid the jail, which was not removed until several years later. In a short time the premises were alive with laborors, masons, bricklayers, carpenters, et al; the hum of industry greeted one's ear on every side, and the work was pushed with vigor in order to get the building under cover before winter set in.

The corner stone of the new Court House was laid at five o'clock Wednesday afternoon, October 3, 1877, with impressive and appropriate ceremonies, in the presence of a large audience. Judge Henry P. Ross took the chair, metaphorically speaking, and made some fitting remarks, when the Rev. Mr. Sheip offered up a prayer. This was followed by music, after which General Davis made a brief address suitable to the occasion. He opened with a reference to the settlement of the county, the organization of the courts and the building of Court Houses, closing as follows:

"If the Court House be a temple, wherein Justice is enshrined, the attorneys are the priests who minister at the altar. The spotless Goddess, which presides in this cloister, accepts the devotion of no unworthy worshipper. A profession, which embodies the legal learning of the world; which has been the safeguard of constitutional liberty since Magna Charta was wrested from an unwilling monarch; which divides, with the christian minister, the last office at the bedside of the dying, and adjusts the most delicate affairs of life, cannot afford to have a blot on its robes.

"The just lawyer, and the christian minister, meeting at the dying bed, the one to give counsel in the proper settlement of worldly affairs, the other to prepare the departing soul for a happy immortality, form a sacred link between the church and the Court House. Impurity cannot exist in either without destroying, utterly, its usefulness. While all ages have lavished wealth in the erection of beautiful temples for the worship of God, is it not meet and proper that we honor the temple of Justice, a co-laborer with the church? This edifice, then, whose corner stone we this day lay, and which is rapidly rising from its foundations to completion, under the hands of skilled mechanism, is a fitting tribute to the sacred profession of the law. When finished, the blind goddess, with poised scales, will open wide her portals, and summon her worshippers to consecrate this new temple to the cause of Justice, Mercy and Truth."

The Honorable Richard Watson now proceeded to lay the corner stone, accompanied by some well chosen remarks. This was followed by a prayer and benediction, by the Rev. V. H. Berghaus, and the affair was concluded.

In the corner stone was put a leaden box containing thirty-six different articles, including a copy of the report of Thomas W. Cernea, one of the architects, concerning the new Court House, July 25, 1875, names of county and borough officers, photograph of old Court House, copy of address at laying of corner stone, copies of county newspapers, school law of Pennsylvania, papers relating to the last legal proceedings in the old Court House, circular of Doylestown Seminary, etc.

The Court House was finished in the early fall of 1878, when the public officers took possession of their offices and the business of the courts went on in their new quarters. The room, now the Sheriff's office, was used for sometime, as the post office, Thomas P. Miller being then the postmaster. During the building of the Court House, one of the laborers, Charles Kiser, accidently fell through the sky-light, and was killed. He was a soldier of the Civil War, serving in Company D, 104th Pennsylvania Volunteers, and "more's the pity" that a soldier of the Union should be killed in this common place way.

The tall and symmetrical flag staff, on the southeast corner of the Court House green, has an interesting history. It was presented to the borough, with permission of the County Commissioners to plant it where it stands, by Dr. Frank Swartzlander, the elder, 1897. He was moved, to make this unique gift to Doylestown, because there was no fitting place, at the county seat, to fly the National flag from, on public occasions. After careful inquiry, the Doctor found, what suited him, in the Spar Yard, of David Baird, Camden on the Delaware, and engaged him to fashion the two sticks into a flag staff, which occupied several months.

The flag staff stands one hundred and sixty-four feet out of ground and ten feet under, embedded in cement. The main mast is of Oregon pine, one hundred and eleven feet long, thirty-three and a half inches in diameter at the butt, and twenty-two at the top, was brought around Cape Horne to Philadelphia, and laid in the Delaware seasoning for seven years. Dr. Swartzlander bought the stick as a log in the water, and had it dressed at Mr. Baird's spar yard. The top mast, bought at the same place, in the rough, is seventy-six feet long, with splice off, of Michigan spruce, five inches in diameter at the extreme top. The flag staff, as a whole, was proportioned by Mr. Baird so as to make it an ideal of symmetry, and is the tallest and largest wooden flag staff in the country. It is rigged with a double set of halyards for two flags. The flag, that flys from the top of the staff, is of the largest garrison size, and was also the gift of Dr. Swartzlander.

The next event of interest occurring, in this decade, was the celebrating of Doylestown's Centennial, March 1, 1878. This date was fixed, because, on this day, 1778, the name, as now spelled, was first written on an official document. Prior to this, the name was neither written, nor spelled, as at present, but, beginning with " Doyles Tavern," the name of the hamlet was written in various ways. The day was pleasant, and the attendance large, of both neighbors and strangers. Preparations for the event had been making for some time.

Our own people were at work, early in the morning decorating their dwellings and places of business, and flags of all nations streamed from the house tops, including a large Papal flag from the Catholic church. The incoming trains added to the crowds that thronged the streets. In the forenoon there was a procession representing trades and occupations, some on floats, led by the Nagle Rifles and a band. The printing offices were represented by a Gordon press; plumbers and tinners by implements of their handicraft; the blacksmiths had a horse mounted on a wagon and undergoing the process of shœing as he passed through the streets, and other industries of the borough were represented by something that reminded the onlooking public of their presence. In the procession were the various Beneficial Societies, the Boys of America in uniform, the Doylestown Hose Company, the machine being drawn by a party of young men; a large display of vehicles from Aaron Kratz's wagon factory and a miscellaneous cavalcade brought up the rear of the procession, occupying an hour in passing a single point.

The literary exercises, of the occasion, were held in the afternoon in Lenape Hall, which a Philadelphia party had decorated beautifully, and was crowded almost to suffocation. Dr. George T. Harvey, chairman of the General Committee called the audience together at two o'clock, and announced the names of the Vice Presidents: Joseph Harvey, John Beatty, John Cox, Samuel Nightingale, Samuel F. DuBois, John B. Pugh, Samuel Hall and Charles Wigton, all now deceased, including the chairman. The stage was filled with distinguished guests.

The exercises were opened with a selection by Brock's orchestra, followed by a prayer from the Rev. Silas M. Andrews, D. D., and an ode by Caleb E. Wright, Esq., whose first stanza ran:

> "Britains may glory in London the great,
>   Frenchmen rejoice in their town by the Sein;
> Russians emboss'd in their ice, view in State,
>   Peter's doomed city on Baltic's rough main.
> We are less lofty, but loving as well
>   Homes that our forefathers won by their toil;
> Town of the hilltop, of all towns the belle,
>   Proud city hereafter, city of Doyle."

This was followed by a poem by Miss Carrie Lœb, Historical Address, by W. W. H. Davis, which covered the leading events in the history of Doylestown, from its settlement; an oration, by Judge Richard Watson, and, upon his conclusion, the exercises were closed with a benediction by the Rev. Levi C. Sheip. In the evening there was a dramatic entertaiment in Lenape Hall by home talent.

Among the prominent people present, at this Centennial celebration, were Count Dassi, of Italy, Ex-Senator Simon Cameron, George W. Childs, Philadelphia, General John Davis, Attorney-General Lear, Judge Henry P. Ross, Hon. I. Newton Evans, State Senators Allen and Yerkes, and many others.

The Society of Doylestown was never more brilliant, if its equal, than in the seventies, the ladies of Saint Paul's Protestant Episcopal church leading in the gayeties. In 1868, the Rev. Hurley Baldy was called to the rectorship, and himself and wife encouraged these pleasures. One of the most important factors was the "Mite Society," organized by the ladies of the church and congregation, married and single, mothers and daughters, all taking equal interest in making it a success. It met at private houses one evening a week, invitations being given without regard to church affiliation. The attractions were vocal and instrumental music tableaux, charades, character plays, etc. The mite box was always on the piano, and it yielded more than the "widow's mite." Refreshments were taboo'd, and no house wife had the courage to break the law. The attendance was generally large, as many as a hundred being present on a single evening, when

"All went merry as a marriage bell."

The leaders, in these social pleasures, were Mrs. Baldy, Mrs. Ross, Mrs. Pugh, Mrs. Davis, Mrs. Brock, Mrs. Lyman, Mrs. Gilkyson, Mrs. Ely, Mrs. James, Mrs. Yerkes, Mrs. Worthington, Mrs. Michener, Mrs. Harvey, Mrs. McCoy, and others whose names we do not recall, forming as splendid a group of women as any society could boast. These agreeable assemblages came to an end at the death of Mrs. Baldy and the resignation of her husband, and were never revived.

The same period was more prolific of lectures than at any other time since I became a resident of Doylestown, some, by subscription, others free. The majority of the lectures were delivered under the patronage of the "T. O. S. Club," of which more is said in a previous chapter, who organized a course for several winters. These young gentlemen did much for the intellectual enjoyment of the people of the borough. They gave an annual hop in Lenape Hall, or the exhibition building, followed by a dinner at the Fountain House. Among the lecturers were Anna Dickinson, at one time a school teacher in Bucks county, but then a star in the lecture field, "Sunset" Cox, on two occasions, one of the most versatile talkers in the country, Richard Vaux, the only American who had the honor of dancing with Queen Victoria, General Nathaniel P. Banks, Henry Ward Beacher, James Whitcomb Riley, Lieutenant Danenhower, U. S. N., an Arctic Explorer and others equally noted. General Banks, Paul DuChaillu and Mr. Cox were the author's guests. The personal character of Mr. Cox, was of the highest order, and his social qualities fascinating.

Doylestown, Old and New.

XXXII
Bi-Centennial Decade.

The wheels of time had hardly turned into the eighties, when another forward step was taken, by the organization of the Bucks County Historical Society, the charter fixing its home at Doylestown.

This had been some time in contemplation, by the lovers of local history, but the movement first took shape at a meeting held in the library room, Lenape Building, January 20, 1880. There is no complete list extant of those present, but, from the treasurer's records the following persons, who were there, may be considered the founders of this now popular institution: Joseph B. Walter, W. W. H. Davis, Alfred Paschall, Richard M. Lyman, Henry C. Mercer, John S. Bailey, Josiah B. Smith, Thomas P. Otter, A. M. Dickie, Mahlon Carver and George McDowell. The erection of a building is now under contract, and the society expect to be in it before the end of the current year. The meeting was organized by calling Josiah B. Smith, of Newtown, to the chair and appointing Henry C. Mercer, secretary. A brief draft of a Constitution and By-Laws was submitted by General Davis, and adopted, and the organization was completed by the election of the following officers: President, W. W. H. Davis; Secretary, Richard M. Lyman, and Treasurer, Alfred Paschall. The society immediately entered upon its assigned work of holding historical meetings, and making a collection of curios of historic interest. In February, 1885, a charter was granted by the Court of Common

Pleas, and, since then, the society has been active in its labors, and is acknowledged to be one of the educators of the county.

For several years, quarterly meetings were held, but finding it difficult to keep the organization intact by meeting so frequently, the number of meetings was reduced to two, midsummer and midwinter, the latter always held in the Court room at Doylestown. While the meetings were held quarterly, the attendance at some were very meager, on one occasion, only three persons being present, General Davis and wife and John S. Bailey. It was a struggle, but, in the end, Faith and Hope triumphed. Under the amended constitution the number of meetings was increased to three each year, May, October and January. It was inspired with new life by the board of County Commissioners allowing the society to occupy a vacant room in the Court House, and, about this time, the ladies began taking an interest in the organization. This gave it the seal of success.

Since that time, interest in the Historical Society has been largely increased, and the meetings well attended. This is especially the case with the mid-winter meeting in the court room, at which there are sometimes an audience of three hundred, and one hundred and twenty-five invited guests lunched by the ladies. Their aid is a telling card, doubtless the most telling of all the factors that have labored in the society's behalf. The Historical Society is prospering on all lines; the membership has been largely increased and public interest in its work grows; its collection, of historic curios, numbers about two thousand specimens, that section, known as "The Tools of the Nation Maker," being one of the most interesting ever exhibited, and we know of nothing like it in America. The paid up members have reached six hundred and the number is increased at each meeting.

The society has been, and still is, cramped for room, and its small income militates against its usefulness, but, in the near future, there will be a change in these particulars. The society's present income, is derived from the admission fee of $2 for each member, and $150 paid annually by the County Commissioners, by authority of the Legislature. There was an effort several years, to raise sufficient funds to erect a building to house its historic collection, and the goal has been reached, thanks to our generous friends. The late James H. Greir, of Warrington township, left the society a legacy of $5,000, for its building fund, which was increased by a gift of $10,000, from the late William L. Elkins, and $3,000 from his son, of Philadelphia. To these sums may be added individual subscriptions of $5,000, amounting in the whole to $18,000. From this outlook, the society's possibilities, for doing good on historic lines, is very flattering. A part of the working machinery, of the Historical Society, is a "Committee on Art," the result of its labors being a large album of photographic specimens that cannot be excelled. The members of the committee are all amateurs, a majority of them ladies, which gives value to its work.

During the past year, additional steps were taken toward the erection of a suitable building; including the purchase of a large lot at a cost of $5,000, the employment of an architect, the drawing of plans and appointment of a building committee, composed of Harman Yerkes, Newlin D. Fell, Samuel Steckel, Hugh B. Eastburn and George Elkins, with Judge Yerkes, chairman. Previous to the purchase of this lot, Edward Longstreth, Philadelphia, presented the society with a lot 150 by 250 feet at the northeast corner of Pine and Ashland streets, joining the later purchased lot and was a part of it. More recently, Miss Elizabeth J. Greir, sister of the late James H. Greir, presented the society with $2,000 for a library fund. The corner stone, of the new building, was laid the 26th of July, 1904, with the proper ceremony.

The first reunion, of the Survivors of the 104th Pennsylvania Volunteers, was held at Doylestown, May 26, 1880, and proved a great success. The day dawned bright and clear, and, with the exception of the extreme heat and dust, the reveilie never ushered in a day more befitting the occasion that awaited it. The citizens had occupied themselves early in decorating their dwellings and places of business, and the borough presented a gay and festive appearance. Flags and festoons were seen everywhere; they were "to the right of us and to the left" of us; while the main streets had been sprinkled and the dust laid. The veterans were on the ground early, each wearing a blue badge, on the lappel of his coat, bearing the state arms and the following lettering in gilt:

REUNION
104th PENNSYLVANIA REGIMENT,
May 26, 1880.

The old regimental band, from Emaus, Lehigh county, arrived at 9.33, and, on being escorted to the monument, played a solemn dirge to the memory of the dead of the regiment; the Durham Cornet Band arrived shortly after, and the two bands made the streets vocal with choice selections. A steady influx of people, in carriages, on horse back, a-foot and by train, had so swelled the crowd by ten o'clock, it was estimated 4,000 visitors were on the streets.

The procession was ordered to form on the lawn in front of the Court House, but the veterans had been so long separated, they felt obliged to re-call their adventures, "by flood and field," chat and shake hands, swing their crutches,

"And show how fields were won."

It took some little time, but they were soon in line, two hundred and sixty-four in number. The first thing was the reception of the regimental flag, with uncovered heads, the band playing the "Star Spangled Banner."

The procession now started for its march round town in the following order:

Doylestown Cornet Band,
Company G, 6th Regiment, N. G., Pennsylvania, as escourt,
Emaus Regimental Band,
104th Regiment.
Officers and soldiers of other regiments, who served in the late war,
Durham Cornet Band,
Invited guests in carriages.

A stand had been erected on old Camp Lacey, near the exhibition building, where the veterns and audience assembled under an extensive canvas. The invited guests seated on the stand, were too numerous to mention in detail, but, among them were Generals Robert Patterson and William J. Hoffman, George W. Childs, Philadelphia, Attorney-General Lear, Judge Richard Watson, Rev. Silas M. Andrews, D. D., Hon. William Godshalk, of Doylestown, and a number of others from home and abroad. After the audience was comfortably seated, General Davis called the meeting to order and announced that the Hon. George Lear would preside. The exercises were now begun, the first the delivery of an appropriate prayer by the Rev. Dr. Andrews, followed by the reading of a letter from Governor Henry M. Hoyt, of Pennsylvania, who was expected to make the address of the occasion, but was confined at home with sickness. As his regiment, the 52d Pennsylvania, fought and marched by the side of the 104th, for nearly three years, his presence would have been every way gratifying and appropriate. A sketch of the regiment was now read by General Davis, its late Colonel, followed by a piece of music

UNION ACADEMY, 1804.

by the Durham Cornet Band, and the literary side of the reunion was closed by a benediction from the Rev. V. Hummel Berghaus, rector of the Protestant Episcopal Church.

It was now announced that a banquet was spread in the exhibition building for the officers and men of the 104th and invited guests, whither they were conducted. In a very few minutes all were seated at the long tables, and partaking of a feast that would have been inviting to daintier appetites than ex-soldiers who had lived on hard tack. The tables were handsomely ornamented with flowers and china, the latter loaned by Rufe & Scheetz. Each man of the 104th had a wooden plate and tin coffee cup, made for the occasion, and presented by Hon. John Wanamaker, and which the veterans took home with them as keep sakes. The tables were arranged for 350 people, and, before the banquet was over, every seat was occupied and the good things had disappeared. Many ladies were present,—without whose assistance the banquet would not have been the success it was. When the feasting was over, Dr. Andrews asked a blessing, the regimental band played several tunes, and the affair came to a close with the blessings of the church, and amid the strains of sweet harmony.

The occasion was marred, to some extent, by the absence of several distinguished guests, who expected to be present. Governor Hoyt we have accounted for, Ex-Governor Curtin missed the morning train by five minutes, and did not come until the reunion exercises were over, but he spent the remainder of the day at Doylestown; was serenaded and made a speech from the porch of the Purdy house and Governor Parker, of New Jersey, was kept away by public business. Among those, from whom letters of regret were received, were the Attorney-General and Secretary of War, Washington, United States Senator Cameron, Major-General Casey, U. S. A., Speaker of Congress, Randall, Col. John W. Forney, General Henry M. Nagle, California and General Wm. H. Emory, U. S. A. The Re-union festivities closed with an instrumental and vocal concert in the evening, in Lenape Hall, in which Miss Ella Heist, Brock's Orchestra, the Emaus band and the Doylestown Singing Society took part. The large audience was delighted.

The most interesting public function, ever held in Bucks county, was the Bi-Centennial celebration of its settlement in 1682. This took place at Doylestown, August 31 and September 1 and 2, 1882 and was largely attended.

It was first publicly[1] suggested at a meeting of the Bucks County Historical Society, held at Newtown, Oct. 1, 1881, in a paper read by W. W. H. Davis. It met with favor, and a committee was appointed, with Josiah B. Smith, Newtown, chairman. They reported favorably with a plan and scope of the celebration, and fixed the time and place. The appointment of other committees, including one for each township and borough shortly followed; the machinery was put in motion, and, for the next six months, there was busy work making the necessary preparations. Besides the literary features, attending such affairs, this was marked by an exhibit of the varied industries of the county, with a display of the manners and customs of the past and present, and of domestic and other curios brought over by the pioneers. To accomplish this, families gave up their priceless treasures to add to the attractions of the occasion. The day exercises were held on the grounds of the "Doylestown Agricultural and Mechanics' Institute," and those of the evening in Lenape Hall.

A general committee, of twenty, directed and supervised the work of preparation, and made the celebration the success it was; composed of Hugh B. Eastburn, chairman; W. W. H. Davis, William Kinsey, William P. Crozier; Algernon S. Cadwallader, John Wildman, Eleazer F. Church, John S. Williams, Edward Boileau, Albert S. Paxson, Alfred Paschall, Nathan C. James, William Godshalk, Dr. Joseph Thomas, Dr. I. S. Moyer, David W. Hess, Sallie J. Reeder, Elizabeth Lloyd, Cynthia S. Holcomb and Anna Eastburn.

The literary feature opened at 2.30 p. m., Thursday, August 31, in a large canvas pavilion, the Hon. Richard Watson, Doylestown, presiding, with music by the Sellersville Cornet Band. After prayer, by the Rev. William A. Patton, Doylestown, Judge Watson delivered the opening address, embracing some pertinent allusions to the settlement of Penn's Colony and Bucks county. He was followed by Dr. Joseph B. Walter, Solebury, and Miss Nellie D. Graham, Upper Makefield, who read poems written for the occasion. The attendance was large. In the evening there was a concert in Lenape Hall, Brock's Orchestra furnishing the instrumental music, several noted vocalist bearing their part.

The Hon. George Lear, Doylestown, presided at the exhibition

---

[1] The late Henry T. Darlington and W. W. H. Davis talked about the Bi-Centennial several years before it came off; were the first to suggest it, and looked forward to it with great pleasure, but, unfortunately, Mr. Darlington did not live to enjoy it.

grounds, on Friday, the Bristol band furnishing the music. The audience was larger than the day before, and on the stand were a number of distinguished persons from a distance, including Governor Hoyt, of Pennsylvania. The Rev. Levi C. Sheip, Doylestown, opened the exercises with prayer. This was followed with an "Historical Address" by General Davis, Doylestown, in which he brieffly reviewed the settlement of the county, referring to the century that gave birth to William Penn, as a "period of great intellectual activity;" the reading of a poem by Samuel Swain, Bristol; an ode by C. E. Wright, Esq., Doylestown, and the Hon. Edward M. Paxson, State Surpreme Court, delivering an oration. In the evening a large company of ladies and gentlemen, prominent in official, social, business and professional life, attended the banquet in Lenape Hall. Mr. Lear, as presiding officer of the day, opened the intellectual branch of the occasion in a few remarks, and, after the plates had been removed, toasts and five minute speeches followed under the direction of the toast master. Among the distinguished guests were Governor Hoyt, wife and daughter; Judges Craig Biddle and Amos Briggs, Philadelphia; Judge Richard Watson, Doylestown; General B. Frank Fisher, Philadelphia; Hon. William U. Hensel, President of Penna. State Editorical Association; Jerome Buck, Esq., New York, and Hon. William Godshalk, U. S. House of Representatives. Robert J. Burdette, the distinguished humorist and lecturer, being unavoidably absent, his response to the toast "woman," assigned to him, was read by Alfred Paschall.

The interest, in the literary features of the occasion, reached its climax Saturday afternoon when an audience of 3,000 persons, gathered about the platform on the exhibition grounds. Dr. Isaac S. Moyer, Quakertown, presided, and the subjects of the speakers were as follows: "Bucks County Abroad," by John A. Burton, Philadelphia; "Our Quaker Ancestry," Miss Anna Eastburn, Langhorne; "Domestic Women," Mrs. Cynthia S. Holcomb, Newtown; an address on "Agriculture," by Eastburn Reeder; the exercises closing with Miss Laura W. White, Newtown, reading a poem on "Grandfather's Spectacles," and a declamation by Miss Alma Sager, the exercises being interspersed with music from the Quakertown band.

In the evening 800 persons gathered in Lenape Hall to participate in "Ye Ancient Tea Drynke." With this closed the Bi-Centennial celebration of the settlement of Bucks county, one of the most successful occasions of the kind held in the State. The list of exhibits in show cases, and otherwise cared for, in the building of the Agricultural Society, was as extensive as rare, and delighted all beholders. The financial committee issued a handsomely engraved certificate to each subscriber, to the Centennial Fund, to the amount of five dollars, which are sure to be preserved as memorials and doubtless some of them will be exhibited, 1982.

Following the erection of a new Court House, 1877-'78, the agitation for a new jail, was continued, and, although it was badly needed, six years were required to get the necessary legal sanction to build it. As in the case of the Court House, the consent, of two consecutive Grand Juries, was required. It was first brought before the Grand Jury at February Sessions, 1882, which reported, unanimously, that "the present building is entirely unfitted for the purpose for which it is used, and earnestly recommend the construction of a new building." This was signed by Thomas C. Ivins, foreman, and filed in the Quarter Sessions' Office, February 10, but no action was taken upon it until a subsequent Grand Jury was heard from. Meanwhile, some opposition was raised to the building of a new jail, while the county was in debt, and, when the question came up at the April Sessions, the liquidation of this debt was made a condition precedent the Grand Jury reporting as follows:

"The question of the building of a new jail has been brought to our notice, and we have listened, with pleasure, to the statements of the gentlemen composing the Board of Public Charities of the State, whom your Honors permitted to come before us, and we have also inquired, with considerable care, into the propriety of erecting such structure, and recommend the erection of a new jail after the present indebtedness of the county is paid at the present rate of taxation." This report was filed May 5, 1882, but the matter lay dormant until the December Session, 1883, when the Court made the following endorsement on the report of the Grand Jury filed May 5, 1882: "And now to wit, January 21, 1884, the within report, and the report of the Grand Jury of February 10, 1882, having been presented and considered, and the County Commissioners representing that the indebtedness of the county has been paid off, the Court approves of the erection of a new county jail as recommended by said report."

By the Court,

(Signed) HARMAN YERKES, P. J.

These were the initial steps in the erection of a new jail; the first, getting consent of the Court, the second, the selection of an architect, the choice falling on Addison Hutton, Philadelphia, who acted in the same capacity when the county erected the new Court House. The plans and specifications were examined by the Board of Charities, at Doylestown, March 8, 1884, the architect being present to explain them; and, after their approval by the board, and so endorsed on each piece of the drawings, they were delivered to Judge Yerkes the same evening for his inspection and approval. They were then filed in the commissioners' office, four weeks before the bids were awarded, for the bidders to examine. The Board of Public Charities previously met the County Commissioners, February 1, 1884, to decide on a site for the jail, and unnanimously agreed on the purchase of the George T. Harvey lot, east side of South Pine street, containing two acres. The price was $1,500, and the location a very eligible one, facing the southwest. The commissioners advertised for proposals for building the jail, on March 4, 1884, the bids all to be in and closed at noon, March 31. They were opened and announced in the papers of April 15, and the contracts awarded as follows: Building the prison, to Henry D. Livezey,[2] $72,000; plumbing, to Kane and Kelsey, $3,950; and gas fitting, $299. The contract for the steam heating was withheld, but, we are not able to say who received it, nor the price.

Work was begun immediately the contracts were awarded, but the jail was not completed until the spring of 1885. One wing was occupied in the early winter, Allen H. Heist being Sheriff, but Elias Eastburn, Sheriff-elect, did not take possession until April 1st. The original plan and specifications called for sixty cells, but the commissioners, believing they would never need so many, had the number reduced to fifty-two. The intent was to have only one prisoner in a cell, but, since then, there have been as many as seventy-two prisoners in the jail at one time, but, despite this change in the number of cells, the plan of the building is such they can be added to without interfering with the original design. The time will come, and probably in the near future, when the cells will have to be increased.

As the new jail approached completion, and before the Commisioners, who had built it, had gone out of office, the Board of State Charities, accompanied by the Hon. Richard Vaux, Inspector of the Eastern Penitentiary, paid it a visit. They came up December 30, 1884. After a careful inspection of the building, as far as completed, they spoke of it in high terms, Mr. Vaux, especially, commending

---

[2] Although the contract for building the jail, was awarded to Henry D. Livezey, James Flack afterward became joint contractor with him.

it. He pronounced it the "most complete county prison in America." and said he "had seen nothing equal to it in Europe." After their return home, the Board of Charities addressed a letter to the County Commissioners, in commendation of the zeal, fidelity and economy displayed in the erection of the prison. In the near future, the Sheriff of Bucks county was written to from Denver, Colorado, making inquiries about our jail at the suggestion of the National Board of Charities, and, since then, other letters have been received on the same subject.

On a stone, in front of the main entrance the following names are cut with the respective official positions held by the persons;—

BOARD OF STATE CHARITIES.

Mahlon H. Dickinson, Lewis Peterson, Jr., W. W. H. Davis, Phillip C. Garrett, Henry M. Hoyt, Thomas G. Morton, M. D., E. Coppee Mitchell, Herbert M. Howe, M, D., Wm. J. Sawyer, Diller Luther, General Agent.

COUNTY COMMISSIONERS.

John Wynkoop, Jones Breisch, Isaac Ryan, J. Evan Zorns, Clerk.

The first step toward organizing the Bucks County Trust Company, the first financial institution of the kind in the county, was taken January 14, 1886. That evening, Judge Richard Watson, George Ross, J. Monroe Shellenberger, Louis H. James, Esqrs. and T. O. Atkinson, met in a second story room of the Lloyd building, East Court street, to consider the matter. Before adjourning, they resolved to form a "Trust Company," and subscribed 1425 shares of stock at the par value of $100. At a subsequent meeting,—the 16th, the above named persons, with the addition of Hugh B. Eastburn and Robert M. Yardley, Esqrs., took additional steps, to furthur the object in view, by resolving that Richard Watson act as president for one year; T. O. Atkinson, Treasurer and Secretary; that the persons, accepted as stockholders, constitute a part of the first board of directors, and, in addition, James B. Doyle, Philadelphia, Aaron Fretz, Plumstead, Joseph S. Atkinson, Buckingham, Alfred Johnson, Southampton, Samuel Steckel, Doylestown, B. F. Gilkeson, Bristol, John S. Williams, Solebury and Joseph Thomas, Quarkertown, were named as directors. At this meeting, a formal subscribed allotment of stock was made amounting to 2500 shares, which each was allowed to dispose of, or retain for himself as he might see fit.

The organization was now named the "Bucks County Trust Company," its purposes specified:—to be conducted under the general corporation laws of Pennsylvania, with a recognized capital of $250,000 and located at Doylestown. In the *Democrat* of January 19th and the *Intelligencer* of the 23rd, a notice appeared that application would be made for a charter. At a meeting held on the 29th of January, the fifteen gentlemen present were declared directors for the ensuing year; Richard Watson was chosen President of the company, T. O. Atkinson, Secretary and Treasurer; Mr. Atkinson was authorized to purchase a portion of the Fox lot corner of Court and Broad streets to erect a building on; Richard Watson, T. O. Atkinson and Joseph Thomas were appointed a committee to procure the necessary papers and books; and Mr. Watson was authorized to prepare an application for a charter, and forward the same to Harrisburg. At a stockholders meeting, March 3rd, the by-laws were adopted. Governor Pattison, who had approved the application for a charter, February 23rd, ordered letters patent to be issued the same day, and the charter was put on record at Doylestown on March 2nd. The new corporation was now clothed with all the power the stockholders had asked for, or the law could grant, and was ready to go to work. The company commenced business in the Mathews' dwelling on East Court street and occupied it until the new building was finished, January, 1887. This building was subsequently purchased by Judge Yerkes, altered, and is now occupied by him as a residence. All things considered, the period, from 1880 to 1890, was one of the most enterprising in the history of the county capital.

Doylestown, Old and New.

XXXIII

Fires and Fire Department.

Compared to most boroughs of its size, Doylestown has had a Providential escape from destructive fires within its limits, or near by.

The earliest fire on record, we have any account of, and heretofore alluded to, was the burning of the farm house of David Kirkbride, 1809, that occupied the site of the present dwelling on the "Chapman farm," adjoining the borough on the north. What gave this fire a more serious feature, was the absence of the parents from home, leaving five small children in charge of two servants. They all escaped, however, but the house and contents were destroyed with the exception of one bed and bed clothes. The dwelling was immediately rebuilt and is the same as that now standing.

The first fire, within the borough limits proper, was at the dwelling of Crispin Blackfan, then Prothonotary of the county, the morning of June 4, 1822, but was extinguished before any serious damage had been done. No doubt the bucket brigade was entitled to the credit of putting out the fire, in the absence of any other artificial appliance for that purpose. Mr. Blackfan lived in a frame house on the south side of East State street, probably in the same house lately occupied by Mrs. VanHorne. Now comes a little by play in Doylestown's fire department, entitled "Locking the stable door after the horse is stolen," which is praticed to this day, and the piece will always be on the stage. As soon as the Blackfan fire was put out, and while the fright was on, Asher Miner, of the *Correspondent*, recommended that "a fire company be immediately formed," but his advice was not heeded. His recommendation was all right, but the villagers had not been badly enough frightened to take his advice.

Seven years later, on the morning of January 11, 1829, a fire of an unique character occurred in Doylestown. On the arrival of the Easton stage, the mail bag was discovered to be in flames and some excitement created, but was put out with little effort. A number of letters and papers were burned, but, beyond that, no damage was done. How the fire originated was never discovered.

The people of Doylestown were now three years cogitating over the recommendation of Asher Miner, in 1822, that "a fire company be immediately formed" before they got to work. They could not have better proved their conservative spirit. This led to the organization of the "Doylestown Fire Engine Company," the first of its kind here so far as we can learn. The meeting was advertized for Monday night, January 24, 1825, at 7 o'clock, at the house of Jacob Kohl[1], the notice stating, among other things, that "citizens disposed to become members are requested to be on hand." In the next issue of the *Patriot*, it is stated "the Engine is in complete repair and the apparatus of ladders, hook, etc., etc., are ready for service in any emergency." The officers elected were: Abraham Chapman, president; Timothy Smith, vice-president; John Pugh, treasurer; and William T. Rogers, secretary. Probably the "Doylestown Fire Engine Company" had come to grief in the next nine years, or been reorganized under a new name. This we infer, for, in 1834, the "Friendship Fire Company," of Doylestown, was undergoing a course of resussitation about the first of the year. The "machine" was refitted and embellished by "Mayer of the Green Tree," the artist-landlord of that popular old hostelry.

One of the most destructive fires, that ever took place in Doylestown, was the burning of the building, occupied by the *Democrat*, on the morning of February 4, 1836. It was then printed in a frame on the East side of north Main street opposite the present Fountain House on the site of the Stuckert building. The adjoining brick store of Charles Harvey, on the corner of State and Main streets, the site of Randall's hardware store, was also destroyed. The fire was discovered about two o'clock. In the building, besides the *Democrat* plant, were the watch making shop of Charles Savage, and the oyster saloon of Nathanial Hubbard. Everything was consumed and no insurance.

The frame building was owned by William H. Powell, and the

---

[1] Who kept the Ship tavern.

Democrat plant by John S. Bryan. The greater part of the store and household goods in Harvey's brick were saved by removal. The weather was intensely cold, but without wind, and the deep snow prevented the adjoining roofs catching fire. The dwelling of Mrs. Sharpless [2], just above, on the same side of Main atreet, was saved with difficulty. The engine turned out and did good service under the direction of Andrew Mayer, Jr., son of the landlord of the Green Tree. This was the first fire in Doylestown that entailed any considerable loss, estimated at $5,315. A public meeting, with Abraham Chapman in the chair, was shortly held at the tavern of Isaac W. James, the present Fountain House, and a committee appointed, for every township in the county, to solicit subscriptions to make good the loss. The exact amount collected we have never learned, and possibly it was not made public.

Our next fire was on the 26th of August, 1839, when an old frame house belonging to Timothy Smith, and the dwelling and barn of a Mr. Whitman, a brewer, on the north side of west State street, a few doors beyond the present Hamilton street, took fire. They were burned to the ground. As the engine was not in working order, the women and children turned out "to a man" and carried water in buckets from the Mansion House pump; and, as the reporter of the period makes no mention of the men doing anything, they probably looked on and "bossed the job" as is sometimes the case at present. The house and barn were insured in the Doylestown Insurance Company, and this was the first loss it met with after organizing.[3] What was the matter with the "machine" is not mentioned.

In 1841 Doylestown possessed a "Friendship Fire Engine Company;" we have no account of its exploits, but doubtless they would be interesting reading could they be got at. That year Lester Rich was president, Theodore T. Kinsey, secretary, and Henry Nightingale, "secretary pro tem," at a meeting held in the spring.

On June 30, 1842, Samuel Yardley's oil mill, near Doylestown, was burned down with the contents. There was a partial insurance on it. Mr. Yardley at the time was a leading merchant in Doylestown

---

2 At Doylestown, January 16, 1849, in the eighty-third year of her age, Mrs. Julia Sharpless, widow of John Sharpless, of Philadelphia. She resided in that city during its occupancy by General Howe's army, 1777-78.

3 The double stone dwelling, belonging to the late Robert Lewis, who occupied one end on the north side of West State street, was the brewery that was burned out.

on the corner of the present Armstrong block. The late John B. Pugh thought the mill destroyed was probably at Mechanics' Valley.

The old frame building that stood on the left hand side of the New Hope turnpike, just beyond the Catholic Church, was burned down the night of April 1, 1845. It was built in 1838, during the "Morus Multicaulis Craze," but, the enterprise proving a failure, the building was sold and passed into the possession of John S. Bryan the owner when it was burned down. The Multicaulis Craze was only second to the California gold excitement while it lasted, but the latter paid better.

The next fire in order, that visited Doylestown, was in August, 1856, when the barn of Jesse Armstrong, on the premises at the crossing of Main and Court streets, was burned by an incendary and completely destroyed with the contents. The town being without a fire engine, or the "machine" out of order, we do not remember which, a bucket brigade was organized and water taken from the "Town Pump," on the Thompson property adjoining and the supply kept up for three hours. The barn only was burned, and no insurance. A man named Weirman, was arrested and convicted of the offence. The barn was rebuilt and a second time burned, in 1885; and it was a curious coincidence, that the man, convicted of burning the barn in 1856, was in Doylestown the night the barn was burned in 1885, but was not arrested. The second barn was insured for $1,000. The following year, 1857, Doylestown was again visited by a fire, a board yard meeting the displeasure of an incendiary. This was the barn of Shade & Rotzell, on their board yard premises, the south side of East State street. It was fired one night in January and consumed with two horses, but the lumber was not burned. The ground was covered with snow at the time.

On Wednesday afternoon, April 5, 1869. what might have been a very destructive fire, broke out in Abel Stover's livery stable. It was discovered to be on fire, but burned to the foundation before the flames could be arrested. It was frame, 60 x 50 feet, nearly new, cost $1,200, and had an insurance of $1,000, but none on the contents. The net loss was $500. All the horses were saved, as well as Hulshizer & Larzelere's agriculture implement factory that was almost adjoining. The cause of the fire was a mystery.

The most considerable fire, the past twenty-five years, was the burning of Lewis Buckman's planning mill and sash factory on the night of January 19, 1881. The alarm was given about ten o'clock, when the fire company and a large portion of the population flocked to the scene of destruction. There was a fine head of water, but the fire had been burning too long to save the building and contents. There was a moderate snow on the ground, and the number of delicate women who turned out to witness the conflagration, was out of proportion to the energy of the men. The cause of the fire was never made known. The insurance covered part of the loss and the building was immediately rebuilt.

In 1893, a new fire department, called, "The Doylestown Fire Company, No. 1" was organized at a meeting held October 11, with the following officers; president, H. P. Beerer; vice-presidents, George Watson and William Raike; secretary, Frank N. Booz; treasurer, John Yardley; trustees, Frank Stover, Frank Hart, S. A. W. Patterson and John Donnelly; auditors, J. Evan Zorns, Walter Darlington, and Evan Morris, Jr. The permanent organization was completed at a meeting held October 18. The meetings were held for some time in the borough Council Chamber, but subsequently removed to the building on the Ross property, North Main street, adjoining the National Bank. It was remodeled and improved at a cost of $600 to fit it for the purpose of the new tenant. This was in 1897, and was still occupied, 1902. Subsequently, the company purchased an eligible lot on Shewell avenue, near Monument Place, to erect a new building on, which is now, September, 1902, in course of erection. The corner stone was laid August 26, with proper ceremony, the Hon. Robert M. Yardley making a suitable address. The company is equipped with all necessary fire apparatus, engine, hose, hook and ladder, etc., of a modern make and is punctual at fires. The officers, at this writing, are: president, Henry A. James; first vice-president, E. F. Taylor; second vice-president, Harry W. Kelly; secretary, A. Lincoln Layman; assistant secretary, George S. Hotchkiss; financial secretary, Silas A. Selser; treasurer, John Yardley; chief engineer, John P. Stillwell; assistant chief engineer, George P. Brock; trustees, W. Harry Cadwallader, W. G. Benner, John Hart, W. Harry Smith and John P. Stilwell. With an active, energetic fire company, such as the present, the borough feels more secure.

The Mount Olivet Colored Baptist Church, a small, frame structure on Lafayette street, in the western section of the borough, was destroyed by fire, with the organ and books, on Saturday evening, August 21, 1897. It was thought to have been set on fire by an incendiary, but the truth was never known. Some believed dissensions in the congregation may have led to it. The building was insured for $150. The last fire, down to that period, was the burning of the barn belonging to the Catholic Church, on Sunday night, October 15, 1897, but we know neither its origin nor the amount of loss. In addition to the fires enumerated, there were a few others, whose date cannot be given. Several years ago the cottage, formerly belonging to the late Commodore Shaw, U. S. N., on the northeast corner of Academy lane and East street, was set fire to and burned to the ground. It was probably the work of an incendiary, as it was burned in the night, and was unoccupied at the time. Who set the building on fire was never known. A building was also burned at the railroad station, either by accident or design, more recently, date not known; and a barn, on the property of James Ruckman, east State street, was destroyed by fire in the early evening, thought to have been the work of an incendiary. The fire department was called out and the adjoining buildings were saved. One of the latest fires, in Doylestown, was the burning of the lunch-box factory of Ex-sheriff Nicholas on Centre street, near West, the morning of November 4, 1899. The building was insured.

On Friday morning, March 28, 1895, a fire broke out in the cellar of John G. Randall's house, on east Court street, but was put out before it had seized hold of the wood work. A leaky gas meter which ignited from an adjacent heater was discovered by a member of the family, who saw the smoke coming up through the floor. She gave the alarm, and two wheelmen, Walter Edals and Samuel Benner, passing by, responded, and, entering the cellar, found the gas meter surrounded by flames. A few buckets of water thrown over it, the gas shut off from the machine, and the devouring element was under control. A few minutes delay might have caused a fire it would have been more difficult to put out. As it was, a large number of persons turned out, and the fire company had the hose carriages taken to the scene. Mr. and Mrs. Randall were from home at the time.

The only fire in our borough, since the new century came in, was an attempt to burn the barn of James Barrett, February 10, 1902. It was doubtless the work of an incendiary. The fire company was early on the ground, and the barn saved with a loss of about $300, fully covered by insurance.

Doylestown, Old and New.

XXXIV.
Odds and Ends of History.

The Town Pump, so called, a name given it in the long ago, but some time passed into history, stood on the premises of the late Robert Thompson, where Shewell avenue debouches into Monument Place at the crossing of Main and Court streets. After being long used by the general public, more than by the owner, so long "the memory of man runneth not to the contrary," the pump tree was taken out and the well covered over. This was many years ago and had been forgotten until uncovered in June, 1897, while digging a trench to introduce borough water into the dwelling. When the pump was in use, several families got their drinking water there, and the *Democrat* and *Intelligencer* offices filled their boilers from it. In the youth of this old well, the water was raised "from the vasty deep" by a long sweep, but, subsequently, a windlass brought to the surface

"The old oaken bucket, the iron bound bucket,
The moss-covered bucket which hangs in the well"

filled with its delightful, cooling beverage. The well was probably dug by Dr. Hugh Meredith, when he built his dwelling near the Armstrong corner, the last quarter of the eighteenth century. When Armstrong's barn was burned, August, 1856, a bucket brigade was organized and the pump manned; and after three hours steady pumping the water in the well was not perceptibly lowered.

Thompson's pump was not the only one that "comes down to us from a former generation," but the author has in mind two others that did duty in the not distant past. The oldest of these, and possibly older than the Thompson pump, supplied the Ship Tavern with water, that stood on the site of Lenape Building. It was probably dug when the old hostelry was built, one hundred and twenty-five years ago, and covered over when the new building was erected, 1874. It was one of the most famous wells in town, and repeated efforts were made to pump the water out, on one occasion with horse power, but without success. Tradition says that when it was dug the water came in so rapidly the well diggers were driven out leaving their tools behind, but were never recovered, and are still at the bottom. This old well is under the Main street pavement opposite the drug store. There are, doubtless, other old wells in town, as ancient as the ones we have named, but we have not struck them.

The third pump, to which we allude, long half tradition, half historic in truth, is at the corner of west Court street and Harvey Avenue, on the lot of Wynne James. On March 13, 1902, while laborers were digging a hole for a trolley pole, they struck a large flat stone that gave out a hollow sound. Investigation showed that it covered an old well, and was probably placed there when Reuben F. Sheetz owned the property, thirty-five years before. It is said to have had a pump in it prior to the water works, and that all the neighbors were supplied with water from it. It is further claimed that the old Doylestown tavern, of 1745, stood on the site of the Wynne James house, formally Pugh Dungan's, and that the well, which supplied it with water, was covered over in the street. There is a little testimony here, as to the location of the Doyle tavern, but not enough to sustain the claim. When Harvey Avenue was opened, a few years ago, another well was uncovered several feet from this. As west Court street that runs in front of the Wynne James house, was not opened until 1807, sixty-two years after the Doyle tavern was licensed, a public house would hardly have been located so far from the highway.

When the Thompson frame dwelling, on the west side of Monument Place, and joint owner of the "Town pump" and the well it stood in, were taken down in recent years, to make some improvements, it was probably one of the oldest frame houses in the borough, almost next to the Russell house in Germany. The date of 1832, on the water spout, when that was removed several years ago, indicated when that part of the building was erected, but the rear part, and the old pork house, taken down many years before, were much older. The Robert Thompson stone dwelling, covered many years with a wholesome yellow wash, was built about the same period. The *Democrat* was published in the building, in the late twenties while General Roger's was its editor and proprietor, and the author remembers, when a small boy, accompanying his father there on one occasion. The door was in the east end. In attempting to remove the Thompson house, in May, 1898, a recent heavy rain had so moistened the ground, the building got out of plum, and fell down with a crash, becoming a total loss.

On Thursday afternoon, September 4, 1816, a large sea eagle perched himself on the vane of the Court house steeple and excited the curiosity of all who beheld it. Some one of the lookers on, belonging to the village, name not given, brought down the strange visitor with a fowling piece. His wings measured six feet from tip to tip.

In 1819, Abraham Myers, owner of the Turk mill dam, advertized he would drain it, as it had not been disturbed since about 1750, if his friends would subscribe liberally enough to cover the expense; he stated he had been repeatedly requested to do so to obtain the extraordinary quantity of turtles, fishes and etc. in it. Myers sent out subscription papers stating the job was to be completed by the 7th of July and the dam would be kept open for three days; but, as nothing more was heard of the affair, the project was probably not carried out. Who knows how often this dam has been cleaned out in recent years?

The 4th of July was celebrated, 1819 at Doylestown; Charles E. DuBois reading the Declaration of Independence, and Samuel Aaron delivering the oration, with a social dinner at the Mansion House, at which Wm. H. Rowland was chairman and Lewis S. Coryell vice-president. The same afternoon the Union Guards, Captain William T. Rogers; met in a wood adjacent to the village. After drilling, Dr. James H. Rich delivered an address, the company partook of a cold repast, and drank toasts, accompanied by music and the discharge of small arms. Magill's Rifle Rangers turned out on the same occasion, but what part they played is not announced.

At that day there was quite a flood of rustic poetry printed in the county papers, dedicated to young ladies, and a newspaper was not thought properly equipped without at least one regular poetical contribution each week. This was kept up, down to the days of the modern magazine. In this regard our county papers kept abreast with the times. In the issue of the *Democrat*, of February 5, 1822, appeared some verses by "Claudine" addressed to an unamed Miss of Doylestown, which opened

> "Yes maiden, I love thee, the rose on thy cheek,
> And the glance of thy dark eye thy loveliness speaks
> Thy lips of brightest coral, that dark flowing hair,
> And thy bosom of snow, says that beauty is there."

In the issue of the *Correspondent*, of September 7, 1823, John Fox was called the "Dictator General of the Democratic party," evidence that politics was pretty warm. On November 13th following, the "Democratic Republicans," a queer combination as we look at politics now, met at Valentine Opp's tavern, and partook of an entertainment on the election of John Andrew Shultz to the office of Governor. Samuel D. Ingham was president, and there was drinking of toasts and firing of cannon.

In the *Correspondent* of March 1, 1824, we find the following paragraph; "The delegates, to the Harrisburg Convention, from Bucks county, started from the public house of William Watts, either the Court Inn, or the Indian Queen that stood on the site of the National bank, on the 28th ultimo, under a cheer from the citizens and loud huzzas for General Andrew Jackson." At that early day there was no public conveyance to carry delegates to state conventions. A Polk and Dallas jubilee was held in the Court House, January 8, 1845; there was a procession with a military company and a brass band: Colonel Reah Frazier, Lancaster, delivered an address, and the affair closed with a banquet at the Mansion house, where toasts were drunk and brief speeches made, Dr. Charles H. Mathews presiding. At that period politics and religion held closer relations than at present, and ministers of the gospel took a part in political functions that would hardly be tolerated now. On April 29, 1828, the Rev. Thomas B. Montanye, pastor of the Southampton Baptist Church, was chairman of a "Democratic Republican" meeting held in the Court house, called to boom the nomination of John Quincy Adams for President.

The people of Doylestown, in the past, were no more unmindful of the calls of patriotism than at present, nor did they hesitate to express themselves through the pocket or otherwise. The struggle, of the Greeks with the Turks, excited universal attention. On Wednesday evening, March 14, 1872, a meeting, held in the Court house to raise funds, was numerously attended. William Watts was called to the chair, Mathias Morris appointed secretary, and a committee, consisting of John Pugh, Abraham Chapman, John Benezet, Charles E. DuBois and William T. Rogers, was raised to receive contributions, and Mathias Morris, Henry Chapman and Robert Bethell, Jr. to prepare an address to the public. The amount collected was not reported.

The newspapers of the period record, as an unusual occurrence, that in the spring of 1830, there was an extraordinary flight of wild pigeons; the *Democrat* of March 30 says Doylestown, with streets, woods, orchards, fields etc. " has been inundated with pigeons, and all persons, saints and sinners, office-holders and commoners, all alike, have been going "pop!" "pop!" "pop!" Pigeons were eaten at every meal, "roasted, fried and on the shell." The editor says, that on Sunday morning a flock of pigeons lit in the orchard of an old friend of his, a church member, and, in spite of the sabbath, he took his gun and killed twenty-two.

The story of Mrs. Ross, rescuing a Jackson hickory pole from its would-be destroyers, as a bit of contemporaneous history is too good to be lost, and fits in with our historic miscellany. It was in 1832, Jackson's second race for President, and politics was at flood tide. The Democrats had erected a handsome hickory pole at the crossing of Court and Main streets, just below where the monument stands. One night the Federalists attempted to cut down the pole, but Mrs. Ross being awake, and hearing them, leaped out of bed, ran down stairs and out of doors, and put her arms around the pole, saving it from the assailants. It created quite a sensation in the political and social world.

The first effort, made in Doylestown, to provide the borough with a town clock, was in 1842, but not successful. Shortly after and we believe in the same year, an article appeared in the *Democrat* of May 18, signed "Punctuality," which spoke of the town clock effort in this wise:

"Not long ago a project was set on foot to obtain a clock by subscription, and a sum nearly sufficient was pledged, when "Cold water," very good in its place, quenched the ardor of those engaged in it, and the matter was abandoned." That project was never revived, but passed into history, and the town clock question slumbered until 1874, a third of a century, when a public spirited and generous woman presented a clock to the Doylestown Improvement Company which was put at the north-west corner of Lenape Building, where it still marks the time, and is in good running order.

Governor Francis R. Shunk, came to Doylestown on a visit to his daughter, Mrs. Chapman, November 22, 1845. In the evening with his suite, he attended the lecture of Colonel John W. Forney, in Beneficial Hall, and, after the lecture, there was an informal reception. The Governor was welcomed with a speech, by the Hon. Samuel D. Ingham, at New Hope, when he came into the state, and his arrival at Doylestown was announced by the firing of cannon. While here he was the guest of Henry Chapman, Esq., his son-in-law. He returned to Philadelphia, via Norristown, the following Monday morning.

An attempt was made on Friday night, November 28, 1845, to rob the store of Samuel A. Smith and John J. Brock, who kept where Metlar keeps on south Main street.

In 1845, after the destructive fire at Allentown, which laid a large portion of the town in ashes, a public meeting was held at Doylestown to contribute to the wants of the sufferers. Abraham Chapman was called to the chair, and John S. Brown, of the *Intelligencer*, secretary. A committee was appointed to solicit subscriptions and several hundred dollars were subscribed.

Although the inhabitants of Doylestown have seldom been the victims of accident that destroy life, we recall two cases in the long past. The first was in the summer, of 1832, when William Cox, while erecting a building in Buckingham, by some mishap fell from it and was so badly injured he shortly died. He built, and lived in, the brick house on east State street, where Dr. Frank Swartzlander, the elder, now resides, the other subsequent owners beside Dr. Swartzlander, being William Stokes and the late General John S. Bryan. Mr. Cox was the father of Charles C. Cox, of Doylestown, who, after a life of varied experience in business and military service in the field during the Civil War, has returned to his native town to spend the evening of his days. The other accident happened to Dr. John B. Pettitt, son of Elnathan Pettitt, landlord of what is now the Fountain House, whose horse ran away with him, Monday evening, May 26, 1845, returning from a professional visit. He was thrown out of his sulky and injured so badly he died in a few minutes. He was a young man, and recently married to a daughter of General Samuel A. Smith, of Doylestown. These fatal accidents are referred to elsewhere.

On the death of Henry Clay, who died June 30, 1852, memorial services were held in the Presbyterian Church the Friday following. Places of business were closed and men of all parties united in paying tribute to his memory. An eulogy was pronounced by Rev. Silas M. Andrews, and an ode, composed by Caleb E. Wright, Esq., was sung;

> List what peal is breaking
> Over the land and sea,
> All hearts to sorrow waking;
> It moveth solemnly,
> Mournfully it swelleth
> Where rosy morning springs,
> Where midday's glory dwelleth,
> And Evening folds her wings.
> The waves seem listening to the strain,
> As silently they sweep,
> Borne by the winds o'er stream and plain,
> O'er mountain dale and deep;
> So all eyes are weeping,
> All hearts are sorrow's prey,
> Long where his dust lies sleeping,
> Columbia mourns for Clay.
> List, list, to the funeral knell.

In Doylestown, December 9, 1834, John Fritzinger at the age of eighty-six.

The deceased was a Hessian soldier captured at Trenton, December 26, 1776. On refusing to be exchanged, or enter the American army, tradition says he was taken before Washington, who asked what his trade was, and he replied he could "make glazed powder;" whereupon he was sent to one of the powder mills on the Perkiomen, and employed there during the war. At its close he married and went to work. In 1805, he purchased, of James Thomas, New Britain, the farm of one hundred acres, now known as the "Fordhook Farm." He lived there until probably the spring of 1832, when he moved into Doylestown where he died. He lived on the east side of South Main street, probably in the house occupied by Mrs. Walton, His will is dated March 27, 1832, but not proved until January 5, 1836, his widow, Catharine, being executrix and Dr. James S. Rich, executor. Among his sons were John W. and Henry, with daughters and grandchildren. His real estate was not sold until 1837. What became of the family, after this time, we do not know.

Peter Jackson was the first colored man of any distinction, in Doylestown, that we have note of. He was here as early as in the twenties, in the service of Judge William Watts, and to his death, off and on. He was a tall, good looking man, and, in the heyday of the volunteer militia, attended the trainings and waited on the ranking officers. Jackson was married and raised a family, and, in later years, we remember when his daughters lived in some of our families. On

SAMUEL HALL.

the reputation of their father they held their heads pretty high. "Sammy" Price, who preceded "Governor" Wells as "Town Cryer," we remember well, but do not recall his history. He did not cut as distinguished a figure as Jackson and Wells.

Richard Wells, sailing under the name of "Dick" Wells, was prominent in colored society, and cut an unique figure in Doylestown for several years; born a slave at Fredericksburg, Va., whence himself and mother escaped to Chicago by the underground railroad. He was in the Civil War, first as a cook and then as an enlisted soldier, and came to Doylestown, 1874. He was proud of his military reecord. On the death of "Sammy" Price, "Governor" Wells, by which name he was known to every one, became "Town Cryer," of which he was as proud as if he were the "Grand Mogul," and held the office to his death in 1895, when he

> "Laid down the shovel and the hoe
> And hung up the fiddle and the bow."

John Walker was probably the oldest man who ever made Doylestown his home, but we do not remember when he came here. He was borne near Carversville, Buckingham township, April 6, 1799; the son of Robert and Asenath Walker and was of English descent. He was brought up on his father's farm, and twice married. At one period in his life he was an extensive limeburner. On his ninty-sixth birthday, April 6, 1895, many friends called on Mr. Walker, and the occasion was a pleasant one to him. He died April 29, 1898.

William Carr, who lived in Doylestown a long time, and was a prominent figure in our village life for twenty-five years, was the youngest son of John Carr, of Warwick township, where he was born September 12, 1789. He was a man of intelligence and excentricities, and served one term as Clerk of the Orphan's Court, besides being deputy in other county offices. He took great interest in Masonry, in which Order he stood high, and superintended the building of the Masonic Temple on Chestnut street, Philadelphia, half a century ago. He died at Allentown, Pa., March 10, 1872, whither he had removed a few years pervious. Mr. Carr was never married. He built the dwelling on the north-east corner of Court and Pine streets in which Mrs. John L. DuBois lives, and also the one that stood on the site of Dr. Groff's house, adjoining, which the Michener family formerly owned, and lived in. It was the first dwelling erected there.

Thomas W. Trego, who died here September 12, 1901, while not a native, was long a resident of Doylestown, and a member of one of the oldest families in the county. He was of Huguenot ancestry which settled here, 1682, and was born at Pineville, May 13, 1816. He received his education at the country schools, finishing at the Park School, Burlington, N. J., with a winters' experience in conducting the Philadelphia school of Charles B. Trego, his relative, while the latter was a member of the Legislature. At twenty-two, Mr. Trego went west, where he had a wide business experience, as a governor surveyor, clerk on a Mississippi steamboat, superintendent of a smelting works, and keeping a hardware store, bringing up at Chicago in the lumber business. He remained there until the close of the Civil War, when his yearning for home brought him back to Bucks county, buying what is now the "Fordhook Farm" near Doylestown. He returned to Chicago, remaining a few years, when he again returned, and settled in our borough, where he resided to his death. He married Elizabeth Baker Betts, of this county, 1851, who with four children, survived him.

Thomas Trego was a student all his life and, while deeply interested in public affairs, was never a candidate for office. He took especial interest in the cause of education, and, at one time, was one of the proprietors of the Doylestown Seminary.

At Doylestown, October 23, 1893, Daniel Smith, in his ninety-eighth year.

Daniel Smith was the son of Joseph Smith, the first person in Bucks county to burn anthracite coal for fuel, and, together with his brother Robert, made the first plow with an iron mould board. This plow, patented, 1800, led to the establishment of the industrial plant at Smithtown, Tinicum township, for their manufacture. The Smith Plow revolutionized agriculture. The patent for the Smith Plow, with John Adam's signature to it, hangs in the room of the Bucks County Historical Society.

At Doylestown, September 3, 1901, Robert Lewis, in the eighty-second year of his age. Mr. Lewis was connected with old historic families of the county, and, for a number of years, his parents, Nathan and Margaret Whittier Lewis, lived in the Keith house, Upper Makefield township, headquarters of Washington in the Revolution, immediately prior to the battle of Trenton.

At Doylestown, January 1, 1902, Mrs. Hannah Paul Bodder, at the age of ninety-one years, the oldest woman in Doylestown.

Mrs. Bodder, the only daughter of James and Susan Bryan, was born in Springfield township, and married Dr. Francis L. Bodder, who died November 20, 1846. He not only practiced medicine but kept a country store for many years. The author remembers their pleasant home, especially the beautiful flower garden that surrounded it. After the death of her husband, Mrs. Bodder kept the store for several years, when she sold out and removed to Doylestown. She was the mother of five children, all sons. The eldest, Lycurgus S., was elected County Treasurer, 1863, serving one term. Mrs. Bodder was a sister of the late General John S. Bryan, for several years one of the Associate Judges of the county.

Among the oldest men living in Doylestown, at this writing, is Jeremiah Gunagan, born in Philadelphia, November 20, 1820. He first came here in 1838, but, after staying a short time, went away; then returned again March 1, 1842, since which time our borough has been his residence.

At Doylestown, September 18, 1837, Isaac Lacey, a soldier of the Revolution, at the age of ninety-seven.

At Doylestown, May 14, 1842, Phebe Dunlap, widow of Andrew Dunlap, in her eighty-first year.

At Lambertville, N. J., August 26, 1827, Rev. James M. Laughlin, of Doylestown and pastor of New Britain Baptist Church, aged about sixty years.

At Doylestown, June 26, 1836, Sarah Newton, relict of Jonas Newton, who had a son a missionary in Northern India.

In the hospital on Staten Island, October 7, 1830, John Godshalk, seaman, formerly of Doylestown, aged twenty-three years.

At Philadelphia, January 8, 1831, Lauretta Kohl, daughter of Jacob Kohl, of Doylestown, aged eighteen years, one month and twelve days.

Oliver P. Hines, son of John Hines, was born on Pine Run, just beyond the borough limits, on March 26, 1812. When quite a lad, he rode post for General Wm. T. Rogers, then proprietor and editor of the Doylestown *Democrat*. He traversed the county on horse back, carrying his bible which he studied in route, for which he was much commended by his Sunday school. At the proper age, young Hines was apprenticed to William Cox, of Doylestown, to learn the carpenter trade, fitting himself for a future business life. When out of his time, he went west, settling at Columbus, Ohio, in 1834. He followed his trade, as a carpenter and builder, until he had a start in the world when he engaged in other business, gradually branching out, finally becoming a banker and amassing a handsome fortune. Mr. Hines married Mary Thomas, February 7, 1837, and died at Columbus, April 24, 1889, in his seventy-eighth year universally lamented. He made occasional visits to the land of his birth and kept in touch with relatives here. Oliver P. Hines was the uncle of our townsman, Charles C. Cox, and first cousin to the late Dr. A. J. Hines. We hope his example may prove a lesson to other Doylestown boys, who are born without the traditional silver spoon in their mouth.

Doylestown, Old and New.

XXXV.
Farewell to the Nineteenth Century.

As we approach the end of the nineteenth century, there is evidence of our business life reaching out on new lines, and other occupations taken up, that will yield profitable employment to those first in the field. This was the case in the world of finance, and there was a call for additional "money changers" with the increase of business. As our readers will call to mind, our first banking institution was established, 1832-'33, and prospered from the beginning. It had the field to itself for a quarter of a century, when the need of an additional bank being felt, one was opened. Following this, was an interval of twenty-nine years, before Doylestown felt the want of another financial institution and there was an immediate response, this time on a new line. The necessity of a trust company, being realized, one was established, its doors opened, and prosperity waited on it. This was the first of its kind in the county. The success, of the Bucks County Trust Company, doubtless opened the eyes of others, who had spare capital to invest, but, whether this was the case or not, the Doylestown Trust Company was established in 1896.

In the fall and winter of 1895-6, several gentleman discussed the propriety of organizing a second Trust Company when they met socially. By the opening of spring, the matter had received such favorable consideration they resolved to emphasize it by calling an informal meeting. This was held in the old Harvey house, west side of north Main street corner of Court, about the first of March, at which a conclusion was reached in favor of taking action and a name agreed upon. The next meeting, by the stockholders, was in the room of the Doylestown Library, Lenape building, on Saturday March 28, Dr. William H. Kirk being called to the chair and Henry O. Harris appointed secretary. Before adjourning by-laws were adopted and some other necessary preliminary work done. At a subsequent meeting of the stockholders the following board of directors was elected; Arthur Chapman, John Hart, C. H. Magill, Harry J. Shoemaker, Edwin R. Jones, Harry Wilkinson, Mahlon K. Dungan, Henry S. Beidler, William Stuckert, Samuel Z. Freed and Henry O. Harris. The directors held their first meeting the same day in the library room, and elected the following officers: President, John Hart; Vice-president, Arthur Chapman; Henry O. Harris, Secretary and Trust Officer; and John Yardley, Treasurer.

At a meeting of the directors, April 8, the Act of Assembly passed May 9, 1889, with its supplements, applying to such corporations, was adopted; the Charter was issued by the Secretary of the Commonwealth, March 24, 1896, and the first Tuesday of each month agreed upon for stated meetings. The old building of the Doylestown National Bank was purchased, in the fall of 1897, the company, previous to that time, transacting its business in the old Hart banking building where it opened in 1896, and removed to the new quarters in the course of a few weeks.

In May, 1895, an additional local society was organized which seemed to be called for by the condition of things. This is known as the "Village Improvement Association," spoken of as the "V. I. A," and was put on foot by the ladies with the intent of improving the good looks of the County's Capital. They began their work by declaring war against throwing waste paper in the streets or on the pavements. Their next move was to purchase a street sprinkler to lay the dust, and is much in evidence from May to September, with beneficial results when it don't rain. The dues are fifty cents a year, families enjoying the benefits of the sprinkler being taxed seventy-five cents a month for the season. There is a visable improvement in the appearance and condition of the streets. The water is given by the Borough Council. The society was organized with thirty-seven members and the following officers: Mrs. Isabella Watson, president; Miss Ella D. Smith, secretary; and Mrs. Henry O. Harris, treasurer. The present officers, 1902, are Miss Mary L. DuBois, president; Mrs. Irvin M. James, secretary; and Miss Miriam Watson, treasurer, with a membership of fifty-four. The society has its quarters in the brick dwelling of Mrs. N. C. James, on north Main street, where the members transact their business and meet socially. During the subsequent winter, the "V. I. A.'s" grafted a new feature on their curriculum, by giving it a literary turn, a paper being read before it on the "Uses of Local History." The room was filled with an audience of fifty attentive listeners.

At this period there were indications of an improved style of buildings for business purposes. We have already noticed the Sheetz and Hellyer mercantile houses and now call attention to the handsome block erected by John Hart, on the west side of north Main street between the Fountain House and Court street. In the meantime Mr. Hart had purchased the Harvey property, and began his improvments on the south end. Pulling down the old frame drug store wherein Dr. Harvey dispensed remedies for half a century, he built on its site, in 1896, a three-story building 28 x 64 feet, of red brick with Indiana lime stone trimmings. The first floor is occupied by a modern drug store, with every appliance the business requires, lighted by a large bulk window of plate glass set in copper frames; the second and third stories are divided into offices, and the building throughout, lighted by electricity and heated by steam. In 1900, Mr. Hart completed his improvements of the Harvey property, by the erection of a larger three-story building of the same material and a corresponding style of architecture, but more elaborate in finish, and mainly fitted up for offices. The two buildings make the handsomest block in the county, and we do not believe it is excelled in the state, in a town of the size.

One of the most interesting events witnessed at Doylestown, took place in the Court House, October 21, 1899. This was the presentation to Bucks County, by the Hon. John Wanamaker, of an historic painting, entitled the " Rescue of the Colors," of the 104th Pennsylvania regiment, at the Battle of Fair Oaks, May 31, 1862. The canvas, eleven by eight feet depicts the scene when the combatants on both sides are reaching out for the flags, the men of the regiment coming off victorous. The painting, consigned to the custody of the Bucks County Historical Society, hangs in the Arbitration room, in the Court House, but will be transferred to the new historical building when the Society moves into it.

The citizens of Doylestown made the occasion a public affair, and the following committees were appointed to conduct it:

Invitation: Fred Constantine, Charles C. Cox, George W. McIntosh, Winfield Donaldson, John G. Randall, John O. James, T. O. Atkinson;

Reception: Dr. Frank Swartzlander, Hon. Harman Yerkes, General W. W. H. Davis, H. B. Eastburn, Esq., Alfred Paschall, Henry Lear, Esq., Hon. Robert M. Yardley:

Finance: George P. Brock, John Yardley, George Watson, C. Howard Magill, Patrick B. Trainor, Richard W. Livezey, Charles D. Bigley, Capt. Moses K. Atler, Fred A. Clayton, William C. Ryan, Esq., James Barrett.

Music: George P. Brock and S. A. Selser.

Court House: Charles A. Cuffel, Willis Wall, Harry Cadwallader, John Bigell, Adam Frankenfield, Henry S. Murfit, Esq., Philip Kellar, E. F. Taylor, Isaiah Sellers, J. Harrison Wilson, H. C. McIntosh, Charles A. Vandegrift.

Hanging Picture: Dr. Frank Swartzlander, General Davis, E. A. Trego.

Luncheon: H. S. Murfit, Esq., Phillip Keller, E. F. Taylor, J. Harrison Wilson, Charles A. Vandegrift.

The following is a copy of the printed programme, as it was carried out:

At the Court House, Doylestown,
On Saturday, October 21, 1899.

Upon the Presentation of Trego's Military Picture, Depicting an Event in the History of the 104th Pennsylvania Regiment at the Battle of Fair Oaks.

"The Rescue of the Colors."

To Bucks County, Whence the Regiment Went Forth to The War for the Union, in 1861.

Music . . . . Germania Band of Quakertown
Opening Remarks . . . . Dr. Joseph Thomas of Quakertown
Invocation . . . . Rev. Jacob Bellville D. D. of Germantown
Music . . . . Band
The Story of The Rescue of the Colors . . . . General Davis
Music . . . . Band
Presentation of the Picture, "Rescue of the Colors," to Bucks County, in the Custody of the Bucks County Historical Society
    Hon. John Wanamaker
Music . . . . Band
Response to Presentation . . . . Hon. Harman Yerkes
Benediction . . . . Rev. N. C. Fetter
Music . . . . Band

The exercises began with the arrival of Honorable John Wanamaker, the invited guests and surviving members of the 104th, who were met at the station by a procession, composed of the Germania Band, Company G, 6th Regt., N. G. of Pa., Bodine Post, G. A. R. and Reception Committee and were escorted to the 104th Monument. In the procession was Sergt. W. Purcell, of White Haven, wearing the medal Congress presented him for saving the colors from the enemy.

The court room, where the formal presentation of the picture took place, was crowded beyond the doors when the band opened the exercises by playing "The Flag is Still There." It was 2 o'clock when Hon. Robert M. Yardley, of Doylestown, stepped in front of the picture which was veiled with an American flag, and introduced Dr. Joseph Thomas, of Quakertown, the presiding officer, in a few complimentary words. Dr. Thomas spoke briefly, in calling the house to order, and the exercises were proceeded with according to the programme. After General Davis had told "The Story of the Rescue," Mr. Wanamaker presented the painting, prefacing it with an eloquent address, in which he paid the regiment, as well as the county, a high compliment, saying, in conclusion:

"The bed rock of American thought is the distinct idea that the loyalty of its citizens is not set upon some men holding power to rule it, but it is imbedded upon a flag, that represents the law and constitution, guaranteeing equal rights to all men.

Kindle newer love for the flag. You are part of an association mighty in its achievements, not to be forgotten long after the last of its members have gone to honorable graves. If we are true to ourselves; if we are true to the teaching of the principles of the government; if we honestly administer the offices, and give obedience to law, the future of this country is safe.

* * * * * * *

"Let us cultivate a stronger love for the flag, and, by example and precept, teach the children never to pass it without saluting it, so that, in course of time, it may become the common custom of all people of America."

The Hon. Harman Yerkes was now presented by the chairman, who accepted the picture, on behalf of the people of Bucks county, in befitting terms, and returned their thanks to the generous donor. There were several telling passages in Judge Yerkes' address, the key note being a quotation from Milton, that

> "Peace hath her victories
> No less renowed than war."

Sergeant Pursell was next called for by the chairman, but was so overcome by the ovation that awaited him, he could only say in response, "I only did my duty." This brought down the house. The artist, William T. Trego, was presented to the audience, which heartily applauded.

Other addresses were made, by Hon. Irving P. Wanger, Representative of the district in Congress, and General B. F. Fisher, of Philadelphia. When the chairman called upon General Davis to tell the story of the "Rescue of the Colors," Miss Susie Swartzlander, the young daughter of Dr. Frank Swartzlander, pulled the cord; and, as the flag, veiling the picture, fell exposing the scene so realistically portrayed by the artist's brush, there was a general exclamation of delight, and applause from the large audience. The exercises were concluded with a benediction by the Rev. N. C. Fetter, followed by the band playing several fine pieces. The audience viewed the beautiful painting with great pleasure. The occasion will never be forgotten by those present at the presentation of the picture.

On the evening of October 23, 1899 a meeting was held in the office of H. J. Shoemaker, for the purpose of organizing a new industry at Doylestown, a worsted mill, at which the following persons were present: R. M. Yardley, H. L. Scheetz, A. L. Martin, S. G. Price, Crossley Holmes, H. J. Shoemaker, S. A. Hellyer, David Davies, H. W. Kelley, H. S. Beidler, J. F. Long, Harry Fluck, William Aveyard, M. K. Dungan, Joseph Wilson and John Yardley. R. M. Yardley was chosen chairman, and John Yardley, secretary. Among other business, transacted at the preliminary meeting was the following:

On motion the meeting resolved to procure a charter, that the name of the corporation shall be the "Doylestown Worsted Company," with a board of eleven directors, viz; Messrs. R. M. Yardley, Shoemaker, Fluck, Hellyer, Wilson, Dungan, Price, Scheetz, Aveyard, Holmes and Beidler who were elected for the first year; Messrs. Dungan, Shoemaker, and Long were appointed a committee to procure a charter, and the treasurer was authorized to collect ten per cent. of the stock subscribed, on November 1, 1899. The meeting now adjourned.

Immediately the meeting of stockholders adjourned, the directors of the company met at the same place and organized by the election of Robert M. Yardley, president; Henry S. Beidler, treasurer; and John Yardley, secretary. On motion, committees were appointed to purchase real estate and erect buildings, draw the necessary papers

MONUMENT 104TH REGIMENT, 1867

and draft by-laws. The company purchased the necessary looms and other machinery in England, Mr. Holmes, being sent there for that purpose. The charter was duly granted and put on record, and by-laws adopted. The boilers were purchased in Boston and the manufactory was in running order by the spring of 1900. Down to the present time the venture has not been a success.

The most impressive memorial services, witnessed in Doylestown, were in honor of the late President McKinley, who fell by the hand of an assassin. They were held in the court room, Thursday afternoon, September 19, 1901, in the presence of a thousand persons, from the borough and vicinity. The room was draped with emblems of mourning, a likeness of the dead President, on an easel framed in crepe and the national colors, and a chorus of fifty singers, accompanied by a violin; and a quartette of horns, occupied seats near the left entrance to the rotunda. The exercises were opened by Hugh B. Eastburn, Esq., chairman of the committee, in some brief remarks recalling the sad event that had called them together. He was followed by addresses from Judge Harman Yerkes, who spoke, particularly, of the lesson to be drawn from the sad and tragic taking off of the President, Henry Lear, Esq., who referred to him as a public man, whose acts of a busy and distinguished career had crowded one another, and whose death had been equally great with his life, and closed by the Hon. Robert M. Yardley, who was in Congress with Mr. McKinley, and spoke of him as a man, statesman and citizen. At intervals, between these addresses, the chorus sang, "Nearer my God To Thee," "Lead Kindly Light" and "Rock of Ages," with organ accompaniment. There was a complete cessation of business from two to five o'clock, and the Court House bell was tolled for three hours. Many private houses, places of business and public buildings bore emblems of mourning for the country's dead President.

Before taking leave of our patient readers, who have followed us through the decades of a hundred and fifty years, we will step across the line into the twentieth century, glance a moment at the Doylestown of to-day and compare the new with the old.

In 1750, what is now the seat of Justice of Bucks county, was but a cross roads, two highways connecting the Delaware with the Schuylkill. The hamlet gathered here consisted, at most, of half a dozen families living in log houses, with a blacksmith shop, a tavern and a pioneer store. By the end of the century, the population had grown to about one hundred and twenty-five with a corresponding increase in the number of neighboring settlers. In order, therefore, to make an intelligent comparison of then with now, we ask the reader to turn back to Chapter five, entitled "Historic Walk" taken soon after the nineteenth century came in. He will notice a remarkable change, and, at first, can hardly realize that it is real.

Doylestown is no longer a "pent up Utica," but a suburban borough and county seat of 3,500 inhabitants, with all the appliances of modern civilization. The streets are lined with comfortable dwellings, many of them handsome, built of bricks or stone, and a few of wood; with paved sidewalks, lighted with gas and electricity, and, in the residential sections, the front yards are smiling with flowers, and every dwelling is supplied with an abundance of pure spring water. The public buildings, court house, jail, high school, National bank and churches are the equal of any county capital in the state; the stores, and other places of business, are stocked with goods that bring buyers from neighboring communities; our public inns would not discredit a more pretentious borough, and the Hart block, where members of the bar "most do congregate," is an honor to the county seat.

The use of steam gives Doylestown easy and rapid transit to all points outside of the county, while electricity is rapidly doing the same within, and, in the near future, all points of importance will be brought in close touch with the county capital. As our borough enters the first decade of the twentieth century, a trolley system that will centre at Doylestown, occupies more and more attention. The future possibilities of extending and improving the means of local travel, at small expense and with safety and despatch, are very flattering. When the trunk line trolley to Easton shall have been completed, it will invite the building of lateral lines to it from the Delaware on the one side and the North Penn railroad on the other, that will send a current of travel down our peninsula to the confluence of the Delaware and Schuylkill. In time, light freight will follow, for that privilege is sure to come to the trolley and will revolutionize minor traffic and travel.

What this may do for Doylestown, both in the way of increase in travel and volume of business, no one can calculate at this early day. At the end of the twentieth century, we have the right to predict, and do predict, that the population of this borough, at least, will reach 10,000, which would be a smaller percentage of increase than that from the eighteenth to the nineteenth century. The last century

LINDEN FEMALE SEMINARY.

came in with a population of 125, and went out with 3,500, and this prospective growth of the county seat is not in the least over drawn. There are several things that point in this direction.

The location of Doylestown is an ideal site for a county borough and cannot be excelled, if equaled. The spot, the Court House stands upon, lacks only a few feet of being six hundred above tide water at Philadelphia. The country around it is picturesque, rich, populous and healthy, and, from the steeple of the Court House, the view is charming, equaling anything Midland England presents. Such, in a few words, is our summing up of the present and prospective Doylestown, whose modest history we have attempted to portray. As we take leave of the volume, and turn it over to the reader and historian of the future, we congratulate ourselves on the conclusion of our labor. "We have nothing to say in its praise or condemnation, leaving that to the reader."

INDEX.

A

Armstrong's Corner, 5, 6.
Army, British, 12.
Army, Continental, 13, 37.
Alms House, 22, 23.
Academy, The Union, 19, 35. 43, 49, 50. First Trustees, 240. Teachers in, 242. Last Trustees, 248-9.
Avenue, Oakland, 240.
Alley, Printers', 50.
Andrews, Rev. Silas M., 53, 93, 241, 245.
Advocate, Public, 67.
Aaron, Rev. Samuel, 75, 81, 241, 251.
Alley, Garden, 83.
Andalusia, 88.
Anderson, John H., 101, 167, 299.
Allentown, 115.
Applebach, Paul H., 8, 153.
Association, Legal, 153. Original Members of 153.
Amusement, The Earliest, 158.
Artillerists, Diller, 159.
Assension, Balloon, 159, 280.
Ashton, Robert, 177.
Adams, Peter, 187.
Avenues, Opened Maple and Linden, 194; Shewell and Harvey, 200.
Andress, Lazarus C., 225.
Anglemeyer, Wm. H., 225.
Art in Doylestown, 254-5.
Association, Doylestown Musical, 260, Concerts, 261.
Association, Amateur Band, 263.
Artillerist, Independent, 275.
Archambault, Joseph, 277.
Atler, Captain B. Frank, 282.
Association, Building and Loan, 324.
Atkinson, T. O. & Co., 325, 326.
Adams, John Quincy, 357.
Association, Village Improvement, 366

B

Biglan, James, 5.
Beal, Joseph, 8.
Business life, Early, 15.
Building lots, 21.
Bachelor, Dr. William, 23.
Britain, New, 33.
Buckingham, 33, 58.
Benner, Isaac, 33.
Brock, Stephen, 33, 135, 136.
Brock, George P., 35, 43, 368.
Building, Lenape, 37,
Bryan, Gen. John S., 38, 64, 281.
Beans, Joshua, 39, 49.
Brower, Davis E., 46, 113.
Bible Society, Bucks Co., 54.
Belville, Rev. Robert B., 55
Beatty, Robert, 55.
Brown, John S., 60.
Brown, Thomas, 61.
Butler, Judge William, 61.
Bryan, William, 64,
Buchanan, President, 65, 68.
Bryan, C. N., 67.
Beans, J. Mathias, 69.
Book Printing, 69, 70.
Buckman, The Misses, 81.
Bar, Philadelphia, 84.
Bank Organized, Doylestown, 96.
Byrnes, Cashier Daniel, 97, Directors, 97, New building erected, 97.
Bankers, J. Hart & Co., 98.
Beneficial Society, Doylestown, 98-9
Blitz, Signor, 99.
Bennett, James Gorden, 104.
Bethlehem, 115.
Brunner, John, 115.
Building, Lenape, 115, 129.
Buck, Samuel E., 132.
Beek, William, 137.
Bridges, Samuel A., 149.
Bench, The, and the Bar, 143-4.

I

INDEX.

Biddle, Nicholas, 152.
Beidler, Henry S., 370.
Binney, Horace, 152.
Bar, The headquarters of the, 153, 159.
Brower. N. P., 162.
Brock, John J., 165.
Burrows, Joseph. 167.
Brock, Jonathan, 169.
Buckman, Lewis, 172.
Barclay, Mr., 180.
Bakers, Doylestown, 183.
Burrows, John Vickers, 186.
Bookbinderies in Doylestown, 187.
Bon, Joe, 192.
Brunn, Thomas, 196.
Beans, Colonel William, 196.
Berkemeyer, Rev. F., 206.
Bartholomew, Wayne, 211.
Bazelys, The, 220-1.
Brown, William R., 220.
Beal, Eleazer, 225.
Brunner, Jr., Thomas, 225.
Berkelback, William, 225.
Barndt, John, 225.
Belville, Rev. Jacob, 227.
Battery, Durell's, 227.
Buck, William J., 242.
Building, Public School, 249-50.
Byrnes, Jacob, 250.
Brass Band, The DuBois, 259.
Band, Cornet, 260.
Baumann, D., 265.
Black, Second Lieut. William, 281-2.
Blackshaw, Randall, 305.
Buckman, Monroe, 306.
Buck, Jr., Nicholas, 306.
Borland, Jane, 307.
Brock Family, The, 315-16-17.
Buck, Jerome, 321.
Beatty, Dr. Reading, 323.
Beatty, Rev. Charles, 323.
Building Period, 326.
Bucks County Historical Society, 337-8-9.
Bailey, John S., 337.
Bodder, Mrs. Hannah Paul, 362.
Band, Germania, 369.

C

Crawford, Isabella, 1, 2, 7.
Civilization, First step in, 2.
Court House, 2, 83.
County Seat, 24.
Courts, The, 29.
Chapman, Abraham, 31, 35, 75, 97.
Cudjo, 36.
Chase, The Fox, 37.
Cornell, Nathan, 38, 189.
Carver, Elias, 39.
Cameron, Mifflin and, 39.

Cholera, Asiatic, 45, 46,
Congregation, Deep Run, 50.
Club, Union Debating, 55, 63.
Correspondent, Pennsylvania, 57, 58.
Company, Intelligencer, 62.
Chapman, Henry, 113, 148, 155, 358.
Cameron, Simon, 63, 226.
Centreville, 65.
County, Chester, 66.
Courier, Jackson, 67-8.
Correspondent, The, 67.
Cricket, The, 69.
Cid Hamet Benengeli, 72.
Canal, Deleware, 77.
Chronicle, Philadelphia, 77.
Cox, Willlam, 82.
Carr, William, 84, 101, 285, 361.
Chapman, Dr. William, 62, 88.
Chapman, Lucretia, 89.
Churches, Methodist, 92-3-4.
Conference, Philadelphia, 93.
Cookman, Rev. Alfred, 94.
Company, The Union Horse, 95.
Company, Doylestown Insurance, 96, 100, 101; Directors of, 101.
Celebration, Democratic, 106; toasts drunk, 107.
Cemetery, Hope, 113.
Coachee, Doylestown, 115, 116.
Company, John Moore &, 116.
Clark, "Benny," 118.
Celebration, Harvest Home, 157.
Club, The Doylestown, 157.
Celebration, Fourth of July, 159.
Committees, Picnic, Names of, 162.
Clubs, The T. O. S., 165; Social Dozen, 165; The Acorn, 165.
Clemens, John, 169.
Cleveland, President, 181.
Cornell, E. Mitchell, 187.
Cox, Asher, 192.
Coheen, Wm., 192.
Carl & Worstall, 193.
Coryell, Lewis S., 198, 356.
Churches, A group of, 201-8.
Church, Baptist, built, 209; Names of Pastors; membership; do. cost of.
Church, Colored Baptist, Pastors, Socities, 210.
Cooley, Rev. E. F., 324.
Croasdale, Samuel, 225.
Coar, Francis L., 225.
Carver, James M., 225.
Closson, J. Wilson, 225.
Curtin, Governor, 227.
Croasdale, Colonel Samuel C., 236.
Cadwallader, General George B., 236.
Cartee, Dr. C. Soule, 244.
Church, Salem Reformed, 246.
Chapman, The Misses, 257.

INDEX.

Concerts, Open Air, 263.
Choral, The Doylestown, 266.
Clench, Colonel, 273.
Cavalry, Union Troop of, 276.
Colfax, Schuyler, 288.
Cuffel, Lieut. Charles A., 293.
Childs, J. M., 302.
Chapman family, The, 310.
Chapman, Judge Henry, 310.
College Log, 323.
Church, Presbyterian, 326-8.
Carver, Mahlon, 337.
Celebration, Bi-Centennial, 341-3.
Convention, Harrisburg, 357.
Clay, Henry, Death of, 359.
Cox, Charles C., 359, 364, 367.
Century, Farewell to the Nineteenth, 365.
Century, The middle of the, 211.
Colors, Rescue of the, 367.
Cuffel, Charles A., 368.

D

Doylestown, 1, 2, 3, 4, 5, 10, 11, 14, 24, 33, 39, 43, 79, 82; Population of, 33, 39, 65, in the past 85; Incorporated, 101; Contiguous land owners, 102; Officers elected, 102; First Council meeting, 103; A Summer Resort 104; What the Newspapers say of it, 105; Literary and Scholastic status, 106; Magnetic telegraph instrument at, 107-8; First Telephone at, 108; Public Cemetery laid out and incorporated, British troops pass through, 273; Fourth of July at, 276; Volunteer Companies in, 282.
Doylestown, Centennial of, 234-35.
Doyles, The, 4, 5, 6, 7, 10.
Delaware, The Fork of, 9.
DuBois, Rev. Uriah, 19, 36, 49, 51, 52, 240, 273.
Dallas, Alexander J., 32.
Dunlap, Moses, 33.
Dublin, 36.
Democrat, Doylestown, 38, 60, 63, 64, 78.
Dick, John L., 42, 52, 133.
Davis, General John, 42, 52, 111, 281.
Dyerstown, 61.
Darlington, Henry T., 61, 324.
Darlington, Dr. William, 61.
Deffebach, Lewis, 63.
Democrat, Bucks County, 63.
Democrat, The, 65, 66, 68, 85.
Davis, W. W. H., 65, 66, 70, 225, 337.
Daubert, Adam, 66, 67.
Dimm, J. C., 66.
Democrat, Independent, 67.
Donat, Ryner T., 68.

Davis, Captain, 69.
Doylestown, Origin of, 72.
DuBois, C. E., 101, 153, 156, 197, 358.
Dwelling, DuBois, 84.
Dwelling, Hall, 84.
DuBois, John L., 84.
Dallas, George M., 113.
Doane, Joel, 115.
Doylestown, Landlord of, 142.
Doylestown, Population of, 218-19.
Doylestown, Social life of, 155, 156; Streets of, 194; An ideal site, 372, 373; Present appearance, 373; Future possibilities of, 372.
Dozen, The social, 156.
DuBois, Samuel F., 159, 257, 267, 268.
DuBois, Henry L., 163.
Dennison, Andrew, 173.
Derrickson, Joseph, 177.
Donaldson, Andrew, 201.
Dana, Rev. George, 209.
Dress Ball, Military and Citizens, 222.
Darling, Edward S., 225,
Dyer, Cephas W., 225.
Davis, Colonel, 226.
DuBois, Robert P., 241.
Donaldson, George E., 259.
Davis, Captain John, 276.
Druggists, The, 299.
Dick, Isabella, 306.
Dick, John L., 306.
DuBois, Uriah, 309.
Dickie, 337.
Decade, Bi-centennial, 337.
Deaths, Several, 363.
Davis, General, 369.

E

Erb, Lawrence, 17, 114.
Evans, Septimus, 35.
Erwin, Miss, 43.
Edwards, William, 46.
Ellmaker, Colonel Peter, 63.
Express, Bucks County, 66, 74.
Express and Reform, 66.
Examiner, Political, 67.
Emporeum, Trenton, 68.
Esposy, Mina, Don Lino Amilio, 88.
Ely, Hugh B., 101.
Eastburn, Hugh B., 113, 266, 371.
Easton, 115, 116.
Eastburn, Charles, 150.
Eisenhart, William T., 180, 302.
Enochs, Alexander, 186-7.
Evans, Dr., 193.
England, Shipment to, 193.
Exposition, Wm. Beek's, 214.
Emory, George W., 225.
Everheart, George A., 225.

INDEX.

Enders, Andrew, 225.
Engineers, U. S. Vol., 282.
Ely, Lieut John, 282.
Eagles, Golden, 293.

F

Ferry, Coryell's, 13, 21.
Freemen, Elizabeth, 5.
Flacks, The, 5, 129.
Fells, The, 15, 17.
Furnace, The Durham, 9.
Forge, Valley, 12.
Farm House, Kirkbride, 13.
Family, Riale, 4.
Fox, Judge John, 32, 36, 89, 90, 151, 196, 273, 312, 357.
Fell, Joseph, 40.
Ferguson, Dr., 46.
Freedom, Star of, 59.
Fretz, Samuel, 60.
Foulke, Rowan, 62.
Fretz, Edwin, 66, 225.
Farmer, Bucks County, 68.
Farm, The Underhill, 80.
Freed, Mr., 81.
Frankenfield, William, 93.
Forney, Colonel John W., 99, 160.
Fell, J. Gillingham, 103.
Frazer, Colonel Reah, 106.
Fox, Edward J., 113, 257.
Feuerbend, John, 115.
Fenton, Ephraim, 116.
Field, William, 116-17-18.
Fox Chase, The, 129, 130, 131.
Fountain House changes hands, 130-1.
Fretz, Joseph H., 131.
Farmer, Bucks County, 133.
Fisher' B. F., 149, 170.
Fox, Gilbert R., 149.
Fencibles, Union, 158.
Fever, Lecture, 160.
Fuzzlegudgeon, Mrs., 163.
Fell, Joseph, 177.
Fretz, Philip, 197.
Folly, Brown's, 220.
Frankinfield, Chris K., 225.
Frankinfield, Lawrence, 225.
Frankinfield, Charles, 225.
Fries, Jacob, 225.
Follis, William, 223.
Fussman, Samuel E., 225.
Firman, David, 225.
Flags presented, 227.
Fisher, General B. F., 236.
Family, A musical, 264.
Ferguson, Frank, 288.
Ferguson, Dr. C. B., 298.
Freman, A. M., 301.
Fox family, The, 311-12.
Firman, Samuel A., 325.

Fires and Fire Department, 348-53.
Frazier, Leah, 357.
Fritzinger, John, 360.
Fordhook Farm, 360.
Fetter, Rev. N. C., 368, 370.
Fries, Aaron, 322.
Flag Staff, 333-34.

G

Gazette, Farmer's Weekly, 19, 57.
Geil, Abraham, 33.
Grim, Webster, 35.
Green Tree, The, 35, 39.
Gilkyson, James, 36.
Gazette, Hunterdon C., 61.
Gazette, Santa Fe, 65.
Godshalk, Samuel, 68.
Guards, Doylestown, 69, 112, 264.
Gazette, The Court, 69.
Gleaner, The, 69.
Gilbert, Benjamin, 70.
Grove, Willow, 73, 77, 116.
Groff, Dr. James, 84.
Goell, Alfred, 107.
Gilkyson, B. F., 143.
Gilkinson, James, 153.
Grays, The Doylestown, 158, 279, 280.
Grove, Harvey's, 162.
Greir, Joseph J., 171.
Gregg, Barzilla J., 178.
Gregg, Mrs., 178.
Garron, Abraham, 188.
Ginsley, Samuel F., 188.
Gaucher, The brothers, 192.
Goheen, J. Warner, 193.
Gries, Rev. William R., 202.
George, Rev. Father, 203.
Geil, William Edgar, 209.
Greeley, Horace, 214.
Green, William Augustus, 225.
Garron, Samuel N., 225.
Gensel, Ira F., 225.
Glase, Jacob W., 225,
Garner, George W., 225.
Groff, Rev. J. R., 266.
Codfrey, William B., 266.
Gaucher, Thomas W., 289.
Gunagan, Jeremiah, 363.
G. A. R., Bodine Post, 369.

H

Hope, New, 5.
Heckman, Samuel, 5, 64.
House, The Fountain, 5, 117, 129.
House, The Mansion, 37, 39, 131.
Hall, Painswick, 4, 305.
Hough, Dr., 6.
Hough, Daniel, 5, 11.
Harvey, Enoch, 5, 14, 74, 83, 129, 300.
Hilltown, 3.

INDEX

Harrisburg, 33.
Hotel, Cold Spring, 14, 41.
House, Titus, Chapman, Lyman, 35.
Homestead, DuBois, 36.
Hall, Isaac, 37, 151; Charles, 37.
Hall, Samuel, 93, 151.
Hart, Wm. Watts, 42, 43, 273.
Hart, Mrs. Ann, 43, 44.
Hendrie, Dr., 46.
Holidays, National, 46-7.
Hyde, Charles, 52.
Hough, Rev. Silas, 55.
Hart, John, 55.
Henry, Hugh M., 60.
House, White, 65.
Herald, Bucks County, 68.
Harton, John, 68.
Harton, Frank, 68.
Heart, John S., 69.
Hatboro, 77.
Harvey, Charles, 83.
Hand, Rev. James, 93-4.
House, Citizens, Temperance, 100.
Hotel, Rotterdam, 116.
Harris, John, 129.
Harris, Hannah, 130.
Heist, Allen H., 137.
House, Citizens, 139-40.
Hart, George, 145, 225.
Hough, Joseph, 148; Death of, 149.
Hall, Goden, 179.
Harl, James, 180.
Huntsman, George A., 180.
Hay, Gilbert, 181.
Hulshizer, Daniel, 181, 259.
Hulshizer, W. Sharp, 182.
Hellyer, Harold A., 189.
Hayes, Thomas, 90.
Hubbard, Samuel, 190.
Heston, Edward, 191.
Hibbs, Aden G., 192.
Hanover, New, 107.
Hatboro, 193.
Hart, Samuel, 197.
Hopkins, Rev. George P., 201.
Huffnagle, Charles, 214.
Hill, Jacob, 221.
Hubbard, Nathaniel, 225.
Hendrie, James D., 225.
Hinkle, Philip, 225.
Hargrave, Henry, 225.
Heany, Henry W., 225.
Hart, Jr., Samuel, 225.
Hoffman, Charles W., 225.
Hogeland, John S., 225.
Haney, William P., 225.
Hough, John S., 225.
Hofford, Eli, 225.
Hart, Thomas, 225.
Harvey, Joseph H., 225.

Harvey, Second Lieut. George T., 225.
Hargrave, John (Drummer) 225.
Hughes, Thomas, 245.
Hall, Beneficiat, 256.
Hicks, Thomas, 270.
Humphrey, Col. Thomas, 274.
Hair, Capt. Joseph, 275.
Hendrie, Dr. William S., 289, 298, 314.
Harvey, Theodore P., 292.
Hines, Dr. Andrew J., 299.
Harvey, Dr. George T., 300.
Hart, Dr. Joseph, 302.
Historic Families, 304.
Hough, Hannah, 306.
Hough, Richard, 306.
House, The Thomas Stevens, 307.
Harveys, The, 308.
Halls, The, 309.
Hall, Samuel, 309.
Hutton, Addison, 126.
History, Odds and Ends of, 354.
Hines, Oliver P., 363.
Hines, Dr. A. J., 364.
Haven, White, 369.

I

Indians, Oneida and Tuscarora, 13.
Irwin, The Rev. Nathaniel, 25, 58.
Ingham, Samuel D., 36, 55, 159, 273.
Intelligencer, Bucks Co., 60, 65, 66, 68, 78, 81, 82, 89, 164.
Institute, Doylestown Scientific and Literary, 108.
Improvement, Spirit of, 113.
Inn, Court, 116, 136.
Improvement Co., Doylestown, 129.
Industries, Our, 173.

J

James, John D., 33, 151.
Joe, Cudjo and, 36.
Jones, Eliza, 43, 45.
James, Mrs. N. C., 38, 58.
July 4th, The Celebration of, 47, 74-5.
Jackson, Elisha B., 60.
Journal, Newtown, 65.
Justice, Joseph, 68.
Jail, Mina escapes from, 87.
James, Colonel Isaiah, 106, 257.
Jackson, Andrew, Death of, 107, 157.
James, Dr. O. P., 113, 285, 299.
Jenkintown, 115, 116.
James, John O., 168.
James, N. C., 177, 259.
Jenks, Michael, E., 225.
Jordan, William H., 225.
James, A. H., 257.
Jackson, Camp, 281.
Jameses, The, 307.

INDEX.

Jail, Building of new, 344-46.
July, The Fourth of, 356.
Jackson, Peter, 360.

K

Kirkbride, Joseph, 3, 4, 5, 40, 304.
Kirkbride, David, 21, 34.
Kennedy, Thomas G., 33.
Kolbe, Frank, 35.
Kuhn, Mrs., 37.
Kiple, Jacob, 41.
Kramer, Samuel R., 59.
Kelly, James, 60, 101, 197.
Keesey, William, 68.
Kuster, Julius, 69, 225, 291.
Kachline, Samuel, 75.
Kendall, Andrew, 108.
Kelly, William D., 113.
Keys, Cross, 115, 141.
Krause, Judge, 153.
Keichline, The, 184-5.
Kachline, William, 225.
Kulp, Moses O., 225.
Kephart, Theophilus, 225.
Kibby, Edgar, 225.
Krauthamel, Emanuel, 225.
Kachline, Thomas, 259.
Kensette, 270.
Keuler, Ida M., 294.
Kirkbride, Mahlon, 305.
Kimmer, Mary, 305.
Kane, James, 211.
Kuhn, Sarah M., 241.

L

Line, Montgomery County, 2.
Langhorne, Jeremiah, 3, 8, 40, 304.
Langhorne, Thomas, 3, 304.
Lacey, Gen. John, 12.
Lyman, John, 35, 259.
Lewis, Thomas, 18.
Lane, The Academy, 21, 49.
Larzelere, Rev. Jacob, 55.
Long, William, 55.
Large, William, 60.
Lukens, Hiram, 62, 285.
Loeb, Moritz, 67.
Luz, Adam D., 68.
Longstreth, Daniel, 76.
Lloyd, John, 81.
Lear, George, 83, 145, 289.
Lore, Rev. Dallas D., 94.
Long, Mahlon, 97.
Lodge, Masonic, 100.
Lewis, "Joe", 120.
Letter Box, The First, 121.
Lawells, The, 129.
Lawyers, Group of, 149-50.
Long, S. Ferdinand, 153.

Lee, Capt. Robert M., 158.
Life, Mercantile, 166.
Lane, Oyster Shell, 181.
Larzere, Harvey, 182.
Luckenback, George, 285.
Lunn, O. P., 189-90.
Lee, Norris, 191.
Lane, Dutch, 194.
Lane, Academy, 194.
Larue, Andrew, 195.
Lancaster, John, 197.
Lynch, Franklin Pierce, 209.
Light, Artificial, 211; Gas, 212; Electricity, do.; Company formed, do.
Laughlin, John McDonald, 213, 225.
Lieper, Col. George G., 214.
Lawsons, The, 220.
Lewis, John H., 225.
Lacey, Camp, 227.
Libraries, 252-3.
Lang, Lewis, 270.
Lashley, Lambert, 277.
Lafayette, Reception of, 277-8.
Livezey, Henry D., 289.
Lodge, St. Tammany, 290.
Liberty, Daughters of, 293.
Life, Our Medical, 296.
Lloyd, Henry C., 301.
Lloyd, E. Morris, 301.
Lear Family, The, 315.
Larue & Co., A. J., 325.
Lenape building, Erection of, 28, 30, 337.
Lyman, Richard M., 337.
Lewis, Robert, 362.
Lear, Henry, 371.

M

Mansion, The Ross, 2, 39, 40, 41.
Maxim, A Roman, 2.
Meadow, Round, 2.
Magills, The, 1, 7, 131, 195.
Meredith, James, 4.
Meeting House, Buckingham, 7.
Miner, Asher, 19, 38, 58, 59, 70.
Mann, John, 33.
Morris, Jr., Benjamin, 33, 102.
Morris, Enos, 43, 301.
Morris, Mathias, 35, 273.
McIntosh, Jonathan, 37.
Murfit, Henry T., 36.
Magill, William, 37, 40, 97, 195.
Meredith, Dr. Hugh, 38, 40, 76, 81, 129.
Meredith, Dr. Charles, 38, 42, 296.
McCoy, Dr. Gilbert R., 38, 298.
Murry, George, 39, 106.
McDowell, E. T., 39, 101.
Miles, Mrs. Sarah, 43, 45.
Montanye, Rev. Thomas B., 42, 55, 273.

INDEX.   7

MacReynold, Nelson, 46.
Moore, Rev. W. Hayes, 54.
Mathias, Rev. Joseph, 55.
Moore, Samuel, 55.
Morris, Enos, 55.
Morris, Edmund, 59.
Messenger, Bucks County, 63.
Mifflin, Benjamin, 63.
Mendenhall, Dr. John D., 66.
Morwitz, Dr., 67.
Mirror, Bucks County, 66.
Morgenstern, Der, 67, 68.
Mills, Franklin S., 67, 68.
Matthews, Rachel C., 68.
McGinty, Bernard, 69.
Morris, Howard, 69.
Mercury, Charleston, 69.
Marple, Mr., 73.
Magill, Captain, 75, 156.
Moore, John, 75.
Mauch Chunk, 77.
Mountain, Schooley's, 77.
Magill, Charles H., 84, 103, 163, 291.
Michener, George H., 84.
Matthews, Dr. Charles H., 84, 88, 101, 196, 197, 207, 281, 292, 306, 357.
Murder Trial, Mina Chapman, 88.
Mina, The trial of; found guilty; execution; military display, 89, 90, 91, 278.
Meeting, Friends, 92.
Martin, Oscar, 94.
McDowell, Rev. W. M., 95.
McCalla, 115.
Michener, Jonathan, 116.
Monroe, 116.
Maddock, Randall, 122-3.
Mail Matter, Quantity of, 126.
Marple, David D., 130.
Mann, C. H., 130, 131, 191, 201.
McLaughlan, Daniel, 130.
Monroe, 116.
Maddock, Randall, 122-3.
Mail matter, Quantity of, 126.
Marple, David D., 130.
Mann, C. H., 130, 131, 191, 201.
McDowell, E. T.,145; poetry of, 145; death of, 147; marriage of, 147-8.
Masons, Benevolent Lodge of, 156.
Menagerie, The first, 157.
Matthews, Capt. C. H., 158.
McMichael, Morton, 160.
Most, Thomas B., 175.
Musgrave, William, 175.
McHenry, William, 176.
Miller, Anthony, 177.
Medary, Isaac B., 179.
Medary & Heath, 179.
McManus, Timothy, 180.
Michener, Nathan, 180.

Moyer, John, 181.
Mellick & Hulshizer, 181.
Maxwell, William, 196.
McCarty, Isaac C., 196.
Markley, Levi K., 225.
Morley, Frederick, 225.
McCoy, John H., 225.
McDowell, William H., 225.
McCarty, William, 225.
Magill, Eugene, 225.
Marple, W. Warren, 225.
Mills, Edward S., 225.
Maugel, Abraham, 225.
McGreggors, 240.
Murray, George, 243, 250.
Music and painting, 254.
Morris, Mrs., 258.
Musical Association, Bucks County, 262; Concert of, 262-3.
Mænnerchor, Doylestown, and organizors, 265.
Music and art, 267-9.
Mann, James S., 277.
McReynolds, Lieut. Abel, 282.
Masonic lodges; the Benovelent, No. 188, page 284; the Doylestown, No. 245, pages 285-6.
McIntosh, George, 257.
Mercur, James W., 258.
Michener, John G., 289.
McHenry, Charles, 301.
Mechanics, United American, 292.
Mater, Dr. W. F. DeLa, 301.
Meredith, James, 305-6.
Meredith, William M., 305.
Meredith, Thomas, 305-6.
Meredith, Dr. Hugh, 306, 354.
McFarland, Mary, 207.
Mann, John, 207.
McIntosh, The, brothers, 309.
Morris, Mathias, 312-13.
Mann, C. H., and family, 317-318.
Moore, Dr. Samuel, 322.
Mercer, Henry C., 337.
McDowell, George, 337.
Myers, Abraham, 356.
Murfit, H. S., 368.
McKinley, 371.

N

Neshaminy, The, 1.
New Britain, 3, 4, 63.
Nicholaus, John, 17, 114.
Nightingale, Rev. Samuel, 36, 208.
Nicholaus, Frederick, 41.
Newtown, 43.
Newspapers, Pioneer, 57.
Naiman, 67.
Norristown, 68.

INDEX.

Natural Sciences, Academy of, 75.
Northrop, George, 113.
Nicholaus, Samuel, 115.
Nugent, Washington G., 225.
New Court House, Erection of, 321-33.

O

Oedipus, 11.
Olive Branch, 67.
Orphans' Court, Clerk of, 83-4.
Opp, Sergeant Peter, 112.
Ottsville, 116.
Opp, Valentine, 133-4.
Officials, Court, 152.
Our Industries, More of, 84.
Orem, James Reed, 225.
Officers, Field, 227.
Orchestra, Brock's, Original members of, 261.
Otter, Thomas P., 269, 337.
Opp, Peter, 275.
Odd Fellows, 286-7-8-9.
Offices, Real estate and conveyancing, 324.

P

Park, Graeme, 2.
Penn, William, 3, 305.
Park, Langhorne, 1.
Pine Run, Valley of, 1.
Pennsbury, 3.
Period, Revolutionary, 12, 13.
Peninsula, Delaware-Schuylkill, 12.
Post Routes Opened, 21.
Pike, Zebulon, 24.
Pugh, John, 38, 43, 55, 111, 273, 321.
Paxson, Samuel Johnson, 38, 64, 76, 188, 259.
Place, Monument, 40.
Philadelphia, 43, 83, 115.
Patterson, Robert, 50.
Presbyterian, Scotch Irish, 50.
Patton, Rev. William A., 54.
Purdy, William, 55, 152.
Potts, Rev. M., 56.
Patriot, Bucks County, 60.
Paxson, Judge Edward M., 61, 65, 152.
Prizer, Enos, 61.
Paschall, Alfred, 61, 29, 337.
Paschall, S. Edward, 61.
Powell, William H., 64.
Paxson, Thomas, 64, 152.
Publishing Company, Doylestown, 66.
Price, Charles, 66.
Purdy, Joseph H. 325.
Policy, Kansas-Nebraska, 68.
Period, A Prosperous, 96.
Patterson, Samuel A. D., 99.
Pugh, John B., 113, 158, 322.
Peters, Jacob, 115.
Post Office, The First, 121.
Postmasters, Names of, 121-4.
Purdy, Thomas, 139.
Performance, Equestrian, 157.
Picnics, The Era of, 160, 257.
Partridge, Captain Alden, 159, 281.
Picnic, 161.
Purdy, John F., 178.
Pollock, James, opens streets and sells lots, 200.
Period, Civil War, 116.
Pierce, A. Jackson, 225.
Patterson, Joseph, 241.
Pawling, George H., 277.
Parades, Military, 281.
Pettitt, D. John, 300.
Parsons, Dr., 301.
Pennsbury, 305.
Patterson, Sheridan T., 306.
Patterson, Dr. Robert, 322.
Pump, The town, 354-5.
Pettitt, Dr. John B., 359.
Pursell, Sergeant W., 369.
Pughs, The, 321.
Population, Increase of, 373.

Q

Quakertown, 67.
Quick, Philip, 93.
Queen, Indian, 41, 116, 134.
Quinn, Emmit, 145.
Quartette, Doylestown, 258.

R

Riale, John
Riale, Richard, 5.
Road, Dyer's Mill, 2.
Road, Easton, 2, 17, 195.
Road, Durham, 3.
Ross, Thomas, 67, 68, 81, 84, 89, 90, 154, 311.
Run, Deep, 9.
Ralston, Isaac, 19, 57.
Riale, Joshua, 33.
Russell, Elijah, 14.
Ross, John, 41.
Rhoads, Dr. John S., 42, 302.
Rily, Captain John, 55. 158.
Rogers, William T., 59, 64, 81, 158.
Record. Village, 61.
Ross, Henry P., 68, 149.
Ross, George, 149.
Railroad, North Penn, 195.
Republican, Daily, 69.
Reaper, The, 69.
Rhett, Colonel, 69.
Rich, Dr. James S., 74, 156, 297, 307.
Robbarth, Captain John, 76.
Roberts, Stokes L., 85, 113, 318.
Rains, Rev. Mr., 93.
Reeside, James, 115.

INDEX. 9

Railroad, Belvidere Delaware, 115.
Route, Mail, 124, 126.
Rodman, Gilbert. 156.
Retreat, China, 159.
Rotzel, Shade &. 171.
Rogers, John P., 178, 314.
Rayton, Burgoyne, 181.
Ruos, Henry D., 182.
Rich, Lester, 185, 197.
Rogers, William T., 196, 215, 323.
Roads, State, New Hope, Port Deposit, Easton, Willow Grove, 197.
Railroad, North Penn opened, 198.
Ross, Mrs. Thomas, 201.
Railroad, North Penn, 212-13-15.
Rogers, Edward L., 162, 225.
Rogers, James M., 225.
Rush, Lawrence, 225.
Regiment, The 104th, 227; Leaves camp, 228; Welcomed home, 229; Monument erected and dedicated, 233; General Emory, 235.
Robinson, John, 241.
Roberts, Mrs. S. L., 257.
Rowbotham, Prof., 259.
Rangers, Bucks County, Roll of, 274.
Rich, Lieut. Anthony, 275.
Kchart, Captain John, 276-7.
Reeder, Captain A. H., 277-8.
Rifles, Nagle, 281.
Republic, Grand Army of, 294.
Road, Almshouse, 306,
Riale Family, 308.
Ross Family, The, 310, 311.
Rogers Family, The, 313.
Regiment, Reunion of 104th, 40, 41, 339.
Rifle Rangers, Magill, 336,
Ross, Mrs., 358.

S

Street, North Main, 1; Broad and Main, 35; South Main, 38-9; Main, 83, 194-5; East Main, 194; Front, 195; York, 195; Court, 194-5; State, 195; Arabella and Louisa, 195.
Shewell, Walter, 4.
Shewell, Nathaniel, 16, 40, 55, 83.
Swanwick, Richard, 5.
Stewart, Barton, 16.
Story, Thomas, 33.
Smith, Timothy, 33, 74.
Smith, Samuel A., 170, 319.
Smith, Amanda and character of, 319.
Shaws, The, 202.
Society, Bucks County Historical, 13.
Ship, The, 37, 129.
Shaw, Josiah Y., 38, 74, 101, 103, 150.
Stewart, Thomas J., 39.
Snyder, Governor, 43.

Stewart, Mrs. Thomas, 49.
Smith, E., 55.
Swarthmore, 61.
Siegfried, Simeon, 63.
Snyder, Manassah H., 64, 66, 67.
Shaw, Francis B., 67, 74, 80, 275, 299,
Sellers, Franklin P., 67, 68.
Seymour, William P., 67, 259.
Spy, The, 68.
Standard, Democratic, 68-9.
Swartzlander, Dr. Frank, 82, 344, 370.
Shewell, Thomas, 83-4.
Street, Shewell, 85.
Sellers, Franklin P., 87.
Sands, Henry P., 93.
Society organized, Beneficial, 96.
Shearer, Conrad, 102 191,.
Sickel, Horatio, 106.
Shaw, James L., 107, 321.
Selser, Silas A., 108, 368.
Stage, The first, 114.
Stewart, Charles, 115, 129, 130.
Shoma, Samuel and John, 115.
Ship, Mathew Hare's, 115.
Stages, Local Lines of, 116-17-18, 80.
Stage, High Grass Line, 118.
Swanwick, Richard, 129.
Stewarts, The, 129, 308.
Spring, The Clear, 133.
Strawn, Joseph, 136-7.
Smyser, Judge, 153.
Scott, Henry, W., 154.
Springs, Yellow, 162.
Society, Bob Narrative, 163.
Smith & Kirk, 178.
Smith, Jervis S., 178.
Smith, Timothy, 178.
Swartzlander, Miss Susie, 370.
Smith, Timothy, 178.
Seitzinger, John, 180.
Shearers, The, 191.
Spoke aud Wheel Company, Worstall & Carl, 192.
Shaw, Harvey, 196.
Shaw, Josiah Y., 197.
Streets, The last group of, 200.
Sheip, Rev. Levi C., 206, 246.
Simpson, John, 211.
Stavely, William R., 225.
Service, Henry S., 225.
Sunderland, George, W., 225.
Shearer, William A., 225.
Swartzlander, Jacob, First Lieut., 225.
Shearer, William K., fifer, 225.
Societies, Agricultural, 237.
Spellier, Louis H., 238.
Schools, Our, 240, 250.
Smith, Eleazar, 241.
Seminary, Doylestown Female, 243, 247-48.

INDEX.

Seminary, Ingham Female, 245.
Seminary, Linden, 246.
Society Orphean, 257.
Siegler, Dr. Charles, 265.
Schooner, William, 265.
Smith, Summers A., 269.
Sizer, Major Asa B., 273.
Smith, Brigade Inspector Samuel A., 275.
Smith, Trumpeter John, 277.
Sons of Veterans, 282-3.
Societies, Beneficial, 284.
Societies, German Aid, 290-1.
Swartzlander, Dr. Frank, 298, 368.
Sotcher, John, 305.
Shewell, Walter, 305.
Sallows, Mary, 305.
Shewell, Betsy, 305.
Snodgrass, Benjamin, 307.
Stewart, Robert, 307.
Snodgrass, James, 307.
Shaw, Lieut. Thompson D., 321, 353.
Society, Doylestown, and its leaders, 335-6.
Smith, Josiah B., 337.
State Charity, Board of, 346.
Shunk, Francis T., 358.

T

Township, Warwick, 1, 3; Solebury, 36; Southampton, 43; Plumstead, 60; Buckingham, 64; Doylestown, 83.
Traders, Free Society of, 3.
Tavern, The Ship, 16, 139, 355.
Tavern, Doyle's, 194.
Titus, Zerick, 21, 35.
Tavern, Charles Stewart's, 17.
Thomas, Jacob, 17.
Taylor, Caleb N., 29, 159.
Trust Company, Doylestown, 37, 60, 145.
Taverns, The Three, 37.
Tree, The Green, 35, 41, 139.
"Town, Doyl," 50, 51.
Taylor, Bayard, 61.
Thomas, Arthur K., 62.
Turnpike, New Hope, 65.
Times, London, 65.
Temperance, The cause of, 85-6; M. S. Snyder comments on, 85-6; Organization of, 87; Sons of, 87.
Thumb, Tom, 99.
Tavern, William Field's, 101.
Tavern, Craig's, 114.
Tavern, Kohl's, 116.
Tavern, John Dungan's, 116.
Tavern, Green Tree, 117; Citizen's House, 119; Fields, 196.
Timothy, Mount, 160.

Thornton, Rutledge, 168.
Thompson, William, 169.
Twining, Henry M., 171.
Tilton, Daniel, 185.
Thompson, Hugh, 189.
Troxel, Jacob, 189.
Tetlow, Rev. John, 189.
Turnpike Company, Doylestown and Willow Grove; Doylestown and Buckingham, 196.
Tavern, Thatcher's, 196; Charles Morris, 197.
Turnpike, Doylestown, Plumsteadville, Dublin, Centreville, New Hope, Newtown, 197.
Tavern, Henry Schools, 197.
Trolley roads: Willow Grove to Doylestown, 198; Newtown to Doylestown, and Doylestown to Easton, 199.
Taylor, Henry J. C., 201.
Tasker, Morris &, 211.
Townsend, Stephen, 225.
Tomlinson, Enos, P., 225.
Tomlinson, Thomas F., 225.
Trego, Thomas W., 238, 361.
Taylor, Franklin, 242.
Teachers' Institute, 260.
Titus, John, 321.
Thomas, Rev. William B , 321.
Thompson, Lewis B., 26.
Taylor, H. J. C., Real Estate of, 226.
Trust Company, Bucks County, 346 7, 365-6.
Tavern, The Doyle, 355.
Town clock, 358.
Thomas, Dr. Joseph, 369.
Trego, William T., 370.
Trolleys, The, 372-3.

V

Valley, Castle, 4, 197.
Village well equipped, 20.
Volunteers, Turn out of, 91.
Vanluvanee, Benjamin, 174.
Vaughan, Rev. Alexander, 204.
Valette, Major, 273.
Volunteers, Companies of, visiting among us, 278-9.
Vandegrift, Captain Charles A., 295.
Vandegrift, Charles A., 368.

W

White, Rachel, 5.
Wirts, Jr., Christian, 15.
Wynkoop, Helina, 16.
Wilson, Judge Bird, 32.
Werner, Ernest, 34, 291.
Watts, William, 36, 39, 41, 43, 55, 82, 135, 151, 273, 357, 363.

INDEX.

Wigton, James, 39.
Wilkesbarre, 58, 59.
War, Civil, 65, 66.
Watchtower, The, 67.
Whig, Bucks County, 68.
Wilkinson, Colonel, 77.
Watts, Arthur, 82.
Wright, C. E., 83, 149.
Winslow, Thomas, 92.
War, The Mexican, 108; Sword presentation, 109, 110; Contribution for soldiers' families, 111; Martial poetry, 111, 112.
Willow Grove, 116.
Wierman, Daniel, 130.
Wyker, George H., 137.
Webster, Daniel, 145.
Wilson, Judge, 151.
Watson, Judge Richard, 149, 289.
Wilkinson, John, 150.
Wise, Professor, 159.
Weikel & Booz, 161.
Wall, Willis, 368.
Wanger, Irving P., 370.
Wigtons, The, 177.
Wigton, Charles J., 177.
Worman, John, 179.
Walton, Mrs. Thomas, 180.
Wetherill & Martin, 183.
White, John, 188.
Williams, Edward, 196.
Wood, Rev. W. S., 209.
Wheeler, Charles, 111.

Water, The introduction of, 215-16-17-18.
War, Civil, Doylestown in the, 223-24.
Widdifield, Henry A., 225.
Walker, William, 225.
Williams, Miles, 225.
Watson, Jane, 266.
War of 1812, 272-4; Raising troops for, 273; Patriotism aroused, 273, 274; Troops return home, 275.
Worrell, General, 273.
Wagner, Captain David D., 277.
Weyandt, Captain Jacob, 278.
War, Spanish-American, Doylestown in, 282; Home, 304.
Welcome, The, 295.
West, Benjamin, 305.
Wright family, The, 317.
Walters, Joseph B., 337.
Wells, Richard, 361.
Walker, John, 361.
Worsted mill, 370.

Y

Yardley, Samuel, 5, 82, 101, 167.
Yardley, Thomas, 33.
Yerkes, Harman, 36, 43, 149, 368, 379.
Young, Joseph, 67, 68.
Yardley, Robert M., 82, 153, 369.
Yerkes, Dr. A. J., 301, 302.
Yerkes, Dr. Hutchinson P., 302.
Yost, Dr. R., 302.
Yardley, John, 368.

www.ingramcontent.com/pod-product-compliance
Lightning Source LLC
Chambersburg PA
CBHW071136300426
44113CB00009B/989